"This is a moving and timely story of that which separates and binds black and white America. *The Hairstons* helps us understand our common past and present."

—Julian Bond

"One would have to be hard-hearted indeed not to be moved by the big story this book tells . . . or by the little stories it tells of individual Hairstons whose lives reveal so much about what it is to be an American. . . . It is scrupulous and honest in all respects, and a powerful testament to what this country, at its best, can be."

—Jonathan Yardley,
The Washington Post Book World

"*The Hairstons* is an epic . . . Enthralling . . . Wiencek creates a profound understanding of slavery, Jim Crow, and the civil rights movement. He uses documents, sometimes centuries old, to bring these Hairstons vividly to life."

—Howard Kissel,
New York Daily News

"Not since *Mary Chesnuts's Civil War* has nonfiction about the South been as compelling as fiction."

—*Time*

"Henry Wiencek's lovingly detailed history of the complicated relationships among various strains of this huge, tragically divided Old South family has been called a metaphor for the nation, but a more accurate description would lie in the words of Robert Penn Warren, who said, 'The past is never past.' "

—*The Dallas Morning News*

"Without sentimentality but with great feeling . . . Wiencek steps gracefully through the intricate web that links two family trees, one white and one black."

—*Publishers Weekly*

The Hairstons

AN AMERICAN FAMILY

IN
BLACK AND WHITE

HENRY WIENCEK

ST. MARTIN'S GRIFFIN ✻ NEW YORK

THE HAIRSTONS. Copyright © 1999 by Henry Wiencek.

Part One, page 1: Unknown Hairstons, 1850s. (Courtesy of Louisa Hairston Breeden)
Part Two, page 133: Ruins of Richmond, 1865. (Courtesy of the Library of Congress)
Part Three, page 217: John Goolsby, 1880s. (Courtesy of Peter W. Hairston)

Book design by Ellen R. Sasahara

Library of Congress Cataloging-in-Publication Data

Wiencek, Henry.
    The Hairstons : an American family in black and white / Henry Wiencek.
        p.   cm.
    Includes bibliographical references.
    ISBN 0-312-19277-0 (hc)
    ISBN 0-312-25393-1 (pbk)
    1. Afro-American Families—Southern States—Biography.
2. Hairston family.   3. Slaves—Southern States—Biography.
4. Slaveholders—Southern States—Biography.   5. Southern
States—Race relations.   I. Title.
E185.96.W54   1999
929'.2'0973—dc21   98-44014
                                                                         CIP

First St. Martin's Griffin Edition: February 2000

10 9 8 7 6 5 4 3 2 1

For Donna and Henry the Next,
with love

CONTENTS

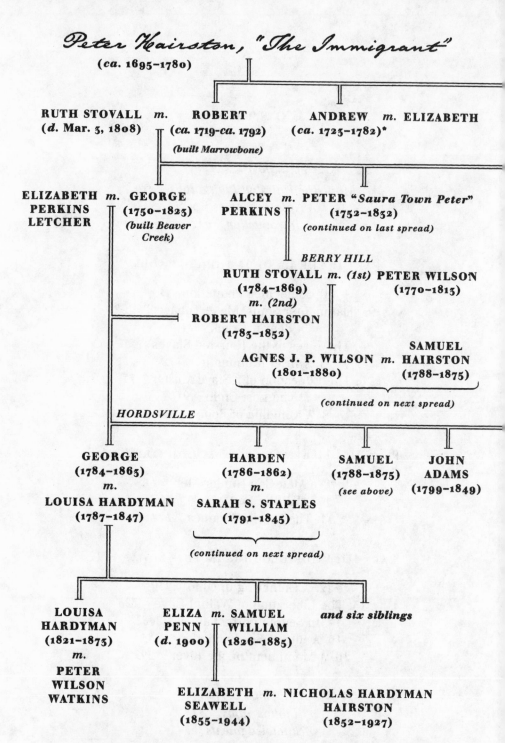

Peter Hairston, "The Immigrant"
(ca. 1695–1780)

RUTH STOVALL *m.* **ROBERT**
(d. Mar. 3, 1808) *(ca. 1719–ca. 1792)*
(built Marrowbone)

ANDREW *m.* **ELIZABETH**
*(ca. 1723–1782)**

ELIZABETH *m.* **GEORGE**
PERKINS *(1750–1823)*
LETCHER *(built Beaver Creek)*

ALCEY *m.* **PETER** *"Saura Town Peter"*
PERKINS *(1752–1832)*
(continued on last spread)

BERRY HILL

RUTH STOVALL *m. (1st)* **PETER WILSON**
(1784–1869) *(1770–1813)*
m. (2nd)
ROBERT HAIRSTON
(1783–1852)

SAMUEL
HAIRSTON
(1788–1875)

AGNES J. P. WILSON *m.*
(1801–1880)

(continued on next spread)

HORDSVILLE

GEORGE
(1784–1865)
m.
LOUISA HARDYMAN
(1787–1847)

HARDEN
(1786–1862)
m.
SARAH S. STAPLES
(1791–1845)

SAMUEL
(1788–1875)
(see above)

JOHN
ADAMS
(1799–1849)

(continued on next spread)

LOUISA
HARDYMAN
(1821–1873)
m.
PETER
WILSON
WATKINS

ELIZA *m.* **SAMUEL**
PENN **WILLIAM**
(d. 1900) *(1826–1885)*

and six siblings

ELIZABETH *m.* **NICHOLAS HARDYMAN**
SEAWELL **HAIRSTON**
(1855–1944) *(1852–1927)*

After Andrew's death, Elizabeth and her children migrated to South Carolina. Their descendants, known as "Andrew's Line," spread across the South as far west as Texas, and lost contact with the other Hairstons until the 1980s.

(The Hairston genealogy is based on information supplied by Frances Hairston, Robert Ervin Hairston Jr., Peter W. Hairston, and Carolyn Henderson.)

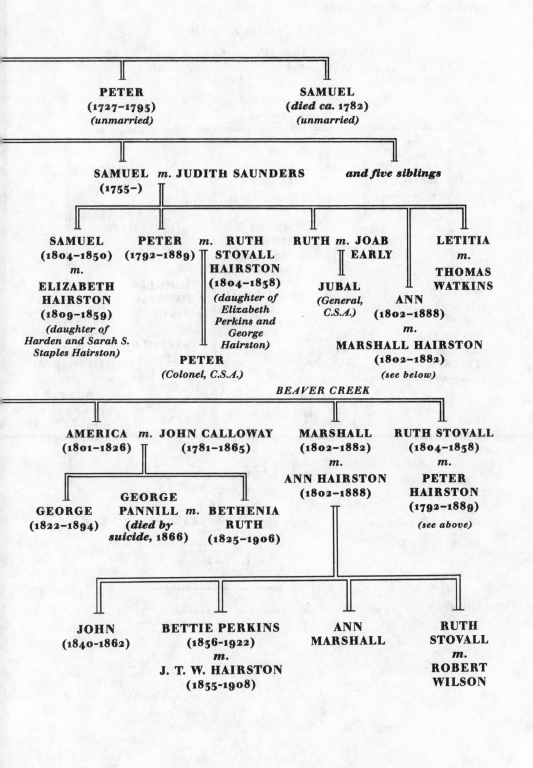

PETER
(1727–1793)
(unmarried)

SAMUEL
(died ca. 1782)
(unmarried)

SAMUEL m. JUDITH SAUNDERS
(1755–)

and five siblings

SAMUEL
(1804–1850)
m.
ELIZABETH
HAIRSTON
(1809–1859)
(daughter of
Harden and Sarah S.
Staples Hairston)

PETER
(1792–1889)

m. RUTH
STOVALL
HAIRSTON
(1804–1858)
(daughter of
Elizabeth
Perkins and
George
Hairston)

PETER
(Colonel, C.S.A.)

RUTH m. JOAB
EARLY

JUBAL
(General,
C.S.A.)

ANN
(1802–1888)
m.

MARSHALL HAIRSTON
(1802–1882)
(see below)

LETITIA
m.
THOMAS
WATKINS

BEAVER CREEK

AMERICA m. JOHN CALLOWAY
(1801–1826)   (1781–1865)

GEORGE
(1822–1894)

GEORGE
PANNILL m. BETHENIA
(died by   RUTH
suicide, 1866) (1825–1906)

MARSHALL
(1802–1882)
m.
ANN HAIRSTON
(1802–1888)

RUTH STOVALL
(1804–1858)
m.
PETER
HAIRSTON
(1792–1889)
(see above)

JOHN
(1840-1862)

BETTIE PERKINS
(1836–1922)
m.
J. T. W. HAIRSTON
(1835-1908)

ANN
MARSHALL

RUTH
STOVALL
m.
ROBERT
WILSON

(continued from previous spread)

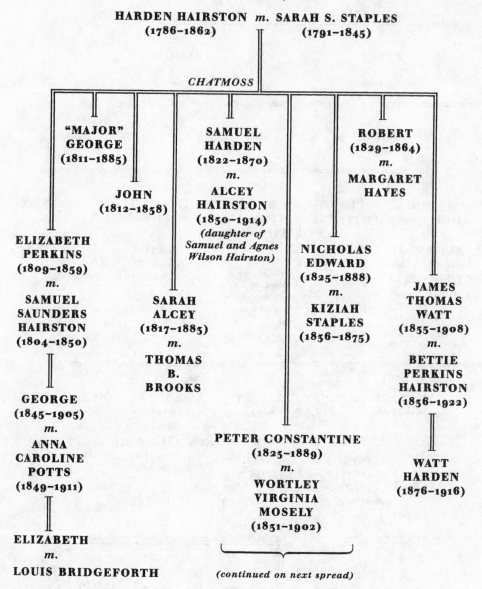

LOWNDES CO., MISS.

HARDEN HAIRSTON *m.* SARAH S. STAPLES
(1786–1862)   (1791–1845)

CHATMOSS

"MAJOR"
GEORGE
(1811–1885)

JOHN
(1812–1858)

SAMUEL
HARDEN
(1822–1870)
m.
ALCEY
HAIRSTON
(1850–1914)
*(daughter of
Samuel and Agnes
Wilson Hairston)*

ROBERT
(1829–1864)
m.
MARGARET
HAYES

ELIZABETH
PERKINS
(1809–1859)
m.
SAMUEL
SAUNDERS
HAIRSTON
(1804–1850)

SARAH
ALCEY
(1817–1883)
m.
THOMAS
B.
BROOKS

NICHOLAS
EDWARD
(1825–1888)
m.
KIZIAH
STAPLES
(1836–1875)

JAMES
THOMAS
WATT
(1835–1908)
m.
BETTIE
PERKINS
HAIRSTON
(1836–1922)

GEORGE
(1845–1905)
m.
ANNA
CAROLINE
POTTS
(1849–1911)

PETER CONSTANTINE
(1823–1889)
m.
WORTLEY
VIRGINIA
MOSELY
(1831–1902)

WATT
HARDEN
(1876–1916)

ELIZABETH
m.
LOUIS BRIDGEFORTH

(continued on next spread)

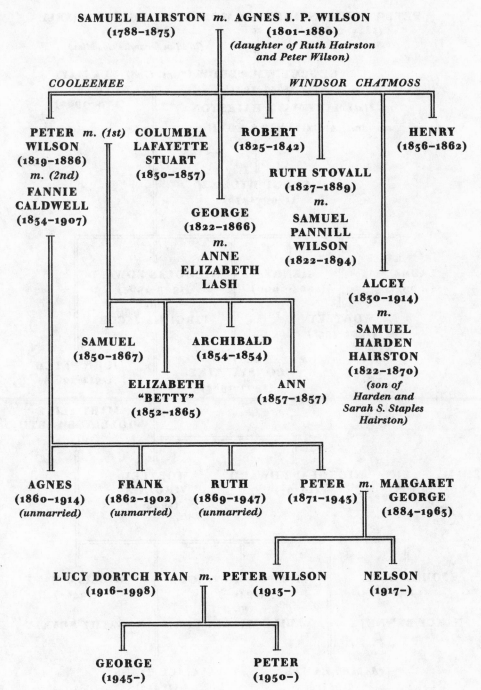

OAK HILL

SAMUEL HAIRSTON *m.* **AGNES J. P. WILSON**
(1788–1875) **(1801–1880)**
*(daughter of Ruth Hairston
and Peter Wilson)*

COOLEEMEE *WINDSOR CHATMOSS*

PETER *m. (1st)* **COLUMBIA** **ROBERT** **HENRY**
WILSON **LAFAYETTE** **(1825–1842)** **(1836–1862)**
(1819–1886) **STUART**
m. (2nd) **(1830–1857)**
FANNIE **RUTH STOVALL**
CALDWELL **(1827–1889)**
(1834–1907) *m.*
SAMUEL
PANNILL
GEORGE **WILSON**
(1822–1866) **(1822–1894)**
m.
ANNE
ELIZABETH
LASH

ALCEY
(1850–1914)
m.

SAMUEL
HARDEN
SAMUEL **ARCHIBALD** **HAIRSTON**
(1850–1867) **(1854–1854)** **(1822–1870)**
*(son of
Harden and
Sarah S. Staples
Hairston)*

ELIZABETH **ANN**
"BETTY" **(1857–1857)**
(1852–1865)

AGNES **FRANK** **RUTH** **PETER** *m.* **MARGARET**
(1860–1914) **(1862–1902)** **(1869–1947)** **(1871–1945)** **GEORGE**
(unmarried) *(unmarried)* *(unmarried)* **(1884–1963)**

LUCY DORTCH RYAN *m.* **PETER WILSON** **NELSON**
(1916–1998) **(1915–)** **(1917–)**

GEORGE **PETER**
(1945–) **(1950–)**

(continued from previous spread)

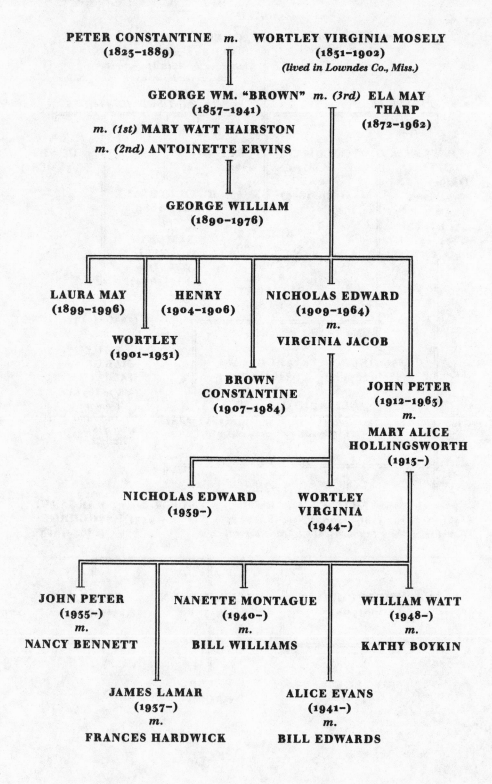

PETER CONSTANTINE *m.* WORTLEY VIRGINIA MOSELY
(1823–1889) (1831–1902)
(lived in Lowndes Co., Miss.)

GEORGE WM. "BROWN" *m. (3rd)* ELA MAY
(1857–1941) THARP
(1872–1962)
m. (1st) MARY WATT HAIRSTON
m. (2nd) ANTOINETTE ERVINS

GEORGE WILLIAM
(1890–1976)

LAURA MAY HENRY NICHOLAS EDWARD
(1899–1996) (1904–1906) (1909–1964)
m.
WORTLEY VIRGINIA JACOB
(1901–1951)

BROWN JOHN PETER
CONSTANTINE (1912–1965)
(1907–1984) *m.*
MARY ALICE
HOLLINGSWORTH
(1915–)

NICHOLAS EDWARD WORTLEY
(1939–) VIRGINIA
(1944–)

JOHN PETER NANETTE MONTAGUE WILLIAM WATT
(1935–) (1940–) (1948–)
m. *m.* *m.*
NANCY BENNETT BILL WILLIAMS KATHY BOYKIN

JAMES LAMAR ALICE EVANS
(1937–) (1941–)
m. *m.*
FRANCES HARDWICK BILL EDWARDS

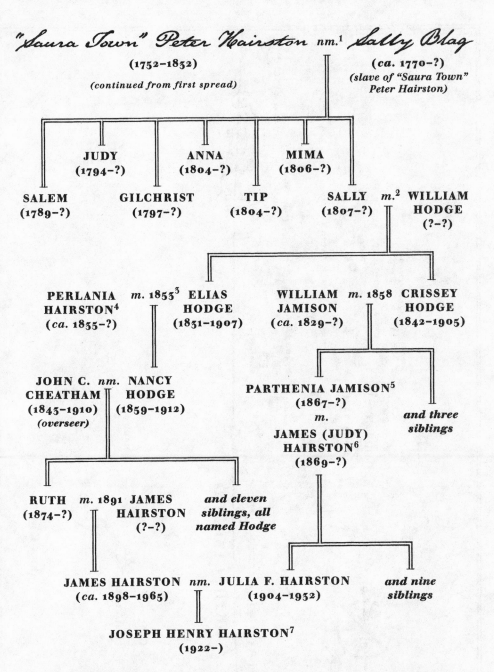

"Saura Town" Peter Hairston nm.[1] Sally Blag
(1752–1832)   (ca. 1770–?)
(continued from first spread)   (slave of "Saura Town"
                                                                      Peter Hairston)

JUDY   ANNA   MIMA
(1794–?)   (1804–?)   (1806–?)

SALEM   GILCHRIST   TIP   SALLY   m.[2] WILLIAM
(1789–?)   (1797–?)   (1804–?)   (1807–?)   HODGE
                                                                                          (?–?)

PERLANIA   m. 1853[3] ELIAS   WILLIAM   m. 1858 CRISSEY
HAIRSTON[4]   HODGE   JAMISON   HODGE
(ca. 1835–?)   (1831–1907)   (ca. 1829–?)   (1842–1905)

JOHN C.   nm. NANCY   PARTHENIA JAMISON[5]
CHEATHAM   HODGE   (1867–?)   and three
(1843–1910)   (1859–1912)   m.   siblings
(overseer)   JAMES (JUDY)
                                     HAIRSTON[6]
                                     (1869–?)

RUTH   m. 1891 JAMES   and eleven
(1874–?)   HAIRSTON   siblings, all
                   (?–?)   named Hodge

JAMES HAIRSTON   nm. JULIA F. HAIRSTON   and nine
(ca. 1898–1965)   (1904–1932)   siblings

JOSEPH HENRY HAIRSTON[7]
(1922–)

1 "nm."=never married. (The author presents his evidence for the "Saura Town" Peter and Sally Blag
  connection in Chapter 14.)
2 Married extra-legally in slavery time.
3 Married extra-legally in slavery time; marriage legally ratified 1866 in accordance with act of Virginia
  legislature and recorded in Henry County "Cohabitation Register." Elias also used the name "Hairston."
4 Perlania also known as Pauline and "Lina."
5 Had distinctly Native American features, still evident in descendants.
6 Judy was James's mother's name; it became part of his name to differentiate him from other James
  Hairstons. He would have been called "Jim Judy."
7 Genealogy of Joseph Henry Hairston, as dictated to him by his aunt, Mattie Bell Hairston, with further
  research provided by Beverly R. Millner and the author. (Not all children are shown in each generation.)

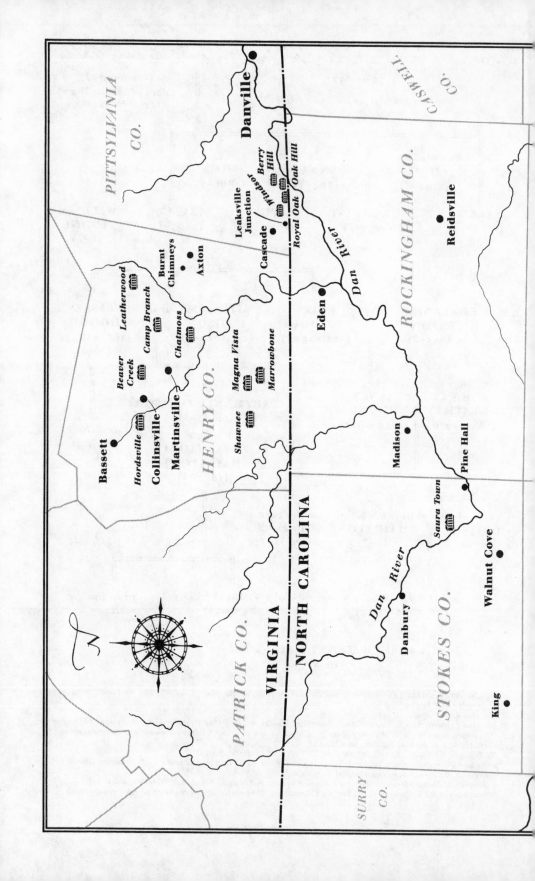

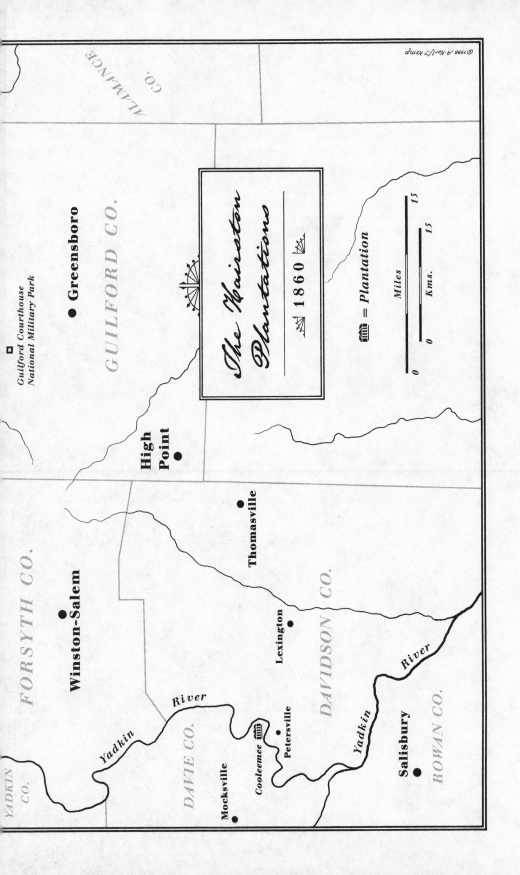

The Hairston Plantations

1860

= Plantation

Miles

Kms.

0   15

0   15

YADKIN CO.

FORSYTH CO.

Winston–Salem

GUILFORD CO.

Guilford Courthouse
National Military Park

Greensboro

High
Point

Thomasville

DAVIE CO.

Yadkin

River

Mocksville

Cooleemee

Petersville

Lexington

DAVIDSON CO.

Yadkin

River

Salisbury

ROWAN CO.

ALAMANCE CO.

A Note on Names

Since almost everyone described in this book, black or white, bears the name Hairston, it is necessary to refer to persons by their first names. No disrespect is intended, although the author is aware that it has been a sign of contempt to refer to African-Americans by their first names.

INTRODUCTION

This is a story of the legacy of slavery, and how that legacy has been passed into our own time.

At a plantation in North Carolina I met the heir to a family of slaveholders, perhaps the largest slaveholders in the South. On the same day, in the library of the old master's mansion, I met the grandson of one of those slaves. Both men shared the name Hairston.

The family saga they began to tell spanned two centuries, from the Revolution to today.

Since that meeting I have spent seven years exploring the past of these two families. I immersed myself in the immense Hairston plantation archive—running to nearly 25,000 items; I scoured the records of counties, states, and courts; I studied the documents left by the slave traders, by the Quakers who aided runaway slaves and freedmen, and by the Yankee officers who imposed freedom on a bitter South. I spent weeks at a time reading the rosters of the slaves, trying to conjure some meaning from the endless litany of the dead. More important, I went out into the old plantation country in Virginia, North Carolina, and Mississippi to seek out the descendants of the slaves and recover the testimony of their exodus.

The black family's story is extraordinary—the true story of the triumphant rise of a remarkable people—the children, grandchildren, and great-grandchildren of slaves, who struggled to pull themselves up from servitude and poverty to take their rightful places in mainstream America. A vast panorama of history unfolds in a narrative that places black Americans at the center of the national experience. Their story touches every facet of American endeavor, from Hollywood to Wall Street, from the coal fields of West Virginia to the battlefields of Europe in World War

II, from a cotton plantation in Mississippi to the computer command center that guided Neil Armstrong to the moon.

In contrast, it has been the fate of the white family—once one of the wealthiest in America—to endure the decline and fall of the Old South. But that was only part of the tale. Beneath the surface lay a hidden history, the history of slavery's curse and how that curse followed the slaveholders for generation after generation. Beneath layers of lies and myth existed a story the slaveholders and their descendants had kept hidden for almost a century and a half. It was not a story of horror, but of love and heroism powerful enough to shake the foundation myth of the South.

In the end, the story of these families is a parable of redemption. It is about the universal human struggle to come to terms with the past. Paradoxically, these families found that one way to transcend the past is to embrace it.

PART I

THE LAND OF THE PHARAOHS

Fear not, for I have redeemed you; I have called you by name:
you are mine.

Fear not, for I am with you; from the east I will bring back your
descendants, from the west I will gather you. I will say to the north: Give
them up! And to the south: Hold not back! Bring back my sons from afar,
and my daughters from the ends of the earth: everyone who is named as
mine.

—ISAIAH 43:1, 5–7

COOLEEMEE
PLANTATION

The mansion at Cooleemee was a commanding presence. Lordly and gleaming, it stood atop a knoll not far from the Yadkin River in North Carolina, at the end of a gravel road that snaked through a pine forest. I emerged from the woods to see the house set on a pedestal of terraced gardens, painted a brilliant white, and guarded by a pair of magnificent trees, a flamboyant maple and a stately Southern magnolia. I approached it from below, like a supplicant.

Tall and heavyset, with a great wave of white hair breaking across his head, Judge Peter Wilson Hairston made an imposing figure as he stood in the doorway of Cooleemee Plantation—the very image of the Old South aristocrat. He wore a bathrobe and slippers—he had been, he explained, polishing the silver—but that did not in the least diminish the gravity of his presence. From the doorway boomed a powerful, resonant voice—truly the voice of a judge. The voice was a great gift, an instrument worthy of an actor, the perfect instrument, as I would find, for telling the old stories of the plantation across a candlelit dining table, with tumblers of bourbon within easy reach. He could adjust its tone and volume from gentle to fierce. It could whisper conspiratorially and roar with pleasure. It was also a voice that had sent men to jail. Now it firmly laid down the law, right in the doorway.

"First things first. My name is spelled *Hair*ston, but it is pronounced *Hars*ton. If you can manage that"—now the smile emerged—"we'll get along just fine."

With this ground rule set down, Judge Hairston led me from the blazing sunshine of a June morning into the cool, echoing dimness of the mansion.

It was a rare privilege to enter this house. Cooleemee is a time capsule, a relic of the dead and untouchable past that has managed to come into our own time because of its isolation and because of the tenacity of its occupants. Many of the furnishings are those that the judge's grandfather put in place before the Civil War. Time has moved so slowly at this house that when you step across the threshold, you can be forgiven if you don't know what century you are in.

The graciousness, the beauty of the house, were breathtaking. The stairhall was a large octagon, three stories high. On one side of the hall a wide door was open onto a view of lush greenery—tall rows of English boxwood, pungently fragrant in the June heat. A magnificent staircase curved along the walls, swirling up to a tower that poked into the sunlight fifty feet above. In the silence a tall-case clock gravely ticked the time. Along the walls hung family portraits, including one that seemed to be of the judge as a much younger man, with jet-black hair and beetling brows. In the dimness it was hard to see at first glance that the clothes were a century off—it was actually a portrait of his grandfather, the Peter Wilson Hairston who built the house. I would later find that there was an uncanny resemblance in the male Hairston line going back five generations.

On the wall at the foot of the stairs was a portrait of a boy about four years old wearing a pale blue suit. This was Sammy, the son of the builder. The artist had posed him outdoors with a favorite toy, a large wooden hoop. Tossed to the ground was a blue hat with a black plume, the jaunty adornment worn in battle by the boy's uncle, General Jeb Stuart, the Confederacy's legendary cavalry commander.

Six doorways opened onto the hall, creating the impression of a stage set for a country-house comedy with drunken, amorous cavaliers rushing about in pursuit of ladies in crinoline. The doors led to a dining room, drawing room, master bedroom, and library, the judge's book-lined sanctum.

In the master bedroom stood a gigantic four-poster bed (to move it requires six men) that the judge's grandfather had ordered from New York. There were porcelain and mirrors from France, paintings from Germany, a set of silver from England, and furniture made in North Carolina by a free black cabinetmaker who once ran the largest furniture-making operation in the state, with many wealthy planters among his clients. And there were even older North Carolina pieces, a tall chest and table from a plantation owned by the judge's great-great-great-grandfather. The table had been made from a cherry tree cut down in 1791. The judge has the receipt from the woodsman who cut the tree.

Cooleemee was one of many houses I was visiting in various parts of the country to write a book about old family homes and the people who live in them. As I interviewed the occupants of these venerable places, I heard history not as a historian would write it but as a novelist would imagine it. I became privy to the secret sorrows of these old families, and I learned also about the strange and cruel maneuvers of money. At one time most of these families had been rich. Money moved like the tide— washing in inexorably, lifting everything in a slow and giddy ascent, then just as inexorably receding, slipping from frantic fingers, leaving only wreckage behind.

A special poignancy suffused the Southern houses. They were the remnants not only of the vanished past but of a vanished society, one that had been destroyed by the Civil War, a war that had left behind what Faulkner called "the deep South dead since 1865 and peopled with garrulous outraged baffled ghosts."

I visited some people who had inherited nothing but the beautiful shell of their forebears' prosperity. They inhabit huge and breezy houses, built as if for a race of giants, with massive furniture ornate with the optimism of boom times, the drawers stuffed with debts. Ghosts pace the halls at night. They live in twenty-four-hour mockery; yet they stay on, pouring their meager dollars into polish and plaster. The houses embody a precious inheritance—it is the past itself that belongs to these families; it is their legacy, their pride, the floor beneath their feet. It has been given to them because of who they are. And the ghosts that walk hold no terror for them, they are guardian spirits.

Amidst all the losses these families have endured, they have been able to take comfort from their tangible links to the past. The strength of their heritage has kept these families together. They know history because it was their forebears who enacted it. They know the family tree going back to the far reaches of Ireland and Scotland and England, and they know where all the third cousins are today. They have to know—one of those obscure cousins might turn up in probate court to challenge a will.

As I sat talking with the descendants of the old planters, I felt all the moral confusion of a spy. I was a Northerner adrift in the heart of the old Confederacy, an honored visitor in stately homes whose legacy I found deeply troubling. America's racial problems had begun here, in the very homes I was planning to write about. It was impossible for me to put that fact out of my mind. Many people, black and white, believe that the key to our racial troubles lies in the past. Some black leaders still talk of the reparations America never paid to the slaves and their descendants for the centuries spent in slavery and the near-slavery of sharecropping.

I wanted to find an African-American family that was descended from slaves on one of the plantations I was writing about. I wanted to hear their testimony about what the experience and the memory of slavery on that particular plantation had done to their family. Was there, in fact, a centuries-old burden still being carried today? Has the past left them with a hatred of white Americans that will never be expunged? Was there anything in their past which they looked upon with pride? Is it possible for an African-American to feel any connection at all to the past, or is it too dreadful even to contemplate? I worried that even if I succeeded in finding such a slave descendant, it might be impossibly embarrassing to ask the right questions.

In any case, I couldn't find them. At the Southern houses I visited, the descendants of the slaves had left long ago. Some might very well have been living down the road from the old plantation, but the white owners didn't know it. There was no reason for them to keep track of the blacks, and they certainly had no interest in doing so.

At one house the only surviving trace of the blacks had been deliberately, though not malevolently, obliterated. There was a burial ground of slaves and free blacks in a pasture by a creek. When the owners rented out their property to another farmer, he told them that he needed that patch of ground too. So the burial markers, iron crosses handmade by the plantation's blacksmiths, were uprooted. Too beautiful to discard, they were stored in the basement of the house—symbols of Christian suffering, iron promises of resurrection—along with a century and a half's worth of odds and ends. The owners meant no disrespect, but certainly no overpowering sense of regard for those particular dead or for their descendants, who might one day come looking for the resting place of their forebears, rose up in their hearts to restrain them. They were poor themselves, they needed to rent out the land, and there was no one around to plead the case of the dead.

The judge ushered me into the library and began to talk about the history of his family. And history poured from him in torrents, as he talked of the family's exploits in the Revolution and the Civil War. The judge's grandfather had fought by the side of Jeb Stuart, his cousin and brother-in-law. He served later with another cousin, General Jubal Early, whose mother was a Hairston. He lost friends and relatives in battle at Manassas, at Williamsburg, and Shiloh. Jeb Stuart himself fell in battle late in the war, hit by a wild shot from the pistol of a federal trooper who had hastily taken aim at Stuart's flamboyant plume.

The judge showed me his most precious heirloom, which went back to the family's origins in this country. It was a crude wooden trunk, hewn from a single log and fitted with hinges and a lock made of iron. The trunk was covered in deerskin, and the inside was lined with faded, worm-eaten newspapers. The first Hairston to come to America, known in the family as Peter the Immigrant, had brought it with him on the journey from Scotland and Ireland. The trunk had contained women's clothing. The clothes were a link to the Scottish past, a link that held great significance for one member of the family, the judge's great-great-grandmother Ruth. "The day before she died she sent the servants up to the attic at Berry Hill [one of the Hairston plantations in Virginia], the old family place, and told them to bring the chest down and air the clothes inside, because that's what she was going to be buried in. And so she was." She had wardrobes full of the finest clothing, purchased with the wealth of her plantations, yet she wished to go to her grave in the simple clothing of times past, when the Hairstons were warriors in the cause of liberty.

Peter the Immigrant had come to America a refugee from war. As a young man of about twenty, he had joined the 1715 Rising, a rebellion of the Scots against English rule. The result was a hideous slaughter of the Scottish patriots at the Battle of Preston. Peter fled to Ireland, where he married and had five children. About 1729 he brought his family to America. They had landed in Pennsylvania, but after a few years, they headed south along the Great Wagon Road to Virginia, where they established themselves as tobacco planters and acquired slaves.

As the judge continued his recitation of the family chronicle, it slowly dawned on me that the beautiful mansion in which I was sitting was a mere outpost and represented but a small fragment of a vast plantation empire, built up over several generations. The Immigrant's children and grandchildren created a network of plantations along the southern border of Virginia, stretching in a broad swath through the counties of Halifax, Pittsylvania, Henry, Franklin, and Patrick. They expanded south into North Carolina, acquiring land in the counties of Stokes, Rockingham, Forsyth, Davie, and Davidson. The Hairstons did not know it when they came here, but by an extraordinary stroke of good fortune they had settled on the best tobacco-growing land in the world, a region of the Virginia–North Carolina Piedmont that would later be called the Bright Belt.

Their plantation empire grew so large that it almost defies description. In Virginia and North Carolina the Hairstons established ten major plantations, and each of these had numerous satellite plantations that might be worked by a dozen slaves or fewer. When Judge Hairston tried to draw up a comprehensive list of the family's pre–Civil War holdings, he came up with the astounding total of forty-five plantations, large and small, in four states. The judge's great-grandfather Samuel Hairston had his headquarters at Oak Hill plantation outside of Danville. His brother Marshall owned Beaver Creek plantation near Martinsville. Another brother, Robert, lived with his wife, Ruth (who was also his first cousin), at Berry Hill, and in the 1830s he went down to Mississippi with yet another brother, Harden, to establish cotton plantations there with a small army of slaves. Other branches of the family were established on hilltops and along riverbanks in southern Virginia, and the judge reeled off the names of the plantations—Windsor, Chatmoss, Hordsville, Marrowbone, Royal Oak.

The Hairstons always seemed to have cash in hand when a parcel of land became available. Dour and devoted to acquisition, they lived by the old Scottish maxim "Money is flat and meant to be piled up." Indeed a Richmond newspaper in 1851 ran an article saying that the judge's great-grandfather, Samuel Hairston of Oak Hill, was probably the richest man in Virginia, and perhaps in the United States, the possessor of land and slaves worth $5 million. He was reputedly the largest slaveholder in the South.

It is impossible to say precisely how many slaves the entire family owned. Judge Hairston consulted over one hundred plantation lists and inventories to compile a roster of the slaves his grandfather had owned. It ran to more than fourteen hundred names, but represented only a small fragment of the family's total holdings. The land and slaveholding records that do exist are misleading and tend to understate the size of their possessions, because it seems that some of the Hairstons were not exactly candid with the tax collector. Still, the judge estimated that the combined branches of his family held ten thousand slaves.

To keep this huge legacy of land and slaves intact, the Hairstons revived one of the old customs of the European nobility—they married each other. The brothers Samuel, Marshall, and Robert all married cousins, creating a family tree of insane complexity. Samuel and his wife, Agnes, built the mansion at Oak Hill. Their first son was Peter Wilson

Hairston, Judge Hairston's grandfather. He combined two branches of the family tree and became heir to the accumulated wealth of five generations. He was to be the culmination of all that had come before, the man they all expected to carry the wealth of slavery through the rest of the century. Then came the Civil War.

Of the family's great wealth, Cooleemee is one of the few surviving relics. The capital of the family empire, Oak Hill, stood empty for many years, and finally burned.

There are no mementos of the Civil War at Cooleemee, no swords or muskets over the mantel, no tattered flags, no sentimental pictures of Robert E. Lee. The memory of the war was vivid enough without such relics. Judge Hairston remembers the visits of an elderly woman, related to the Hairstons by marriage, who wore black mourning clothes in memory of her brother, who had been killed leading a cavalry charge at Manassas sixty years earlier. The judge's grandmother was, he said, "the most unreconstructed Southerner that ever was." She never let go of her anger at the North. A young girl visiting Cooleemee on the Fourth of July was imprudent enough to show up with a small American flag pinned to her dress. She was stopped at the door by Fanny—"Child, take off that *Yankee rag* before you put foot in this house." Judge Hairston's father wished simply to put an end to the era. "Dad objected so to the bitterness over the Civil War that when I was growing up, you could not mention it in this house."

In the last days of the war, a Yankee raiding party approached Cooleemee and may have entered the plantation but did no damage. No one knows exactly why the house survived, but the judge believes that the plantation's manager may have offered the Yankees provisions in exchange for sparing the mansion. What is known is that a slave named John Goolsby risked his life to save the family silver. Goolsby, the plantation coachman, had served throughout the war with Peter Hairston as body servant and horse handler. He loaded the family silver in a wagon and drove sixty miles to Stokes County, dodging Yankee raiders, and buried the silver in the vegetable garden at the Saura Town Plantation. Goolsby lived into his nineties, and Judge Hairston remembers seeing him as a very old man at Saura Town. The silver Goolsby hid from the Yankees, usually kept in a bank, is brought out for family functions at Saura Town. The judge was polishing it the morning I came to the house.

I had heard such stories of "the faithful slave" at other plantations. Supposedly such servants begged the Yankees to spare the master, spare the house. They hid the furniture, the mirrors, the silver, and brought it all back when the Yankees had passed. It was hard to believe that people on the brink of freedom would cling to their masters and shun the liberators, but that is what the whites all maintained. Since the slaves and their descendants had gone, no one could say otherwise.

So I asked the question that had drawn only blank looks at other Southern houses: Did the judge have any idea what happened to the slaves and their descendants? Indeed, he did. Quite a few descendants of Cooleemee slaves were still living in the vicinity. Most of them were named Hairston, but they pronounced the name in their own way. "The whites follow the old Scottish pronunciation," he explained. "I believe that the blacks originally used our pronunciation, but when the Yankee schoolmasters came down here after the war and got their hands on them, they made them say it as it is spelled."

It suddenly made sense that the judge had insisted, almost as a condition of my entering the house, that I get the Scottish pronunciation of the name right. I thought that this may have been the white family's way of distancing themselves from the blacks who had adopted the name but had given up the odd way of saying it.

So there were dozens of slave descendants, perhaps more, still living here. What stories would they have to tell? Did they have a sense of their family history as strong as the judge's?

I was about to ask for the telephone book so that I could get the addresses of black Hairstons and write to them for appointments when the judge surprised me by saying, "I'll call my old friend Squire Hairston and ask him to come over."

I found it hard to imagine that a prominent judge and landowner could be on such good terms with a black man that the latter, out of pure friendship, would drop whatever he was doing and rush over for a chat with a total stranger. Perhaps Squire Hairston would feel that it was in his interest to answer this sudden summons. I felt uneasy interviewing Squire on these terms—I felt that he was being called in to give a command performance, to regale a visitor with old plantation stories at the behest of the master. Squire might tell me only what he thought Judge Peter would want me to hear. And it occurred to me that the judge's reference to Squire as "my old friend" was window dressing, intended to show an outsider that he could be a man of the people, of the black people to boot.

Before long, our conversation was interrupted by the sound of voices in the stairhall. The judge's wife, Lucy, ushered Squire Hairston into the library. The judge rose to welcome his guest, and the two men shook hands warmly.

This meeting was not what I had expected. Here were two men with the closest possible ties to slavery, the grandsons of slave and slaveholder, greeting each other cordially in the library of the old master's mansion. How did this come to pass?

Of average height but solidly built, Squire was dressed in work clothes, neatly pressed green pants and shirt. Although he was seventy years old, he still worked a few hours a day as a custodian at the Davidson County Community College.

Squire settled into one of the library's worn leather chairs. The judge excused himself, leaving us to talk in private.

I started by asking about his family. Squire said his father was born on Cooleemee Plantation in 1886. His father worked all his life as a sharecropper here, and on the side he planted tobacco on two acres of his own land, which he had bought for $20 in the early 1900s. Squire's grandfather, named Franklin, had been born a slave in 1851. Squire had been able to trace back to his great-grandmother Louisa, Franklin's mother, born in 1833. The judge had shown him the plantation ledger that recorded Louisa's birth. But beyond that he could not go. His deeper ancestry might be somewhere in the older plantation ledgers, but no one had been able to trace a family tree among the thousands of names.

Squire spoke slowly and chose his words carefully. He talked about his lineage but offered few details about anyone's life. He had heard the story of Goolsby hiding the silver and had no reason to doubt it, but he had no direct knowledge that it was true. As I listened to him, I was trying to form a tactful series of questions. From the judge, history had poured out in a flood—like many white Southerners, the judge possessed a rich storehouse of plantation tales to draw upon. Asking the grandson of a slave about whips, chains, and the humiliations of slavery was another matter. But this was my one chance and I took it. I asked Squire what he knew about the old days on the plantation.

"An old lady used to sit down and talk to us a lot about what they went through."

"What was her name?"

"Victoria."

"What were some of the stories that she told?"

"Well, she told how they went out in the fields . . . worked hard and everything . . ." Squire looked away and, to my surprise, broke into a quiet laugh. "Well—she told a lot of stories." He fell into silence.

"Nothing you want to tell me?"

"Well, I've got a lot of memories."

He would say no more. I imagined that generations of memories were flashing through his mind, memories that might not be the sort of quaint and poignant anecdotes that writers like to collect for books about old houses. Perhaps he did not realize that I was willing to listen to anything he cared to say, that I was not interested in stories that were merely charming. Then it occurred to me that Squire had laughed at the idea that I expected him to explain, in a few minutes, his family's experience during slavery time and afterward.

Squire Hairston's warm greeting to the judge—indeed, his mere presence in the old master's mansion—seemed to indicate that he had made his peace with Judge Hairston over what had happened in the past, but obviously he was inclined to keep his family's past private. Just before Squire arrived, I had asked the judge about how his grandfather had treated the black Hairstons in slavery. He said I should ask Squire, that he would not presume to speak for them. The tradition in the white family was that they had treated their slaves well, but he acknowledged that the blacks might think differently. Only they could tell me.

I was reluctant to press the matter with Squire—perhaps he would never talk about such things to a white person—but I made one more try.

"I guess there are some stories that will never go outside the Hairston family?"

"Never will . . . never will, no."

That seemed to be the end of it. But as he stood up to signal an end to the interview, he said there would be a reunion of the black Hairstons in a few months, and he invited me to attend. If I wanted to gather stories of the old days at Cooleemee, he said, there would be people at the reunion with ties to the plantation. He would see if anyone would talk with me.

After Squire left, I went up to the tower. It had a panoramic view—on one side of the house were old barns and stables; on the other, open fields that ran down to the Yadkin River a quarter of a mile away. At its peak just before the Civil War, this plantation had six hundred slaves and forty-two hundred acres. Since then the land and the house had changed hardly at all—so I could actually touch the objects the slaveholder had touched and see the very things he had seen. And I wondered about the mind and soul of such a man. How different was the mind that looked down from this great height through this window and saw a white boy rolling a hoop for fun and a black boy sweating in a cotton field? In 1860 it seemed that the order of things would never change. The order of the world was good and could not be otherwise because Peter Wilson Hairston believed that God Himself had imposed the existing order on the world, and it was not for man to tamper with His design. "Thank Him who placed us here," wrote a Southern poet, "Beneath so kind a sky."

Before leaving I asked the judge, if he had been his grandfather, would he have freed his slaves?

"He had so many, it would have been all but impossible to free them, even if he could have hired them right back. The law required that if you set people free, you had to send them out of the state. How would they provide for themselves? And he didn't own the slaves outright—his title was all mixed up with his grandmother and the rest of the family. And of course, slavery was simply the accepted system back then."

I asked him the question that he had been asked many times before: Did he feel any guilt about his family's past as slaveholders?

"You can't repeal history!" he thundered.

And then, in a quieter voice, he said, "I can't go back and unwind it."

As the day of the Hairston reunion grew nearer, I realized how fortunate I was to be invited to it. If a friendly connection actually existed between the white and the black families, it was certainly rare, and it would be a privilege to document it. More valuable still was the chance to interview some of the last surviving people who had actually seen and spoken with slaves. But I also began to have some misgivings. Whatever the blacks told me would end up as a short postscript to the tale of a white slave-holding family—a black stamp of approval, solicited by the white author, on the plantation days. And in my story, as in so many others, black

13

people would be remote figures viewed at a distance as the whites dominated the scene. But as far as I could tell, the history of a black family was largely unrecoverable. The documentation simply did not exist. So I put aside my misgivings and persuaded myself that I was doing some small service to the black family by setting down the memories that did still echo from the past.

The Hairston family was meeting at a large hotel on the outskirts of Baltimore. Off the lobby at a registration table, two women sat wearing "HAIRSTON CLAN" buttons. A few people milled around, but there was no evidence of a bustling reunion. It seemed that I had come for nothing.

Squire emerged from an elevator. I had last seen him in his work clothes, but he was dressed now in a gray business suit. He hurried me into the elevator, saying that some people were waiting for me upstairs.

Gathered in the living room of a suite were about fifteen men, all in business suits, and two women in silk dresses. Unsmiling, they eyed me silently as I came in. Most were middle-aged; a few appeared to be about seventy. Three were in their twenties. I had expected an interview; instead it seemed I had been called before a tribunal.

Squire introduced me and said a few words about the family background of the people in the room. Verdeen Hairston, a neighbor of Squire's in Petersville, was the great-grandson of a Cooleemee slave. He was a farmer. A tall, powerful man, with a broad face set in a scowl, he did not look happy to see an outsider coming into this family gathering. A speech impediment made his words come out in a strained, basso growl, tending to increase the fierceness of his expression. A woman in her forties with reddish hair and yellow skin, named Ever Lee Hairston, also wore a serious expression and listened to the conversation with great intensity, but she said nothing, and I noticed that she never looked at me. Squire said she had grown up at Cooleemee.

The president of the clan was Collie Hairston from Camden, New Jersey, where he once served as an assemblyman. Born at Cooleemee, he was about the same age as the judge. His sister Marie was in the room as well. Their parents had been Cooleemee's housekeepers, the last of the black domestics to be part of the everyday life of Cooleemee. Collie's great-grandfather had been John Goolsby, who was the patriarch of six branches of the Hairston family. Collie told me the story I had heard from the judge, about Goolsby hiding the white family's silver in the last days of the Civil War. This seemed to be the agreed-upon plantation-days story that both the whites and blacks told to outsiders. I thought that the white family might have made up the story, but Collie said that he had heard it from Goolsby's son.

"There were twelve children in my family, all born on that plantation," Collie said. "My mother spent eighty-five years on the plantation. She was born in Stokes County, and when she was six, she moved into Cooleemee. My grandfather drove a mule team for the plantation; he used to take loads up to Virginia."

Collie's account of his family background was interrupted by the arrival of a short, bald, elderly man who walked with a cane. The room rose to greet him. This was Jester Hairston, the family celebrity. Nearing ninety, he was a regular on the television comedy *Amen,* in which he played the character of Rolly. Everyone called him "Cousin Jester," but he was introduced to me as "Dr. Hairston," in recognition of his four honorary doctorates in music. He was one of several Hairstons who were well-known. The others were sports figures, but I found Jester especially intriguing because he had had a long career in theater, radio, in Hollywood, and as a performer of Negro spirituals. He had figured prominently in two films I remembered well from my childhood. He had appeared in John Wayne's 1960 movie *The Alamo,* playing the role of Jethro, the archetypal "faithful slave," who remains by the side of his master, Jim Bowie, despite being granted his freedom and with it the chance to leave the death trap at the Alamo. In one of the final scenes, as a horde of Mexican soldiers closes in on the injured Jim Bowie (played by Richard Widmark), Jethro hurls himself over his former master to take the death blow meant for the white man. Five years earlier, Jester had conducted the chorus for another movie that dealt with slavery—the Howard Hawks film *Land of the Pharaohs,* an epic of ancient Egypt written partly by William Faulkner, which portrayed a pharaoh's mania for wealth and the labors of an enslaved people in bondage to the master's obsession.

I had not expected that Jester Hairston would turn up at the reunion, and I was pleased when he was guided to the chair closest to mine and the conversation was turned over to him. He said he had been to Cooleemee and knew the judge.

"About three years ago I did a concert near Cooleemee, and Peter wrote me and told me he wanted me to stay at his house that night. He came down and got me and brought me up to the plantation, and I spent the night and slept in his bed. And I didn't know it until he told me, 'Jester, I was born in this bed.' I didn't feel it was any great honor, but it showed me we were friends."

I asked him how he felt about staying in that house, given its history.

"It's a part of my ancestry, and it's a part of me just as much as it's a part of Peter. My folks were there in a different capacity, but that was the way of life in those days. It's the way it came up. Why look at it with hate? If you hated everyone who had us in slavery . . . that was the system in those days. I don't know a better man than Peter."

Dr. Hairston was a raconteur of the same high order as the judge. He launched into a series of stories about meeting Hairstons, white and black, on his travels around the country over the last sixty years. As a young man he had gone out to Hollywood in 1936 with an all-black choir from Harlem to sing in the film *Green Pastures*, which led to an offer to perform on a radio comedy.

"After we finished the picture we got a radio program with Irving S. Cobb. *Paducah Plantation* was the name of Cobb's show. He'd say, 'Brother Hairston and the Hall Johnson Choir will perform so and so.' I got a letter from a woman in Long Beach who was thrilled to hear the name Hairston on the radio and wanted to know if she was related to me. I told her to meet me after the show. I saw this tall redhead standing with her husband. I'm sure they thought I was the janitor come to turn up the seats, and she just froze—I put my arms around her and said to her husband, 'Can you see the family resemblance?' And he said, 'No, Jester, that will have to grow on me.' "

The room erupted in laughter. They must have heard that story a dozen times, but Jester's polished delivery never failed to get a laugh. He went on to more reminiscences, and I realized that I was truly in the hands of a brilliant performer. He had succeeded in putting me at arm's length. He could entertain an outsider with stories and send him home smiling, without ever revealing an ounce of himself. From reading clip files on Jester Hairston I knew that he had not collected four honorary doctorates and been invited to perform around the world just because he had cracked jokes on *Amos 'n' Andy* and carried a spear in Tarzan movies. He had spent his lifetime collecting, arranging, and performing Negro spirituals. He had said that the Negro spiritual expressed the deep religious faith of the slaves, even though their masters thought they could use religion to keep the slaves docile. He was a profound scholar of the African-American slave experience and had struggled with the ambiguities and contradictions of that history. But he was keeping all that hidden from me. When he saw a white man with a notebook, his guard went up.

Jester had put everyone at ease, and I was soon filling my notebook with the family's recollections of plantation life. They jogged one another's memories, recalling for each other half-forgotten ancestors. Soon I could not keep up with the outpouring of memory as ghostly generations, white and black, rushed past. They remembered "Marse Peter," the judge's father, who insisted that the blacks address him by that title left over from slavery time, even though he was born ten years after Emancipation. Some knew stories of "old Peter," the judge's grandfather. Eventually they seemed to forget that I was in the room and made no effort to explain to me what they were talking about. I heard them speak of lost relatives in Mississippi; about the distant era before Cooleemee existed, when their forebears lived in "Sorrow Town," or Saura Town, as I knew it; and about some of the other Hairston plantations, Oak Hill, Berry Hill, Beaver Creek, and Chatmoss. Collie and his sister tried to sort out a long and hopelessly complex story about a spat with the judge over who would have the right to bury their parents. All the talk about ancestry, about Sorrow Town and Mississippi, about who would bury whom—it all baffled me, but among themselves they were unfurling the tapestry of their private history, and they could see vividly into a past that was invisible to me. Then Collie turned to me and said suddenly, "Peter will tell you everything. He'll tell you some stories you don't want to hear."

His sister resumed talking about the plantation, but I was barely listening to her. I was trying to puzzle out what Collie had meant. Something they had just said among themselves had provoked this remark, but I could not fathom what it was. Squire must have been thinking about it too, because he answered my question before I had a chance to ask it. He began indirectly, talking about his ancestry, running through the dates when his ancestors were born, until he had gotten back to slavery time. He recalled a conversation he had had with an old man many years ago, and as he recounted it, he briefly took on the voice of that man, his low drawl shifting up the scale to a melodic singsong. And as he spoke, the atmosphere in the room changed completely. The people in the room recognized the names he was speaking, and they knew what he was leading up to. They realized that he had made a decision. He would not wait for the judge to tell me what I didn't want to hear; he would tell me himself.

"I have the names of all the slaves," Squire said. "And the names of those who were born as a *mulatto*." He pronounced the word slowly, so that I wouldn't miss it. "I have the names of all of those who were born half-white. And some of *my people* were half-white. My foreparents. They

17

were born from the masters by the kitchen women. They would take our mothers and get children just like they wanted to."

Another man broke in to say, "If you look at us, we are not purebred Africans." He was almost fair-skinned himself. I had noticed as soon as I had walked in the room that the people in it were a spectrum of browns, blacks, and yellows. I had thought the subject was taboo, but this man now spoke of it openly.

"You have Peter's book?" Jester asked. He was referring to a history of Cooleemee written by the judge and published with the help of the Hairston Clan. A third of the book was taken up with a roster of his grandfather's slaves.

"The names are in there of the people whose mothers were the slaves and the Hairstons were the fathers. It happened on that plantation. That's what happened on all the plantations."

"I didn't know that," I said. Of course, I had no way of knowing it; and I would never have known it if they had not told me. So the slave roster that Judge Hairston had compiled for his book contained the names of his own relatives.

"But you know . . ." Squire seemed unsure of what he wanted to say. "Time changes everything. . . . They would take our mothers." He stopped. "And just like they would take our foreparents and get children just like they wanted, now our black boys can take the white girls and get babies on them. It's just coming back. It all started with the white master on the plantation." He shook his head and said in a loud voice, "Whatever you do, *you're going to reap it*."

Verdeen spoke up, and I strained to hear his words. "White people say to me, 'God wanted you to be with your own.' And I reply, 'It's funny—it took you all two hundred years to learn this.' "

Jester nodded his head and remarked, "That's what you call 'reality.' "

Verdeen looked at me and said, "You asked us the question, 'How do we feel about it?' How do *you* feel about it?"

Sadness is what I felt, and shame that I had picked open an old wound. I had been foolish enough to take Squire's meeting with the judge at face value. I knew that the abuse of black women by the slaveholders had happened on plantations, but I looked upon it as part of the remote past. For the people in this room history was not an abstraction, it was personal, and bitter. I felt humbled by the courage of Squire's admission. In my own past there was no equivalent, and I avoided Verdeen's question by saying that I had no right to answer it.

"My family has been here only since around 1900. You're more American than I am. You go back farther. Your people go back, I don't know, maybe two hundred years or more."

"*Sixteen nineteen,*" Jester declared. This was a date burned in his memory. "*Sixteen hundred and nineteen*—when the first boatload of blacks from Africa was brought to Virginia."

Another man spoke up: "You say we are more American than you. But *you* are accepted. We didn't come here by choice. We were chained and brought here. We are a long-suffering and a forgiving people. But we are still not totally accepted."

There was the briefest pause as they reflected on this remark, on the trials that their family had endured that had not been sufficient to make them fully American in the eyes of many, and someone joked, "But we're working on it."

Laughter spread through the room, and they let the tension go. Collie announced that they had to start their business meeting. He said that if I wanted more information the family would cooperate. I shook hands with Collie and Squire, nodded to the others, and left.

I had come to ask for their absolution over a history I did not know. I knew only the inside of a house in North Carolina, where I had witnessed what now seemed merely a ritual of courtesy enacted by two elderly men of the South. I had been arrogant enough to assume that an additional hour of chatting with the black Hairstons would be sufficient for me to seal a pact of forgiveness between the races. They knew why I had come. In their view I was an emissary of the judge, and at first they were content to give me what I wanted, but Squire decided it would be wrong. He wanted me to know the truth. He had opened a door to his family's history, and I now felt obliged to go through that door and seek out as much of their history as I could. No sooner had I made this decision than I discovered how large a task lay before me.

The hotel lobby that had been almost empty earlier in the day was now filled. Buses were arriving from distant parts of the East and the South. Several hundred people crowded the huge space. Their name tags listed hometowns from all over the North and the South—New York, Philadelphia, Washington, Detroit, Baltimore. There were large contingents from Ohio and from rural Virginia and North Carolina, and a few people from the West. As I walked through the lobby, people greeted one another with hugs and kisses, showed off their children, and hailed long-lost cousins. The size of the family astounded me, and I was moved by the strength of family feeling that could draw so many hundreds of people together across great distances. This gathering could not have sprung from nothing. It had to be the culmination of something that began deep in the past. Where were its roots? In slavery? In what came later? What fires had forged the links that held the family together?

I went from one person to another, asking where they were from and how far back they could trace their roots. I met coal miners, ministers, businesswomen and salesmen, a young surgeon, farmers and mechanics. One man's appliance business was failing; his nephew was applying to MIT. A frail man in a wheelchair, dying of cancer, talked about his grandfather, who had gone off to college in 1900 with fifty cents and a sack of flour, become a minister, and ended up a trustee of the college. He pointed me toward a sprightly woman in her nineties talking with a cluster of gray-haired men. He said they had been her students in a one-room schoolhouse seven decades before. At last the lobby began to empty as people dispersed to prepare for a banquet. The moment was slipping away, and I had been able to gather only fragments of their story.

I was approached by a courtly gentleman in his sixties whom I recognized from the earlier meeting. His name was Joseph Henry Hairston. He was the light-skinned man who had spoken up about their mixed origins.

"You're interested in plantations," he said. "So am I." His line of the family was from Chatmoss and Beaver Creek, two of the largest Hairston plantations in Virginia. As we sat in the darkening lobby of the hotel, he talked of his origins. His starting point had been a log cabin in Burnt Chimneys, Virginia, where he was born the first son of young, illiterate sharecroppers. He remembered his aunt cooking at the fireplace, tugging at a heavy iron bar to swing out the cook pot. He would sit there in front of the fire, and she would tell stories of his forebears, who lay buried in graves behind the cabin. As an adult, Joseph kept going back to visit his aunt, in her nineties and widowed. One afternoon he sat down with some paper and she recited from memory the names of his forebears, some of whom had been the slaves of the judge's grandfather. She was barely literate but her memory was prodigious and the roll of begats she recited that afternoon stretched back to people from before the Civil War. Later Joseph checked the names against census records, as much as possible, and found that she had been absolutely accurate. She had passed on to him a map of his family's history. Whenever he went to a reunion, he brought a copy with him, and now he handed it to me.

By this time people were gathering for the dinner, and Joseph hurried off to join his family. I stood in the lobby outside a vast banquet hall, as last-minute arrivals hurriedly showed their invitations to the doorkeepers and searched for places at the farthest tables. Nearly a thousand people were assembling for the dinner, which would be followed by speeches, awards, and festive music. I could hear Squire's voice welcoming the family as the doors to the banquet hall closed and I was left alone in the lobby.

I had crossed a line into a region where the past was still felt to be alive and where the ghosts of the past still governed events. Some of their names were written on the sheets of paper that Joseph had given me. On the train ride back I studied those names, and when I reached home, I unfolded a map of the South and plotted a route into the past.

"DAMN YOUR SOULS, MAKE TOBACCO"

Hairston country was once called the Land of Eden, having ac-quired that name in 1728 when a famous Virginia gentleman, William Byrd II, journeyed along the Dan River to survey the boundary line between Virginia and North Carolina. He was swept away by the region's beauty and fertility. "The great felicity of the Climate," Byrd wrote, allowed the inhabitants to support themselves with only the slightest toil—"surely there is no place in the world where the inhabitants live with less labor." So lovely was this land that Byrd and his party made a habit of ascending every hill and ridge they encountered so they could enjoy the view "in more perfection." Byrd intended to found a colony of Swiss farmers here. Instead, Scots-Irish poured into the region, among them the Hairstons, to establish tobacco plantations worked by slaves. Since then the Land of Eden has lived out a destiny determined by to-bacco. When a church leader in colonial Virginia appealed to the king for funds to "save the souls of Virginians," back came the royal reply: "Damn your souls, make tobacco."

The Dan River winds through this proverbial Land of Eden, crossing the Virginia–North Carolina border six times. From its headwaters in the Blue Ridge on the Virginia side it plunges south into Stokes County, North Carolina, which was once the home of the Saura Indians. The river passed through their main settlement, which was purchased after the Revolution by one of the founders of the Hairston empire. He called his plantation Saura Town, a name that was pronounced and sometimes written "Sorrow Town."

From Saura Town the Dan turns northeast, rolling placidly through the hamlet of Belew's Creek, where Jester Hairston was born, then east into Rockingham County, where it loops north into Virginia. On the Virginia side the Dan might as well have been Hairstons' River. Along with their in-laws and cousins, the Wilson family, the Hairstons owned much of the land on both sides of the river from the state line to the outskirts of Danville. There were three family mansions on this stretch of the river—Windsor, Berry Hill, and Oak Hill, the mansion where Judge Hairston's grandfather had grown up. This was the eastern edge of their private realm.

Many of the black Hairstons I had met at the reunion traced their roots to this part of Virginia. Although they lived in such places as Ohio, Pennsylvania, New York, and Washington, D.C., they kept close ties to this stretch of southern Virginia, their ancestral homeland. They returned here from time to time for local reunions with relatives who had remained in the old plantation country. I had the names of two men in this area, Daniel Hairston and Dean Hairston, who were descended from Oak Hill slaves. I was told that they both had vivid stories of life at the plantation.

Before meeting them, I wanted to see the countryside, and I wanted to see the ruins of Oak Hill, which had burned mysteriously in 1988. On my visit to Cooleemee the judge had marked an X on my map at a place near the Dan River where the plantation could be found.

I came into Pittsylvania County by a back road. It was autumn, well after the tobacco harvest, and the fields were stubbly, yellowish brown blank spots. I had expected a landscape as flat as an Iowa cornfield, but it was very hilly. The narrow roads rolled and banked, dipped into shady valleys and pitched up into the sunlight, offering a sudden view of the Blue Ridge in the distance. Much of the land was forest, and the area seemed uninhabited, which was a characteristic of tobacco country because the planters had to keep large tracts of land in reserve. "No crop is so well adapted to a sparsely settled, primitive community," wrote one traveler who passed through Pittsylvania in the 1880s. "There are great forests," she wrote, "stretching away as far as the eye can reach. Often one sees no human habitation except a log cabin in a little clearing, as if the sturdy pioneer had just reached a new country." It seemed that many of those log cabins were still here, close to the road but hard to spot under thick veils of kudzu vines.

There were many peculiar log structures of another kind—tall, narrow, and without windows. These were curing barns where racks of tobacco leaves were heated until they attained the proper dryness and color. Some of these log barns were still in use, equipped with propane heaters and thermostats. But in the antebellum days human thermometers monitored the precious weed. A slave lit a fire in a trench in the floor. The barn quickly became a hothouse, but the slave had to stay with the tobacco to make sure the heat went high enough to cure the weed to the right color, but not so high that the barn burst into flames.

In the eighteenth century the Hairstons sold their tobacco to the French, who were notoriously finicky about what they smoked. A local planter wrote that curing had always been dangerous, but it was made doubly so by the demands of the French. A fashion in France was colored tobaccos, which led to much experimenting in the curing barns to produce fancy variations such as "calico," "straw," "green streak," and "fawn." To achieve such subtleties the slaves had to sit in these tinderboxes for a week. The planter wrote, "Were a stranger suddenly to open one of our barns, where the fires had been unremittingly kept up, from Monday morning until Saturday, and see one of the hardy sons of Africa, with his red eyes and sooty locks, he would imagine himself on the borders of the infernal region."

As I traveled through this landscape, I carried with me a trunkload of books and copies of hundreds of pages of the Hairston family's plantation papers. Judge Hairston had gathered documents from scattered family members and deposited them for safekeeping in the Southern Historical Collection at the University of North Carolina at Chapel Hill. There were diaries, letters, plantation ledgers, account books from stores, Civil War records, tax records, business receipts, photographs, newspaper clippings, and thousands of loose scraps of paper. It seemed they saved every piece of paper that had to do with money. The judge's grandfather, Peter Wilson Hairston, kept two diaries and was a prolific letter writer. All together the family papers ran to some twenty-five thousand items, covering events from the Revolutionary War up to the 1930s. Although they rank among the premier collections of plantation records, the Hairston papers have largely been overlooked by scholars. I found only a handful of references to them in scholarly books and articles.

I was just beginning to make my way through this enormous trove of documents. It was like watching a series of disconnected film clips—people and events would emerge full-blown, and for a few moments I would gaze in wonder at a richly detailed scene from the past—and then it would break off to be replaced by something else. From time to time one of the whites described what the slaves did and said. These were precious fragments, and I tried to make sense of them, but the blacks were almost always minor figures, phantoms that came and went, uttering a few words before they vanished.

I found a letter from 1852 describing the courtship of a white Hairston woman and her handsome cousin Jeb Stuart, then a West Point cadet. The scene was the purest distillation of Southern romance. The two young lovers sat chatting in a garden, watching the fireflies flitting in the twilight; and all of a sudden they could hear the slaves coming in from the fields, singing a harvest song. The romantic chitchat of the young plantation aristocrats meant nothing to me, but I would have given anything to hear those slaves singing.

Some testimony from the slaves themselves has survived. In the 1930s interviewers hired by the federal government fanned out across the South to locate former slaves and ask them about their experiences in slavery. The interviewers were hired by the Federal Writer's Project, under the auspices of the WPA, the Work Projects Administration, founded during the Depression to put the unemployed to work. The WPA's art and construction projects are legendary—they constructed the Blue Ridge Parkway, for example—but the ambitious project to document the lives of former slaves may be the WPA's greatest achievement. For the last three decades, historians have meticulously sifted through the thousands of interviews to construct a portrait of the enslaved people. The WPA interviews are now regarded as some of the most precious documents of American history, despite some shortcomings in the way the interviews were conducted.

Many of the interviewers were white. A few were the children or grandchildren of slaveholders, sent to interview the very people their families once held in slavery. Not surprisingly, this situation led to a candor problem. Poor blacks knew it was in their interest to tell white people what they wanted to hear. One former slave admitted that they spoke the truth only among themselves: "Lots of old slaves closes the door before they tell the truth about their days of slavery. When the door is open, they tell how kind their masters was and how rosy it all was."

The situation, however, was different in Virginia. The supervisor of the program to interview former slaves was a black man named Roscoe Lewis. He hired mostly black interviewers. He also tossed aside the official questionnaire drawn up at headquarters in Washington, which had 333 queries ranging from "What time was bedtime?" to "Did slaves press their clothes?" Lewis wrote to headquarters that what the former slaves had to say on their own was infinitely more important than the questions they were being asked. He sent his people into the field with six questions, but their basic instruction was to just let the people talk.

Lewis focused his efforts on eastern Virginia, but a few of his interviewers, all of them black, reached Pittsylvania County. One of them called on an old woman in Danville, who delivered her blunt recollections of the plantation days.

"Tobaccy? Used to get sick of seein' de weed. Used to wuk fum sun to sun in dat old terbaccy field. Wuk till my back felt lak it ready to pop in two. Us black people had to luk arter dat 'baccy lak it was gold. Git a lashin' effen you cut a leaf fo' it's ripe."

As I drove through long stretches of pine forest, I recalled the stories told by former slaves from Pittsylvania County. According to their accounts, these forests would have been full of runaways in slavery time. One former slave said that many people who had been mistreated did not try to make it to "freedom land," but stayed here in the forest. His own grandmother, as he recalled, ran away and lived in the woods because her masters treated her "like a dog." The runaways were taken care of by slaves who slipped away from their plantations at night.

The forest was a world apart, a place of refuge where the slaves had their own society, largely invisible to the whites. They had dances in the forest, with music provided by fiddlers and banjo pickers, guitar players, and men who played the bones. Young women were dressed in calico with ribbons in their hair—each one danced with a glass of water balanced on her head. The young men placed bets on which dancer could keep the glass in place the longest. When that was finished, they all danced a six-handed reel. Sometimes these dances were held with the permission of the masters, but often they were not, and the slaves had to dodge the dreaded "patrollers" who roamed these roads.

Riding patrol was a duty all white men had to do on a rotating basis. Every night a group of them prowled the roads and lanes of the county looking for gatherings of blacks or an individual slave walking without his master's written permission. They poked into barns, corn cribs, and kitchens looking for runaways and peered into the woods for the flicker of a torch that would betray a meeting. The patrollers were armed, carried whips, and had the authority to mete out punishment on the spot.

The masters had their spies in the slave quarters, who would alert the master to a meeting in exchange for favorable treatment. The blacks had their spies, too—the house servants who saw and heard everything. The blacks used a code right under the noses of the whites to alert each other to trouble: "bugs in the wheat." A former slave in Pittsylvania remembered the time the blacks were planning a nighttime dance in the woods. That afternoon the footman on the plantation returned from the court-house with his master; he had heard the patrollers were going out that night, and they knew about the dance. Standing with the mistress of the house, the footman said to one of the other slaves, "Did you know dey was bugs in de wheat?" The mistress was puzzled: "What are you talking about?" "Nothin'," said the footman. But the slave knew, and she stayed home from the dance, "an' she was glad of it," recalled the slave, " 'cause de patterollers caught some of de slaves an' lashed 'em terrible."

The forest I was riding through had been the scene of an intermittent, undeclared guerrilla war between the slaves and the hated patrollers. A former slave recalled the night when a group of blacks set a trap for the patrollers on a road near the place where the slaves were having a secret meeting. They left a lookout standing in the road, and sure enough the patrol came down. The patrol spotted the lookout, which was part of the slaves' plan. The patrollers spurred their horses to a gallop and pursued the lookout around a bend. He vanished into the woods as the horsemen rode at full speed into a low barricade of vines. Scattered in the woods, the slaves watched as the barricade tripped the horses and pitched the riders to the ground. After falling victim to this trick a few times, the patrollers learned to tether their horses at a distance and make their explorations on foot. When they did that, the slaves crept up on the horses and cut their throats.

The patrollers were not only looking for meetings and dances, but also for worship. The slaves went into these woods to hear their own preachers, who compared their sufferings to those of the children of Israel, whom the Lord had led out of bondage amidst plague and pestilence. This was the most subversive message of all, and the patrollers were ruthless in suppressing it. One night they crept up on a religious meeting and beat as many slaves as they could catch. "You ain't got no time to serve God," one of them said as he applied the lash, "we bought you to serve us."

For miles at a time I was the only person on these undulating back roads. I thought my map would be sufficient to guide me through the mazes of this back country, but I was driving through a web of twisting, forking roads where the map showed only a blank spot. I could see the Blue Ridge far to the west, so I knew roughly what direction I was traveling, but I couldn't find a road that would take me south to the main highway. In another part of the world a crossroads might have meant a store or a gas station; here it was just a crossroads. I passed an orange construction sign, and just around a bend was a road-repair crew.

One of the men took a break from spreading hot top to help me with directions. He noticed the camera I had on the backseat.

"You a photographer?"

I told him I was a writer doing some research on a family he might know of.

He chuckled when he heard the name. "*I'm* a Hairston!"

He told me his full name and I couldn't believe my luck—not because he was a Hairston but because of his first name. I asked him to spell it.

"J-I-L-L."

He showed me his driver's license. "Jill Hairston." This was not a woman's name but a modern echo of an old name from slavery time—Gilblas—the name of a highly respected slave who had managed plantations for the white Hairstons and owned land himself. This man was a descendant.

I knew about Gilblas from reading Judge Hairston's book, and Jill knew him from family lore. Gilblas and another slave known as Tinker had received bequests of land from the judge's grandfather's great-grandfather in 1832.

Tinker could read and write—the judge had printed a photograph of one of Tinker's letters in his book—and I was tantalized by the possibility that Gilblas had also been literate. Had he left behind any letters? If so, perhaps this man leaning on a shovel would know where they were. But Jill didn't know of any letters or anything else that had been passed down from slavery time beyond his name. He said the only person who might have known was his father, who had died some years ago. Still, this accidental roadside encounter had the feel of something dictated by fate—I had the sense that it would unlock a door further on.

Oak Hill eluded me. As far as I could tell, I was on the right road, but as I drove back and forth several times, all I could see was a solid wall of pines. Disappointed, I headed south until I crossed the North Carolina line and swung off on a side road to find the house of Daniel Hairston, a descendant of Oak Hill slaves. South of the Dan River the forest gave way to open fields under cultivation. In the distance I spied a house, a neat brick bungalow, on a rise next to the road, nestled in a grove of fruit and chestnut trees.

Daniel was seventy-five and had suffered a stroke. He remained in his easy chair in the living room as his wife, Betty, and son Arthur greeted me. Betty was short and energetic, with a bright, vivacious voice. Her husband and son were tall and heavyset, though Arthur had an air of delicacy about him. His parents would mention later that Arthur had been a sickly child with a respiratory problem. For a time Daniel had to take him to the doctor every day. Daniel and Betty had four other children, who had moved away many years earlier.

Sitting in his easy chair, dressed in a plaid shirt and overalls, Daniel still had the look of a powerful man who could do a day's work. Though his stroke made it difficult for him to move, he did not seem disabled but merely at rest. Nor had the stroke affected his memory. His words shaped a rough music, flowing so fast I had a hard time keeping up with him. He spoke in the old way, in the accent preserved in the interviews with the former slaves—tobacco was "baccah," join was "jine," Oak Hill rhymed with "heel," and tears were "tayers."

Betty and Arthur must have heard Daniel's stories many times, but they sat down to listen again. Before long they were joining in, adding details Daniel had left out, prompting his memory with suggestions, attesting to the truth of what he said. Storytelling was an old, honored ritual in the family. When Daniel was a boy, his grandfather would call the children together to tell them stories of his life in slavery time.

Daniel was born in 1920, fifty-five years after slavery had ended, but as a boy he had known survivors from that era. Three of his grandparents were former slaves who had reached great age. Both of his grandfathers, Gus Hairston and Jube Adams, had been slaves at Oak Hill. When Daniel was a boy, he worked by his grandfather's side, learning to grow tobacco.

"Grandpa Gus was a good tobacco man," Daniel said. "When the plant got knee-high, he'd dust it with arsenic and lead and lime. That would keep the flea bugs off it. If it didn't have no holes in it, it was wrappers for the cigars. In the wintertime he would come down to the river and cut ice in two-foot squares for the icehouse at Oak Hill. Doesn't get that cold anymore. There used to be a ferry across the Dan. You'd holler for the ferryman across the river. There's a bridge now."

His family's fate was tied to tobacco. From a distance of sixty years he could still remember how much his family was paid for their crops.

"We sold tobacco at four cents a pound in Hoover's time. In FDR's time, Pop went to Danville and sold it for thirty-five cents. He came back and said, 'Poor man rich today—I sold tobacco for thirty-five cents a pound.'"

I asked him what his grandfather had told him about the slave days.

"He was working in the garden one day, and he got himself some butter—I guess they wouldn't let him have butter. He had it under his hat. He done something the old boss didn't like, and they whupped him, and the butter fell out from his hat and they whupped him again."

All three of them broke out in laughter. They thought the story was funny. Daniel said his grandfather often told that story, and he always told it as a joke on himself.

"Didn't your grandparents think the Hairstons were cruel masters?" I asked.

"No. They didn't act like they was cruel."

"Even though they whipped some of their people?"

"They had to take it," Betty and Daniel said at the same time.

"They had to take it," Daniel repeated. "If they wanted to live."

Arthur reminded his father of another story: "Sometimes if they wanted something extra to eat, they had to take a fence rail at night . . ."

Daniel picked up the story. "That's how they got their meat. They'd go out at night when Ol' Marse and them would be asleep, and ten or fifteen of them would get together and take a fence rail and kill them a hog and cook him and eat him up, and burn up the hide and bones till there's nothing left. They'd be enough of them to eat the whole hog."

This story, oddly enough, connected with an incident that was described in a diary kept by the judge's grandfather, Peter Wilson Hairston, in 1845. He wrote that a neighbor told him he had caught some slaves burning fence rails. Peter did not speculate on the slaves' motives, but the implication was that they burned them out of spite or from pure laziness, because they did not want to carry them the next day. (As punishment the slaves were made to carry fence rails for a night.) The rail-burning seemed to be just another example of the indolence and cussedness of the slaves, when actually it was part of the secret life of the slave community.

Religion was another part of that hidden life. The slaves were forbidden to pray together and had to worship in secret, in fear of the lash. Daniel said that when the blacks at Oak Hill wanted to worship, they had to go out into the forest. The men carried with them a large cauldron used for washing clothes in the slave quarters.

"When they got ready to pray, they turned over the pot so the sound would go in it and the white people wouldn't hear. They turned it bottom up, and they'd get on their knees when they were singing so the sound would go under it."

One of the first things the freedpeople at Oak Hill did after Emancipation was to build their own church—Piney Grove Primitive Baptist—where Daniel had worshiped since he was a child. Daniel's grandmother, Grandma Rose, taught him his religious faith and made sure that he was active in the church, which occupied a central place in the life of the community. "When I was eight years old, I began to help Rose out at the church every Sunday and Thursday. She would always tell me, 'Dan, don't forget to pray.' She always talked about the Lord. She would walk five or six miles at night and it would never bother her. She said, 'The Lord will take care of me.' " Rose had worked for the white Hairstons as a nurse at Oak Hill. "She used to hold the babies in slave days," Daniel said. She preserved some of the old-fashioned folkways: "She told time by a mark in the yard—she'd watch for the sun to hit it, then she'd know it was time to make dinner."

Daniel had been close to his grandmother. When Rose died in 1937, no one knew how old she was, but Daniel wanted to find out. He went to Oak Hill and asked the Sam Hairston, the grandson of the slaveholder, who then owned the place to look in the records from slavery time for Rose's age. Daniel was just a teenager when she died—and a sharecropper—so it must have taken some courage to go to the door of the mansion and ask the owner to put aside what he was doing and look up some old records. Sam Hairston pulled out the ledger books and ran his finger over the pages looking for Rose's name. Sam found the notation he was looking for and said Rose's age was 107. She had been born in 1830. Daniel had known someone who was alive when Andrew Jackson was president.

Daniel said that Rose was never angry; religious faith gave her the strength to endure the travails of slavery and sharecropping with equanimity. His great aunt, Rose's sister, was not so peaceful; but when she found herself in trouble, she too was rescued by her faith. "Grandma Rose's sister—one day Ol' Miss smacked her, and she stuck her fingernails—she had long fingernails—and she stuck her fingernails into Ol' Miss's satin dress and they went right through." When the slave realized

31

what she had done, she was terrified. "She left and stayed away hiding for two years," Daniel said, "and nobody knew where she was. And the Lord said to her, 'Go on and go back.' He would be there when she got home. And Ol' Miss didn't bother her. Having faith unlocks the door." I heard Daniel murmur to himself, "They had it tough then."

His thoughts turned to his own life. He said that when he was a teenager during the final years of the Depression he had had to take a job on a distant farm to help support his family. "I would leave my family Sunday evening and I wouldn't see them again until next Saturday night at ten. I'd come home with three dollars and fifty cents in my pocket— a week's wages—and I'd hand it to my dad. He had a whole lot of kids to take care of. Those were rough days. Yes, sir, I have been through . . ." Daniel stopped, as if reluctant to compare the difficulties of his own life to what his grandparents had gone through. But I asked him to talk about it.

"I didn't go no higher than seventh grade. My daddy didn't care for it. He wanted you to work. He couldn't read his own name if you wrote it on the wall in big letters. But you couldn't beat him counting and he could build anything. He built the rock wall up the road on the Sims farm. He was seven feet tall and weighed three hundred pounds—but rawboned, no fat on him. He could do anything with tobacco, and he could make anything grow. He planted the fruit trees here. He had one of his legs amputated and walked on crutches, but he still worked. We'd be working in the fields, pulling the suckers that grow between the to-bacco leaves, and he could walk on one leg and break suckers as fast as we could. He never owned his own land. He moved a lot, like the Gypsies, forty-nine times."

Daniel's image of his father was heroic, but that brand of heroism was required in Daniel's youth. He grew up during the Depression when, for many people in rural Virginia, times were as hard as they had been in slavery. He spent his teenaged years working and dreaded his leave-taking every Sunday evening.

"Going out on Sunday—I hated that so bad. Bunch of us boys would be playin' and Momma would come out to me and say, 'Come on and get your clothes now and go.' I had to walk twelve miles through some woods. Too dark to see, but I knowed the way. I've gotten scared by a lot of things, but the Lord was with me. I'd sleep in an old stable with the mules. Wouldn't be no chinking or nothing. I'd just have an old straw tick and some covers. Next morning I'd start the stove for the man I was working for. Get the breakfast ready. He'd work the food out of you.

Plowing tobacco and corn—he had plenty for you to do. I was sixteen, seventeen years old. I tell it to my kids and they laugh.

"I cut wood for a year for ten cents an hour, sunup to sundown, clearing new fields. If you got to work late, you'd get nine cents. The owner—he'd watch you make the first cut, and if he didn't think you could do good work, he'd send you away. I saw grown men crying because they couldn't get work. There was no other work. They'd say, 'Let me cut a pile of wood for a meal.' A whole lot of kids died because the parents didn't have enough for them to eat. Times was tough, but we survived. Now I'm going to tell you how I raised my family."

For much of his life Daniel did farm labor. When he was in his thirties, he started work at a brickyard in Eden, North Carolina. For twelve years he had a job "cookin' bricks," loading giant kilns with unbaked bricks and stoking the fires. A heart attack forced him into what he called retirement when he was in his late forties—what that meant was he gave up the brickyard and went back to "pullin' tobacco" as a sharecropper. He had five children to support and he wanted to see them through school. He didn't want them to fall into his trap.

"I had two horses and two cows, and I sold them and bought my own tractor and moved over here and went to work on shares. This man I farmed for, he had nine sharecroppers and two rows of tobacco. We worked one row for him, and we nine had to divide that second row. We had to live off it and pay half of it to him. Nine of us had to survive off that one row."

The owner habitually cheated his sharecroppers on their accounts. "He had a long pencil," as Daniel put it.

"He thought I couldn't read. When I paid him a bill, he would never write on the bill what it was for, and I would go straight back to him and say, 'Look, you ain't got on here what this bill's for.' He had one sharecropper, his wife had to count his money for him because he couldn't count.

"But I survived, got my kids through school, and they all went to college. I planted me two acres and a half of sweet potatoes, and I raised me six hogs. I raised everything we ate. I raised chickens too. That's how I survived.

"I want to tell you a story that's true. One day I was in the field and my brother come by to get me. Daddy was in the hospital. I didn't have any money. I walked through the field worried where I would get the money for the doctor. And a voice spoke to me. Twelve o'clock in the day. I started to ask somebody, 'Did you hear that voice?' This woman I farmed with—that's where the voice directed me to get the money. I went to her and she let me have fifteen hundred dollars to pay his hospital bill. And I sold a crop, and I was blessed to have money left over after I paid her." With that he finished his stories. Betty and Arthur set out a meal in the kitchen. Daniel hobbled into the kitchen and took his seat at the head of the table.

As we sat eating dinner together, I was thinking about the story Daniel had told of Grandpa Gus and the whipping he got for taking butter. No man laughs when he is being whipped, but when Gus passed on his story of being whipped, he made a joke about it. The laughter made sense when I realized exactly when the story had been told to Daniel—it was during the Great Depression. Grandpa Gus had passed through slavery, but in his old age he had come into a time when grown men cried because they could not feed their children. He wanted his children and grandchildren to know what he had endured. He wouldn't boast about his courage, so he spoke to them in parables. If he could laugh about the trials he had passed through, then some of his courage would be imparted to them, to the grandchildren like Daniel who would soon be cutting wood for ten cents an hour and traversing dark forests, whose bed would be a pile of straw in a stable. Now, in his old age, Daniel rested in a comfortable house, in the shade of his father's fruit trees.

That night in my motel room, I recalled Daniel's story of the Oak Hill slaves worshipping in the forest in secret. One part of his story—the way the slaves used a washpot to protect themselves from discovery—struck me as significant. It made no sense, and yet Daniel had spoken of it clearly. I had the feeling that it was more than just a minor detail of Southern black folklore—it had a meaning that I couldn't see. I pored over the WPA collection of Virginia slave narratives for the descriptions of secret worship in the forest. Eleven people from different parts of Virginia mentioned the use of the pots to deaden sound. A footnote to one of the accounts said that the practice had nothing to do with science—it was a relic of the religion the Africans had brought to America.

As containers of water, pots were sacred to the gods of the rivers, who were believed to be the deities with the greatest sympathy to mankind. An upturned pot invoked the protection of one of these gods; the Africans put them on the floor to protect a house.

Daniel was telling of a custom that had come across the ocean with the first slaves. It was a link to his deepest past on another continent in another time, and it was also a link to the entire African-American world of the South. The custom was so old and had been passed down through so many generations that its precise meaning had been forgotten, but the memory of its power remained. Daniel's foreparents had been profoundly devout Christians, but the upturned pot had allowed them to pray, as if an old god had turned his people over to a new one, giving his blessing at the very moment his power melted away. A historian traced the use of these pots to Africa. They brought good health and prosperity, helped people to achieve their destinies, and allowed them to "live out their allotted spans of life on earth." When I read that, I remembered that Grandma Rose's span had reached a century and seven.

Following my visit to Daniel, I went to the town of Cascade to find Dean Hairston, another descendant of Oak Hill slaves. I had been told that he had a keen interest in the family's history and had collected a large amount of information. The confident dot on the map led me to believe that Cascade was a proper town with a center and stores and perhaps a flag fluttering in front of a quaint rural town hall. But in fact it was a carpet of farms. The "center" was a wide place in the road with just enough room to turn off into an old and ramshackle general store.

I came to a cluster of houses set back from the road behind broad lawns. Fields stretched out beyond them, and in the distance a lone farmer maneuvered a tractor through this ancient landscape, shaping ovals around some obstacle I couldn't see. In the old days this was one of the outlying sections of Oak Hill plantation, but now the black Hairstons owned it. This cluster of houses was their family compound. The newest house belonged to Dean Hairston.

In his early thirties, he was a stocky man of medium height, with short hair and a neat mustache. He walked briskly and had the look of a middleweight boxer. He kept in good shape because he was a detective on the Danville force and a member of the SWAT team.

From his lawn he pointed to the houses around his.

"That was my grandparents' house, that's my uncle's house, my father's house, my cousin's house, my other uncle's house. All this is part of the original plantation. We've been here for six generations. We are all descendants of a slave named Major Lewis Hairston; that's how we define our branch of the family. Just about everybody in Cascade I know or I'm kin to." A mile and a half down the road was the ruin of Major Lewis's cabin. He was born a slave in January 1835.

Dean and his family had just moved into their house a few weeks earlier, and packing boxes were still in the rooms. He showed me around the house, a bright, spacious place with windows overlooking the fields. He mentioned that he wanted to set up a studio for himself in one of the rooms. In college he had studied commercial art and graphic design, but he had put that career on hold for a more practical job in police work.

We sat at a coffee table and he spread out some of the documents that had been passed down to him, and some others that he had unearthed himself. He had made several visits to the Pittsylvania County courthouse in Chatham and returned with census records, marriage and death certificates, and deeds for the purchase of the land his house stood upon.

"When I was a child, my grandfather told me that Major Lewis was 'one of Sam Harston's niggers'—that's the terminology he used. He said we came from Oak Hill. I didn't know what that meant until I was old enough to drive, and I went down a road near here and saw a mailbox that said Oak Hill. I stopped for a look, and I saw that it was an old plantation.

"After the Civil War a lot of slaves left, but our set stayed on at the plantation. We've always had a strong sense of family." His grandfather told him that Sam Hairston gave one of their ancestors as a wedding gift to a white relative. Around 1850, about seven hundred slaves were marched from Oak Hill to Martinsville—another wedding gift from Samuel Hairston, this time to his daughter Alcey and her husband and cousin, Samuel Harden Hairston. They founded a plantation to the west called Chatmoss. Later on, I would learn more about what the slaves went through at Chatmoss.

Dean's family owned about 165 acres. The first section was purchased around 1870 by Major Lewis. His descendants have been working that land and expanding their holdings ever since. The 1910 census shows his son Essic Sr. living here with his family. Essic was Dean's great-grandfather.

The oral history passed on to Dean chronicled generations of hard work. Dean said that in the late 1800s and early 1900s the family farmed in the summer and cut wood in the winter. They built and operated a sawmill and hauled the lumber into Danville, where they sold it along with their vegetables and eggs. They hauled stones for road building. Essic also raised horses and earned a reputation as one of the best horse breeders and trainers in the region. Dean said not long ago he was at the scene of a traffic accident in Danville, talking with witnesses, when one of them noticed his name tag and asked if he was related to old Essic. The man said that Essic was still remembered among people who knew their horses.

Essic hit some lean years, in the 1920s. At one point his land was put up for auction, but at the last minute a brother came down from the North and paid off the debt for him. Earlier, the brother had migrated to New Jersey and started a trucking business. To pay off his debt to his brother for the land, Essic traveled to New Jersey several times to work at the trucking company, making the journey by horse or by hopping a freight train.

Despite their hard work and good reputation, the Cascade Hairstons still had to contend with abuse from whites. One of Essic's sons, George Hairston, had had to flee Cascade for his life in the 1930s. He was a handyman and chauffeur for a white doctor who worked at the black hospital in Danville. The doctor's wife was having a party one day, and she called George in from the yard and slapped him in front of her guests. She just wanted to show her guests she got submission from her help. George punched her and knocked her out. For three nights the Ku Klux Klan circled George's house. He fled to West Virginia, then to Pennsylvania, and finally to Ohio, where his descendants live today.

The story seemed to remind Dean of something, and he said, "Let's pack up and go see some places, and I'll tell you some things my grandfather told me."

We headed east through the fields, past the family's old sawmill, which was abandoned and falling in, and past the stretch where Major Lewis's cabin was.

"This area is thirty years behind the times. A lot of the older people here, both white and black, have not been exposed to what's gone on in the rest of the world. A lot of them still feel like it's the 1950s—the language they use is what they knew when they were growing up. If they call you 'boy,' that's all they know. But black and white get along real well in this area. Danville is a different story. You have a rough edge between the whites and blacks in Danville, and every now and then something will pop up. Of course they're having the Confederate-flag issue now. That's been a big problem.

"You see, Danville was the last capital of the Confederacy. When Jefferson Davis was on the run from Richmond at the end of the Civil War, he stopped in Danville, at Sutherlin's mansion. He stayed there five days and convened his cabinet one last time before the surrender. So Danville hails itself as being the last capital, which a lot of Southerners take a lot of pride in. Sutherlin's place was later turned into a museum, and they fly the Confederate flag there. One of the black city council members saw it one day and objected to it, saying that public funds should not go toward flying the Confederate flag. So it was taken down, by the decision of the museum board, and that's when all the rip-roar started. Now you've got people with huge flags on their vehicles going up and down the street, and they parade.

"In 1963, Danville was one of the places that had a lot of trouble. They had one incident with the police officers and sanitation workers—they gave them clubs. When the blacks tried to march on city hall, they beat them with clubs and washed them down the street with fire hoses.

"Danville is one of the lowest-income cities, with the lowest level of education, that you're going to find in this part of the country. I'm surprised we haven't had some type of race war here. If you were to look at the achievement of blacks in Danville versus the achievement of blacks in Greensboro, you would say the blacks in Danville are at least thirty years behind. When blacks in Danville get an education, they leave.

"I have mixed feelings about racism in this area. That's one reason I *didn't* leave. I've had offers from outside, but I have no desire to leave this part of the country. If blacks are going to progress here, we can't migrate out and then expect to come back. Somebody's got to stay and pay their dues and work their way up. Plus I have a strong sense of family. My family's been here a long time. You're not going to see blacks progress in this area until a lot of the powers-that-be die out. If I see it in my lifetime, then I'll be happy."

We pulled off the road a few miles from his house. I could see nothing but tall grass by the roadside and fields in the distance. Dean led the way through the grass until we reached a cemetery. All of the people buried here were black Hairstons. We walked among the graves in silence for a moment until we reached the edge of the cemetery where, right next to a fence at the edge of a pasture, a small stone marker was set flush with the ground. There was no name on it.

"I spent a lot of time with my grandfather, working around the farm, and he told lots of stories. He told me how this cemetery got to be here.

This is our land here, but the white neighbor who owned that field would come over at night with some men and move the line markers."

To put a stop to the theft of their land, the Hairstons buried a stillborn child at the property line in the early 1900s. It was the only marker the whites would respect. So that the child would not lie alone, the family made this spot into their burial ground.

"That was typical of those times. If there was some problem with the whites, the blacks would have to figure a way out of the situation without offending someone who was white. If you offended someone who was white, maybe you would see the knights of the Klan.

"My grandfather said that his father, Essic, was a proud man, which got him into some trouble with whites. He said a bunch of whites tried to get Essic one time. They came to his house on horses and called him out."

That was a custom of the Klan. They would surround the house of their victim and call him out to get his punishment. It was a sign of the submission they expected from their victims.

"Essic came out with a double-barreled shotgun and said, 'Get off the horses if you want to, but I'll kill you.' So the men rode off.

"I always heard people talk about the Klan, and I've heard of meetings, but I only saw them myself when they marched in Danville in 1989." As a member of the Danville police department's SWAT team, Dean was on duty at the march. Ironically, his job was to protect the Klan.

We walked among the graves. The founder of this branch of the family, Major Lewis Hairston, was buried here. Dean explained that "Major" was not a military title but part of his name. Dean said that in slave days the blacks heard whites addressing one another by these titles and assumed they were names—but special names that brought respect, so they adopted them.

"Major Lewis married a woman whose father was white," Dean said. "Her father was one of the overseers. My grandfather told me about it."

The slaves did not name themselves capriciously. They took a last name if they regarded it as the correct one, even if it was a painful reminder of their origins. I thought of this when we came to the headstone for Rachel Staples Hairston, who was Dean's great-grandmother, the wife of Essic. She had been born on the Chatmoss plantation. Dean showed me an account of her origins that Rachel had written in 1952. The pages virtually shake with anger when she tells how her family got the name Staples in slavery time:

"You know in them days the Rich White People had Poor White Men to boss the colord people and those poor white men did just what they wanted to an they got lots of children by the colord girls. So my dadys father was a white man he was Boss for Miss Alcy Hairston and his name was George Staples."

From the graveyard, we headed farther east along a lonely road. No houses were in this area. The fields dwindled, giving way to pine forest, and finally the pavement ran out and we bumped along for a while on a rutted gravel road until we got onto another hard road that seemed familiar. We were driving through a tunnel of pine forest, with Dean peering at the right side of the road. I recognized it now; this was the road where I had looked for Oak Hill.

"They've cut some timber here," he remarked as if some landmark had been removed.

He slowed and pulled over. When I got out of the car, I could see faint traces of ruts that led off the road into the trees. Dean stepped to the edge of the forest, edged sideways through some brush, and swept aside a curtain of vines. I followed him in through the curtain.

"This is the old Harston plantation," he said. "This is where my family is from."

What I remember from that moment was the strange quality of the light. The road had been a dark tunnel, shadowed by a forest that seemed to close in on it. Here, on the other side of the curtain, the landscape was suffused with light, not a harsh, glaring sunlight, but an illumination that seemed to emanate from the land itself.

The plantation had reverted to forest. Dean pointed out huge magnolia and holly trees, old cedars and oaks, evidence of the great age of the place.

"This has such a stillness to it," Dean said. "A place that used to maintain such activity, and no longer does. It's almost like you have gone through time and returned to a place that you once knew, but you look for people and there's no one around. It has that feeling to it."

Amid the twisting branches of the trees I could make out a different kind of form, something man-made—a slender brick chimney thrusting into the sky. Dean pushed his way through dense brush, warning me of snakes, bursting through a chest-high tangle of vines, with knots of creeper and roots laying snares below. We emerged in a clearing. A grand avenue of old boxwoods—about 170 years old—flanked a broad, grassy path that led to Oak Hill mansion, a grand approach to what was now a shell. The broad brick facade showed none of the stylishness of Cooleemee. The house would have looked old the day it was built—its design of plain walls with a severely symmetrical row of windows was more at home in the 1700s than in the 1820s, when Samuel Hairston established the plantation. Unlike his son Peter, Samuel obviously cared nothing for architectural fashion. His house was a bastion, a declaration not of beauty and graciousness but of the eternal solidity of wealth. Now, with the roof gone and the upper row of windows stripped of their lintels, the house looked like the battlement of a sacked and ruined castle.

We ascended the steps for a look into the ruin. Fire had gutted the house, burning everything within the brick walls. No floors were left. If we had stepped across the threshold, we would have plunged to the earthen floor of the basement, littered with the charred remains of great beams. Nothing was left but the outlines of doorways and staircases that zigzagged up the walls to nowhere. Higher up the walls, fireplaces gaped out over the emptiness.

Dean ran his hand along the wall. "This house was finished in 1823. All the brick was made on the plantation. That must have taken a long time." He said the mansion stands on the highest point in the area, surrounded by a series of terraces that once formed an elaborate garden.

"You know an awful lot about this place. How did you learn so much about it?"

"From what we're doing now."

He pointed out another brick structure a short distance away. We plunged back into the thicket of brush and made our way to it. It was a long, narrow brick building, one and a half stories high, with four doorways and windows.

"This was the slave quarter." Dean thought that this building might have been the residence for some of the house servants, because it was so close to the mansion. It still had its roof.

We went inside and found the interior littered with the rusting parts of old farm machinery and wagon wheels. A steep wooden stairway led to a sleeping loft.

"My grandfather used to talk about Major Lewis. He said he was a big, muscular man, and he had large whip marks on his back, where he had been beaten. The people who owned the slaves had very little to do with the day-to-day running of the place. It was the overseers who ran the plantations, and my understanding is that they had some very rough overseers. But the Hairstons always treated their slaves well. I was told that if one of the overseers was caught abusing a slave, they were let go. I think that's one reason why my group of people stayed on with them in Reconstruction."

We headed down a path that led toward the Dan River. Dean said that in the old days all the land we were passing through was cultivated, and from the mansion you could see all the way to the Dan. We passed the remains of a stable and stopped at a railroad track. More forest lay beyond.

"There's talk that there's a cemetery here, but I've never been able to find it. You know, if you have relatives buried on a place, you can't be charged with trespassing."

We walked back from the railroad track toward the house. Dean turned off the path and pushed through the brush. Under the shroud of brush and vines there lay some invisibility worked on the land, something unseen that shaped the landscape powerfully. I could feel the land ascending, gradually at first, then in a series of giant steps, some so steep that we had to grab hold of vines and haul ourselves up. We were rising through the forest. Dean had led the way into what was once the garden, and we were ascending massive terraces the slaves had built. They had sculpted this landscape. As we walked along the earthen platforms, Dean pointed out the contours of the land that had been shaped by his forebears. He knew this landscape intimately.

I would have thought that the plantation where his people had been enslaved was the last place a man would want to revisit.

"You obviously feel a very close connection to this place."

"Well, if all your history is in it . . . Major Lewis worked on this plantation, and his foreparents, and so forth."

Dean now owned some of the land that his forebears had worked as slaves. It had been bought by one of those slaves; its borders were marked off with the bones of their offspring; and it had been handed down in an unbroken line for five generations—Dean's children would be the sixth. They were the heirs of people who had worked this land and died with nothing to show for it. Several generations of them lay buried in a cemetery somewhere in this forest. It was their resting place that gave Dean the right to come here.

He had repeatedly explored this hidden place to find the remnants of their labor. Their labor had imbued this land with a peculiar gravity, a gravity Dean felt as a powerful "stillness" that drew him back time after time. That the lives here were lived out in slavery did not disgrace the labor that was done. That labor had not been in vain; it would not be as evanescent as sweat but as permanent as memory—it was like the law of the energy of the universe, which can never be lost but only changes form, from sunlight to plant to human flesh, then back to dirt, dust, plant, and perhaps through a law we don't know about yet, to a light that illuminates a forest from below. This is where they worked.

We went back through the forest to the road. When we pulled away, I looked back at the spot we had gone through. I couldn't see anything beyond it. Several months later I returned to the area and drove down this road looking once more for Oak Hill. I went back and forth through the tunnel of pine trees, and I was never able to find the way in.

BEAVER CREEK

From Oak Hill I headed west toward the foothills of the Blue Ridge and the town of Martinsville, where I was told I could find other remnants of the Hairston plantations, and where more descendants of Hairston slaves still lived. Martinsville was founded after the Revolutionary War as the seat of Henry County, Virginia. In antebellum time, the town stirred to life for a few days each month while the circuit court was in session, then returned to its slumber. When the Danville and Western Railroad finally built a line to Martinsville in 1882 (many parts of the far West had better rail connections by then), it spurred a boom in tobacco manufacturing. Several factories produced flavored chewing tobaccos that were esteemed around the world. Explorers carried tins of a Martinsville brand to Africa as gifts for local rulers. When the vogue for chewing tobacco faded, the tobacco manufacturers shifted their capital into furniture factories, which still turn out household and office products today, and in 1941 the giant chemical company DuPont built a nylon plant at the southern edge of town on the Smith River.

The white Hairstons, however, took part in none of this industrialization. They were planters first, last, and always, firmly rooted in the agrarian ways of the nineteenth century. They trusted that their landholdings—"land without end, amen," as a family saying went—would insulate them from change. It was said that before the Civil War you could walk from Danville to Martinsville and never leave Hairston land, and once you got to Henry County, the Hairstons owned virtually everything. Before the Civil War the Hairstons' holdings represented about 85 percent of Henry County, according to the local historian, O. E. Pilson. By the 1980s, however, there was not a single white Hairston remaining in the county. When I asked Pilson how that happened, he could not explain it beyond saying, "They just faded away."

Some of the Hairstons' houses, however, can still be found. Marrow-bone stands on the top of a hill outside Martinsville. The view is sweeping and magnificent, a stunning panorama of rolling fields set amidst mountains that seem to enfold the landscape and close it in, creating the sense that what you see is the entirety of the world. On this hilltop the Hairston women created hanging gardens, terrace upon terrace of flowers cascading down in a profusion of colors, kept in check by borders of dwarf boxwood. Elsewhere in the garden they planted giant boxwood that grew twelve feet high. When John D. Rockefeller was restoring Colonial Williamsburg in the 1920s, his gardeners scoured the Virginia countryside for colonial boxwood and found just what they wanted at Marrowbone. They up-rooted all the hedgerows and took a few grand cedar trees as well. A frame house painted white, Marrowbone was the first house the Hairstons built in this part of Virginia. Not as large as the houses that would follow, Marrowbone had the unpretentious air of a humble ancestor, the hard-working founder. It was built in 1749 by a son of Peter the Immigrant. It passed to his son George and to four Georges thereafter, until the family lost the house in 1881. Fifty years later one of the last occupants drove down from Roanoke to see once more the threshold she had crossed as a bride and the room where her two sons were born. Standing in the ruined garden, looking at the empty house, she thought of the generations that had passed through the place—"All are gone but memories!"

Hordsville, a handsome, two-story brick house, was built in 1836 but harkens back to the old colonial Virginia style. Its builder, one of the many Hairstons named George, owned plantations and a large ironworks in the mountains. He married a ward of President John Tyler. The last Hairstons to occupy Hordsville were an elderly brother and sister, Peter and Mattie Hairston. In the early 1960s a Hairston from Texas was trav-eling through Virginia, and on a whim he decided to see if he had any relatives in the old homeland. He opened the Martinsville/Henry County phone book to the H section and found whole columns of Hairstons. At that time the phone book was still segregated. Beside the listing for Mattie and Peter was the word *white*, so he called them. They were delighted to see him. They talked about the Civil War as if it had happened the day before yesterday, showing him the charred spot on a second-floor ceiling where Yankee raiders had held a torch in a failed attempt to set fire to the house. Mattie, who died on 1979, is thought to be the last white Hairston who lived in Henry County.

Chatmoss survives only as the name of a country club. When the house burned in the 1930s, the family sold the land and the remains of the mansion to the club, whose architect salvaged the stairway of the old house but nothing else. The antebellum master of this place, Samuel Harden Hairston, was said to be cruel to his slaves. He once threw a rock at a slave who was running away from him, hitting the man in the back of the head (the only recorded occurrence of a white Hairston striking one of his slaves). The oral history of the black Hairstons painted an even grimmer picture. Dean Hairston's ancestor Rachel Staples Hairston was the daughter of two Chatmoss slaves. In her brief 1952 memoir, she recorded the family's bitter experience at Chatmoss: "My parents told me, I remember very well, they said that Mr Hairston was so mean to the colored people. He would make the overseers beat the colored people unmercaful then lock them in a barn for three or four days without food or water." She also remembered the retribution that befell this master: "Mr. Hairston was in the White House after Lee surrendered fussing with the Northern white people for freeing the colored and one entire floor of the White House in Washington calapsed and killed him and lots of other men both North and South." There was no such incident at the White House, but Rachel's memory was wrong only in the details: It was not the floor of the White House but the floor of the state capitol in Richmond that collapsed. It happened in 1870, and sixty-three men and women were killed, including Samuel Harden Hairston, state representative from Henry County.

There had been another house in Martinsville itself, of which only a photograph survives. Two women, wearing long white dresses that appear to be from the 1890s, sit on the porch on a brilliantly sunny day. The photograph was taken from too great a distance to see their faces clearly—the photographer had to move far away from them to get the entire house in his frame. The house was immense, with eight lofty columns in the front and windows that appear to be about ten feet high. A spinster named Ann Hairston lived there alone. After her death in 1907, the family emptied the house and rented it; but the tenants left after only a brief stay—they said the place was so huge that their furniture appeared tiny and they were always feeling lost. The Hairstons then donated the mansion to the town of Martinsville as a hospital. It burned in 1918, leaving only the photograph of two unknown women on a sun-splashed afternoon.

The plantation I was most interested in seeing was Beaver Creek. At the reunion I had met several people descended from Beaver Creek slaves, and they had given me the name of a relative, Flo Cahill, who could take me there. More important, Flo had an elderly aunt who had worked at Beaver Creek and supposedly knew some of the old family stories. On my way to Flo Cahill's house I decided to take a look at downtown Martinsville.

The old center of Martinsville is not quite a ghost town, but many of the storefronts are empty, victims of the generic shopping malls that ring the town. But the old courthouse, erected in 1824, still presides over its square. A two-story brick building fronted with white columns, it is the very image of a plantation manor. I imagined that it was built that way to remind one and all about the source of the county's power and wealth—the plantation. George Hairston, who founded Beaver Creek in 1776, donated the land on which the courthouse stands, which is not surprising, considering that the courthouse would be the family's own safe-deposit box. It contained all the deeds, wills, indentures, and other documents that gave paper permanence to the ownership of the land and slaves.

Accustomed as we have become to weightless, disembodied, electronic record-keeping, it was fascinating to see the accumulation of two hundred years of paper—deed books the size of half a door, and entire walls taken up with old-fashioned narrow drawers, stuffed with legal documents tightly rolled and bound with red ribbon. The clerk's office bustled with lawyers and title searchers digging into the strata of old documents and depositing their own fresh layers of paper.

I took my turn at the unwieldy indexes to court records and deed books, in search of information to augment what Judge Hairston had told me about George Hairston, who was the judge's great-great-grandfather. George had served as a captain in the Revolutionary War, leading a regiment of men from the Piedmont in several battles, including the final victory at Yorktown in 1781. Arriving at George Washington's lines with his regiment, George was ordered by some fancy officer to get his frontiersmen in proper file. "File, hell!" George exploded. "I came here to fight and I don't aim to file." He was a veteran of the murderous partisan warfare in the mountains between American loyalists and patriots. When a patriot was shot down in his cabin by a loyalist, George led the posse that hunted down the killer and put him to death. They hung the man's body in chains from a tree as a warning to other loyalists. George returned to the murdered patriot's cabin to bring his young widow and her infant daughter to safety. He soon married the woman, Elizabeth Letcher, and adopted her daughter, who became the grandmother of the Confederate cavalry general Jeb Stuart. Age did not diminish George's martial spirit: when the United States and Great Britain went to war again in 1812, George rushed to arms, though he was then sixty-two years old. An officer who served with him in that war described George admiringly as "a Tower of Duty."

Before departing Beaver Creek for the War of 1812, George Hairston had come face-to-face with a different sort of violence—an aborted slave rebellion in Henry County, an unsuccessful precursor to Nat Turner's revolt in 1831. Serving as acting county coroner, he was summoned to view the body of a neighbor, John Smith, whose skull had been bashed by a slave wielding a tobacco hoe. George counted the fatal wounds and wrote a report on the case. The slave, named Tom, not a slave belonging to the Hairstons, was captured sixty miles to the west, trying to make his way into the Allegheny Mountains. He confessed to the killing and declared that he was part of a large conspiracy against the slave masters of Henry County. George Hairston was one of their intended victims—they planned to poison him. From talking with poor whites and from hearing newspapers read aloud, Tom said the slaves in Henry County knew that war between the United States and Great Britain was imminent. They had gathered a few guns and planned to get more weapons and powder by breaking into a general store. They planned to coordinate their rising with the expected British invasion. The core group numbered between thirty and forty people, but they were certain that once they had risen up, they would have an army of blacks behind them. A wagon driver had made contact with blacks in Lynchburg, who said they would join in also. Their grievance was simple, according to Tom's statement: "They were not made to work for the white people, but the white people were made to work for themselves, and that the negroes would have it so." The arrest of Tom, who was executed, and two other conspirators—one of whom was acquitted at trial and the other punished with a public whipping— brought an end to the plan.

At the courthouse, a clerk's assistant immediately recognized the name George Hairston and pulled out a history of the county that had a brief note about the wealth amassed by the founder of Beaver Creek: "George Hairston purchased 30,000 acres from the crown of England for 10 cents an acre. He became the largest land and slave owner in the State. At one time he owned 238,000 acres of land in Henry County alone. He had twelve children and to each he gave an estate in land and negroes valued at about $500,000 when they married." One of those children was Samuel Hairston of Oak Hill, the judge's great-grandfather. Another was Marshall, who inherited Beaver Creek plantation in 1827. Following Samuel's example, Marshall married a first cousin, whose name I had seen in some records as Ann Hairston Hairston.

A series of misfortunes struck the male children in Marshall's line. Two of Ann's sons died in infancy. The only son who survived to adulthood was killed in the Civil War. One of Ann and Marshall's daughters married a first cousin from Mississippi and had one child, a son named Watt, born in 1876. Watt owned the first automobile in Martinsville (it was the second car registered in the state of Virginia—he had license plate #2). The town passed speed laws specifically against him. The story is told that the constable waved him down one day as he was zipping into town flagrantly above the speed limit. The constable fined him $5 on the spot. Watt handed him a ten—"so I won't have to stop on the way out." Watt enjoyed a drink, and he liked to drive when he had had a few. He was only forty years old, and unmarried, when he got himself killed, not surprisingly, in a wreck. The estate that would have been his then passed to a female cousin who had married a Covington from North Carolina. The Hairston name departed from Beaver Creek, but I would soon find that the family's ghosts remained.

Flo Cahill lived atop a hill about a mile east of Martinsville that offered a spectacular view of the Blue Ridge and a relief from the dusty atmosphere of the archive. The morning air was fresh and clear, and a caravan of fleecy clouds stretched across an enormous blue sky. Her house lay outside of town, at the end of a steep road that ascended to a group of small clapboard houses painted white. Like Dean Hairston's community, this too was an old family compound. The ridge had been the family farm of the Kings—her mother's family—for several generations. Everyone who lived on the ridge was related in some way to the family.

Flo was an attractive woman in her late forties with smooth, dark almond skin and straight black hair. She looked at least ten years younger than her age, and I was taken aback when she mentioned that she had just retired. The DuPont plant was downsizing, and Flo had taken the company's offer of an early retirement package. So on a midweek morning she had the time to take me around.

Flo's father was descended from Beaver Creek slaves, and members of his family continued to work at the plantation until the 1970s. Flo's uncle had been the caretaker, and his sister, Aunt Clara, had been the housekeeper. Meeting Clara was the chief purpose of my visit.

As we drove down the hill from Flo's house back into Martinsville, Flo described how she used to visit her aunt and uncle at Beaver Creek when she was a child. Her uncle used to tell her ghost stories. He said at night he could hear the sounds of horses galloping up the gravel drive to the house. The ghost of Marshall Hairston occupied a window in the attic. Aunt Clara used to take Flo up there to see the strange image of a man marked on the glass.

Although Flo was a relatively young woman, the childhood she described seemed to be from another era, when family farms were self-contained and self-sufficient. Flo recalled that they raised their own chickens, hogs, and cows. They had no refrigerator and kept their milk chilled in a spring. Her grandmother churned butter by hand. The only food they bought was flour, which her father brought home by the barrel.

There was no school bus for the black children in the 1950s, but by getting up early Flo was able to catch a public bus to her segregated school. Since she arrived early, it was her job to gather brush and start the fire in the stove to warm the room before the teacher and the rest of the children arrived. The bathrooms were outhouses. There were no lights in the school, so on the days when it was too cloudy and dark to see, the teacher would just tell the children to lay their heads on the desks.

I asked her if it bothered her now, looking back, that she was compelled to attend segregated schools.

"Not really. I never wanted to go to school with the white children. But I wanted to have the same books they had. *That's* what I wanted."

The textbooks had stuck in her memory for a good reason. She had mentioned in passing that when she was a girl, she had spent her summers in New Jersey. I had assumed she went there on vacation. I was wrong.

"From the age of nine, I went to Glassboro every summer to pick berries to get money to buy my schoolbooks. Every morning I'd get up at five and get on the back of a truck and pick berries on a farm. My sister did it too."

I pictured a truckload of third-graders, compelled to labor for the textbooks their government refused to provide, being brought to the fields at dawn. It would be unthinkable today. But Flo spoke of it without any apparent resentment. As a teenager in the early 1960s, she joined demonstrators carrying picket signs in front of the downtown restaurants that refused to seat blacks. Even that memory was not bitter. She maintained that, despite segregation, race relations in Martinsville had been good.

"When we were picketing, a lot of white people slipped notes in our pockets saying, 'If you need help, we'll give it to you.' In Danville they were dropping snakes out of windows onto the heads of black people. We never had violence here."

After high school she went to work at the DuPont factory because her parents couldn't afford to send her to college. It was in the early 1960s, and the company was just then dismantling its in-house apartheid system. There had been COLORED ONLY water fountains and a separate cafeteria for the blacks. Until that time most of the black employees had been groundskeepers, cooks, and janitors; but in the 1960s the company began to open assembly-line and clerical jobs to blacks. Flo was in the first wave of blacks able to take advantage of these opportunities at DuPont.

She talked about relatives who now had prestigious careers—a literature professor in Maryland, a bridge contractor in West Virginia, local teachers, and police officers. "There's a Hairston girl who's a judge in Richmond. I have a niece who works in a radio station, a nephew who's a promoter, a niece who is a social worker, and another who works for a paper company in New Jersey. Two of them graduated from UVA."

As she reeled off this list of young people who had benefited from the breakdown of racial barriers, had gotten fine educations, and were now embarked on good careers in places far from Henry County, I felt a stab of regret for Flo. She was part of the last generation that had suffered under segregation and had helped to overthrow it, but had not fully reaped the benefits.

"You retired so young," I said, "you can go to college now."

"I *am* going to college. It's part of my layoff package."

Flo and I made a brief stop to see Gloria Hairston. She too was descended from Beaver Creek slaves, but the main reason Flo wanted me to meet her was that she had been directly involved with the integration of the local schools. She was the first black teacher at one of Henry County's elementary schools when the system was integrated in the mid-1960s.

Flo had taken a generally positive view of race relations in the area. When Gloria spoke, some of the sunshine went out of the conversation. "We're in Ku Klux territory," she said bluntly.

She said that overall there was no problem integrating the school she was assigned to, but for her the first year was an ordeal. Some white teachers circulated petitions to have her removed. Some resorted to nasty, personal slurs.

"They wanted to know—'Why are you this color?' 'Why is your hair sort of curly?' 'How did you get to be this way?'"

Gloria was very fair-skinned, with almost straight, light hair. Her tormentors knew very well how a black person inherited such features. What galled the other teachers was finding themselves on the same professional level with a black.

"The only way they ever saw black people was as the maid or janitor. The only black person they could tell you about was 'Aunt Susie' or 'Uncle Tom.'"

She mimicked the tone of a condescending white: "'My mother just *loved* Aunt Susie. She lived in our house and did *all* our work.'

"The school system sent me in so the children would see a black person as something other than a maid or a cook. Some teachers went out of their way to be nice to me. I'm still in contact with them. And by the end of the year things were smoother. Still there were little, subtle things, but if you dwell on things like that, it makes life pretty hard for you."

I asked her what she meant by her remark that this was Ku Klux territory. She said that a small group of Klansmen had paraded through Martinsville a few years ago—just a handful, but they got attention. In recent weeks the television station had carried a report about a local white man hanging blacks in effigy from a tree in his yard.

Flo drove me out to Beaver Creek. The Covington family—the Hairston cousin and her husband from Richmond—had kept the house until the 1980s, when they sold it to a prosperous plastic surgeon, who turned the mansion into a private clinic. A four-lane road had been built across the plantation. South of the road, fields and wetlands rolled gently down to a creekbed, with forest in the distance. On the northern side, the mansion stood on a hill, surrounded by large cedar trees, magnolias, and maples. It was a broad frame house, painted white, with four columns flanking the entrance. We had not made any arrangement with the doctor to visit the house, but we assumed that he would not turn away a descendant of people who had worked on the place for two centuries.

A room off the entrance hall had been converted to a reception area. When the doctor's secretary heard why we had come, she immediately recited a litany of ghost stories. The house, it seemed, was thoroughly haunted. Patients who spent the night at the house recovering from surgery had heard gunshots, the sounds of children playing under the trees, horses galloping up the gravel drive, and a piano playing in the downstairs parlor. One patient had been so terrified that he pushed a dresser against his door. Another, who claimed she was followed home by a ghost, returned to the clinic in the hope that he would follow her back and stay there.

After a few minutes the doctor appeared in the hall and readily agreed to take us around. He was clearly proud to be the owner of such a fine house, but he was just as clearly immune to the "mystique" of the old plantation. He did not fancy himself a country squire. He had modernized the house from top to bottom. Before he bought it, the Covingtons had removed every piece of furniture; no relics of the old days had been left behind, except the ghosts.

"Your secretary told us a ghost followed one of your patients home."

"Something like that. People exaggerate, but I believe in ghosts. He's been seen by too many people for too long a period of time. He's on the third floor in the window."

"Do you sleep in his bedroom?" Flo asked.

"Oh, no, I wouldn't do that. I'm fairly bold, but not that bold."

On some nights he has heard footsteps approach his door, stop, and then go away.

"Do you hear the piano play?"

"No, I haven't, but I've heard about it." He chuckled, but he added quickly that he treats these stories with the greatest respect. "After all, it's God's world. And if He wants to do these things, I'm not going to check on it." The doctor said that a lot of the nocturnal noises were just the natural sounds made by an old house at night when the temperature dipped. But the noises bothered him enough that he kept the air-conditioning system running all year, making just enough noise to drown out anything the house could utter.

He ushered us down a hall and into a spacious operating room, where he pointed to the floor—it was pink marble. This had been an apartment, added to the house in the 1930s. The doctor had been able to make a pair of large operating rooms out of it. We looked through bedrooms on the second floor, where apparitions had supposedly terrorized the patients, and saw nothing out of the ordinary. The doctor then led the way to the attic.

The window I had heard so much about was also entirely ordinary. A double-hung dormer window with twelve panes, it overlooked the rear of the house and the fields beyond. Supposedly Marshall Hairston had had his face pressed to the glass, watching the slaves at work, when lightning struck, stunning him and leaving his impression forever imprinted on the glass.

Flo knew which pane to look at and saw the image immediately.

"Part of his jacket is down here." She pointed to a spot on the pane. "Can you see it?"

I couldn't.

"See where I'm pointing?"

I stared and squinted, moved forward and back, but I could see nothing but clear glass and the greenery behind the house.

The doctor led us outside to a double row of boxwoods that towered fifteen feet high, shading a long, narrow walkway. We walked single file down the path to an iron gateway that opened onto a small family cemetery. In this walled compound, sixteen white Hairstons lay buried under obelisks along with two black Hairstons, named Surry and Esther, who had been slaves of the family and remained after Emancipation as house servants. There was a bronze plaque on the tombstone of George Hairston, the family progenitor and Revolutionary War hero. It had been placed on the stone a few years earlier, with pomp and circumstance, by the Daughters of the American Revolution. A representative of the DAR had called the doctor to ask permission to hold the ceremony.

"I expected a couple of dozen people would show up. But on that Sunday afternoon there were four hundred people here from Virginia, North and South Carolina, West Virginia—politicians, two marching bands, etc."

We looked around at the other graves. I found the stone for George's son Marshall, who lay here but prowled the house, and the marker for Marshall's son John, who fell in the Civil War. The family went to great effort and expense to have his body brought back from the battlefield and buried here. I later found that John had lost his life largely because of his commander's vanity and thirst for glory. His commander was his cousin

Jubal Early, his mother's nephew. John's mother harbored no ill will toward her nephew on account of her only son's death. At the end of the war, when Early was desperately fleeing the Yankees, he came to Beaver Creek for help. Ann Hairston gave him $200 in gold to aid his escape—her last contribution to the cause that had taken her son's life.

Flo Cahill's aunt lived with her daughter in a rural area on the western edge of Henry County. In her mid-eighties, Aunt Clara was a fair-skinned woman, with thin, straight hair brushed back to reveal a broad forehead. She was demurely dressed in a pullover shirt and slacks, with silver earrings and a thin gold necklace. She was slightly hard of hearing, and until she adjusted to the sound of my voice, she sometimes answered questions I had not asked.

We began by talking about her family background. Born in Martinsville, she had been raised by an older sister in West Virginia after their mother died when Clara was seven. At the age of thirty-five, she and her husband moved back here, and Clara got a job as a seasonal housekeeper at Beaver Creek. Her father, and his father before him, had worked there also. She could not trace her family any further back than that, but she knew the names of scores of aunts, uncles, cousins, and all their children.

Clara called Beaver Creek by an old name, Hairston's Bottom, which referred to the fertile bottomlands along the creekbed, but beyond that it seemed she had no stories of the old days. Flo reminded her about the image of Marshall Hairston's face in the attic window. Clara said you couldn't wash that window—the cloth would stick to it.

I asked her about the ghost stories, hoping that she would have some explanation for the noises and apparitions that afflicted the house. She knew about them—the cook had told her that she heard ghosts and the sound of horses coming up the drive at night—but Clara herself had not heard the noises and didn't know what their origin might be.

The conversation lagged. It seemed that Clara had exhausted her store of recollections; and after an hour of conversation she began to seem tired. Before leaving, I mentioned my accidental roadside meeting with Jill Hairston several days earlier, and the conversation we had about the slave with the unusual name, Tinker, who could read and write.

"I remember Daddy calling that name—*Tinker*," Flo blurted out.

The name produced an instantaneous response; it summoned a buried memory. Clara suddenly answered a question that had not been asked.

"You know they said there used to be slaves down at Miss Covington's house when Marse Harston was living."

She was speaking to us as if we knew nothing of the history of that house, as if we didn't know that there had been slaves there. And this was the first time she had mentioned "Marse Harston."

"They say he was so mean—Grandfather said it—that he was so mean he was looking out the window and the lightning struck, that's why his picture is there. They said he was the meanest man. Downstairs, I noticed some dirt. You go down there, back in a room in the basement, there's blood. There was blood when there were slaves there."

I waited for Clara to say what that bloody event was, but she did not. As abruptly as this door to the past had swung open, it closed. Something had happened at Beaver Creek that had left a stain in the family's memory. The mention of an old name from slavery time had been enough to conjure it up, but the details of the event had been blotted out. There was, however, another place I could look. As Flo and I drove back to her house we talked about what Clara had said. I recalled that, among Ann and Marshall Hairston's papers at Chapel Hill, there was a thick ledger of Beaver Creek slave records. It contained lists of names and accounts of the daily work done by the slaves. Perhaps it contained some key to explaining this haunting memory, some clue to the lives of people not yet celebrated by plaques and marching bands.

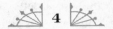

4

THE LIVES OF THE
HAIRSTON SLAVES

The lives of the black Hairstons as enslaved people were written in the plantation ledger books. They appeared mostly as lists of names—bookkeeping entries, pure and simple. Slaves aged twelve to fifty were taxable, so the master had to make a list of them every year; twice a year the slaves were clothed, so the mistress made a list of who got pants, shirts, shoes, and coats; when a child was born, it got a blanket—and so a notation was made on the list. When the master died, an inventory was made of all his property, including the slaves, who were called together by the officers of the court and counted, their names written again in the ledger in long columns, with long columns of figures—the dollar value of each man, woman, and child.

The white Hairstons tracked every aspect of their plantation business, and they were constantly toting up the profits and losses of their plantations. The measuring rod was how much profit they derived per slave. Of course, the slaves themselves created profit; the masters kept careful track of what they called the "increase," adding the number of black children born every year and subtracting the old ones who had died. The ledgers were, in effect, bankbooks of human souls.

And so we have lists of names—thousands of them, column after column, page after page; bare evidence of existence, in records as inscrutable as the clay tablets of Babylon. We know how much corn they ate but do not know how they felt to see the sun rise. The chronicle of slavery is so large that people vanish in it, and the old crime of the slaveholders is perfected—individual humanity is denied, lost, swallowed up in the whole.

At first glance these records seemed to be melancholy proof that there were no families, or very few, among slaves. It has been said that slavery so demoralized the Africans that they could no longer form a family and hold it together. This belief in the absent family haunts black history. But the oral history of the Hairstons was rich with family recollections. When asked how the Hairstons could have such a strong sense of family feeling today, an elderly man said it was not new, that it went back to slavery. But where was the evidence of it?

I had been reading the annual tax lists in the ledger of Beaver Creek plantation. Marshall Hairston was the master, but it was his wife, Ann, who kept the ledger for thirty-seven years from 1831 to 1868. I turned the pages looking for some other type of record. I came to a section of household accounts and found more lists of names. Slowly, I read them aloud, saying the names, calling a litany of the dead, trying to summon some meaning from these pages. Some names had dates written next to them. The eye instinctively locked onto a pattern: a short list of four or five names, each name followed by a date, and the notation "blanket." The dates were a few years apart. Years of birth? At the head of this list, two names, female and male, without dates. With a shock of recognition the pattern emerged: *mother-father-children.* Down a little on the page, the same pattern: mother-father-children. Another list was headed by three names: mother-father-grandmother and children—all apparently living together; this one by four names: mother-father-grandmother-grandfather and children. On another page, one of the daughters had a child—here was the note for "Jinny's blanket"—so now there were four generations connected, and from these pages life burst forth—it cannot be suppressed—and the pattern was found that leads inexorably to us: *mother-father-children.*

Ann never wrote the words *husband, wife,* or *family.* She was distributing blankets—valuable items she counted with care. She gave them to the mothers, and as she handed out the blankets, she wrote down who was in each woman's household and the birth dates of the babies. By this accident of record-keeping she made a genealogy of the black community.

Here were Mat and Kit with their six children; Ned and Patsy with their four children; Patrick and Grace—two of the oldest slaves—with their children and grandchildren; Daniel and Sarah, Charles and Franky, Ben and Penelope, Old Aggy and Crocket, Sampson and Hannah, and on and on.

One name leaped from the pages—Sam Lion—a resonant name suggesting bravery, strength, and ferocity. He was a field hand. His work was planting, cutting, hauling, lifting, wielding his ax to clear new ground.

He was married to Kate and they had a cabinful of children—ten of them, from thirteen-year-old Cornelia to the newborn twins, Delila and Cloe, born on March 17, 1837. Kate took care of the children, the cabin, and almost certainly had her own vegetable garden—but she did all this work on nights and Sundays because by day she worked in the fields along with her husband. So did the children, except for the infants, who were cared for by an old black woman.

To help his family, Sam did extra work. Field hands raised their own crops of tobacco, corn, or vegetables, which they sold to the master for cash or traded for goods at a country store. Sam Lion used his extra earnings to acquire his own woodworking tools. He might have made simple furniture to trade with friends and relatives for eggs, chickens, or vegetables; or he could have done carpentry jobs at the big house for meat, cloth, or cash. As the ten children came along, he was busy building beds, making toys, and almost certainly adding a large room or two to his cabin. He got along well with Beaver Creek's white overseer, Craven Wyatt. If Wyatt needed a tool, Sam would lend it.

A man named Ned was the wagon master at Beaver Creek. He was in charge of the horses (there were nearly fifty at Beaver Creek), and the ledger recorded his long journeys, lasting several weeks at a time, to sell the plantation's produce and buy goods. Since there was no reliable postal service, it was the wagon master's job to carry letters for the masters from one plantation to another. News of the black community went with him as well, so he was the link between scattered friends and family. On the road he was, to a certain extent, his own man. He could earn a substantial amount of money using the plantation's wagon to haul loads for other planters. The white Hairstons permitted such financial independence in order to keep their wagon drivers—who were considered elite workers—contented. The drivers handled cash and negotiable goods all the time, so it was in the master's interest that the wagon drivers be allowed a certain latitude. If the master had something to buy or sell, the driver often did the bargaining and made the final decision on price.

Another wagon master, named Clem, was an exceptionally good haggler. When Clem went to a tannery to buy shoe leather, he bargained down the price, to the annoyance of the tanner. Clem could not be fooled because he had traveled all over the area and knew that leather prices were lower across the line in North Carolina. On the receipt for the leather the tanner scribbled, "25 cents for our best sole is lower than we usually sell but the boy said it could be had at Leaksville for that." Despite his condescending reference to "the boy," the tanner did not dare contradict him—Clem knew the market well and had no qualms about speaking up. On his own account Clem was a beekeeper on the side. He kept his own hives and sold the honey, a prized luxury in both the black and white communities. He expanded his business when he ordered a honey press, for which he paid ten dollars and two gallons of honey.

I found a receipt from a white storekeeper recording a transaction with two slaves named Ben and Andrew. The receipt said they had exchanged a quantity of corn for calico, thimbles, knitting pins, and fine cotton cloth. They made the purchase in mid-December—and it seemed plain to me that Ben and Andrew were trading a portion of their private crop to get material for their wives to make clothes, something softer and fancier than the coarse work shirts the mistress doled out, something with a burst of color—calico dresses to be put on at Christmas.

The ledger opened a window on the daily life at Beaver Creek. Ann recorded in detail the multitudinous labors that went on from dawn to dusk, as the slaves worked to produce virtually everything necessary to support themselves and the seven white people in the big house. They raised hogs, cattle, and chickens to get bacon, beef, and eggs. They produced corn, wheat and flour, lard, butter, honey, potatoes, and wine made from currants and blackberries. They raised peas, peppers, horseradishes, pears, and yams. At one time they tended over a thousand yam plants. For the master's table they raised turkeys, ducks, and geese. They plucked the geese to make pillows; when they slaughtered cattle, they boiled the fat to get tallow for candles—in one day the slave women made 660 candles.

Every commodity on the place was weighed, measured, and counted at every step of production and kept under tight control. If a slave wanted something extra, she had to work for it. The slaves raised their own chickens and vegetables and bartered them with Ann for extra rations of lard and bacon. One chicken would fetch a pound of bacon. In her book, Ann wrote down that she had advanced a slave named Dice $2\frac{1}{3}$ pounds of lard, for which Ann expected to be paid in chickens.

The slave quarters were a rural textile mill. They planted cotton and flax and tended flocks of sheep for wool. The cotton was the short staple variety, from which it was difficult to extract the seeds. Cotton gins could not do it, so slaves had to do it by hand, extracting the seeds with "cards," which were wooden blocks studded with tiny hooks. Ann did not record at what time of day this was done, but other planters made seeding an extra job at the end of the workday. One mode of measuring production was to have each slave seed cotton until he or she could stuff a shoe with it—there is a record of a slave with big feet complaining about the unfairness of the system. In 1833 the five plantations under the aegis of Beaver Creek produced over 3,700 pounds of cotton, all of it for use on the place.

Much of the spinning and weaving at Beaver Creek was done at this time by two women, Grace, the wife of Patrick, and their daughter Julia, but other women pitched in as needed. They spun the raw cotton into "hanks," cleaned it, and rolled it onto a large reel. Ann noted the weight of each bundle of raw cotton she gave to Grace and Julia and wrote down the amount of thread they handed back. They made two grades of thread: the common grade was kept in the lumber house; fine thread was kept in the attic of the mansion where the slaves could not easily get their hands on it. The fine material went into making sheets, tablecloths, and curtains for the main house, and diapers and crib sheets for Ann's children. Grace and Julia wove the coarse material into fabric for the slave clothing. Ann kept her eye on the cloth. She cut out the fabric herself and turned it over to the black women to be sewn up. They made shirts in two sizes, large and "common." If the homespun ran short, the mistress had to buy "Negro cloth," a coarse, cheap combination of hemp woven with cotton that was made specifically for the slave states in the textile mills of New England. She also bought osnaburg, another cheap cotton fabric that came from England. Both fabrics irritated the skin. In at least one category of clothing the Hairstons were more generous than many other masters: they gave their slaves good shoes. Their accounts show large purchases of leather for making uppers and soles. On other plantations slave shoes were generally made of leather uppers nailed to wooden soles. They were clumsy and uncomfortable, if the slaves had them at all.

Almost nothing was wasted on the place. At one time Ann had fifty pounds of cow's hair stored up, and she put Julia to work spinning the hair with wool to make blankets for the black children and coarse carpeting for the house. Blankets were guarded with care. The mistress kept careful track of which slaves had been given blankets and when, so no one would be tempted to request a second blanket.

The output of the black weavers and seamstresses was prodigious—linens and pillows, blankets and curtains, diapers, bonnets, frocks, "suits," shimmies, bed ticking, and carpets. In summer they made winter clothes; in winter they made summer clothes. Yet all of this work was done in service to another crop, the one the planters called a tyrant.

There was never enough time to do all the work needed for raising tobacco—the planters said it was a "thirteen-month crop." Everybody worked—men, women, and children: Sam Lion, Kate, and their children; Mat and Kit and their children; Simon and Julia and their children; and on down the list. As a rule black children went to work in the fields at age five or six. They picked cotton, carried water, cleared stones, pulled weeds from the corn rows, and helped to stack the harvested stalks of wheat. Children were put behind the plow even before they were tall enough to reach the handles. One would wrap his arms around the sides of the plow and another would guide the mule. Their short stature and quick, small fingers made them exceptionally useful for plucking and crushing tobacco worms. Certainly some overseers and masters thought they could make this into a game, but children do not last long at any game and want to do something else. One slave on a Virginia plantation could not forget the method her master had of keeping the children attentive to their work. If the master found that a child had missed a worm, he would gather up a handful and stuff the green, squirming things in the child's mouth with the command "Chew." Even if there was nothing in particular the children could do, the master wanted them out in the field just to get used to it. There was a saying then among the blacks: "Slave young, slave long."

The cycle of tobacco planting began in January when the slave families went out to prepare the seedbeds. The overseer, Craven Wyatt, divided the people into groups to prepare several fields at once. They scorched the earth, pulling sleds loaded with burning wood across the seed ground to sterilize the earth, killing dormant insects and the roots of weeds. Then the plowmen came out with the mules; behind them people chopped away at the furrows with hoes until the clods of earth were completely pulverized. Meanwhile, children had been gathering up ashes to mix with the tiny tobacco seeds. Tobacco seeds are too small to be strewn about—ten thousand of them would fit into a teaspoon—so the slaves had to mix them with ash before they could spread them over the carefully groomed ground. Then they covered the plant bed with brush to protect it from frost.

While waiting for the tobacco to sprout, the people planted corn. Lines of men and women slogged through muddy fields, soaked by spring rains. Those in the lead dropped the kernels and were followed by workers with hoes to pull earth over the seeds, then by mules pulling harrows to crush any remaining clods. The people moved quickly because the work was watched closely by flocks of crows, circling above and ready to dive at the seeds if given the chance. At the same time, other gangs were sowing wheat.

By the time the corn and wheat were planted, the tobacco seedlings had sprung up. The slaves transplanted the shoots from the seedbed to plowed and fertilized fields. This job could be done only in damp weather when the ground was wet, else the delicate slips would die. The women pinned up their dresses while doing this work so their hems would not brush against the slips and break them. They gathered up the seedlings as if they were infants, cradling them in their skirts as they carried them to oxcarts.

By hand, the slaves sculpted the earth to receive the plants. For each seedling they made a little hill, one foot high, three feet from the next one. The slaves molded handfuls of dung and wet earth to form the mounds—filthy, backbreaking work, carried out quickly and on a vast scale. At one of the Hairston plantations one spring, about four hundred slaves made three hundred thousand tobacco hills in a few days. The slaves poked a hole in the top of each hill with a stick or with their fingers, gently inserted the plant, and tucked it in. This work also had to be done in damp weather; and the overseer made the slaves hurry before the earth dried. In a single day of transplanting, a slave would bend over four to five thousand times. When the wet season had passed and the ground was dry, the people came back and scraped each hill just hard enough to break the crust of dried mud so that the meager summer rain would trickle in. The slaves groomed the soil gently with their hands, clearing away insects and weeds. Everyone feared drought. The whites feared losing the crop; the blacks loathed the extra, backbreaking labor of hauling casks of water through the fields—no wagons could be brought in among the rows—to sprinkle the ground, taking care as usual not to knock into the precious plants or wash them from their hills.

In late summer the master inspected his crop every day, scrutinizing the yellow spots that were emerging and spreading over the leaves, waiting until their size and color told him that the exact moment of perfect ripeness had arrived. Then the hands swarmed into the field wielding long knives. They split the stalk almost to the bottom, then hacked the plant from the earth and moved on, leaving a trail of stalks to dry in the sun. After a few days they gathered up the stalks, piled them in oxcarts, and brought them to the curing barns.

Autumn brought the wheat harvest, and once again long lines of men, women, and children wound through the fields, led by the strongest men, such as Sam Lion and Sam Mountain, swinging scythes in rhythmic motion, singing to keep up their strength and spirits. Behind them came the women and children, gathering up the stalks and tying them into sheaves. The songs set the pace: if the women and children began to lose strength and fall behind, their men would gradually slow the tempo of the song— so gradually that an overseer might not notice it. The black plantation communities had subtle ways of helping one another, of ensuring that no one fell behind and got into trouble. A master, looking over his fields on horseback, might see a regiment of disciplined workers, but their order came from within and was not so much discipline as it was cooperation among the people themselves.

They worked together as families, which explained a great deal about slavery that was otherwise inexplicable. One wonders why there was not more resistance and rebellion among the slaves. The whites attributed this lack of resistance to the benevolent regime of the masters. This explanation implies that enslaved people were so grateful for minimally decent treatment that they accepted slavery gladly. It makes more sense that the slaves acquiesced to the system because they had their families to protect and keep together. Sabotage, resistance, and running away would only bring reprisals and a hundred other hardships to spouses, children, and the elderly. Across the South, a large percentage of slaves who ran away from their masters did so not to seek freedom, but to find family members separated by sale.

The whites and the blacks had different reasons for doing the same thing—the whites needed to keep the plantations peaceful and functioning smoothly to increase profits year by year; the blacks needed to keep the plantations peaceful to preserve their families and their community. They endured much for the sake of family and community. There was, in the black community, a sense of duty as strong or stronger than in the white.

The slaves held their families together, nurtured them, and strengthened them, out of the purest love and devotion; they built nothing but a family, they owned nothing but the feelings they had for one another, they could look forward to nothing but the continuation of what they had known, done, and lived already. Yet in the face of this they did not yield to despair, but held their families and their communities together.

Scholars have struggled to understand the dynamics of the enslaved family. Some scholars believe that the slave system all but crushed the family and relegated the father in particular to a marginal role. They point out that an enslaved family was supported not by the father but by the master, and that the father had no real authority over his own family in his own house. As a result, the institution of the family was undermined, if not destroyed outright.

But just how much a father would sacrifice for his family was revealed in the story of Sam Lion, the field hand listed as the father of ten children. A cryptic note in the plantation ledger from the winter of 1842–43 indicated that Sam Lion was in the county jail awaiting trial. He had a chance at freedom and did not take it—given a choice between freedom and his family, he chose his family. His fate rested in the hands of a Beaver Creek overseer, Craven Wyatt, who had been the only white man to witness a sudden, horrible death in the forest.

In the weeks before Christmas, 1842, the slaves had gone into the forest to clear new seedbeds. It was a hateful task. Outside of a mine, no labor was more arduous than this. The slaves first cut down everything in sight, chopping down trees, hacking at brush and saplings. This was old-growth forest, so the trees were large and the undergrowth was dense. When they had finished cutting, they faced a field of stumps and the tangled roots of scrub. All this had to be laboriously hauled up with hoes, axes, and picks, then set on fire, so the land could be made as clear as a beach to receive the tobacco seeds.

Marshall Hairston must have thought that his people were working too slowly, because he hired a new overseer, Beverly Brown, to work along with Craven Wyatt. Brown brought with him a large whip with a heavy handle. When Wyatt saw the whip, he thought it might have a "loaded" handle—one with a core of iron. A loaded whip had only one purpose, to club slaves, being deadlier than a whip itself.

A few days before Christmas, Brown and Wyatt had a large crew at work, burning great piles of roots, saplings, stumps, and brush. The piles were wet, and Brown had the men chopping dry kindling to keep the smoky fires going. Brown needed an auger, and Craven Wyatt told him that Sam Lion owned one. Sam did not care at all for this new overseer, so when Brown told him in a peremptory way to get his auger, Sam refused, saying that it was his own. He had bought it with his own money and he was not obliged to lend it.

Sam had defied the overseer in front of everyone, and Brown was not inclined to let it go. He told Sam to pull off his shirt because he was going to get a whipping. To this also, Sam said no.

Sam turned his back on Brown and resumed his work, chopping kindling. He would do the work that was expected of him but he would not submit to a beating.

Brown was furious. He sprang at Sam, who had his back turned, not to whip him but to kill him. He had his club raised to strike. At the last second Sam heard something—perhaps someone shouted a warning—and turned from his work. He was holding his ax in both hands. Just as Brown was upon him, Sam reacted. He swung his ax to ward off Brown's blow. The blade plunged deep into Brown's chest.

The overseer staggered backward and fell into the arms of Wyatt. Within seconds Beverly Brown was dead.

Kate Lion would have been working there with the children. We can only imagine the awful shiver that went through them, as they knew that they were probably seeing their father for the last time. There was nothing for Sam to do but run. He fled through the smoke of the burning forest, kicking up sparks from the charred stubble, and hid himself in a cave. He had done nothing more than defend himself, but a white man lay dead as a result.

Sam Lion could only save himself by fleeing North. For help he could seek out the Underground Railroad, which had been active in the Hairstons' area for twenty years. The Underground could have provided a disguise and counterfeit travel papers. There were "conductors" in the region willing to risk their lives to help slaves escape. A mere five miles to the west of Beaver Creek lay the foothills of the Blue Ridge. From a high point there Sam could look across the Shenandoah Valley at the rugged mass of the Allegheny Mountains. This had been the highway to the North for hundreds of black refugees. If Sam could make it across the open fields of the valley, which at that point was narrow, he could pick his way north along the mountains. In the part of the state that would become West Virginia during the Civil War, many people were opposed to slavery and were willing to help runaways reach Ohio or Pennsylvania.

But Sam did not try to reach freedom. One man running alone could escape, but traveling through the wilderness with a wife and ten children would have been all but impossible. He stayed in hiding in the forest for nearly two months. He could not have survived in midwinter without people surreptitiously bringing him food and blankets. They also brought him startling news: if he came in, Craven Wyatt would help him at his trial. The universe of slavery was capricious. Slaveholders wielded total power over people who were totally powerless. But from time to time the legal system rescued individual slaves from unjust punishments, and in this case, Sam had an ally who was white. Sam came in.

A special county court of "oyer and terminer"—a slave crime court—convened immediately. Only one witness appeared, Craven Wyatt. The overseer described the killing in great detail, with clear sympathy for Sam Lion's case. Almost everything he said tended to exonerate Sam. Despite prodding by the prosecutor, Wyatt refused to say that Sam Lion had raised his ax first. Wyatt testified that Brown sprang so fast that Sam did not have a chance to react in any other way. But a crucial piece of evidence had vanished. When the prosecutor displayed a whip in court, Wyatt said it was not Brown's. He declared that the one Brown carried that day had a much larger handle that might have been loaded with iron. He said plainly that the overseer brandished the handle like a club. But without the whip itself in evidence, there was no proof that it was a deadly weapon.

The court was not moved by Wyatt's testimony. The killing of the overseer had opened a breach in the regime of slavery. The breach had to be sealed. Sam was convicted of murder and sentenced to death by hanging.

At this point, Marshall Hairston could have intervened. The court, if asked by the master, could have forwarded the case to the governor for a consideration of clemency. But no request for mercy was heard. Sam Lion was sent to jail to await his execution in three weeks.

Sam's situation was hopeless, but his courage had not yet left him. He now attempted to do what he could have done before—he tried to escape. Somehow he broke loose from his cell, but he had not run more than a few steps when a guard raised his gun and cut him down.

At Beaver Creek, Ann Hairston took out her ledger book, crossed out Sam Lion's name, and wrote, "Condemned to hang for killing overseer." She thought he had cheated the hangman because she added, "Died in jail before time arrived." Three months later Ann opened her ledger again to that page and scratched out the name of Kate Lion. She too was dead. When a slave died, Ann wrote the cause of death next to the name, but this time she did not, so we don't know if Kate died from an accident, disease, or from unendurable grief.

Ann Hairston occasionally wrote in the ledger next to a slave's name the word "Sold." She and Marshall broke up at least four families by selling a spouse. In another instance they sold both husband and wife (although there is no way of telling if the couple were sold together), and they sold the oldest surviving son (aged nineteen) of a woman who had died, leaving his younger siblings to be taken care of by others.

Nothing indicates that Marshall ever felt any remorse over selling slaves. In the winter of 1845, a rumor swept through the extended white family that "Uncle Marshall intends selling off all his negroes except his house servants." It never happened, and on its face it was highly improbable, but the mere suggestion of a mass sale would have sent a wave of dread through the black families, which may have been precisely what Marshall intended—to remind the people of just how much power he had at his command and how capriciously he could wield it.

Several slave traders were active in the Hairstons' part of Virginia. A trader from Pittsylvania County named Philip Thomas traveled through Virginia and into the Deep South buying and selling with great enthusiasm. His main markets were Richmond and Montgomery, Alabama; he envied the New Orleans traders who made the big profits. Thomas's reports glow with his enthusiasm for the market:

> The auction is now going on. 14 year old girls bring from $1250 to 1275. #1 women $1300 . . . #1 Men from $1500 to $1600 . . . You write me to buy Boys not less than 100 lbs weight, but you say nothing of the prices. Write me immediately what sort you think best to buy and what such will bring. . . . I have bought [for resale] two women [with] a child apiece and both in the family way again, also 1 girl. I am buying slow and I think I have nailed Christ to the + on them.

This last expression meant that he had made the deal of his dreams.

The Virginia banks were heavily involved in financing the slave trade and derived large profits from the fees they charged for accepting checks on distant banks. The slave traders cultivated personal relationships with their bankers. "I think I have raised our reputation some in the Danville Bank," Thomas wrote. "Sutherlin [the president of the bank] says as long as we let our exchanges pass through his bank we can get his money. . . . The more exchange we let the Banks have, the more indulgence we can get, and the more negroes we buy." He estimated they could pass $40,000 to $50,000 ($635,000 to $794,000 in 1998 dollars) in checks through Sutherlin's bank, which would get them enough goodwill to borrow $30,000. A black man from Danville remembered seeing slaves led south to be sold in the cotton states: "Over de hills dey come in lines reachin' as far as you kin see. Dey walk in double lines chained tergether in twos. Each one have an old sack on his back wif everythin' he's got in it. Truly, son, de haf has never been told."

Marshall Hairston sold a man named Jim to a North Carolina slave trading company, Jarratt and Puryear. This company did a brisk business buying slaves in Virginia and North Carolina and selling them south to the booming cotton states. Jim was fortunate, as such things go, in that he did not end up in a chain gang heading south; he was bought by a North Carolina man. Jarratt and Puryear bought many hundreds of slaves in southern Virginia and Stokes County, North Carolina, but none of the other Hairston planters turned up in the thousands of documents kept by this company. Marshall was the only member of the family who turned a man over to them.

It was probably Marshall who had dealings with a Pittsylvania County slave trader, James Mitchell, several years earlier. The record for this is not among the family papers but in an account book the slave trader kept of his expenses for bringing a slave coffle from Virginia to Mississippi in the winter of 1834. Mitchell listed the names of forty-nine slaves he took south, including Frank, Ephrem, and Mary Hairston. They left on October 18 and arrived in northern Mississippi thirty-eight days later on November 25. It was a miserable journey, rainy most of the way and the people nearly always cold, wet, and covered with mud.

Mitchell's first stop in Mississippi was the plantation town of Washington, near the center of the state, where he sold a fourteen-year-old boy named Henry Lang to a planter named James Bland. Then Mitchell went on to Jackson and Port Gibson, where he found buyers but none who had cash. Everyone wanted to buy on credit, but Mitchell operated on a "strictly cash" basis, so he continued on to Natchez, the elegant city on the Mississippi River that was the center of Delta plantation society and commerce. There he found what he wanted. He sold some slaves individually, then sold the rest of his consignment, including the three Hairstons, all in one transaction for over $18,000. Mitchell did not record the name of the buyer, but such an expensive purchase would probably have been made either by a large-plantation owner or another slave trader who had access to bank funds.

A letter written by Mitchell's daughter depicts him as a kindly man who liked to sit by the fire with his children and tell them his hopes for their future. Another item paints a different picture. He had to pay a refund to James Bland for the purchase of Henry Lang. Lang became acutely ill just a few days after Mitchell left town. Bland called in a physician and spent $100 on treatments and medicines, but the boy died. The doctor said Lang's illness had been chronic, that the boy had been sick for a long time before his arrival in Mississippi.

When Mitchell refunded the money, Bland noted on the receipt that Mitchell was an honorable man. His definition of an honorable man included someone who had walked a sick boy in chains for over seven hundred miles in winter.

All these transactions had long been forgotten in both the white and the black families. What remained was Marshall's face etched by lightning on a window at Beaver Creek and the memory of a bloodstained house. Perhaps it was not a bloody beating that had left this memory—the black Hairstons had endured such things and had shrugged them off—but the destruction of a family, the rupturing of blood ties.

I had not been able to see Marshall's face in the glass, but I was soon troubled by ghosts. One night three people, a woman and two men, appeared in my room and said their names, Mary, Frank, Ephrem—the names of the three Hairstons sold into Mississippi by the slave trader Mitchell. I saw them as adults, but I clearly heard them say, "We are children." I sat up and realized I had been dreaming. I went to the file where I kept a copy of Mitchell's account book. Nothing in it indicated that the three Hairstons were children. They had been sold as part of one lot for a single price. I divided the price by the number of people sold—thirty-one—to get the average. It was the price of a child. They were all children.

It seemed that the moral blindness of these slaveholders was total. Marshall Hairston, having sold children, still remained serene in his religious beliefs: "Remember thy *Creator* in the days of thy youth," he wrote to his daughter, "do not neglect your bible, read it regularly and endeavor to be profited thereby." He could cite numerous passages that showed divine approval of slavery.

The slaveholders' bedrock was the belief that blacks were ordained to slavery by God. In the documents they left behind, the Hairstons rarely used the word *slave*. They wrote "servants," "men," "hands," and "blacks." To refer to their slave holdings as a whole they wrote "negro property," "black family," or "the people." The word they most often used was *negro*. The rosters at various plantations were headed, "List of Negros at————" and even when they bought slaves, the receipt would read, chillingly, "Bill of Sale for Negros." For them, the word *negro* equaled "slave." It quite literally meant the same thing. They clung to their belief in the natural inferiority of the black race even as they grew more and more dependent on the skills of the black people, saw the growth of the generations in their black family, and felt the stirrings of emotion when one of them died.

The Frenchman Alexis de Tocqueville, traveling through the South in the 1830s, was baffled that the slaveholders had created a system that contradicted all the ideals America stood for. Such a society was doomed. Slavery, he wrote, was "cruel to the slave," but inevitably it would be "fatal to the master."

5

A BRIEF

ILLUMINATION

In the preceding months of my research, I had been a frequent guest at Cooleemee. The judge seemed pleased that I was at work on a book about his family, but warned me that it would be more arduous than I thought, given the size and complexity of the story. Generous with his time and advice, he had taken me to Chapel Hill to show me the family papers and introduce me to the archivists in charge of them. He had directed me to local historians and to remote family members who might have recollections. It occurred to me that this might be his way of controlling what I found, but that was not the case. He never asked me what the black Hairstons were saying about him or his ancestors, and when I offered to show him a portion of my work to see if I had made any errors, he firmly declined. "I'm not going to serve as your editor," he said.

Starting early in the morning over coffee in the columned dining room, and continuing into the afternoon in the library, the judge and I spent many days discussing his family's past. He was no mere storyteller. He was a serious student of Southern history, especially the legal history of the South as it related to slavery. He lent me a scholarly book on the slave laws of North Carolina, which he had carefully studied himself. He had also collected books about the condition of the slaves, the Civil War, and the philosophy of the slaveholders. Most of all, the judge was a student of his own family's history. Whenever I came up with what I thought was a discovery, I would find that he had been there first, and I would hear a familiar refrain: "I can tell you all about that."

On some points we sparred over interpretations, and he would overrule my objections politely but firmly. Only on rare occasions did I feel a blast of irritation roll down from the bench, as when I did not recognize the name of a slave called Dorcas, and he thundered, "It's in the Bible!" An enormous eighteenth-century Bible from one of the old Virginia plantations was in the library. In the evening of the day he had chastised me for my scriptural ignorance, I slipped into the library and gently opened the heavy tome to find the passage where Dorcas is raised from the dead. I had thought that the judge kept the Bible purely as a historical relic. He derided open displays of religiosity. Still, he knew enough of his Bible to recognize the obscure name of Dorcas.

I provoked another of his blasts when I repeated to him a story I had heard about his great-grandfather from a black Hairston woman in Virginia. I collected a great deal of oral history from the black Hairstons and felt no obligation to "check" this material with the judge, but occasionally I would mention something I had heard to see if he could shed additional light. The woman had told me that some of the land her family still owned had been given to her great-grandfather after the Civil War by the judge's great-grandfather, Samuel Hairston of Oak Hill. "I can tell you all about that," he barked. "By that time he was senile!" There was no more discussion of the matter, and I was left to ponder the meaning of his remark. On the one hand it reflected the ancient Hairston belief that giving away land was the height of foolishness, and on the other it seemed to be a warning to me: write whatever you want, but please don't try to make things sound better than they really were. On the subject of slavery, the judge was a realist, not a romantic.

One December, Judge Hairston asked that I bring my family to Cooleemee for a special event—a Christmas-tree lighting in the traditional antebellum style, not with electric lights but with candles. On the appointed evening we arrived to find the house filled with guests. A seventeen-foot pine tree rose up in the hall, with scores of candles attached to the branches. When darkness fell, all the lights in the house were extinguished. The old tall-case clock gravely ticked the time. The guests began to sing a hymn as two of the judge's grandchildren and my son used long tapers to light the candles on the tree, gradually illuminating the curved staircase that spiraled up into darkness, and casting a gentle glow on the portrait of the judge's grandfather displayed in the hall. Many times I had stood in the hall and studied that portrait. The judge seemed to possess many of the same traits I thought I could detect in the portrait: authority, dignity, a sense of duty. To these I thought I could add practicality, generosity, and honesty. Like his father and grandfather before him, the judge had shouldered the duty of managing this plantation. I felt uneasy because my research—not by my wish—was assembling a posthumous indictment against his ancestors. But because the black Hairstons enjoyed close relations with the judge, I assumed that his grandfather had been "a good master." I expected that my research would separate him from the despised class of slaveholders, that I would find some redeeming feature that would rescue him, not for his sake, but for the sake of his grandson.

For a few moments, the hall blazed with light. I wished that I could step outside to see this illumination from afar, to see exactly what a visitor would have seen a century and a half ago, but there was no time. As soon as every candle had been lit, the children began to douse them one by one, and the house slipped back into darkness. On our way home after the party, my wife related to me something the judge had said to her privately in the dining room as we had awaited the lighting of the tree. "I'm terrified," he had said to her, "of what will be in that book."

THE EDUCATION OF
A SLAVE MASTER

Peter Wilson Hairston, the judge's grandfather, was barely thirteen years old when he inherited Cooleemee Plantation in 1832. By then he was already well trained in the racial hierarchy of the South. As a small child his playmates were black. They swam together and fished, wandered through the woods, and explored the attic of Oak Hill. As he was learning his ABCs, he played school with his companions, teaching them the rudiments of reading and writing. It was all a great game, until the day when his black friends did not show up. From an attic window he might have been able to see them, far off in the fields, beginning the first day of their real lives as slaves. From then on he was their master.

Peter attended a boarding school in Hillsborough, North Carolina, filled with planters' sons—teenaged slaveholders whose dinnertime talk ran to secession. In 1833, he wrote to his mother from school that "there are three boys from South Carolina here, one of them is a Nullifier [someone who supported a state's right to nullify a federal law within its own borders—one of the issues that led to the Civil War] and the other two are Union men." Peter had already been at boarding school when his great-grandfather, "Saura Town" Peter, died the previous year, leaving him the two-thousand-acre Cooleemee Plantation and four hundred slaves. His father, Samuel, directed him to leave school immediately to see that his plantation and his slaves were in good order. He rode by himself the fifty miles from the school to Cooleemee. He inspected the plantation, rode twenty miles to the town of Salisbury to bargain for hats and shoes for his slaves, and then returned to his studies, a thirteen-year-old of independent wealth. More would someday be his. Later on some murmured that he was to receive too much, but the older generation had watched the growth of the next one and had taken note of Peter from the start.

Peter was the heir to an obsession—a mania for building an empire. In the Hairston family, all else took second place. Peter's forebears had married each other to keep the land in the family. Peter himself was the offspring of an arranged marriage—his parents, Samuel and Agnes, were first cousins (once removed). Their marriage in 1818, which shored up the foundations of the burgeoning Hairston empire, had been brokered by the Peter Hairston known in the family as "Saura Town" Peter (1752–1832). He was Agnes's grandfather and Samuel's uncle. Saura Town Peter himself had only one child, a daughter named Ruth, born in 1783. She married Peter Wilson, whose family was among the most important land- and slaveholders in Pittsylvania County (the Wilsons had helped establish the city of Danville), and Ruth had given birth to Agnes in 1801. As the years went by and Ruth had no other children, it became apparent that Agnes would be the main heir of two great fortunes from her Hairston and Wilson foreparents.

A crisis arose, however, in 1813 when Ruth's husband died, leaving her a widow at the age of thirty. Saura Town Peter fretted over the enormous amount of money, land, and slaveholdings in the hands of two women who were now unattached. His fears were justified. He soon began receiving inquiries from suitors eager for the hand of Agnes, who was only twelve. All of the land and slaves he had laboriously accumulated would slip from the family's grasp unless he could quickly find a Hairston husband for his only grandchild, and therefore, he fastened upon his nephew Samuel. Despite Agnes's enormous wealth, Saura Town Peter had to be persistent to focus the twenty-five-year-old Samuel's attention on the charms of his barely adolescent cousin. One of his letters on the subject, despite its garbled syntax, clearly conveys Saura Town Peter's growing irritation with Samuel along with an implied threat that it was highly unwise for Samuel to disregard the request of a rich uncle: "This is the third letter I have wrote to you on this subject and conclude from your not gratifying the meaning that my wishes for your welfare is not thought so well of." Saura Town Peter went on to say, in an apparent reference to romantic love, that it was natural for a man to wish for "Happiness during Life," but that the paramount concern was money—"riches," he wrote to Samuel, were "now in your power to marry." He wrote that by marrying Agnes, Samuel would obtain "one of the Best ackomplished girls in Virginia as well as a great fortune." Peter's letter combined sternness with a sense of panic: he had received a letter from an outsider expressing interest in Agnes just the previous day—"delay breeds danger the sooner the better."

A betrothal was apparently agreed upon in 1814, and the outside suitors were put off. Accordingly, the cousins Samuel and Agnes married four years later in 1818, when Agnes had attained an age that made the transaction seemly. A year later they celebrated the birth of their first child, Peter Wilson Hairston. Saura Town Peter was delighted. He would watch this young Peter closely for the signs of firmness, steadiness, and devotion to duty that would make him a fitting heir.

The marriage of a cousin to a cousin was common in the Hairston family, but the alliance of Agnes and Samuel had a bizarre corollary: Agnes's mother, the widowed Ruth, married Samuel's brother Robert. Their marriage produced what Saura Town Peter so devoutly wished for—the consolidation of Hairston lands with the Wilson lands that Ruth had inherited from her late husband. In these dynastic marriages, mother and daughter became sisters-in-law; Robert became the father-in-law of his brother Samuel—and all became tightly bound to Saura Town Peter, and to each other, in a complex, interlocking directorate of legacies. Later on, when a crisis arose in the Hairston family, it would become supremely difficult to sort out precisely who owned what. The ownership of the Hairston slaves was particularly muddled—it was virtually a collective ownership.

Their financial ties to each other—bonds that would determine the fortunes of five generations of white Hairstons, born a full century apart— suppressed personal independence and dissent for decades, especially on the subject of the slaves. Judge Hairston, in my first conversation with him at Cooleemee, had revealed how effective these links were when he alluded to the economic and legal difficulties posed by freeing slaves. Referring to his grandfather's situation and sidestepping the inherent morality of the issue, the judge had said, "He didn't own the slaves outright— his title was all mixed up with his grandmother and the rest of the family." And in terms of marriage, the judge's grandfather, when he was a young man, was well aware that the family's financial, legal, and social interests would partially determine his choice of a wife. As he wrote in his diary, "Marriage—parents have the veto."

Samuel Hairston expected a great deal from his first child, Peter, and held him to high, sometimes harsh standards. He went to the University of North Carolina, garnering academic honors. At age eighteen, having gotten a master's degree in 1837, Peter was sent off to the University of Virginia to study law. His father had no intention of making a lawyer out of him, but a good working knowledge of the law was essential to running a plantation empire. Peter made a special study of the law of dower—an aspect of common law that had critical importance for the Hairstons. The law of dower determined property rights of married women—it governed what they owned personally, what their husbands could take from them, and what they could inherit and bequeath. A large portion of Peter's future wealth would descend to him through his mother, Agnes, and his grandmother Ruth.

Homesick at the university, Peter wrote to his grandmother in 1837 that he missed his hunting dogs, saying that when he looked out his window on a fine crisp morning he sighed for his pack of hounds. He was looking forward to Christmas, but he got a shock when he wrote to his father asking for permission to come home. To this appeal Samuel wrote back frostily, "Your letter of the 3rd instant has been duly received and contents noted." There followed several densely written pages about de-votion to duty, pointing out Peter's deficiencies in that department. It had come to Samuel's attention that Peter had been absent from class four times in a single month. Samuel thought that a dose of isolation at holiday time would be good for his son.

Peter's absence from home that holiday hit hard on his mother, Agnes, a sensitive woman who felt lonely in the splendid solitude of her plan-tation. Samuel was occupied with plantation business that often required him to travel to North Carolina or to another Virginia property. During Peter's first months at the University of Virginia his father was away, building a mill on another plantation. As winter descended, Agnes felt the isolation keenly. By January she couldn't wait for the ground to thaw so that she could return to her great solace, her garden: "I shall soon begin to plant bushes and then I shall not feel lonesome," she wrote in 1838. The one visitor she had was of dubious comfort: "Your Grand Mother [Ruth] is here," Agnes wrote to Peter, "she has been a good deal complaining."

Agnes also had trouble with Peter's younger sister, who was moody and suffered from bouts of fatigue and vaguely defined spells. She used her "illness" to bully her mother—"if she is crossed in the least thing it appears to make her [sickness] worse," Agnes once wrote in exasperation.

What should have been a festive occasion—a trip with her two daughters to Philadelphia and New York to buy clothes and jewelry—became torture. "I have just returned from shopping," Agnes wrote to her mother, as if she had just returned from the field of battle. "I do not think I ought to be blamed for what [my daughter] does, as she will listen to nothing I will say. If I can find rest in the grave all will be well. It is useless to expect it here." Agnes was also bracing herself for Samuel's grumpiness over her expenditures. She passed up a piece of jewelry, one that she wanted more than anything else, because the price was $250 (about $4,500 in 1998), a sum her husband could easily afford. She let her daughters order several dresses, but bought only one for herself, already thinking of justifying herself to Sam—"he may call me extravagant, but must not call me selfish."

In this age a son dared not to openly contradict his father, and Peter signed his letters, "your dutiful son." But a letter written to Peter by one of his friends from UVA indicates that Peter, at least briefly, chafed at the idea of devoting his life to the pursuit of money. The friend wrote to Peter in 1838 about the great fortunes being piled up in Mississippi, saying that if a man were disposed to risk his health in that climate, he could make more money there than in Virginia—but this prospect, the friend concluded, "would please your Papa better than you." Although Peter may have felt some youthful misgivings over the necessity of earning money, he was hardly loath to spend it. While a student, he withdrew $100 at a time from his own tobacco account with a Lynchburg merchant and provoked a scolding from his father over his spending habits.

The dutiful son remained forever grounded to a path he ultimately did not wish to leave, but throughout his life a streak of melancholy never left him. When he was twenty-eight, Peter wrote to his brother that he was reading a book about the tragic life of the English poet Byron. In it he found "many thoughts and feelings which come home to me. Driven an exile from his own country, a morbid sensibility and suspicious irritability seems to have seized upon him and destroyed the peace of his mind." Two years later, Peter was traveling in Alabama to conduct some unpleasant negotiations with a family member over land and slaves— negotiations that required him to be less than honest with his relative. At a boardinghouse he spied a copy of Leonardo's painting of the Last Supper, which led Peter to reflect upon the betrayal of Christ by his own disciples: "He was pure and yet was crucified. . . . Why should we, who are frail & endued with strong passions, expect better things from our fellow creatures? With the best intentions we sometimes deceive others & are deceived ourselves."

As Peter advanced through his twenties his father gradually turned the plantation businesses over to him. He assumed the task of investing his father's money in Virginia land, negotiated with Lynchburg traders to sell the family's tobacco and wheat, and undertook the delicate business of extending credit and collecting debts. Converting paper profits into ready cash was a chronic problem, since no national currency existed until after the Civil War. Local banks issued notes that were negotiable at face value only where the bank was well-known. People of wealth who had distant business interests had a difficult time getting their hands on cash they could use. When the Hairstons pursued a debtor from North Carolina to Tennessee and won a court settlement, the debtor handed over $5,000 in Tennessee notes, which, if brought to Virginia, would have been worth less than half their face value. The Hairstons' lawyer in Tennessee set about hunting for Virginia or North Carolina banknotes he could acquire in exchange for the Tennessee paper. The family had problems even on its home ground. The Hairstons built up large balances with their Virginia tobacco agents. At one point Samuel had a $12,000 balance (equivalent in 1998 to more than $210,000) at a Lynchburg trading firm but could not withdraw a penny of it because the firm had no cash on hand. He had similar difficulties getting access to funds deposited with the Danville Bank.

The intricacies of foreign commerce were something else Peter would have to master. Selling tobacco and wheat was an international business. Peter and his father received regular notices from their agents in Richmond and Petersburg about events in Europe that affected the prices for their commodities. War, the threat of war, the rise and fall of governments, and the mischief of European speculators all determined how much money they made, if any. Their Richmond agent wrote in 1847 that the latest bulletins brought by steamship revealed that prices in England for all kinds of produce, including Virginia tobacco, were stagnant because of "the deranged state of the currency." Rampant speculation in food commodities had weakened many of the richest British banking houses, forcing them to suspend business. Some months later, Virginia planters closely monitored the violent overthrow of the French monarchy in the Revolution of 1848 and the shaky start of a republican government in France. The Hairstons' agent wrote to them, "We confess the late advices via steamer from Europe are not as favorable for the continuation of peace. . . . If the French Republic stands, 3500 hogsheads of Tobacco will be required in [Richmond] to supply the French market."

Although Peter was learning to be the manager of a large financial enterprise, with interests in several states and markets overseas, his foremost duties were those of a slaveholder. At his father's side he learned all the aspects of his personal responsibility for men, women, and children who were enslaved. The master tended slaves when they were sick or injured. If a slave wished to marry someone from another plantation, the master had to approve. Overall, he had to give sufficient consideration to maintaining the well-being of "his people" while keeping them enslaved. It was a contradiction typical of the paradoxical world they all inhabited. In his writings, Peter never expressed any misgivings over slavery, but he was aware that such misgivings did exist in his family. One letter that his mother, Agnes, wrote to him contained a brief, but nonetheless extraordinary, hint of doubt over the family's ownership of slaves. For just a moment, the mask slipped: "I feel their situation deeply without having it in my power to relieve them any." Such thoughts were dangerous; they undermined the rigid mental discipline that the slaveholders had to maintain; and Agnes banished this vague rustling of doubt immediately. Her next sentence reads, "They behave themselves very well to me, and are more obedient than they used to be." The mask was firmly back in place.

There arose, unexpectedly, an opportunity for Samuel to impart a crucial lesson to his son when one day word reached them that the overseer at Cooleemee, an Irishman named Grief Mason, had killed two slaves. The death of two slaves was an extremely serious matter, and Peter and his father went down personally to investigate. Mason told them that he had given permission for the slaves to have a party. He provided liquor and wished everyone a good time, but he warned that he would not tolerate any fighting. The entertainment progressed in fine fashion until slaves from across the river turned up and began to help themselves to the food and drink. A fight broke out. Mason heard the commotion and came running, putting a stop to the fight by killing two men.

Peter was furious with Mason. He told him that under no circumstance was he to kill a slave. Mason replied that if the master did not approve of the way he ran the plantation, he would quit.

At this point Peter's father intervened. "You let Mason run it his way," Samuel said. "If you don't, you won't be able to put foot down here yourself."

Samuel believed that if Peter failed to back up his overseer, the slaves would lose respect for both overseer and master. He regretted the death of the slaves, but knew that a plantation always had the potential for violence. Without question, when the lives of slaves had to be weighed against discipline, order, and control, then the slaves lost. The slaves already knew this. But the young master had to learn that lesson. The unexpected incident at Cooleemee had provided Samuel with the opportunity to test his son. Peter spoke first, and when he was inclined to stand up for the slaves, his father had to contradict him in the presence of the overseer. Peter was naive. He knew that he was inheriting property, that he was coming into possession of certain legal rights and responsibilities, but he did not fully understand the scope of his ownership. He knew that his people, his black family, were his property, but he did not yet know the full implications of mastery. But after his confrontation with a man ironically named Grief, Peter could not fail to know that what he had inherited was the power of life and death.

In 1843, at the age of twenty-four, Peter went off on a grand tour of Europe. For the first time he mixed with people who were not Southern slaveholders, and even though we can assume these people were of a similar social class, he was immensely shocked to find himself treated as a pariah. During the voyage to England it quickly became known among the passengers that the young Virginian was a slaveholder. While this did not stop a Yankee named James J. Roosevelt (the great-uncle of future president Theodore Roosevelt) from forming a friendship with Peter, the English passengers made clear their disdain. At the dinner table, one of the Britons asked him if he hitched his slaves to the plow instead of oxen. The remark left him seething with indignation: "The fanatic bigot," Peter scribbled in his travel diary that night, "his mind is filled with confounded notions of liberty and freedom, neither of which he fully understands. . . . In no subject do foreigners display greater ignorance than slavery. Prejudice and misrepresentation have so biased their minds that they will not believe the truth."

Once ashore, Peter became convinced that the English were thorough hypocrites for criticizing slavery in America. He had never seen a slave forced to live in the conditions of the English worker. The poverty of English cities shocked him. In Manchester there was "wretchedness on a grand scale"; in Liverpool, "we cannot step out into the streets without being annoyed by beggars with their piteous tales. Mothers with little children in their arms, little girls, and stale, stout looking men, all asking for a penny to buy them some bread." His diary sounds like the rantings of a socialist: "Palaces and poverty are closely united—splendours and penury. These grand edifices tell the tale of oppression, that while the few are revelling in all the luxuries of life, the many are suffering the bitter pangs of want. And while we may be dazzled by the splendour of royalty we can but shudder at the wretchedness of its subjects."

Everything he saw tended to confirm the widely held Southern view that plantation slavery was not nearly as evil as the factory. The workers, he saw, took their midday meal ("dry bread with a little coffee") on the factory floor amidst dead air and thundering looms. In a London newspaper he found an article that confirmed his opinion of English iniquity. "White Slaves of London," he wrote, copying down the story of needleworkers starting their shift at four in the morning, working eighteen or nineteen hours a day, "plying their needles without a ray of hope to cheer them," prey to diseases of the lung and premature old age. "Where is the slave in America," he asks, "with whom these unfortunate creatures would not willingly change lots?"

In the countryside he passed rows of farmhouses. Their small windows and thatched roofs struck him with their antique appearance. But far from thinking them quaint, he thought them uncomfortable and unkempt. He took a hard look at the farmers too, as they came home from the market in their broad-wheeled carts. Strong and hale looking, he thought, but ignorant and rough—"they are the supporters and yet the slaves of the country's tyranny. Though oppressed, they love their oppressor and hug the very chains which bind them."

In Italy he met another American, a New Yorker named Glover, and the discussion turned one more time to the potentially troublesome topic of slavery. On this occasion, however, the conversation steered clear of the American version and focused on Old World slavery. Glover had traveled in the company of a Turkish nobleman, who had with him an entourage of six or seven slaves. Slavery in Turkey was very mild, Glover said, a luxury known only to the palaces "among the higher order." The slaves did not till the soil, a task carried out by peasants. The slaves ate at the same table with their masters, and they all said their prayers together. Whenever a female slave had a child by her master, she was at once liberated. Slavery was worse in Russia, Glover maintained. Peter wrote down Glover's remark that the serfs in Russia were white but no less subject to the will of their masters. Glover had overheard a Russian princess talking about slavery. She was asked if they ever beat their slaves. "Yes," said the princess, surprised at the stupidity of the question. "What else do you expect?"

Peter's grand tour lasted nearly nine months. He talked to some of Napoleon's veterans, asked the price of a Raphael painting ($20,000), saw the queen dowager of Genoa, and attended royal balls in Naples, where he was surprised to see military officers kissing the hand of the king.

He returned to America very much the same man he had been when he left. The unpleasant discussions over slavery had not altered his views in the slightest. In fact, scenes and events he had witnessed in England only served to buttress his philosophical and racial conception of slavery. In particular, he had seen the footmen of English nobles, clinging to the rear of carriages clattering through the streets. What struck him were their uniforms. They dressed in knee breeches, stockings, and fancy coats. Each lord had different colors, so his servants would be readily identifiable. This harmless custom made a deep impression on Peter: "It is abhorrent to my feelings to see a white man put on a badge and declare that he belongs to another." The footmen in their livery of servitude horrified him because the white man was not meant to assume the mark of bondage. As for the black man, Peter thought, his skin was the badge of servitude, divinely ordained: "God has marked [him] in such a manner that he cannot wash it out."

The reflections Peter set down in his diary were not meant to be private. A nineteenth-century traveler, upon his return, customarily shared his travel diary with friends and family so that they could read about his experiences and benefit from them. Peter's reflections on slavery have the forceful tone of a man anxious to convince himself and his family of their moral purity.

Other events, personal family matters, were probably on Peter's mind. He never mentioned it in his diary, but his trip, which left him feeling so embattled but so justified on the question of slavery, came at a time when the Hairstons were grappling with dissension within their ranks. There was an enemy within the family itself, a master who had grown sick at heart over slavery. It would be Peter's task to contend against him, to defend slavery against a man who desperately tried to undo it, who would call upon God to hear his declaration that slavery was not divinely ordained, but an evil and an abomination.

At Christmas in 1845, Peter joined his family at the Virginia plantation of his cousins, the Broadnax family. For several days the men amused themselves by hunting and target shooting, while the women stayed inside and talked. In the evenings, the men played backgammon while the women sang. Peter's father, Samuel, discussed business. It was the end of the year—the time to take stock and settle accounts. Accordingly, Samuel had been riding around his properties on a tour of inspection, and he gave the family his report. He had passed a farm where he did not like the way the tenant was managing things. He went into the man's house and screamed at him—"You will impoverish my children!"—as if the Hairstons were teetering on the abyss of bankruptcy.

Peter himself undertook some family duties. He rode out to see the black sheep in the family, Powhatan Hunter, a drunkard whom Samuel had taken pity on.

> He is one of the poorest persons I've ever seen. He was no doubt just
> on the point of starving when my father gave them money. They had
> no axe nor tool of any kind and only one bed and two bed quilts.
> He's old, palsied and unable to work but has two sons who are strong
> and hardy looking boys and if they would work could support their
> parents handsomely. My grandfather tried to make something of Pow-
> hatan but could not as he became dissipated.

In Peter's mind, Powhatan's degradation served as an example of what could happen to those who were weak, and he reproached himself in his diary for his own lapses: "How many days have been misspent and how often have we strayed from the path of duty?"

Later that day, Peter went to visit someone who, along with his father, had become a mentor to him—his grandmother Ruth. He rode through miserable sleet and rain to reach her mansion just a short ride away at Berry Hill. Ruth's great wealth had bought her not an ounce of jollity at Christmas. Peter found her entirely alone except for a large black cat sitting at her feet. She immediately launched a stream of complaints: "She told me she remained there ten days at a time without seeing a single white person when the weather was very bad." She lived in a widow's solitude, although her husband, Robert, was still very much alive.

As night descended, Peter sat with her in one of the dark, frigid rooms, for Berry Hill was a great cavern of a house, impossible to heat. In mid-winter one could not stray more than a few feet from a fireplace. The house exuded antiquity—even then it was considered ancient. At the core of the mansion was the log house Ruth's great-grandfather Nicholas Perkins had built in 1740. The place later got its name not from any wild fruit that grew nearby but as a corruption of "Bury Hill"—it stood near a burying ground where British soldiers had been laid to rest during the Revolution.

The past preyed on Ruth's mind that night—the past and the ebb and flow of fortune. "We conversed," Peter wrote in his diary, "about the changes which time had made." She talked about the Revolutionary War when her grandfather had billeted militia troops in the house, when one of the soldiers had cut the throat on the old picture of the king. The portraits were long gone. Ruth had no idea what had happened to them— they had simply disappeared, along with many of the old furnishings she had known as a girl, in a financial catastrophe that had struck her grandfather Peter Perkins. Ruth lacked not at all for money—she could furnish the house ten times over if she wished—but the loss of the things that had been so familiar in her youth had convinced her of the instability of the world. All could be swept away.

Peter had absorbed the family's history deeply, but as he sat with his grandmother in the dark, cold parlor of Berry Hill, she told him a familiar cautionary tale of wealth and poverty, recalling again for Peter the story of her grandfather. She wanted to drive home its moral one more time.

She recalled that her grandfather had been "more handsomely fixed than any man in this part of the country." But she stressed that he had lost everything. Perkins put all his money into building iron forges and then went bankrupt. He wrote a piteous letter to Ruth's father telling of his deep humiliation. "I have managed my business very badly," he wrote. "My intent was to do rite and justice to all mankind." Fortune's wheel had turned, and Perkins left in disgrace for Tennessee. The moral of the story was clear—it revealed the foolishness of the man who would try "to do rite and justice to all mankind."

Ruth was not just a querulous old woman. She possessed a sharp, penetrating, and far-seeing intelligence. She ran her plantations herself, and not a hog was moved to market without her knowing it. She understood land, crops, livestock, markets, and money as well as anyone else in the South, and she could manipulate the intricacies of the law far better than Peter could, for all his studies at the university. She understood the ways of wealth and the lengths that men and women would go to grasp it. Wealth had to be kept in those hands strong enough to grasp it firmly, and out of those hands whose kindness or weakness could undermine the family's position. She had done exactly that and was paying a price for it. Her solitude was the price for having won an intricate legal game against her husband, for Robert had left Virginia for Mississippi, taking with him hundreds of slaves.

Robert had predicted that wealth would be the family's destruction. The pursuit of wealth had tied him in invisible, unbreakable coils. Wealth was wreaking its havoc upon generation after generation: "You and I know not what hour we may leave this world," he had written to his brother Samuel, "and both have as much of it as necessary—and what we leave behind us, if left as it is, had better not be left." This cryptic utterance was typical of Robert. He spoke in riddles. He always meant more than he could say—but despite the ambiguity of his remark, the significance of it was plain enough. Money—and his own desire for it—had only brought him misery, and he foresaw bitter feuding after his death. The family relentlessly sought more land, more slaves, more wealth. Robert's pronouncement that wealth would do them harm was the most egregious heresy. At the root of his misery was slavery. Some years earlier, in 1832, he had done something no Hairston had ever done before—he had set some slaves free.

He had made contact with the American Colonization Society, a group devoted to the gradual abolition of slavery by sending blacks to Africa with the permission and support of their masters. The society had purchased land on the western shore of Africa and established the colony of Liberia in 1821. It solicited donations to support the colony until it became self-sufficient. Some abolitionists such as those organized by William Lloyd Garrison, denounced the group as a fraud, a mere sop to the consciences of slaveholders willing to free a few people but unwilling to part with slavery itself. But to many slaveholders, such as Robert Hairston, who felt misgivings over slavery, the society's program seemed to be the only reasonable and practical way to bring an end to the "peculiar institution."

In late September 1832, Robert received a letter from the agent of the Colonization Society in Lynchburg, William M. Rives: "I hope you have seen the last accounts from Liberia—every new arrival is more and more satisfactory & encouraging. The country is now more open—better cultivated—better homes for the people." Rives informed him that the next ship bound for Liberia, the *Jupiter*, would set sail from Norfolk in about two weeks and would have room for thirty passengers. Robert responded immediately:

> Dear Sir,
>
> I received last night a letter saying that the *Jubiter* would be in Norfolk about the 13th and that the negroes that I wish to send to Liberia can have a passage. I shall start them Monday next, but my calculation is that they will not reach Norfolk before the 16th, which is as soon as I can possibly get them thare. I shall also send the money to pay for thair passage and 6 months support. . . . I shall take it as a favor if you will have them settled in Liberia according to plan.

Far from wanting to wash his hands of them, Robert was concerned for the well-being of the people he was sending on this voyage. He felt uneasy about them and wanted to make certain that the society would take good care of them—"They have all been raised on my plantation and have seen very little of the wourld." He inquired what accommodation would be made for their spiritual needs, pointing out that "one is a member of the Babtist Church in this neighborhood." And Robert wished to be kept informed of what became of them: "On the return of the *Jubiter* please send me such information as you received of them."

Robert and the six people he freed—he did not record their names—scrambled to make their preparations. It was his habit to be late, to ignore urgent correspondence, and to put off dealing with matters that were unpleasant, but to this task he leaped. Getting these six people equipped, provided with cash, and expeditiously onto the *Jupiter* seemed of paramount concern to him, as if he was afraid that someone might stop him. Some years later, when a man who married into the family quietly tried to send off seven slaves to Liberia, his Hairston in-laws immediately got an injunction against him and had the slaves pursued on the road to Norfolk and arrested.

Such was not the fate of these six slaves, who left the Leatherwood Plantation in one of Robert's wagons. On October 16, Robert was notified by the society's agent in Norfolk that his people had come in safely:

This day your six freed servants arrived here in your waggon, and the ship *Jupiter* in which your people will embark arrived also today. I received your letter containing two hundred and twenty Dollars, which sum will be applied in the payment of passage and furnishing them with provisions and other articles suitable for their comfort after their arrival there; your liberality will furnish them sufficiently until they can do for themselves. The ship will sail in about eight days from this place.

Robert's act shocked Ruth and the rest of the family. His small-scale emancipation came just months after the death of Ruth's father, Saura Town Peter, who had left her fifteen thousand acres and several hundred slaves. Robert was not one of the beneficiaries of the will, but this was a mere technicality. Under the laws and customs of dower, a husband was entitled to half ownership of, and total control over, anything his wife possessed, so half of whatever Ruth inherited from her father would immediately become Robert's. It was too late to recapture the slaves Robert had freed, but his wife could prevent him from ever freeing a slave that was hers.

Ruth devised an ingenious plan to keep her inheritance entirely out of Robert's hands. Enlisting the support of family members who were the executors of her father's will, Ruth delayed indefinitely the formal adjudication of the will. By this simple expedient, she held the will in limbo. Meanwhile she had the use of her father's land and slaves and received the income from his plantations; but because Ruth technically did not own them, Robert never took formal ownership of the husband's portion.

The Hairston family closed ranks against Robert to protect the future, to ensure that all the wealth so laboriously piled up would pass intact to the next generation. But Robert laid a plan in secret. He trained a young slave to be a carpenter and tried to move him, along with many other slaves, from one state to another. Ruth refused to allow it. She kept an eye on every event on all of her plantations, and she could sense, correctly, when something was awry. Robert had not broken off his contacts with the Colonization Society.

In the fall of 1840 a representative of the society, Mr. W. McKenney, made a speech to the Quaker meeting at Guilford Court House, about forty miles from the plantations Robert and Ruth owned. The Quakers had been generous in their support for Liberia, and McKenney appealed for increased contributions to improve conditions there. The program was succeeding, he said, and would reach even greater heights if they would redouble their efforts to develop Liberia. To encourage the Quakers to greater effort, McKenney held out a shining hope of what they could achieve: "In this state there is one gentleman, who owns nearly one thousand [slaves], who has determined, should the colony continue to prosper, to send them to it. He is now training them with that view."

Robert was planning a gradual emancipation of the slaves he controlled; he was training them for freedom, and moving some of them to obscure corners of the Hairston holdings where he could quietly let them go. But he was not able to carry out his plan. Several months after McKenney's speech about the massive emancipation planned by an anonymous slaveholder, Robert and Ruth had a fierce argument at Berry Hill. Robert stormed out of the Berry Hill mansion in a rage. He mounted his horse and disappeared, heading north. He never saw Virginia again.

He went to Philadelphia, then to the resort at Saratoga, and then to New York City. Whatever peace he was looking for, he could not find it—"I am not satisfied anywhere," he wrote. He had no idea how long he would stay away, but he sent his brother Samuel detailed instructions for the management of his property. Hire the best managers, he said, no matter what the price. He told him where to find thousands of dollars in bonds that he had left behind. "I am on the decline," he wrote, and "I never expect to plague myself about money."

He left America and traveled through Europe. Exactly what he saw and what he did are not known except that, in Paris, he sat for one of the early daguerreotype portraits. The image was lost, which is unfortunate, because it would be fascinating to gaze upon the face of the wanderer, the exile from the slavocracy, to see if his face showed any sign of the peace that had eluded him at home. After a year of traveling, Robert landed at New Orleans and made his way to one of the plantations he had started several years earlier in Mississippi. It was a new land there, and a man could live as he wished.

THE LOST
CHILD

The way was opened for the great land rush into Mississippi by a three-week outdoor "party" that General Andrew Jackson threw to debauch the Indians. It was the fall of 1820, and only a few years earlier the Choctaw warriors of Mississippi had been some of the staunchest allies of the United States in the War of 1812. They had been by Old Hickory's side in the Battle of New Orleans, in January of 1815. But now the Choctaw were in the way. So Jackson called a conference of Choctaw leaders and several hundred of their warriors. They probably thought the general wanted a reunion.

Jackson spent $20,000 for food and liquor to put the Choctaw in the proper frame of mind to hear the government's plan for them. The Choctaw, however, were stunned at Jackson's demand that they leave Mississippi and move to lands in Arkansas and farther west. Jackson then cast aside the mask of genial host and began to threaten. If the Choctaw did not agree to leave peaceably, he would carry out the government's program at the point of a gun. The Choctaw reluctantly gave in, signing papers that ceded to the United States the west-central part of Mississippi. Ten years later at Dancing Rabbit Creek the Choctaw signed another treaty ceding northern and eastern Mississippi and removed themselves to the west.

The first white settlers were overwhelmed by the beauty and fertility of the land they now possessed. "The Richest Soil I ever saw—it can never wear out," wrote one newcomer. "Providence has been very Bountiful to this Country," said another. They gaped at a panorama of grassland—they compared it to gazing out over the ocean—and were more than a little unnerved by the openness of it. "This is such a singular country to a stranger," one woman wrote after her wagon had passed nothing but grass for thirty miles. For Robert Hairston, it was the land where he could create himself anew.

He lived apart from civilization on the Mississippi prairie, like an old Scottish knight on the moor. He surrounded his house with an eight-foot brick wall, topped with iron spikes. He disdained displays of wealth; his home was a log house with a large brick dining hall, where he entertained his friends. In speaking of him people invariably used the word *plain*. His house, they said, was "a neat, comfortable, though plain residence." His furniture was all "plain and common." One of his acquaintances said, "He was a plain man and his residence was in accordance with his habits." He wore homespun clothes made for him by his own people on his plantation—even in Mississippi his garments were so far from fashion that people laughed, though not to his face. He never spoke of the wealth he left behind in Virginia, and if anyone asked him about his old home, he said he intended never to go back. He loved hunting and doted on his pack of hounds. A gothic novelist might imagine him in his crude baronial hall, with candles flickering against the Mississippi night, surrounded by hunting companions with a pack of dogs lounging at his feet, dispensing Madeira to a jolly company.

It caused comment that he did not live according to his means. When someone asked him why he did not build a mansion, Robert replied that old men who build fine houses are apt to die soon afterward. He built almost nothing for himself, but he did erect what he called a hospital for his slaves, a row of cabins near the mineral springs he owned, where the sick could take the waters and rest.

Robert was not the only Hairston in that part of Mississippi, for his brothers John and Harden had also settled in Lowndes County, about ten miles away from Robert. John would later move to northern Mississippi, to Yalobusha County, but Harden remained in Lowndes with his wife, Sally, and some of their children. Their oldest son, known as Major George, was already a grown man in his twenties. He had studied law but decided to seek his fortune instead as a planter in Mississippi. Major George became a close friend of his uncle Robert.

Life on the Mississippi frontier in the 1830s wrought changes in some white people. It was a far harsher place for slaves than Virginia. The overseers whom Robert brought down from Virginia became cruel—they apparently felt there were restraints in Virginia which did not apply in Mississippi. A number of blacks tried to flee—some attempted to get back to Virginia to be reunited with their families; while others fled south.

Robert's presence would keep things running smoothly, but as soon as he left a plantation, there was trouble. When he was away, Harden and John kept an eye on his plantations, and on the overseers. John became so disgusted by the cruelty of the overseers that he met secretly with the slaves and urged them to resist and run away. Harden took a firmer hand. Tucked among the accounts for food and goods that Harden bought for Robert's plantations is a line item for "1 negro whip."

Robert allowed his slaves a degree of autonomy and freedom of movement and had trouble with the more rigid control over slaves that was expected in Mississippi, where masters never gave slaves any autonomy. The roads were infested with bounty hunters, who would snatch up any black person not carrying travel papers from a white. One black Hairston, seen alone on the road to Columbus, was assumed to be a runaway and was "taken up" by a bounty hunter, who put the man in jail and expected the master to reward him for the catch. An acquaintance of Robert's happened to recognize the unfortunate man in the Columbus jail, wrote out the necessary travel pass for him, and sent him back to the plantation with a stern warning to Robert never again to allow a black man to travel without written authorization.

In the 1940s the historian John Hope Franklin combed the records of plantations and discovered a phenomenon he called "slaves virtually free." He said that some slaveholders would have set their people free if they had not been totally hemmed in by the rigid code of laws restricting emancipation and the lives of free blacks. These slaveholders treated their slaves as free people in everything but name. Within the plantation they managed themselves, enjoyed family life, and held property. Robert Hairston tried to accomplish that in one of the most hostile environments in the South.

Robert put black Hairstons in charge of one of his plantations on the Tombigbee River. They quickly became targets for abuse by white men from nearby farms who could not abide the idea of black men running a plantation. They repeatedly went onto the place and whipped the blacks until Robert sent his most trusted manager to confront the whites and put a stop to it.

Robert's family now consisted of his slaves. It was not at all unusual for a white man to live alone with slaves, but the Mississippians noticed that Robert carried this relationship beyond the limits of acceptability. With evident disgust, people took note of how he lived and saw where his affections lay: "The house was not suitable for a family of his wealth but would do for such an one as he had with him—composed entirely of servants." One of those black servants Robert took as his wife. Her name was Elizabeth. Although he was still legally married to Ruth, it was said that he regarded Elizabeth as his true wife and gave her a ring. Around 1845 to 1847 they had a daughter, named Chrillis. Robert made no secret of his relationship to Elizabeth, and he was delighted, in his early sixties, to be a father at last. He knew that it would cause conflict with his family if he announced how he would treat his daughter, so he put off dealing with the issue. He thought he had time, but he was wrong.

Robert did not expect death to come when it did. In March 1852 he went to his Moore's Bluff plantation on the Tombigbee River, several miles from his home place, to supervise his cotton warehouse there. The overseer, who owed Robert money, had abruptly run off. It was an un-healthy location. Robert's chief manager, who had earlier served him loyally by protecting the black Hairstons against hostile farmers, flatly refused to go there, saying that he had no doubt that the Bluff was a death sentence. So Robert went himself. After working several weeks by the river, he came down with pneumonia. He did not at first think that he was dying, but his health deteriorated precipitously. Harden Hairston hur-ried to the Bluff with his sons and a son-in-law to look after him.

It soon became apparent to the Hairstons that they were at a death watch. Robert became feebler, losing consciousness from time to time. He called for Harden's son Major George and said that he wished to write his last will. George, who had studied the law but never practiced it, sat next to him and took down what his uncle said. Robert told George he would give him some property and four slaves. As for the rest, all the slaves and all the plantations—Hairston's Bend, Moore's Bluff, Hisha-homa, Coxes, Coleman's, Nashville, Leatherwood, and all the other land in North Carolina and Virginia—all would go to his child, and she was to be set free.

George wrote out the will immediately and read it aloud to Robert, who expressed his approval and signed it. George left his uncle's side to show the document to his father, Harden, and the other relatives who had gathered to witness Robert's passing. Stunned by this amazing doc-ument, which dashed their expectations of instant wealth and dynastic consolidation, they burst into Robert's room and raged at him as he lay on his deathbed—they told him that the bequest to his daughter would not stand, that it was illegal in Mississippi for an enslaved black to inherit property, and that Robert could not legally set his child free in a will.

Robert responded, "Major George says it can be done." Incapacitated as he was, Robert suddenly became frightened, frightened that his daughter would remain a slave.

Major George suggested that the bequest might go through if the girl were carried off to a free state. This prospect tantalized Robert, but he realized that his will would have to be written by a skilled lawyer if it were to stand. He instructed that a messenger be sent to the town of Aberdeen, twenty-five miles away, to fetch a lawyer. It was already night, and the man could not leave until daybreak.

Hardly had the messenger left the next morning when it became apparent to Robert that he would not live out the day. He sent for another lawyer, named Gilmer, who lived close by. Gilmer arrived about eleven in the morning and went directly to Robert's bedside. Robert dictated a new will. There was no time left to him for any details—he was drifting into a stupor. He declared simply that it was his final wish that the girl be made free and that she possess his entire estate. And then he directed Gilmer to write something he had omitted the previous day: "I will my body to its mother dust and my soul to my father Almighty God." But as Gilmer hastily wrote these words, Robert lost consciousness. He had not signed the paper. Gilmer shook him awake and showed him the will. With tremendous effort Robert strained and squinted, but could not read it. He asked for his spectacles. When he had them on, he scrutinized the parchment and pronounced himself satisfied. Gilmer put a pen in Robert's grasp and guided the dying man's hand to sign the will. Robert sank back on his bed and drifted into unconsciousness for the last time. He had turned the world upside down—a slave girl was now one of the richest women in the United States.

Freed from slavery and placed in possession of immense holdings, Chrillis would have had it in her power to emancipate at least hundreds and perhaps as many as a thousand slaves. She could have punched troublesome holes in the map of slavery, creating a patchwork of free colonies in Virginia, North Carolina, and Mississippi.

If Robert had wished only to have his daughter freed, sent to a free state, and comfortably maintained for life, he could have specified exactly that. He could have followed the example of other planters who had quietly bequeathed land to their slave children, while letting them remain slaves. But he gave his daughter everything—land, money, freedom—

without restriction. He was dismantling his part of the Hairston empire and threatening the hegemony of America's slaveholders; and as he commended his soul to Almighty God, he was not doing so as a slaveholder. The wealth that had so burdened him would dissolve, and freedom would take its place.

News of Robert's death hit the Virginia clan like a thunderclap. Peter was riding along a road in Henry County with a cousin when a man rode up and joined them. He said he had word from Mississippi, brought by a slave trader, that Robert Hairston was dead and had left all his property to a slave girl.

Peter's cousin exploded with fury and declared flatly that the will would be thrown out. He went on a tirade against Robert and implied that he was insane.

Peter galloped home to Cooleemee, where he sent letters to his family to put them "on their guard." He arranged to hire the finest legal minds in North Carolina to find a way to break the will, and then he set off personally to Mississippi.

As Robert had predicted many years earlier, his death did indeed open a chasm in the family. The family split into factions, each vying for a portion of Robert's wealth. His widow Ruth's maneuver with her father's will came back to haunt her. The family all knew it had been a legal fiction, and now they insisted that everything she had inherited from her father in 1832, and from her first husband in 1813, had always been hers, and so half of it was part of Robert's estate. In North Carolina and Virginia, slaves were called out and counted, their value assessed, and their names written in the ledgers. The family went about its work of dividing the spoils on the assumption that they would find some way of dealing with the problem of the girl.

Major George, however, stepped forward and submitted the deathbed wills to the court in Columbus, Mississippi. He took it upon himself to be the girl's protector.

The legal proceedings promised to be long, so to protect the value of the slaves while the case was going on, the family requested that Robert's slaves be divided up among the claimants. When the case was finally decided, the losers would either hand over the slaves to the winners or pay them. Major George objected strenuously, but the probate court ordered it done. Court-appointed commissioners assessed the slaves and parceled them out by lot.

By an accident of the lottery, Robert's black common-law wife, Elizabeth, was allotted to his legal wife, Ruth, who wanted nothing to do with the woman. Major George approached Peter, who was acting as his grandmother's agent, and bought Elizabeth from him. She was fortunate.

Peter had no intention of bringing any slaves back to Virginia. He separated out the young, strong men and sold them individually at premium prices. The rest he sold at auction.

He wrote to his grandmother that he was worn-out after months of tedious negotiations over the case and simply wanted to get rid of the excess property. He apologized to Ruth for the low prices he got for some of the people: "A bad disease had broke out among them and I could not warrant them to be sound."

He was the most cultivated of them all—the handsome embodiment of the best of the South. And yet he had not the slightest stirring of conscience in him as he carried out the deed. He described the people he led to the auction block: "There were a great many old ones, and diseased ones, and a good many children."

I had reached the end of the documents about Robert and his daughter. There was no further trace of her in the papers at hand. But *something* had happened to Chrillis. With all their power and wealth, the Hairstons could not simply make her vanish. The fates of the two families, white and black, converged in that child. I wanted to know what had become of the legacy of freedom Robert had bequeathed to her.

I went to Cooleemee to see Judge Hairston and find out from him what had become of the child. I thought he would be surprised—infuriated—by the revelation that his grandfather had sold slaves. Among the descendants of aristocratic planter families, such as the Hairstons, it remains an important point of honor to be able to say, "Yes, we held slaves, but we never sold them." But he knew all about what his grandfather had done. "He had to settle his uncle's estate," the judge said flatly, and that was that. The family was not in the business of selling slaves, he insisted. Whenever possible, his grandfather and the rest of the family kept the black families together. They recognized marriages. When one of their slaves married someone from another plantation, they would sometimes purchase the spouse so the family could be together. He maintained that his grandfather sold the slaves in Mississippi because he was compelled by necessity. The judge was impatient with people, such as me, who did not fully understand what it meant to be responsible for large properties, to be the person whose actions determine whether a place survives or goes broke, whether the next generation inherits wealth or only debts.

And then he said something that astounded me. A curtain parted, and I heard the voice of someone I did not recognize, the voice of command—command so total that it could nullify by pure declaration what others took to be unalterable truth. I had misunderstood the events in Mississippi, the judge said. As for Uncle Robert, "He was paranoid." As for Chrillis, she may not have been Robert's daughter: the house servant could have fooled an old man into thinking that he was a father.

But no sooner had the judge uttered this strenuous denial than he admitted that he had often wondered about the fate of the child. If I wanted to solve that mystery, he continued, then I should go to an upcoming event in Mississippi. His relatives down there, the descendants of Harden and Sally Hairston, were having a reunion.

In a curious coincidence, on the night I arrived at my motel in Mississippi, a local television station was showing *Land of the Pharaohs*, the Hollywood epic directed by Howard Hawks from a screenplay by William Faulkner, with choral music conducted by Jester Hairston.

It tells the story of a tribe, the Kushites, whom the Egyptians defeated in war and forced into bondage. Seeing the film in the South, I realized that Faulkner's script was a fascinating meditation on slavery. The film questions the apparent loyalty the slaves display toward Pharaoh. Pharaoh promises to grant the Kushites their freedom if they will build a tomb for him that will be impregnable to grave robbers. He believes he will go on to live in eternal pleasure, if only his slaves can construct an impregnable tomb to safeguard his hoard of gold, wine, and food. He will sacrifice anything to guarantee his eternal happiness. But he has no illusions about what is in the hearts of his slaves. When one of the slaves rescues Pharaoh at the risk of his own life, Pharaoh says to him, "I know you didn't do it out of loyalty to me, but to save your people."

The Egyptians repeatedly notice how the slaves sing, how they express their pain in their music. It haunts the masters because it cannot be suppressed; they try to ignore the music, but it has a power they cannot comprehend. Indeed the music at times seems to take over the film. The mournful singing of the slaves constructing Pharaoh's tomb was Jester's music; the voices were those of Jester's choir, some of whom were the grandchildren of American slaves.

The slaves succeed at their task. They design an impregnable tomb, but the problem is, it can only be sealed from within. Pharaoh's monument to himself and to his eternal mastery will be a tomb for his own living family and his followers. As his queen leads the funeral procession into the heart of the tomb, the mechanical apparatus designed by the slaves closes off all exits with immovable walls of stone. The queen suddenly realizes that she is to be entombed alive, along with Pharaoh's entourage, to serve him in the afterlife. As a look of horror comes over her face, the camera cuts from the tomb to long lines of freed slaves walking toward their homeland, leaving the land of bondage behind them.

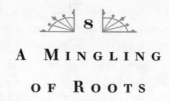

A Mingling

of Roots

About twenty white Hairstons had gathered in the cemetery on a fiercely hot afternoon, protected from the sun by the shade of a lone cottonwood as they scrutinized the gravestones of their ancestors. They were the heirs of a dead dynasty, the descendants of men and women who had ruled over this part of Mississippi like pharaohs.

No special event had summoned these family members from their homes across the country. No will was to be read aloud, no inheritance quarreled over. They gathered on this summer weekend to search together for bits of their lost past. At the motel the night before, they had huddled over old photographs, looking for resemblances in the shape of a nose, the curve of a smile; they pored over a large family tree pinned to the wall of a room. Four feet wide and eight feet long, it sorted through a tangle of family ties in the marriages of five or six generations ago.

The Hairstons had once owned tens of thousands of acres in Lowndes County, but today about all that was left to them was the cemetery. The last Hairston left in the nearby town of Crawford did not make his living from the land. He was the postmaster. His route stretched across the southern part of the county, through lands his family had once owned. Black farmers owned some of it now; but the biggest chunks had come into the hands of a corporate agricultural company.

The cemetery was not a carefully groomed Victorian park, but a small patch of land, bounded by a sagging, rusted chain-link fence, set in the middle of a vast field that had once been part of a Hairston plantation. Thirty-six Hairstons were buried here, including the founders of the Mississippi dynasty—Robert and Harden Hairston, and Harden's wife, Sally. It had been sixty years since the last burial, and perhaps twenty years since someone had come with a wreath or a prayer. The surrounding fields were being cultivated, and the banged-up condition of the fence showed

that this old graveyard had been an annoyance to the tractors and har-
vesting machines. Over the years of neglect, thick vegetation had taken
root—huge cedars, oaks, and cottonwoods had crowded together in this
preserve, enmeshed in an impenetrable thicket of brush. In preparation
for the visit, Nick Hairston had come in with a chain saw and a flame-
thrower to clear the graves. The Hairstons that afternoon stood on
scorched earth. Nick had left a large cottonwood to spread some shade
over the gravesites, and its brittle leaves made a ghostly rustling sound at
the slightest breeze.

Nick passed out copies of a map of the cemetery, showing the location
of each grave. Robert was buried next to Major George, the nephew who
had helped Robert write his will freeing his daughter. Major George had
never married. The two men were buried at a slight remove from the rest
of the family.

After reading the gravestones for a short time, the visitors were eager
to get out of the heat, but one of the cousins called for attention and said
they had an unexpected guest, a man from nearby Brooksville who said
he had some stories to tell. A tall, middle-aged stranger in a pale blue
shirt, with erect and proper bearing that could have come from a military
background or from a lifetime of enacting the fine points of Southern
courtesy, stepped forward, holding in his hand, incongruously, a Cool
Whip container.

"I'm not a Hairston," he began. "I'm not even related to you, but I'm
probably more interested in your family than you are, and I may know
more about it than you do." His name was Reuben Triplett, and he was
a local historian. The stories he was about to tell, however, did not come
from books, but from the lips of a childless widow he had known fifty
years earlier.

From the Cool Whip container he removed a delicate piece of blue
medallion china—a match holder—and held it up for all to see. They
recognized the pattern. It was part of the enormous set of Limoges porcelain shipped from France to Harden and Sally Hairston before the Civil
War. Many of the Hairstons at the cemetery had inherited portions of
the set.

"From the time I was a small child I knew Miss Lizzie Hairston Bridgeforth. When I was a little boy, she gave me this match holder. It's the
badge that gives me admission to this party."

In 1940, Aunt Lizzie, Robert's grandniece, and Harden's granddaughter, was in her sixties, living alone in a suite in the Brooks Hotel in

Brooksville. On rainy afternoons Aunt Lizzie would have Reuben come up to her suite and give him hot chocolate and fudge. They played old maid and she told him of the Hairstons. She had chosen a seven-year-old boy to hear the old plantation stories. The storytelling Reuben described was right out of Faulkner. In *Absalom, Absalom!* the elderly spinster Rosa Coldfield summons Quentin Compson to her dilapidated mansion and makes him listen, she says, "about people and events you were fortunate enough to escape yourself," about how Colonel Sutpen "came out of nowhere and without warning upon the land with a band of strange niggers and built a plantation—(Tore violently a plantation, Miss Rosa Coldfield says)—tore violently." And Quentin realizes he has been summoned not just to keep her company: "It's because she wants it told." Reuben was there that afternoon in the cemetery because he had been made the messenger for things that Lizzie Hairston Bridgeforth wanted told someday. He held the Hairstons spellbound as he told them tales of their family that they had never heard.

Aunt Lizzie told him how her grandfather Harden and his brother Robert had come down from Virginia with a thousand slaves in the 1830s. The old slaves and the white folks rode in carriages, she said, and the young slaves walked. They came like a conquering army into this Mississippi wilderness, took possession of eighty thousand acres of land, and commenced planting cotton. From Columbus, Harden sent letters to agents in New York, Philadelphia, and Europe; and in response, many months later, steamboats labored up the Tombigbee River from Mobile, stopping at Hairston Bend to disgorge their cargoes of furniture, carpets, wallpaper, woodwork, porcelain, jewelry, books, paintings, and statues.

The cemetery where the Hairstons stood that hot afternoon would have been in the shadow of a mansion called Mooreland, which Harden built for Sally, and which passed down to Miss Lizzie and her husband. It was hers until it burned. To prove to Reuben that she was telling the truth, that an old woman living alone in a hotel room actually knew about the plantation days and had not just read about them in books, Miss Lizzie would take out a big metal cracker box filled with photographs of the family's old mansions in Virginia. And she took him through the suite, showing him the valuables that had been rescued from the fire at Mooreland.

"She had the most gorgeous china in the world—service for twenty-six! She had a Bible table—I never have seen another one like it—it held a big open Bible. And there were life-size oil portraits of the Hair-stons, so large that Miss Lizzie couldn't hang them in her apartment. They put them up for her in the lobby of the Brooks Hotel. She had beautiful pieces of jewelry. One was a cameo set, and I never have seen as many cameos in my life. There was a cameo necklace, two cameo bracelets, a huge cameo brooch, and cameo earrings. And she had another set of jewelry with a necklace and a bracelet and earrings. They were solid gold.

"But Miss Lizzie did not have the Hairston diamonds. There was a basket full of them. She wouldn't have the diamonds because she said there were too many dirty stories attached to them. Miss Lizzie was the kindest, sweetest, most gentle human being on earth, the most sensitive and the most beautiful old lady who ever lived—her eyes looked like *agate*, they were so glassy blue—and she didn't want a thing on earth to do with those diamonds. She said that the Hairston men who gave their women those diamonds did not always treat the women right."

Miss Lizzie never forgot her dead kin. One day she bundled Reuben into her car, with a lunch basket and flowers in the backseat, and drove out to decorate the graves. As they tugged at weeds and placed the flowers, she told him the stories of each person buried there. The first Hairston laid to rest here was Sally, the wife of Harden Hairston. "Miss Lizzie told me that he was so grieved he buried her as close to the house as was decently possible, so he could watch her grave."

The cemetery was a frightening place for a young boy—overgrown and dark under its canopy of trees, with the gravestones fallen over and the lonely column standing over the graves of the twins Constance and Constantine, born, baptized, and died on July 20, 1872—and Reuben decided that he didn't want to visit there again. But Lizzie had barely begun to tell her stories, and she was determined to pass them on to someone. So to take the fear out of the place, Miss Lizzie promised Reuben a treasure. In her hotel room she handed him a map with dotted lines and an X on it, which she said she had found in her cracker box. Reuben eagerly climbed into the car and could barely wait to get to the cemetery, where he paced off the lines until he got to the marked spot and, just as Miss Lizzie had promised, dug up a wooden box full of coins. He was too excited to read the dates on the coins and see that they were new and to guess that Miss Lizzie had buried them the previous day.

Everyone in the group hooted at this trick of Aunt Lizzie's. But Reu-ben continued with utter seriousness. "There is rumor that there *is* gold buried here." He said that almost every Southern family had some story about buried gold, but this story was different—this treasure belonged to a slave. Every summer in the years before the Civil War, Harden Hairston took his daughters to the fashionable summer resort at White Sulphur Springs in Virginia. They traveled in a coach with a slave as the driver. Miss Lizzie said that the slave was such a favorite with the patrons at the resort that they all gave him gifts of gold. The slave supposedly buried that hoard here.

Harden Hairston did not live to see the end of the Civil War, but his daughters did. Their genteel upbringing left them ill prepared to cope with the upheaval in the postwar South—their field slaves ran off, their livestock was stolen, and their precious Limoges became a mocking reminder of the abundance they had once so easily commanded.

"When Reconstruction came, they had nothing. Miss Lizzie told me that the two aunts who were left—of course they'd never worked in their lives, they didn't know how to do anything except fold their hands and fan, and probably sip mint juleps—they had to go to work because they had nothing to eat. They had nothing to plant until they remembered that their old dolls were stuffed with seeds, so they tore them open and got the seeds. They had an old broken-down mule. One of them rode the mule, and somehow they hitched a plow to it, the other one held the plow, and they turned some of this land up.

"And they boiled the dirt. They tore the floor out of the smokehouse and boiled the dirt to get salt, because they had no salt, they had nothing. People don't realize how *destitute* the South was when the Civil War was over. It's too romanticized. And we didn't have a Marshall Plan or a U.N. to help us. We are just now—I know this sounds farfetched and romantic and too Southern and rebel ['Don't apologize,' says a voice from the crowd]—but we are just now in this wonderful country recovering from the effects of the Civil War.

"You don't see many cabins in the South anymore, but that's in the last twenty-five years. It took us a long time to get over that war. Well, anyhow, those ladies had to make do the best they could. If you think *Gone with the Wind* and Scarlett O'Hara eating turnips and all that is fiction, that is not fiction. That's true. That is the truest portrayal of what really happened in the South. The truth is stranger than fiction, and even though I realize *Gone with the Wind* is considered fiction, it was based on truth, and these folks were among them who had to go through it.

"I've been asked a lot of times why I became a historian, and I've never been able to answer that except to say I loved old folks from the earliest childhood, and Miss Lizzie was one of those, and they filled my head full of this stuff and I never got over it. These people out here were almost alive to me when Miss Lizzie talked about them. She was a grand lady, and you all come from a grand family."

Triplett had one last tale to impart. He held up the map of the graveyard that Nick Hairston had distributed to the visitors and pointed toward the grave of Harden, the man who had led the odyssey from Virginia to Mississippi.

"I've had time to scratch and find the marker at the foot of the grave of Mr. Harden Hairston, the first one to come here. That grave right next to his belongs to Davy Hairston. Well, I guess all of you think that's one of your relatives. He isn't. He was Mr. Harden Hairston's body servant. He was a slave. And there's a heartrending inscription on Davy's tombstone. I scratched it out a while ago and I can read it now. I'd forgotten it; I hadn't been here in twenty years."

Davy Hairston's grave was right next to his master's, as close to it as the grave of Harden's wife, Sally. Etched into the slab were the words:

DAVY HAIRSTON
DIED APRIL 1865
AGE 58 YEARS
BUT IS HE DEAD? NO NO HE LIVES
HIS HAPPY SPIRIT FLIES TO HEAVEN
ABOVE AND THERE RECEIVES
THE LONG EXPECTED PRIZE.

Triplett paused and looked around the cemetery, taking in the piles of brush, the tree stumps, and the sagging fence that separated the burying ground from the soybean field. He waved his hand in the direction of the place where Mooreland used to be.

"You know that poem by Shelley about the pharaoh? 'My name is Ozymandias, king of kings: look on my works, ye Mighty, and despair!' I've thought of that so many times at the power and wealth of these folks. And then look, look at this. Devastation.

"They were the biggest slaveholders in the South. Miss Lizzie's grandpa brought a thousand slaves with him. Well, that was a sizable colony of slaves. A young male was worth from thirty-five hundred to five thousand dollars in gold, and an average worker slave was worth fifteen hundred to twenty-five hundred dollars. Multiply all that times a thousand, and you'll see how much money they had invested in slaves.

"There's so much *myth* involved in slavery in the South. There's so much *romance* involved in it, it's hard to separate fact from fiction. But if you read that inscription on Davy's tombstone, do you think that Mr. Harden Hairston—and that man was his slave—do you think he loved him?"

The question hung in the air, no one willing to answer it. What comfort could there be in saying *yes*? What absolution could be uttered over the graves of these slaveholders, on whom the judgment of history had fallen, whose mansions were dust, who would lie forever near a treasure that was not theirs, but a slave's?

But that was the message Lizzie had been so desperate to impart to the future—they had loved their slaves. It was her key to understanding her family's past. It was the bedrock of her belief in the goodness of her forebears, in the goodness of the world she had inherited, and in the goodness she saw in herself. Perhaps it was just such an absolution Lizzie yearned for.

She wanted the world to remember the tragedy of their fate. She believed that something valuable had been lost forever—an old social order of wealth, grace, and gentility, in which blacks and whites coexisted in harmony and in love.

The devastation Reuben described was evident when we passed through the town of Crawford, or what remained of it. The center of the Hairstons' plantation empire, it had once been a bustling rural hamlet, with a railroad depot, bank, cotton gin, and several general stores. Crawford was now a virtual ghost town. A long brick row that had at one time housed the town's stores was almost empty and partly collapsed. Houses on the main street were entirely swallowed up in vines.

Nick Hairston, the man who had cleared the family cemetery, wasted no breath on the "glory" of the plantation days because he had lived through the aftermath. He was surprisingly bitter about his family's past. The people of his generation—he was in his fifties—had been bound to a dying system. He said that none of the people of his generation had been allowed to leave Crawford and get an education. They had to stay and tend the land that had been in the family for five generations.

He said the man who had carried the plantation empire into this century was his grandfather Brown Hairston. A grandson of Harden and Sally, he was born three years before the Civil War and lived until World War II. Brown had inherited only eighty-nine acres from his father, but he had made himself the twentieth-century patriarch of the family by repeating the old family pattern of marrying a first cousin to get her inheritance. He acquired more land from what he called his "depleted cousins." As relatives, one after another, hit hard times, Brown bought them out. When one of his sisters lost her land, she literally lived off the past—she moved into a rented house and paid the landlord with old family china, a few pieces every month, until it was gone.

Brown was the largest landowner in Lowndes County, owning most of the southern portion from the Noxubee River to the Tombigbee. Brown was obsessed with keeping the land in the family and determined that his twelve children (by three wives) would perpetuate the family legacy through this century. He delivered stern lectures to his children on the subject: "Don't *ever* sell a *bit* of your land. They don't *make* any more of it. You can't replace it!"

Brown was determined also to preserve the plantation way of life at all costs. Thus, he made a decision in the 1930s that set the course of the area's history. A food-processing company approached Brown with a proposal to build a factory in southern Lowndes. They needed to buy some land from him. The profits from such a sale would have been considerable, but Brown said no. If a plant opened up, he would lose his workers, and the county would depart the nineteenth century for the twentieth. Brown Hairston wanted this part of Mississippi, *his* part, to remain exactly as it had always been, and so he would not agree to a plant. His decision kept the sharecropping system alive for three more decades. It kept the blacks in their economic place and kept his own family tied to the land.

Brown used the land to control his children. When his son Pete married, Brown put him in charge of a broken-down farm that was mostly sagebrush. But Pete wasn't happy running a small operation under his father's nose. He made plans to attend a technical school in New York to learn cotton classing, a skill that would at least allow him to supplement his income and might one day take him out of the fields and put him in the professional class. Brown was adamant against any of his children doing anything but farming the family land; but Pete was just as determined to go. He and his wife closed up their house and said their good-byes. On the night before their departure Brown called Pete in for a talk. When Pete came home, he told his wife the trip was off: "Papa just gave me a lot of land and we've got to stay here and look after it."

His widow, Mary Alice, remembered that night vividly—it was the turning point that never came in her husband's life. As an outsider to the family she had looked upon the Hairstons with a cold, observant eye. She watched as the family's history grew to be a heavier and heavier burden. She watched as the family legacy destroyed one person after another, including her husband, Pete. When she spoke of the past, she spoke so vividly that people long dead seemed still alive, and I had the sense that she wished she could go back and change things.

She had raised five children on a dairy farm where money was always tight, when it was around at all. Pete drank, so heavily that she put him in the hospital several times. She knew he was drinking himself to death.

Brown divided his property among his children. After his death in 1941, some of Pete's siblings tried to revive what they thought to be the grandeur of the plantation days. To finance their dreams they converted land into cash.

"When Mr. Hairston gave them the land, what did they do but go out and soak it. They mortgaged it all for jeeps and things that they didn't need. They needed tractors and equipment to work the land," Mary Alice said. They built a tennis court and bought a generator so they could light it at night, but meanwhile most of their houses still didn't have indoor bathrooms—which didn't bother those who had house servants to empty the slop jars.

Pete's half brother George clung to the old customs, living out a fantasy of antebellum plantation life. Even into the 1960s his daily life followed the ancient rhythms. He hunted and drank, hunted and drank—bourbon at breakfast, then onto the horses and after the fox. At noon his hands brought him fresh horses and dogs, a basket of food, and bottles; then he was off again for the rest of the afternoon. Whenever he needed money, he sold a chunk of land, until there was no more land.

Mary Alice remembered a young woman from a genteel family who married another of Pete's brothers. She was an excellent tennis player and pianist who knew nothing about running a farm or a household. "She was raised to live in a fantasy world," Mary Alice said. She slowly went mad. "She used to iron things like a maniac, trying to smooth out the wrinkles of her life."

Pete's sister Laura May lost all of her land to her illusions of the past. "She and her husband were going to live like gentlemen. Everything on her place was white—white fences, white geese, white turkeys, white chickens, white jonquils, white narcissus, white flags. They used to invite people from Nashville to come down here and hunt. She fixed it up, but you can't make money out of a white fence. Pete used to shake his head: 'They're gonna lose it. They're gonna lose it.' And they did."

Laura May's disappointments and frustrations were reflected in her anger toward blacks. When she wrote a sketch of Crawford for a history of Lowndes County, she placed the blame for the town's deterioration on the blacks and the civil rights movement. In the old days, she wrote, "there were very few crimes. Children, both black and white, had some parental training and discipline in the era before 1960. Demonstrations and mobs developed, calling for 'rights' and 'freedom'—whatever that may be. They brought in politicians, do-gooders, and activists from outside of the state. Today, after the civil rights revolution and after hundreds of thousands of government dollars have been poured into Crawford we are now a crime community focussing on beer, whiskey, gambling, rock and roll, and the jungle beat music."

In a private memoir written for her children, Laura May looked back fondly to the 1930s, when "law enforcement was decisive." She described with approval the fate of a black man, a stranger in town who had been convicted of murdering a local black. The court was an informal one, convened under a tree in Crawford. When the verdict was reached, on what evidence Laura May did not say, the defendant was put in a car to be conveyed to authorities in Columbus. The car paused on the bridge high over the Tombigbee, and its manacled passenger was dropped into the river.

In her memoir Laura May revealed the degradation that had taken hold among Crawford's white families. (If she knew of any Hairston crimes or indiscretions, she did not mention them.) She described a white lecher who was dissuaded from approaching a pair of young girls only when one of them fired a pistol in his direction. A member of the town's banking family embezzled local funds and killed himself. A doctor and his wife died of drug addiction. Another prominent white habitually visited the black district to drink and gamble. The blacks were terrified of him. In a rage after losing a card game he pulled a pistol and killed a black woman. Brown Hairston saw to it that the shooter was tried and convicted. Amidst the morphine, gambling, and shootings, the old aristocracy was falling to pieces; some of them went as mad as the woman who played her piano all day and sang at the top of her voice, "Listen to the mockingbird sing coo-coo-coo."

As the planter aristocracy fell, what remained was the absolute domination of white over black. The chief recreation for the Hairstons and the other planters in that part of the county was hunting, accompanied by titanic drinking bouts and more sinister entertainment. Loaded up with liquor, the hunters would amuse themselves by making a black man sing and dance. One landowner whipped people for sport, until an angry group of blacks descended on his farm and threatened to kill him. Mary Alice remembered him well: "He was a mean man, and yet, around us, he was the most polite old gentleman."

It baffled her that people had the capacity to be "so split up, so compartmentalized," to divide their souls so completely. It had shocked her to find that the vicious abuse against black people was not being carried out only by white-trash thugs, it was being done by people she knew, from her own social class, sometimes from her own family. It frightened her that the line between the good people and the evil had blurred. One of her husband's half brothers, the oldest of Brown's sons, had a secret side that Mary Alice could not penetrate. She only knew the signs of it.

"George was scared of the blacks. *Scared* of them. He slept with a gun under his pillow all the time. . . . He rode with the posse when a white man got killed out on the prairie by a black. They went looking for the killer. *Lord have mercy.*"

A friend of the Hairstons' was killed by one of the blacks who worked for him. The shooting might have been accidental. Trying to break up a fight, he was shot when he entered a cabin. The whites gathered a posse and hunted down the shooter that night. They found him in the woods by the road to Columbus and killed him.

Many of the white men in Crawford were alcoholics, sinking under the weight of a dying economic system. More than most, Pete Hairston took his legacy to heart. His father had entrusted it to him and he guarded it carefully. He worked hard and did without the luxuries his cousins bought with loans. He also took seriously his obligation to his black tenants. He took sick children to Columbus for treatment and personally cared for an aged tenant farmer who had lost part of his throat to cancer.

Mary Alice remembered the day when Pete's drinking had once more spun out of control. He refused her plea to go into the hospital, picked up a gun, and left the house. She was on the phone asking the doctor to come over right away when she heard the shot that ended her husband's life. In her mind the bullet was put in the gun when Brown Hairston used a gift of land to prevent Pete from going to New York and escaping the clutches of the old order. "If he'd gone," Mary Alice said wistfully, "he might have been better off."

The South changed and the white Hairstons did not know how to change with it. They depended on cheap labor, but after World War II, young blacks began to leave the farms for jobs in Columbus and the North. The blacks who stayed behind were landowners themselves, working their own acres.

The last white Hairston to work the land in Mississippi was Nick, who finally gave up after his father died in the early 1960s. "I closed the gate and turned the key on the whole era," he said. He sold the last of their land and went to work for a Columbus building company.

Some blacks in the area enjoyed a modest prosperity while the whites were declining. Many of those blacks were Hairstons whose roots here ran as deep as the whites'. None of them had turned up at the white reunion in the cemetery to claim a lost inheritance. Mary Alice knew the story of Robert and Chrillis. When Brown died, Pete went to the courthouse to check the titles on the land and discovered the story of Robert's will. When he came home and told the story, his sister Laura May was enraged. She said he should have torn those pages out of the record books. She said he was never to mention it again, and he never did.

I wandered through the prairie going from house to house. In another part of the world they would have thought that I was mad, knocking on doors asking about a black girl who had been missing for a century and a half. But here the quest seemed reasonable. This was a world cut off. The same families had lived here for 160 years.

When I visited black families, I had difficulty at first because, once again, I was seen as an emissary of the whites. One of the white Hairston women tried to help me by making contact with black Hairstons whom she used to know, but she reported back that "everybody's clamming up." I visited one woman who led me into her living room, turned on the television, and ignored me until I left. Others courteously but firmly refused to see me or made appointments and then repeatedly turned out not to be home when I arrived. A woman in her nineties who everyone said was "a gold mine" of stories turned out to have lost her memory.

One person the white Hairstons did not want me to see was a politician who promoted black causes with a little too much vigor. His mother was a Hairston, and he had grown up on a plantation in Crawford. To my surprise he spoke highly of the whites. "There was a closeness," he said, between the white and black Hairstons. "Even today it exists. Because of that closeness, attempts were made to make things bearable for the blacks." His grandfather had told him that the only time trouble arose was over voting. The blacks organized a voting drive in the 1930s, and the whites put a stop to it. He said the blacks fared reasonably well, given the circumstances. "There was a standard of living that might be equated to middle class." Still, blacks could not really get ahead until the 1950s, when good jobs began to open up for them in Columbus. Many left the declining plantation country for the city, while others used their earnings in the city to buy their own land.

I asked him how the blacks and whites could feel such a closeness in a place as rigidly segregated as Mississippi. "It was no secret," he answered, "the blacks were direct descendants of the white Hairstons." His own great-grandfather was so fair, he said, "you would think he was white."

The archivist who had, many years ago, prepared the index card for Robert Hairston's will had rewritten the past, perhaps inadvertently, or perhaps because the clerk could not believe his eyes. Where the will stated that Chrillis was to be "manumitted," or set free, the clerk had written "maintained." The index card was the first place a white or black Hairston would look in tracing the past, and with a few strokes of his pen the archivist had turned an emancipation into a monthly allotment of cornmeal and bacon. No one would be tempted to look further.

A clerk at the courthouse led me into a storage room with steel shelves holding enormous volumes of deed books and probate records. I located the book from the 1850s and slid it carefully from its place.

The book contained more than the will. It had pages and pages of court testimony about Robert. The Hairstons tried strenuously to prove that he was insane, but the court had ruled that he was competent when he died and admitted the wills to probate. Robert's bequest to his daughter would have been unknown except for Major George. He could have torn up the wills and shared generously in his uncle's estate. But he took the two wills Robert had written on his deathbed and submitted them to the court. His actions made me believe that on his deathbed Robert had begged his nephew to look after his black family when he was gone.

A great many mysteries surrounded Robert's daughter. In the first place, the records disagreed on the most basic point—what her name was. In some places it was clearly written "Chrillis," but elsewhere there was a variety of spellings, as if the name were unfamiliar to the lawyers and clerks who had to write it down—Chrimbell, Chrimbill, Chrimbiel, Chimchild, Chemiel, Chrischil, and several unintelligible variants. In one document, otherwise written flawlessly, it seemed that the hand that wrote the name began to shake.

After a certain point the records stopped mentioning Chrillis at all. The court fight was entirely between the Virginia and Mississippi branches of the white family. I had missed something. I glanced backward in the court records and found nothing at first, but then I scanned the pages in an earlier section. Buried in the middle of a complicated document outlining the competing claims of the Virginia and Mississippi branches was a single, offhand sentence stating that the girl named Chrillis, the heir to a vast fortune of land and slaves, was dead. The document gave no explanation, no details, no date of death. She was simply gone.

Her death would have been an easy act to bring about, as easy as suddenly losing a prisoner on a bridge over the Tombigbee. They could have used her father's ferry. The boat would have gone out onto the river with her and come back empty.

Until then I had seen nothing in any of the plantation records to hint that the Hairstons would deliberately have killed a slave. Never before had a slave stood in the way when so much was at stake, but I was certain that the murder of a child was beyond what they would do.

Confronted with documentary evidence that Chrillis had died, I was forced to retrace my steps to try to find the origin of the oral history that she had lived. At the white family's reunion, Mary Alice Gibson had told me the story of a wedding ring being passed down through Chrillis's descendants. When I called and asked her where that story had come from, she said she had heard it not from a Hairston but from Betty Thomas, an archivist who had moved away from the county some years earlier. Her son, however, visited Columbus from time to time. By luck, I met someone who knew the son, Blewett Thomas; and by better luck I found that Blewett would be visiting in a few days to attend a memorial service for an old blues player from Crawford, "Big Joe" Williams. Blues fans had raised the funds to put a tombstone on Big Joe's unmarked grave. Oddly enough, the name Blewett was familiar to me. I had seen it on documents in the archives among Hairston legal papers. His family had had business dealings with the Hairstons dating back to Reconstruction.

Big Joe's service was being held at the Crawford library, a cramped building fashioned from a converted trailer. I had misread the schedule and arrived late, just as people were heading to their cars to drive to the cemetery. I asked someone—a blues fanatic who had traveled all the way from Germany for Big Joe's service—where Blewett Thomas was.

"That's his car there."

I had missed him. Blewett was pulling onto the road and heading out of town.

"Follow us," the man said. "We're all going to the cemetery."

I followed my guide out of town, past the local cemetery I had assumed we were heading toward, and into the country. We were soon off the hard road. It had been raining much of the day, and the road had turned into a waxy gumbo that stuck to the sides of the car and clogged the wheel wells. My guide's car fishtailed as he struggled to keep the vehicles ahead of him in sight. Like me, he was an outsider and unused to speeding down these dirt roads in the rain. At one point we lost the lead cars, ended up on a narrow side road that just petered out, and had to drive in reverse for a quarter of a mile to get back out. This was the poorest part of the county. Far from everything, even a paved road, scattered families lived in shacks surrounded by their chickens, hogs, and an occasional cow. Wide-eyed children in tattered clothes watched as we slithered by.

At last we came to the cemetery. About fifty people milled around a hillside. Tombstones were here and there, in no particular order. Some graves were marked just with a single, small, bare stone, and other burials were not marked at all. Big Joe's had been one of them until that day.

Blewett Thomas, a heavyset man in his thirties, was posing for a photograph in front of Big Joe's shiny new stone. This old country cemetery seemed the perfect setting to approach a stranger and ask about a long-lost child from slavery time. When I told Blewett I was looking for Robert's missing daughter, an odd guardedness came over him. He looked around as if he didn't want to be accidentally overheard as he repeated a story that had been passed down in his family for well over a century.

Robert Hairston, he said, had disgraced his family. He had crossed the color line and lived exclusively among the blacks. When he fell in love with his house servant he made no secret of it. It was acceptable to have a black mistress and black children but it was unthinkable to treat them like your family. The final humiliation was the deathbed will, giving everything to the girl. The Hairstons had to get rid of her.

I told him that I had found in the county records that she had died. He looked startled.

"They absconded with her."

"They did what?"

"Took her to another one of their plantations. They never told her who she was."

So she was not dead after all. The Hairstons had stolen her land but they had not killed her. They lied to the court, and the judge did not care to pursue the matter. If the Hairstons said a slave was dead, then she was dead—case closed. Anyone looking at the official record would take for granted that the record was correct and assume that the girl had died, tragically, of one of the diseases that periodically swept through the slave quarters.

Despite all the money and land at stake, the Hairstons could not bring themselves to kill her. When they moved her to another plantation they would have given her a new name to obscure her connection to her father and to the past. But she was still here, waiting somewhere to be found. I knew that now as a certainty. But I had already gone from one corner of the county to the other without turning up any other trace of Chrillis. I had ransacked the archives and the courthouse records. On my list of people to see, there was only one person left, an old sharecropper named Thattis Hairston. He had been born on the plantation of George Hairston, the half brother of Peter and Nick, who had died in 1976. George was the one who had slept with a gun.

I had directions through the prairie to a dirt road that led to a small yellow house where Thattis Hairston lived. He was short and strong, a gruff man with an iron handshake. He wore denim overalls and a black baseball cap over gray hair. A dark mustache curled around the corners of his mouth. Born around 1920, he went to work in the fields alongside his parents when he was seven. George Hairston, whom he contemptuously called "Georgie Boy," routinely cheated Thattis's parents. But this was not unusual. Referring to all the people who worked on plantations as sharecroppers, he said, "None of them got what they were supposed to get." A small act of cheating finally got to Thattis's father—the sheer pettiness of it infuriated him. One Christmas Thattis's mother told his father to go to George Hairston's plantation store and pick out a gift for himself. He chose a two-dollar pair of overalls. A week later, at the annual settlement of accounts, he got the store bill from George with a charge of $25 for the overalls. Thattis remembered his father flying out of the house in a rage to confront "Georgie Boy."

George's father, Brown Hairston, was a different sort of man. Thattis remembered Brown's generosity during the Depression. "Brown Hairston—he would help people. A *free-hearted* man. On a lot of the plantations they weren't feeding the people, especially the old people. They would go to Brown and he would feed them. The white folks would tell him he was going to end up in the poorhouse from feeding all the blacks, and he'd just say, 'That's all right.' He was feeding folks from Noxubee River to the Tombigbee."

Thattis's parents had scraped together enough money to buy their own farm. Thattis remembered his mother and father working ceaselessly—they would "plant, plant, plant, plant"—and they raised enough food to give some away to poorer neighbors.

On one point Thattis was in complete agreement with the whites—this part of Mississippi was beyond the law. "If you did something wrong, there was no court, no jury. They'd just say, 'Well, take those niggers and carry 'em on back down there and give 'em ten or twelve lashes and turn 'em loose and have 'em go to the fields.' " One of his cousins disappeared, just vanished, and no one would tell him directly what had happened. But Thattis overheard the adults talking about it among themselves. His cousin had been castrated and hanged by the river. The people could not do anything about it or even talk openly of it. "Back in them times, they had to drop it. Forget it—as much as they could. They forgot it, but it stayed in them."

When Thattis was a child, a series of civil rights meetings was held at the black church in the country. "That was the first of the civil rights movement," Thattis said. "Thirty years later, Martin Luther King came up with the same thing." At each meeting a spy would turn up, a white man who stood at the back of the church, listening to the preacher, the Reverend Mr. Wright, urge the people to organize for their voting rights. One night a large crowd gathered to listen to Wright, but from the darkness emerged a gang of white men, wielding whips. "George Hairston was the leader," Thattis said.

The mob laid hold of the minister. They pushed the women away and grabbed the men, leading them into the night to "straighten them out" with their whips. But as George was leading the men away to be whipped, one of his uncles suddenly appeared. "You aren't going to whip any of my colored!" he yelled, and he moved through the group separating out "my people." The rest he left to the mercies of his nephew. He could have put a stop to the whole thing, but he did not. The minister and his followers were led away and whipped. That was the end of the civil rights movement in that part of the county.

The public humiliation of their minister was a wound the people had to hide. They could not speak of it, even to other blacks. In the 1950s, when the NAACP tried to organize a voting drive in Lowndes County, they were surprised at the resistance they met in the black community. "The minds of the people are enslaved," one civil rights worker wrote.

There were many secret wounds that had "stayed in them." But wounds cannot heal if they stay hidden. Thattis groped his way forward to another story, a story of a private crime and its punishment. Before telling it, he was careful to separate morally the perpetrator from the rest of his family.

"The others didn't do like George. He was the only one who did that kind of stuff. Every family has a black sheep. He was the *leader*. He did some things . . . *uncalled for*. But he paid before he left.

"He was a rich man. All his life. Brown Hairston's son. He was rich. And he died poor. Just like the Bible says: Lazarus lay at the gate and then asked the rich man for the crumbs cleared from the table—that's where he wound up." Thattis's voice fell to a whisper. "Poor, poor, poor. Didn't have nothin'. Didn't even have a coat on part of his back. Shoes? He was walkin' on the sides of the shoes—instead of walkin' on the heel he was walkin' on the side. He went to the poorhouse. Folks called it the poorhouse. It was the nursing home. And what he did, he paid off right there. Do you remember what I said about Wright, the man who got whipped? Well, Wright helped kill him."

Day and night the nurses heard George cry out, "Let me alone, Wright, go ahead, go ahead, Wright, let me alone." Thattis said the nurses wanted to know, "Who was Wright?"

"Wright and this baby killed him. The baby would crawl on his plate—he used to crawl all over him. Daily. Night. Wright and that girl rode him in. George Hairston—rich man—but they rode him in—that girl and Wright—that little baby. Used to tell the nurse, '*Get the baby back, get him back!*'

"He'd be layin' in bed and he'd try to read the paper, and the baby'd be all over the paper. He couldn't read the paper. He had to put the paper down, he couldn't read it.

"He couldn't eat. He'd tell the nurses, *'Get the baby back! He's playin' with my food!'* The nurse would say, 'I don't see no baby.' *'That baby that's playing on the plate!'*

"They stayed on him all the time. Wright and that girl, they rode him in."

Thattis had related the story haltingly. He was holding back some part—the part about the baby. I asked him who the baby was.

"There was this man who worked on George's place. He had a daughter, a teenager. When the father went to the field, George would go and have sex with that girl. She got pregnant. George didn't want the white folks to know he had a child by this girl. He went and dropped that live baby in the well."

I left Thattis's house and drove to the main highway. I pulled off at the edge of a field, where the prairie rolled gently into a distant line of trees. Looking south, I could see the highway curve and disappear, its path marked by the tall crosses of telephone poles, following the land as it rolled on into infinity. No other human marks were on this land. This place had been one of the American frontiers—a vista of fresh, new, open land that formed, as one writer put it, "the geography of hope."

The search for Chrillis had led me this way. It was as if she were leading me through this place deliberately and methodically, leading me through an invisible maze built in the past and occupied in the present. It was as if she would not let me find her until she had led me through the lives of others, so that I would know that hers was not the only story. She was a missing child herself, and she led me to the story of the nameless child dropped in a well, a story of unspeakable brutality. It seemed unspeakable to me, but Thattis wanted it told. The crime had already been paid for, he said, and I thought that he wanted the story told because he understood that it was part of a larger, more painful process, a process that the writer Ralph Ellison called "the persistent drive to define human hope in the United States." That process takes place, Ellison wrote, "not through avoiding those aspects of reality which were brutal and dehumanizing, but taking that too as part of the given scene, and then determining to go beyond it. Not to ignore it, not to pretend that it didn't exist, but to humanize it, to take it in, to make it connect with other aspects of living—with the dream, with the sounds of the future and the sounds of hope."

Amid the brutality of slavery, the love Robert Hairston obviously had for his daughter stood out as a brief flicker of humanity. Chrillis provided the answer to the question Reuben had posed in the cemetery about Harden Hairston and the slave, Davy Hairston, buried by his side: "Do you think he loved him?" That question lay at the core of the plantation myth—supposedly, the love that masters felt for some of their slaves redeemed the masters from utter depravity and made them, along with their slaves, victims of an infamous system that they could not throw off. That was the myth Lizzie Hairston Bridgeforth had extracted from the past and conveyed to Reuben. But if Harden "loved" Davy, he also kept him enslaved. His feelings toward his slave—whatever name can be attached to those feelings—served to sustain the corrupt illusion that his mastery was just, good, and humane.

Robert's love for his daughter made him see the humanity of his slaves—even those he did not know and did not love—and attempt to set them free. Robert was dangerous because he exposed the profound corruption that slavery had wrought—it had corrupted even the idea of love. He could see that the supposedly privileged elite among the "servants"—the unacknowledged children of the masters who acted as body servants, butlers, and housekeepers—were not beloved but merely enslaved. He could foresee such a fate for his daughter, and the vision of it horrified him on his deathbed. He alone was sane, but they called him a lunatic. The others had made themselves mad in denying the humanity of the slaves. That kind of madness had allowed a man to drop his own child in a well.

Robert believed that Chrillis's blood tie to the family would protect her, that it was the only tie they would respect. But the girl was abhorrent to them precisely because she was their own flesh and blood; she was their dark-skinned equal; and if she had the right to freedom, then so did all the others.

I felt certain that Lizzie Hairston Bridgeforth had known what had happened to Chrillis and had taken the story to her grave. But she had passed on a clue to Thattis.

Thattis said that he knew Lizzie Hairston Bridgeforth very well. He knew her before Reuben did, when she lived in a crude frame house with no running water. The Mooreland mansion that was so much a part of her history was long gone. Lizzie was always embarrassed when her fancy relatives from Virginia came to visit. The house was almost bare of furniture except for the few things that had been rescued from the fire at Mooreland. Old, elegant china and family silver stood out incongruously in the primitive rooms.

But Lizzie tried to hang on to her pride. What she did have was a set of servants, mostly children of dirt-poor tenant families. When the Virginia relatives visited, the servants enacted a well-choreographed routine of old-fashioned hospitality. A houseboy about twelve years old would scurry out to collect luggage. A maid in a white cap and starched apron greeted guests at the door and showed them to a room. The maid asked if they wished breakfast served in bed. Another black girl was assigned to be a personal servant, to fetch anything the guests might want, and to help the ladies dress and undress. It was a sad parody of the old plantation life. A cauldron of water had to be kept boiling in the yard day and night in case cousin so-and-so wanted tea or a hot bath.

Lizzie was living through the disintegration of the old order, and she built a fantasy that she was a plantation mistress, the heiress to a great line of benevolent masters. She had woven a shroud of myth to cover a reality that was too complex and too painful for her to bear. At the core of that myth was the supposed love between blacks and whites.

She responded to the old story of Harden's "love" for his servant because she too felt that love. If someone was sick, Lizzie and her husband would drive him to the doctor. If someone needed medicine, they would make a special trip into Columbus to get it. They picked up pension checks in Columbus and distributed them to the people. During a flu epidemic they brought food to people who were too ill to cook for themselves. Lizzie drove into Columbus to pick up dresses women had ordered for the "8 of May"—an old African-American holiday in honor of Emancipation. She was so hard up she tried to sell her family silver—finding no takers—but when some poor black children came to the door offering chickens for sale, Lizzie bought them, even though she had a yard full of chickens already. She also bought a bit of antique glass from them and gave them a meal before they left. She felt an obligation toward the black people as long as they remained in their place. When word reached her that the blacks were organizing for their voting rights, she felt betrayed. Her love, like Harden's love for Davy, had a limit.

Lizzie had passed down to Reuben the old myth of the plantation, a myth that she desperately wanted to be true, because she—and the rest of her family—had used it to keep the future at bay. They clung to a myth of an old orderly world, and that myth became their plague. It split them from reality, substituting a dream. As the real world came crashing down around them, they lived more and more in the dream. The slave's treasure of gold coins was part of the dream, a yearning to keep the slave's legacy buried safely in the past. Lizzie knew the secret of another treasure far more precious than a sack of coins. It was a legacy of love, not buried, but standing in plain sight.

She often passed Thattis's farm and always said hello. One day he asked her where she was headed, and she replied that she was on her way to visit Rob Hairston and his family. It was a black family. She said to Thattis, "They're my first cousins."

Thattis told me, "I'd known them all my life, but I never knew they were her cousins. I knew they were mixed race, but how, I didn't know." Once Lizzie had told him her secret, Thattis was amazed he had never noticed it before: "They looked just like she did, but they were black."

A ghostly genealogy, an invisible map of two families of different race, was spread over this county with barely discernible lines connecting one person to the other. Those lines converged at a house on Plum Grove Road where Lizzie had frequently gone to see her cousin Rob and his daughter. The daughter was still alive, living in the same house Lizzie had visited. Thattis told me how to get there.

Two farmhouses stood side by side on a quiet road where the black schoolhouse used to stand. They faced a broad expanse of fields fringed with woodland. Behind the farmhouses a pair of horses grazed quietly in a pasture. I went onto the porch of the second house, rousing several cats from their afternoon nap.

A short, almond-skinned woman, wearing a cotton dress, answered my knock. Her name was Aldia Hairston Adams. She owned the farmland across the road, and much else besides. She was in her early eighties, but her body had the same ageless energy I had seen in ranchwomen who ran their own places out West. She had a high-pitched, raspy voice—raw notes that could get livestock to do exactly what she wanted them to do. She invited me to come in, and I came face-to-face with the girl I had been searching for. Her photograph was on the wall.

Chrillis had grown into a beautiful woman. She looked out with a strong, firm gaze, with warm, dark eyes. I guessed that she was in her late thirties, judging by the strands of gray that lightened her wavy hair. She was dressed elegantly in a velvet dress with matching velvet bow, a lace collar, and gold earrings. Her features were delicate. It seemed that she had inherited her color from her father, but he could not have been the source of her fine, kindly, delicate face. Her mother must have been a beautiful woman.

Aldia said it was a photograph of her grandmother.

Aldia led me into another room to show me a photograph of her grandfather. She pointed to the picture and said, "Major George Harston."

In all the genealogies and family trees drawn up by the white Hairstons, Major George was always shown as unmarried. A generation ago, the whites had managed to expunge that part of their past from their collective memory. The white Hairstons I had been interviewing simply didn't know. But these two portraits brought to life all the fragments of truth and half truth, the scraps of paper and lore that had come down from slavery time. In the division of slaves after Robert's death, Major George had purchased Robert's black wife. Chrillis was taken to another plantation and given the name Elizabeth. The name Chrillis could never be spoken again. Her past had to be erased, but the white Hairstons could not break her connection to her mother. When Emancipation set her free, she left the plantation where she had been kept and rejoined her mother at George's place. She was then a young woman of about twenty, and George fell in love with her. They lived until his death as husband and wife. She bore six children.

"Major George put all their children in his name," Aldia said. There were other interracial couples at that time, she said, where the children were given the mother's last name to maintain the fiction that the white man was not their real father; but Major George insisted that his children carry his name, and that everyone know who the father was. He gave all of them land. Her father was the second son, named Robert.

When Aldia was young, the white Hairstons visited her father, Rob, every weekend. She mentioned their names—they were the parents of the white Hairstons I had been interviewing.

Even old Brown Hairston knew the connection and honored it. Aldia told of the time when her father was put in jail in Columbus for speaking disrespectfully to the sheriff. Word reached Brown Hairston, and he immediately telephoned the jail. "Don't you give Rob Hairston none of that slop you feed the prisoners on," Aldia recalled him saying. "He's not gonna be in there long." When court opened the next day, Brown sent one of his sons to bring Rob home.

Aldia took me outside to show me where her childhood house had stood. "It was a big, two-story log house. Major George built the place. Over where the pecan trees are." A gusty wind had blown up, kicking up dust from the field and obscuring the road in the direction where Aldia waggled her finger. The house was gone anyway, and all that stood to mark its spot were two pecan trees growing side by side.

There was a big front porch, she said, where another frequent visitor from the white side of the family used to sit for an afternoon chatting with her black relatives, a woman who used to ride over alone on horseback—Lizzie Hairston Bridgeforth. Lizzie came without her husband, "who didn't cotton to colored people," Aldia explained. As for Lizzie herself, "she didn't deny her colored kin."

Weeks earlier I had found a legal paper in the county archives about a lawsuit brought against the Hairstons by a "colored" woman for back wages in 1885. I had thought nothing of it except that this black woman, named Elizabeth, must have been a bold one for suing the Hairstons. I left Aldia's house and raced back to the archive.

The archivist brought out a large cardboard box. Inside were ten thick legal folders that held a long-buried family secret. The box contained hundreds of pages of documents, depositions, and transcripts of testimony from three lawsuits Elizabeth brought against the Hairston family.

Elizabeth and Major George had lived together for twenty years. She had borne his children and had run his plantations for him. He had promised to give her land in his will, but after his death in 1885, no will was found in his papers. His relatives, led by his younger brother James Thomas Watt Hairston, known as J.T.W., promptly evicted Elizabeth from the property, sending her off with some livestock in recognition of her years of service. But she refused to go quietly and sued them.

The court testimony provided a fuller picture of the character of Major George. I understood now why Robert had selected his nephew Major George to write his will. They shared a love and an empathy for the enslaved people. Major George had been the type of master most feared by the whites—he subverted all their illusions of racial mastery. Like his uncle, he "married" a black woman and lived among blacks, whose company he preferred to that of his white family. One witness said, "He had no white friends that visited him except on business." He hired a private teacher for the black children on the plantation, the workers' children and his own. Like his uncle, he tried to create his own island of racial equality.

Lowndes County was one of the most violent places in the post–Civil War South. In the 1870s the Ku Klux Klan conducted a savage, well-organized campaign against blacks and their white sympathizers. The Klan specifically targeted interracial couples, people like Elizabeth and George, for whipping.

Gangs of fifty or sixty Klansmen would ride up and down the roads at night, stopping at plantations along the way to "straighten out the niggers," by which they meant whipping everybody, men, women, and children—twenty-five or thirty people at a time. The people were so terrified that many took to sleeping in the woods.

Some blacks were whipped for working too slowly, some for working too hard. A community of blacks had formed partnerships to farm large tracts of rented land, and they too got whipped so that the Klan "could always control the labor themselves." According to U.S. Congressional hearings that investigated Klan activity in Mississippi in the 1870s, the Klan whipped a black man one thousand times for improper language toward white women. A black schoolteacher was killed and thrown into a well. A black political leader had his throat cut and was then disemboweled while his wife watched.

One night a party of thirty Klansmen rode by a farm a black Hairston was renting. He saw the procession of mounted men in their white robes and hoods, the leaders sporting horns on their heads and cow's tails dangling down their chests, making weird whistling noises like whippoorwills and screeching like owls, jabbering in a broken language. Hairston called out, said he wasn't afraid of them, and what the hell were they doing near his place? Exactly why he did this foolhardy thing is difficult to explain because he got whipped on account of it, "pretty severely," witnesses recalled. Word went around the county that this fool Hairston had, at night when he was alone, called out to thirty of the Klan. A witness in the Senate investigation said, "This man Hairston said something to them—that he was not afraid of them. They fell upon him and beat him terribly."

Further testimony revealed that not long after this incident, the Klan dragged out a man named Stewart, a hardworking, quiet man who had sued a planter who didn't pay him. The Klan wanted to straighten him out. The work of "straightening out" one black man required sixty Klans-men—they whipped people in relays—but the gang this time attracted attention. They were spotted taking him away, and a party of black men quickly formed up. The black men ran to get their guns and within minutes hatched a plan. They knew that the Klansmen would leave their horses in one place with a few men to hold them and take Stewart down a road someplace deeper in the woods.

The Klansmen were whipping Stewart when the black men opened up on them. The Klansmen shot back into the woods, but they couldn't see any targets and kept getting hit themselves. A witness who described the attack recalled, "Well, the firing was pretty sharp by the freedmen." So the Klan chief gave the order to scatter and they ran for their lives. All along the road freedmen were hiding behind trees firing at the Klansmen as they ran—the moon was bright that night and the white robes of the Klansmen glowed against the dark background of the forest—and other blacks were already shooting up the men who were holding the horses.

The victory proved temporary. The Klan, groups of Confederate vet-erans, and other well-organized white groups conspired to steal the state and local elections of 1875 and install white-supremacist governments across Mississippi. In the weeks leading up to the election, black leaders frantically appealed to the federal government to send troops to stop the torture and murder of black political organizers. Their telegrams to Wash-ington, detailing hideous atrocities, read like a desperate SOS from a sinking ship. President Ulysses S. Grant—the Sword of Emancipation—delayed, considered, and then refused. Taking the political pulse, he de-cided that the North was tired of "the Negro Problem." It was an issue for the states to settle on their own.

The whites were, therefore, free to do as they wished in the elections of 1875, with no fear of federal interference. A column of Confederate veterans rode into southern Lowndes County from Alabama to take con-trol of the polling places. At the election site near the Hairston planta-tions, two white men, with the assistance of the white man in charge of the voting, hid in the polling place after it closed and replaced all the ballots. In the northern part of the county, white paramilitary groups made up largely of war veterans fired cannons at groups of black voters. White-supremacist politicians handily won offices across the state, taking control of the legislature. Blacks formed a majority of Mississippi's pop-ulation, but after the election of 1875, in the words of one historian, they "once more lay at the mercy of the white minority."

A brief era of promise had come harshly to a close. Immediately after the war, the blacks of Lowndes County had gathered in a mass meeting at Columbus and issued a public statement: "We want peace and reconciliation with the whites." They were, they stated, willing to put aside the bitterness over generations of slavery and work together with the whites to build a harmonious society. But their call for reconciliation brought no response from the whites. The attitude of most white Mississippians was embodied not by men such as Major George, but by men such as his brother, J. T. W. Hairston, who complained bitterly about conditions in Mississippi after the war. Theft was rampant, he wrote to his wife in Virginia. Most of the thievery was the work of poor whites—he knew that for a fact, but that did not alter his thinking. It became fixed in his mind that the blacks were the source of all his trouble, and he wrote to his wife, "We must exterminate the Negro."

The whites looked back with nostalgia on the antebellum period and on the institution of slavery, viewing it as a necessary restraint on the savage tendencies of the ignorant blacks. There was a deep irony in this view. Slavery had indeed been a restraint—on the savage tendencies of the whites. When the war ended, many ex-slaves tried to forgive their oppressors, but the whites unleashed a tide of hatred against the blacks seldom matched by anything in slavery.

Elizabeth survived this reign of terror in the 1870s. She raised a family and prospered. Strong-minded and independent, she stepped in when her husband faltered. Discouraged by debts, by failed real-estate investments, and by the machinations of his own family members who tried to "break him up," George simply gave up. Elizabeth refused to accept failure. She took over George's plantations and made them successful.

It was said that Elizabeth "did the work of a man and the work of a woman too." She hired hands and managed them in the fields. She put hands to work fencing pastures, repairing old cabins, and building new ones. She ran a store and a mill; she had her own stable of horses and mules, which she fed with corn she raised herself. She worked more hands than anyone else in that section. She always had work available because she was always opening new land—"weed land," which George had regarded as useless. Elizabeth put into cultivation between three hundred and five hundred acres that George had neglected.

She raised her own cotton, only to see it taken when George's creditors pressed him. She had stored up six bales of cotton as down payment for a farm of her own, but George was hit with another financial crisis.

He had bought a new cotton gin in Mobile and couldn't pay for it. If he did not send the manufacturer some payment, he would lose the engine, so he sent Elizabeth's cotton to Mobile. Then George used three years of her crop to pay off another debt to a merchant in Columbus.

A witness at the lawsuit following her husband's death in 1885 testified that George had acknowledged his debt to Elizabeth and had meant to pay her back: "I heard him say that he intended to leave her a home. He went so far as to tell me what land he was going to give. He said she had let him have the greater part of what she had made while she was there."

Elizabeth lost her first suit to claim some of George's land. In the third and final suit, filed in 1889, she asked for repayment of loans and for "wages," which she substantiated with detailed accounts of the time she had spent working on her husband's behalf. The whole issue of "wages" was a legal fiction; it was a humiliation for Elizabeth to be compelled to make her claim on that basis. She had not been George's employee, she was his wife, except that the law forbade their marriage. Unable to claim the widow's portion, she calculated what her labor had been worth to George as if she had been a "hand."

Elizabeth's lawyers maintained that most of the white Hairstons recognized that her claims were legitimate and were willing to pay her, but that a faction of the white family was adamantly against her. They were determined to take Major George's land. In their dry language, Elizabeth's lawyers stated, "Certain of said heirs believing they can defeat the claim, have concluded an agreement by which they were to undertake to fight the claim, and receive as their reward certain lands of decedent."

Two family members appeared in court to contest Elizabeth's claim, one of them being George's brother J.T.W. On the witness stand he was blunt in his contempt for Elizabeth: "Common report was that she was his mistress." He denied that she deserved any settlement, and the court agreed.

Rebuffed by the court, Elizabeth refused to accept defeat. A resourceful and energetic woman, she went out and bought a 1,120-acre plantation on an eight-year mortgage, payable in cotton. She put fifty hands to work in her fields.

When Elizabeth's lawyers were making their final, fruitless arguments before the judge, present in the courtroom was none other than Brown Hairston, then a young man. His subsequent concern for Elizabeth's children made sense. They were his nieces and nephews, and he knew that some of the land he had inherited or bought from his "depleted cousins" had been stolen from their mother.

The secret of Elizabeth and Major George had been so well kept for so long, I wondered what the effect would be when I told the whites. I went to see Nick Hairston, the man who had cleared the old family cemetery.

Seated in Nick's living room, looking over old family photographs, I waited for what I thought was the opportune moment to bring up the matter. As we were reviewing the pictures of relatives, I blurted out, "I met a new cousin of yours today, over on Plum Grove Road."

Nick was puzzled. He knew he didn't have any relatives in that part of the county.

"She's black."

I told him how I had found Aldia Adams, that I had seen a photograph of a white man from the nineteenth century, whom she called Major George.

"There should be records. Can you substantiate this in the records? Does she have any documentation?"

"She has the photograph."

He sat silently for a minute and then said, "There's the connection right there." He smiled. "Frances has got to put this on her family tree." Frances was married to his cousin Lamar, the Crawford postman. She knew more of the family's history than most blood Hairstons, and she had drawn up the elaborate family tree I had seen at the reunion, a tree that had blank spaces next to Robert and Major George where their families would have been. We were about to fill in those blanks in an unexpected way.

"She carried the name?" Nick asked. "Her maiden name was Hairston?" I told him that it was.

"I've never had any doubt in my mind that we were kin to the blacks in some way. But I never knew how. Is she a very light-complected person?"

"She said her father was very white."

I told him that his father, Nick Sr., had visited them often.

"I want to go down and see her," Nick said. "She'd probably like to see Nick's son. I'd like to sit down and talk with her and show her the photographs of all these people here that she's connected to, and the pictures of the houses in Virginia that she's from. I'd like to meet her and tell her who I am."

The next Saturday morning we drove down from Columbus to see Aldia. We stopped on the way to pick up Frances. The night before, Nick had broken the news to her about the family's new relative. He could barely contain his glee at Frances's reaction—which was dumbfounded disbelief, then annoyance that this upstart wished to join the Hairston family. Nick reminded her that Aldia had a photograph of Major George that proved her relation. Frances replied testily, "Well, let's go out there and see what else she's cooked up, or faked, or bought from some store."

But overnight some transformation took place. When we picked up Frances, she carried with her the family tree and projected an air of excited anticipation. Whatever hostility she had felt the night before had evaporated.

As Nick pulled up at the house, Aldia emerged onto the porch and called out an enthusiastic greeting in her high, raspy voice. Aldia's niece Jean and great-great-nephew emerged from the house next door.

"How you doing?" Nick called in response. "Are you Aldia? My name's Nick Hairston. I guess you're a long-lost cousin."

I half expected a thunderclap from the sky when these two branches of the family finally met.

Aldia and Frances stared at each other for a second.

"I *know* you," Aldia chuckled.

"I have seen you before, too," Frances replied. Both burst into laughter when they realized they had known each other by sight for years, had never said a word to each other, and turned out to be related.

Nick looked across Aldia's field and realized that he had been here before. "I used to come down here in the 1960s to measure the cotton crops," he said to Aldia. "I'm sure I checked your cotton at least two or three times."

Aldia invited everyone inside. She spread out photographs of her father, her uncle, and far-flung cousins. They peppered Aldia with questions: "That's your mother's mother? What was her name? Who was her father's mother?"

Aldia noticed Nick studying the portrait of Elizabeth. "She passed right after I was born," Aldia said. "I took my color from her." She explained that as Elizabeth grew older, her skin darkened.

Aldia brought out the large portrait of Major George in its ornate, nineteenth-century frame. "Every child Grandma Liz had," Aldia said, "he put in his name." Nick had brought with him photographs of his great-grandfather, who was Major George's brother. "Aldia, this is your great-uncle."

Frances unfurled the Hairston family tree and pointed out Major George's name. She traced Aldia's roots back to the Mississippi founders, then to General George Hairston of Virginia, who had fought in the Revolution, and back to the original immigrant from Scotland. Nick opened his album of photographs of the Virginia and North Carolina mansions.

Aldia described her roots on her mother's side. She could remember her great-grandmother, who had been a slave, dancing in the joyous manner of slavery time. She would balance a glass of water on her head, sway to the music, and wave her arms, never spilling a drop from the glass. Aldia's great-grandfather was a Cherokee from Alabama, a medicine man who kept a shed full of snakes from which he made his cures.

Nick and Aldia went outside to pose together for a picture, holding the portrait of Major George, and then Aldia led both families down the road to see the spot where George and Elizabeth had lived.

"See the pecan trees there? That's where I was born. That's where their house was."

The site was empty save for the trees, which had a story of their own that Aldia wanted to tell. Elizabeth had traveled to the New Orleans Exposition in 1884. It was a great display of the South's industrial and agricultural progress, with a special pavilion devoted to the achievements of the African-Americans. Elizabeth returned from the fair with two pecan saplings. She planted the pair side by side in front of the house she shared with Major George. Aldia pointed out that Elizabeth had planted them so close that "they growed in together." I could see the separate roots, and where the trunks had curved themselves to join and form one enormous tree.

As we walked back to the house, Nick looked over Aldia's fields with a professional eye. The crop was ripe and Aldia was about to gather in her harvest.

"How much land have you got here, Aldia?"

"We're supposed to have one hundred fifty."

Nick knew that asking about landholdings could be an impolite question, and I knew that Aldia's family held more land than that—she just didn't care to admit it.

Something unspoken was lurking beneath that exchange. The blacks had succeeded at an enterprise where the whites had failed. They held the land. Aldia mentioned that she was making plans for a grand Thanksgiving dinner, with relatives coming from across the South for a reunion. They were coming back to their ancestral homeland, to enjoy Thanksgiving dinner together and celebrate with her the abundance of the land passed down from Elizabeth.

Elizabeth had refused to accept defeat and humiliation. By her own sweat and effort, she had reclaimed the countryside after the Civil War, opening new land and putting people to work. With her own hands she rebuilt a plantation her husband was too weak to manage; and when that plantation was taken from her, she had started over and bought another, which she had handed down to her children. The shape of her life and character struck a familiar chord in my memory. I had read of such a person before, a woman by the name of Scarlett O'Hara, the mythic heroine of the South. Elizabeth was not a fictional character; she had actually lived that heroic life, and she was black. How many others like her have been forgotten?

Much more than land had been taken from Elizabeth and her offspring—history itself had been snatched away from them, history and a rightful share in the myth of the South. Myths would not be so dangerous except that we live by them. Myths determine the beliefs people have about themselves and tell people what place they have in the world. Myth bestows ownership of the past and declares who are its heirs today. For that reason myth is closely guarded by the people who see themselves as the sole heirs of the past. The myth that only white people built the South remains alive. It is the reason why the Confederate flag can be hoisted again over courts and statehouses. As I returned north to Virginia, I could see it fluttering from cars and trucks on the interstate. We may not realize it, but we travel on very old roads. The interstate lay over the mountain road the slaves had taken to Mississippi. They crossed these mountains in winter, walking without shoes. Their feet froze and the bones stuck out, leaving a trail of blood. We revere places like Valley Forge, where in a bitter winter the barefoot patriots of the Revolution left bloody tracks in the snow; but there were no markers by this highway where the slaves had left their own red trail in the snow. Theirs too was American blood, shed in the cause of opening new land. Their descendants hold it today.

I headed to the University of Virginia, in Charlottesville, to continue my research on the Hairston family. I was retracing the steps of the judge's grandfather—Peter Wilson Hairston had gone to Charlottesville 160 years earlier to study law at the University of Virginia, and now I was going there to continue my research into his life. The university's archive contained copies of many of the Hairston plantation papers. But I was also in pursuit of someone else, a figure who had emerged by surprise in Mississippi.

In my search for Robert's daughter, I had looked through many obscure documents. I had scanned hundreds of pages of dusty, barely legible records, hoping for the appearance of the name Hairston. I was looking for information about Chrillis, but I stumbled upon someone else, someone whose story led me in an unexpected direction. When I found him, I had the sense that Chrillis had pointed me toward the discovery, that she had had one final secret to disclose before she faded away—she wanted to reveal the name of her emancipator, the man who achieved what her father had failed to do. It was someone she had known when they were both children on her father's plantation. He was one of the children she could have set free, had the white Hairstons honored her father's deathbed wish. But instead, he was among the surplus marked for auction. They sold him into more distant slavery; but—in a supreme irony—by doing so, the Hairstons set in motion the machinery of their own destruction. As his story unfolded, the fates of the two families became woven into a larger tapestry.

PART II

"I TREMBLE FOR MY COUNTRY"

The Southern slaveholders proudly presided over the greatest enormity
of the age. As deeply believing Christians, they . . . pronounced slavery
ordained of God. [Their records] reveal the people who presided over that
enormity as, more often than not, admirable men and women who struggled heroically to build a Christian civilization. . . . They qualified, by any
reasonable standard, as good and decent people who tried to live decently
with their slaves. They were doomed to fail, for, at bottom, their relation
with their slaves rested on injustice and violence, and therein lay the
tragedy that has made them, individually and as a class,
the most arresting of Americans.

—EUGENE GENOVESE, *"Decline and Fall of a Slaveocrat"*

So Moses left Pharaoh, went out of the city, and stretched out his hands
to the LORD; then the thunder and hail ceased, and the rain no longer
poured down on the earth. But when Pharaoh saw that the rain and
the hail and the thunder had ceased, he sinned once more and
hardened his heart, he and his officials. So the heart of Pharaoh
was hardened, and he would not let the Israelites go.

—EXODUS 9:33–35

"No Man Can Hinder Me"

One of William Faulkner's most famous sayings is that "the past is never dead, it is not even past." As a lifelong Northerner, a resident of cities constantly renewing themselves by obliterating the past, I had doubted Faulkner's wisdom, which I took as a mere rhetorical flourish and nothing more. But I came to realize that the South and the Southerner possess something the Yankee is born without. A Faulkner scholar expressed it as "a sense of the presence of the past, and with it, and through it, a personal access to a tragic vision. For the South has experienced defeat and guilt, and has an ingrained sense of the stubbornness of human error and of the complexity of history."

One of the first things I noticed when I arrived in Charlottesville was that I had exchanged one set of statues for another. In my old Brooklyn neighborhood I had lived within sight of the imposing triumphal arch of the Grand Army of the Republic, the collective name Union veterans adopted after the Civil War. From my apartment window at dawn I had been able to see the first rays of light illuminating the bronze figure of Victory, a robed woman facing south atop the arch, driving a four-horse chariot. Concealed in overgrown shrubbery on the traffic circle below stood Victory's attendants—Union officers whose names I could not remember. All the time that I had lived there, I had never thought to look at the names engraved on the marble bases, and I could not recall a single commemorative event. Just two blocks from my new home in Charlottesville stood a statue of Robert E. Lee on his horse; and a short stroll from Lee would take me to the memorial to Thomas Jonathan "Stonewall" Jackson, who was fatally shot, in error, by one of his own men on the night of his greatest triumph—the famous flanking maneuver that won the Battle of Chancellorsville, in 1863. Nearby, a bronze Confederate foot soldier, flanked by cannon, guarded the county courthouse. Occasionally, gunfire echoed through the streets as men in Confederate garb gathered at one statue or another to fire salutes in tribute to the South's leaders.

At a county fair thirty miles south of Charlottesville, I came upon blue- and gray-clad men re-creating a cavalry skirmish from the Civil War, with booming cannon, the sharp crackle of muskets, and men of the North and South on the ground feigning wounds and death. More than just a pageant—with the noise of men and horses, and the scary discharge of a lone weapon—whose bullet will that be?—it was a determined attempt to leap into another dimension and, with unconquerable will, revive extinct glory. Though the field be lost, the mind and spirit remain invincible. There is a saying among the Confederate reenactors: "Lee surrendered; we didn't." In the South, history is politics: taking note of the resurgence of Confederate sentiment, and brushing aside the furious objections of black leaders, in 1997 the governor of Virginia proclaimed April—the month of the Surrender—as "Confederate History and Heritage Month," a time to reflect upon the South's "struggle for independence and sovereign rights."

The South might win the war if it were fought today. In battle reenactments, Confederates often outnumber Union troops—a reversal of the historical fact—because many Northern reenactors now choose to put on the uniform of the Confederacy. I discovered this odd fact when I met a journalist, Tony Horwitz, who had written a book about the reenactors. Horwitz asked the reenactors about their reasons for fighting the war over again and found that in a handful of Southerners and Northern turncoats, their motive was racist. But the vast majority insisted that they were not doing symbolic battle in defense of slavery. They chose the gray uniform out of sympathy for the underdog, admiration for the heroes of the South, nostalgia for the simple agrarian society destroyed by the war, and as a symbolic protest against a federal government once more viewed as tyrannical.

The fall of the Old South remains nonetheless a great tragedy of American history. Its poignance resonates still, and the gallantry of the Southerners, such as the Hairstons, in defending their homes, touches us to this day. So we watch the mock battles, knowing the inevitable, unchangeable outcome, with pity and fear—pity for the doomed Southerners, with so many noble attributes, and fear that Americans who believed they were good could be so utterly destroyed. Simply to watch these events and feel these emotions entraps the onlooker in a moral labyrinth. With full knowledge that the defeat of the Confederacy ended slavery—the vilest evil in American history—the reenactors roll back history and hold it in suspension at the moment when that evil still existed, when victory hung in the balance. Certainly the Confederates were gallant, but if they had won and the South had become sovereign, they would have preserved slavery. Some Confederate apologists maintain that the institution of slavery was waning and that the South would soon have relinquished it anyway. But scholars now think that slavery was actually strengthening, because the slaveholders were finding ways to adapt the old institution to a modernizing economy. The South in the years preceding the Civil War was rapidly industrializing, and in response, masters were hiring out their slaves to work in factories. Slavery might have continued for several more generations, enshrined in law, ratified by a successful war, and condoned by a society that refused to admit that anything was wrong with slavery. Indeed scholars are baffled that, in the immensity of letters, diaries, and other documents from slavery time, the masters left little evidence that they thought slavery was wrong. Were they blind to it? Americans deeply believe in the goodness of history, which has dispensed so many blessings on this country, and in the goodness of our forebears and the Founders. The planters held slaves, but did they do it in innocence? The Founders excluded slaves from the "inalienable rights"—did they do so in innocence? Thus, when the modern Confederates hurl themselves into mock battle—their ranks swelled by fresh recruits from the North—their long gray lines pose the central question, a mystery as old as the Book of Exodus: How is it that so many men, proclaiming the best motives, will choose to stand not with Moses but with Pharaoh?

These questions might well be posed to a reenactor from an earlier era. In Charlottesville I once caught sight of him loping through the streets in his costume of powdered wig and knee breeches. No heads turned but mine; everyone knew who he was—the descendant of Thomas Jefferson who regularly put on performances as the Founding Father. Even without the reenactor, Jefferson's presence hovered over Charlottesville. From many parts of town I could catch a glimpse of his mountaintop plantation, Monticello, a magnificent architectural achievement where the author of the Declaration of Independence had surrounded himself with books, paintings, sculpture, and scientific instruments.

I visited Monticello many times and learned a great deal about slavery from the guides and historians there. I was surprised to discover that Jefferson did not pass all his time sequestered in his study with his books and instruments. He rode out to inspect his plantation daily, spending many hours in the saddle to see the work of his overseers and slaves. He personally supervised a small nail forge he built just a few steps from the mansion. He started the nailery because he was perpetually broke, and he staffed it with slaves he could spare from field work—children. Jefferson knew "the nail boys" well: each morning he visited the forge to dole out the raw iron; in the afternoon as he labored in his study over issues of rights and liberty, his thoughts would have been punctuated by the clinking of the children's hammers; in the evening he returned to the forge to weigh the finished nails. As hard as the boys worked, they were never able to catch up to their master's indebtedness.

Jefferson was surrounded by slaves: his white family of nine people shared the mountaintop with more than a hundred African-American slaves, some of whom are likely to have been Jefferson's own children. The debate over the question of Jefferson's black children flared up at a conference about his legacy, when a black man in the audience identified himself as a Jefferson descendant. A white historian disputed the notion that Jefferson could have had black offspring; he recoiled from the thought of it, asserting that Jefferson was not the kind of man who could enslave his own children. Then Julian Bond, the former civil rights leader and a lecturer at the university, who would later assume the chairmanship of the NAACP, rose to say that Jefferson had already enslaved other people, and from there it was but a short step to enslaving his own children. But if Jefferson had children whom he held in slavery, he made no mention of them. No solid evidence for such a relationship survived, and the assembled scholars continued to debate the mystery of the slaveholder's mind.

Something in Jefferson's daily contact with the enslaved people made him uneasy. Mastery required effort that was difficult to maintain: "The spirit of the master is abating," he wrote, and "that of the slave [is] rising from the dust." He made that observation in his book, *Notes on the State of Virginia*, which included a long section of his scientific arguments espousing the natural inferiority of the black people. Jefferson tried to justify slavery through the power of reason. But in the midst of his ruminations, Jefferson's carefully crafted intellectual edifice abruptly began to crumble.

It was as if the very idea of slavery pushed the "Sage of Monticello" beyond reason. The turmoil that plainly surfaces on the printed page of Jefferson's book reflects a struggle with some knowledge of slavery's evil—a knowledge he could neither suppress nor admit. His writing suddenly took a mystical turn. Having lived through one revolution he foresaw another—"a revolution of the wheel of fortune, an exchange of situation, is among possible events." He was seized by a dread that some biblical cataclysm would befall the nation over slavery: "I tremble for my country," he wrote, "when I reflect that God is just: that His justice cannot sleep for ever. . . . The Almighty has no attribute which can take side with us." He thought that sometime in the distant future slavery might end peacefully, with the blacks being sent to Africa. He feared, however, that slavery would end violently, not with the consent of the masters, but "by their extirpation."

Late one evening, emerging from the University of Virginia library after a long day reading Peter Hairston's letters and diaries, I heard the sound of singing. A soft yet powerful music, wafting on the warm air of a spring night bursting with fragrance and stars, drew me through the grounds of the venerable university in search of the singers. Jefferson had designed these buildings in the 1820s, nearly five decades after he had written the Declaration of Independence. I walked past serpentine brick walls enclosing the gardens of the professors, and toward the looming white dome of the Rotunda, a massive, templelike brick edifice Jefferson had modeled after the Roman Pantheon. I passed through a covered arcade and entered the Lawn, the heart of the old university, where a broad greensward unrolled from the Rotunda and through Jefferson's "Academical Village"—the nation's greatest architectural achievement. Here, Jefferson proclaimed the ideals of the new republic in the classical forms of ancient Greece and Rome, an august setting for the education of the elite of the slavocracy—young planters such as Peter Wilson Hairston. Here, I found the source of the beautiful sound that had drawn me through Jefferson's creation. A massed chorus of African-American students was singing on the steps of the Rotunda. Gravely, respectfully, they gave voice to a spiritual—"No Man Can Hinder Me"—a song composed by slaves about the apocalypse that would sweep slavery away.

When the concert was finished, I walked up the steps of the Rotunda and found that, just behind the chorus of African-American students, the fulfillment of Jefferson's prediction was embossed on the wall of his Rotunda. Under a broad colonnade, I noticed a pair of bronze tablets with a list of names—the 503 students and graduates of the university who had died defending the South in the Civil War, young men who had been extirpated so that history's wheel could turn. By the flickering light of a match, I saw that two of the names on that grim roster were Hairston.

I wondered: Could the story of this family answer the questions that on a larger scale, were unanswerable? What would this family have done if they had been given a vision of slavery's evil when there was still time to act upon it? What if they were sent a sign, a private revelation—the opportunity to redeem themselves? What if, one day, bringing terrible knowledge, there had appeared among them a prophet?

Indeed, this had occurred; and I already had the answer. I felt that such a revelation had happened when Robert Hairston revealed that one of the slaves was his daughter, the Hairstons' own flesh and blood, and had commanded the family to let her go. And so the Hairstons were tested, not knowing that *this* was their trial. They could not have foreseen that the test would come veiled in something as common as a business transaction, the settlement of an estate. From the moment they looked upon the child's face and saw, perhaps, the outlines of their own, they could never say that they did not know what they were doing, that through some defect in their perception they did not comprehend that the African-Americans were human. Knowing that Chrillis was Robert's daughter, they hardened their hearts and sent her back into slavery. They willingly stepped into a labyrinth of denial. William Faulkner described in *Absalom, Absalom!* the agony of a man "who knew but still did not believe," who struggled with knowledge that "would be like death for him to learn." The slaveholders were not blind to slavery's evil; they knew it well, and they were able to live with it because they had grown accustomed to it; and when they had to sell children, even their own, they steeled themselves for the distasteful task. Their tragic flaw was not blindness, but refusal to believe: it was hardness of heart—Pharaoh's curse brought to America.

Despite the evil the masters perpetrated, we are moved by the tragic spectacle of their downfall because we are compelled to admit that the proprietors of the "peculiar institution" were not an exotic breed; they were fully in the American grain. They pursued their manifest destiny

Samuel W. Hairston, ca. 1845. *(Courtesy of Louisa Hairston Breeden)*

Columbia Lafayette Stuart Hairston, with Samuel
and Elizabeth, ca. 1856. *(Courtesy of Peter W. Hairston)*

From left to right: Samuel Hairston, master of Oak Hill; "Saura Town" Peter Hairston; Peter Wilson Hairston, ca. 1880. *(Courtesy of Peter W. Hairston)*

Stair hall at Cooleemee, ca. 1923. *(Photograph by Bayard Wootten, courtesy of North Carolina Collection, University of North Carolina Library at Chapel Hill)*

Ruth Stovall Hairston. *(Courtesy of Peter W. Hairston)*

Louisa Hardyman Hairston Watkins
(conjectural), 1850s.
(Courtesy of Louisa Hairston Breeden)

Bettie Perkins Hairston Hairston,
1916. *(Courtesy of Mrs. Elmo H. Shivar)*

Ann Hairston mansion in Martinsville. *(Courtesy of Mrs. Elmo H. Shivar)*

Graveyard at Beaver Creek. *(Courtesy of the author)*

Stair hall at Cooleemee with portrait of Peter Wilson Hairston, ca. 1923.
*(Photograph by Bayard Wootten, courtesy of North Carolina Collection,
University of North Carolina Library at Chapel Hill)*

Slave cabin at Cooleemee. *(Courtesy of George R. Hairston)*

Betsy Hairston, servant of the
Samuel W. Hairston family.
*(Courtesy of Bassett Historical Center,
copy image by Desmond Kendrick)*

Rev. Samuel H. Hairston.
(Copy image by Desmond Kendrick)

John Goolsby, ca. 1880. *(Courtesy of Peter W. Hairston)*

Preston Ridge School, Henry County, Virginia, 1910.
(Copy image by Desmond Kendrick)

Hairston ferry on the Yadkin, ca. 1900: "Marse" Peter Hairston sits at right, his sisters Ruth and Agnes are at left, and his brother, Frank, sits next to ferryman, Righteous Hairston.
(*Courtesy of Peter W. Hairston*)

Collie L. Hairston Sr., Clarence Hairston Sr., and Nelson Hairston at Coolomee, ca. 1924–1925. (*Photograph by Bayard Wootten, courtesy of North Carolina Collection, University of North Carolina Library at Chapel Hill*)

Cooleemee, 1969. (*Photograph by Mike Clemmer, courtesy of the* Salisbury Post)

William T. and Charming Hairston at Cooleemee, 1968.
(Courtesy of Peter W. Hairston)

Dean Hairston at Oak Hill ruins. *(Courtesy of the author)*

Joseph Henry and Ann Hairston with daughters Nancy and
Naomi, Japan, 1948. *(Courtesy of Joseph Henry Hairston)*

Jester Hairston, John Wayne, and Richard Widmark on the set of *The Alamo*. *(Courtesy of Ashley Ward Collection)*

Jester Hairston receives an honorary doctorate, University of the Pacific, 1964. *(Courtesy of Richard J. Hatch)*

Ever Lee Hairston and Lucy D. Hairston. *(Courtesy of Otis L. Hairston Jr.)*

Squire Hairston in an old slave cabin at Cooleemee.
(Courtesy of Otis L. Hairston Jr.)

Squire Hairston, Collie L. Hairston Sr., and Verdeen Hairston
at Cooleemee, 1988. *(Courtesy of the* Salisbury Post*)*

Joseph Henry Hairston and Peter W. Hairston at Cooleemee.
(Courtesy of Otis L. Hairston Jr.)

Jester Hairston at Los Angeles Hairston reunion, 1980. *(Courtesy of Bonnie Schiffman)*

to create a strong and prosperous society, just as the Founding Fathers, of the North and the South, made a pact to exclude the slaves from the "inalienable rights" so that national enterprise could go forward. In examining *Absalom, Absalom!* the eminent literary critic Cleanth Brooks asserted that the slaveholder at the center of the story was not meant as an archetypal Southerner, but as an archetypal American— a man consumed by his plan to create a grand enterprise. To preserve his burgeoning plantation empire, the novel's slaveholder, Thomas Sutpen, rejects his own son because he is a mulatto. In explaining this rejection Brooks wrote, "He does not hate just as he does not love. His passion is totally committed to the design. Not even his own flesh and blood are permitted to distract him from that." Like Sutpen, the Hairstons had been so corrupted by their obsession with building an empire that they refused even to recognize their own offspring. Their financial enterprise required slavery, or so they believed. Slavery corrupted the idea of love, the idea of truth; and slavery had so corrupted the masters that they led the South into an apocalypse to save slavery.

I had searched the documents left by the judge's grandfather for an answer to the question "Did this slaveholder go to war for slavery?" In a letter to his wife from the battlefront in 1861, Peter Hairston wrote a sentiment suitable for a banner at a modern reenactment: "We are exposing our lives for what we deem the holiest cause in the world—our homes and our firesides." But I only had to look a little deeper to find that Peter Hairston's bedrock was slavery. To preserve it, he would even undo the Revolution: "Should a dissolution of the Union ever take place, *we could place ourselves under the protection of Great Britain, she guaranteeing us our slaves* [italics added]." In 1849, after the House of Representatives had passed antislavery resolutions, Peter wrote, "I fear the late resolutions passed by the lower house of Congress place us nearly on the verge of a civil war, which to the South would be disastrous in the extreme." As early as 1842, when Peter was only twenty-three, he had written in his diary of the South's determination to preserve slavery. He predicted correctly the place where North and South would meet in an Armageddon. His beloved Virginia would become a "bloody battleground."

He could foresee the disaster, but weighing in the balance against it was the wealth slavery could dispense, if only Robert Hairston's emancipation plan could be thwarted. In his will Robert had, to a significant extent, overthrown slavery within the Hairston family. The Hairstons desperately tried to restore the dead regime, but all their effort could not restrain the onrushing force of history. The only real effect of their acts was that they condemned themselves to join in the coming apocalypse, to sacrifice themselves and their children to it. It was their last chance to save themselves. As I examined the slave records drawn up after Robert Hairston's death, when the white Hairstons gathered in Mississippi to divide his land and slaves, I could see what they could not: history's wheel had already turned—*the emancipator was already there*. He was one of the slaves walking among them, one of the children. That was the discovery Chrillis had pointed me toward.

After Robert's death the officers of the court called the enslaved people together and counted them, writing their names in long columns in a ledger, with long columns of figures—the dollar value of each man, woman, and child. I studied those names, especially the names of the children. Some of them were sold into distant slavery by Peter, split from their families and from then on numbered among the lost. One of the children was named Thomas. Later on, an archivist showed me the first record of black marriages in Mississippi, a ledger kept during the Civil War in the Yankee stronghold at Vicksburg. There in the ledger was "Thomas Harston"—the clerk had written it down the way Thomas pronounced it—joining himself in marriage to a woman named Annie Saunders in 1864. Giving his age as twenty-one, he said he had been born in Virginia. Next to his name was a notation I didn't understand: "3rd USCC." I asked the archivist what that meant, and she said it was a Union military outfit—Third Regiment, United States Colored Cavalry. The child sold into distant slavery would return as a soldier to overthrow his masters.

Peter Hairston's fortunes reached their zenith in the decade after Robert's death in 1852. He had helped preserve the family's wealth from the crisis Robert had brought on them, and some of that wealth then went into the construction of his mansion at Cooleemee. Several hundred slaves set to work sculpting a knoll near the Yadkin River into a fitting pedestal for the mansion. They carved out enormous blocks of stone and manhandled them into place to form the foundation. They carved out terraces for the gardens; felled trees and hewed planks. They built kilns to produce the three hundred thousand bricks needed for the mansion. Day after day their children hauled bricks up the hill and piled them up for the bricklayers. From Italy Peter ordered a marble fireplace, and from Philadelphia he ordered columns for the entrance and walnut banisters for the majestic spiral staircase that would sweep him up to his tower and its lofty view of his domain. The columns and banisters came by ship to the coast of North Carolina, where they were loaded onto wagons and hauled by oxen over a new plank road to Cooleemee. There the slaves, as if enacting scenes from ancient Egypt, carried the columns up the hill to the house and set them upright at the entrance. They carried the banisters into the shell of the house, where skilled white craftsmen were anchoring the stairs to the brick walls. The supports were hidden, so the stairway seemed to soar aloft by itself in a masterful illusion of architecture.

When Peter sold the black children in Mississippi, he had recently become a father himself. He had married his blue-eyed cousin Columbia Lafayette Stuart, who gave birth to three children. He had erected Cooleemee for her, but no sooner was the house finished than Columbia died there, giving birth to a daughter who lived long enough only to be named and baptized. I had seen a picture of Columbia, a delicate glass ambrotype of her and the children Sammy and Betty. A vibrant personality blazed from that image. Columbia, in defiance of the conventions and technology of the time, had managed to hold a slight, shy, beguiling smile through the long exposure. The smile meant love and laughter. But her son Sammy, merely seven years old, glared straight at the camera with an expression of perfect aristocratic hauteur. By that time he was already a slave master, with his own manservant. Born to ease and leisure, he held himself with the pride of a prince, and I thought I could detect in his unwavering stare a hint of cruelty, an innate feeling for mastery. But neither child survived adolescence: Betty fell from a tree in 1865, and Sammy succumbed to typhoid fever in 1867. The image of the three of them struck me as the portrait of a catastrophe. I hesitated to form the connection—it seemed to arise of its own accord—but that calamity bore a fearful symmetry to what Peter himself had done to the black families in Mississippi when he felt compelled to sell the elderly, the sick, and the children.

Peter was living at Cooleemee in April 1861 when word reached him that Virginia had seceded from the Union. He went into the library and pulled out his ledger. "Went to war," he wrote, "kept no further accounts." At the end of May, Peter wrote to his second wife, Fanny, from

Virginia that his unit had received marching orders. "Should we never return," he wrote, "I commend my children to your charge and care and remember if I fall my last farewell was to you and my last remembrance is my affection of true and devoted love to you."

Looking through the Confederate records, I counted eighty-three Hairstons, from branches of the family across the South, who wore the uniform of the Confederacy. In Mississippi the Hairstons helped organize a regiment from Lowndes County, called the Prairie Guard. J. T. W. Hairston came north with them as a captain. Two other Hairstons served in the unit as privates. In northern Mississippi other cousins joined the Fifteenth Mississippi Infantry—one of them fell at Shiloh and had his name added to the roster of the dead on Jefferson's Rotunda. At Beaver Creek plantation in Virginia, Marshall and Ann's only son, Jack, joined the Twenty-fourth Virginia under his cousin, Colonel Jubal Early, and marched off to northern Virginia. Jack had been drummed out of the Virginia Military Institute for insubordination—he had sneaked off the grounds to attend a tea party. Although his father could easily have paid for a substitute, he joined up to redeem his honor. He too was killed, and the cousin who went to look for him died of disease after his futile search. In this fashion, the tenth plague fell on the house of Hairston.

I found a brief memoir written by a Hairston woman who was a young girl when the war broke out. She remembered vividly the day her uncles, not much older than herself, marched off to war with the Twenty-fourth Virginia: "I can see as if it were yesterday, my Grandmother and her four daughters striving, with faces rigid with effort, to suppress their tears and to control their emotions, as they follow the soldier boys to the gate for a last embrace and a 'God Bless You.' As the carriage rolled away out of sight the brave Mother dropped in her tracks as if her very life had gone with the last sight of her boys. It was her last sight of one of them, for the youngest was brought home in his coffin, and a letter came from the wife of the surgeon who ministered to him in his dying moments, saying she had 'kissed him for his Mother.' "

It was the destiny of the white Hairstons to enact the downfall of the Old South. Their gallantry and sacrifice exemplify the character of the Southerners, whose tragic fate gnaws at the nation's memory. What kind of people could endure such sorrow in service to their country? We must understand them if we are to fathom the character of the nation. And, for their part, it was the destiny of the black Hairstons to enact the exodus embedded in our national story—the miraculous, astounding rise of the African-Americans from the dust of slavery. Slavery could not crush them, nor anything thereafter. What kind of people could endure such evil and still cling to the country that dispensed it? What manner of man is *this*?

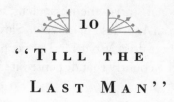

10

"TILL THE LAST MAN"

Peter Hairston's Civil War began with a burst of glory. He galloped into the war by the side of the Confederacy's greatest cavalry officer, Colonel Jeb Stuart, the brother of Peter's late wife, Columbia. Peter and Jeb had known each other since childhood. Although they had followed very different paths, they remained close friends. As a lieutenant in the United States Army before the Civil War, Jeb had been an officer under Robert E. Lee in the unit that subdued John Brown's violent rebellion at Harper's Ferry, in 1859. Jeb confiscated Brown's bowie knife when he took the abolitionist into custody, and as a token of friendship he had given the knife to Peter. So, ironically, one of the richest Southern slaveholders carried John Brown's knife into the Civil War. Like Lee, Stuart had resigned his commission in the U.S. Army to serve in the armed forces of Virginia. Peter Hairston's prewar cavalry experience consisted of fox hunting. Amateur or not, Peter rushed to take up arms. With the rest of the First Virginia Cavalry, he was encamped at Manassas, Virginia, on July 21, 1861, when the federal and Confederate armies clashed in the first battle of the war. Southerners called the engagement the First Battle of Manassas; in the North it became known as the First Battle of Bull Run, after a creek that runs through the battlefield.

At dawn on the twenty-first, the distant sound of gunfire awakened the camp of the First Virginia. After several hours of awaiting orders while the noise of battle grew louder and louder—a delay that drove the impetuous Stuart to distraction—a rider galloped into the camp with orders from the Confederate commander. "Colonel Stuart," the rider called out, "General Beauregard directs that you bring your command into action at once and that you attack where the firing is hottest."

They only had to follow the sounds; but before the First Virginia could reach the fighting, the regiment first had to pass through "a sickening ordeal," as one of the officers remembered. They rode through a shady little valley where the surgeons were "plying their vocation." On tables about breast high, set up in the shade, "screaming victims were having legs and arms cut off." The surgeons and their assistants were stripped to the waist, smeared with blood, and wielding long knives and saws, dripping with blood. One of these surgeons was a Hairston cousin from Henry County who had volunteered for service despite poor health. The surgeons went about their work quickly, and there was already a pile of limbs, the product of a single morning. The air rang with curses and hoarse prayers, amidst a swarm of flies and a sickening stench. The men of Stuart's regiment leaned from their saddles and vomited.

They rode on toward the sound of battle and came to a valley shrouded in smoke, making the combatants invisible. A gust of wind blew the dense cloud aside, and they caught sight, a mere seventy yards ahead, of the strangely clad Zouaves, dressed in Turkish style, with scarlet caps and trousers, and blue jackets heavily laden with gilt. Stuart and his officers could not tell if they were friend or foe, as both armies had Zouave units. Then they saw the Stars and Stripes suddenly unfurl and flutter in the smoke. Stuart called out the order, and the regiment charged into them. The Zouaves saw the "Black Horse," as they called the Southern cavalry, bearing down on them, and they leveled a volley. A red sheet of flame leaped toward the Southerners; they did not pause or waver, but plunged directly into it. At the moment of impact, with the Yankees struggling to reload, the horses of the Southerners knocked them end over end. One of Peter's comrades never forgot that moment of impact, when the two armies collided and he saw a bayonet coming up at him. He fired his carbine and felt a twinge of sorrow at the death of his enemy, "as he lifted his handsome face to mine."

They scattered the Zouaves and captured their artillery; but the larger battle at Manassas was still undecided. Peter Hairston galloped back and forth across the battlefield, carrying orders and dispatches from Stuart to other commands. Nearby, the Virginians of General Thomas Jackson threw back a Yankee charge, winning for their commander the name "Stonewall." But the Yankee pressure showed no signs of abating, and Confederate reinforcements were bottled up, miles away, by congestion on the rail lines. Captain J. T. W. Hairston was waiting angrily on one of those trains with the Lowndes County Prairie Guard. As the day wore on and reports reached them by telegraph of the desperate fighting at Manassas, their frustration turned to fury. Convinced that the delay was the result not of traffic but of treason, the Prairie Guard marched up to the cab of the locomotive and shot the engineer.

Atop a ridge overlooking the battlefield the Confederate commander, General Beauregard, nervously watched the approach of a strange column. If those troops were federal, he would have to abandon the field, and the Confederacy would lose its first fight. A staff officer stood by to carry the order to retreat. Once again the wind picked up, causing a distant flag to unfurl. The column was marching under Confederate colors. It was Jubal Early's Twenty-fourth Virginia.

Jeb Stuart had spotted that flag as well. He sent word to Early that he had captured enemy guns and could use them in combination with Early's infantry. Early's Virginians, howling the rebel yell, charged the federal line while Stuart's men fired at the flank. The whole Yankee army was soon fleeing pell-mell back to Washington in a defeat that stunned the North and elated the Confederates.

For Peter, the glory of the moment was dampened by news that his wife's brother-in-law, Colonel Charles Fisher, had died on the field of battle. One moment Colonel Fisher was leading his regiment in a noble charge against the Yankee line, and in the next he was slumped across his horse. In tribute, his men drove a post into the earth on the spot where he died. Peter later returned to the battlefield to find that marker. He was seeking some token, some small fragment of the place, to assuage his wife's grief at the loss of her brother-in-law. To obtain it, he first had to walk through a valley owned now by the dead. He wrote that the scene before him presented "a horrid spectacle." Everywhere bones rose from the ground. Rain had washed away the few inches of earth the victors had tossed over the corpses of the vanquished. Hogs had unearthed others, "exposing clothes, shoes and other things belonging to them." Amidst the carnage Peter could plainly see the distinctive red uniforms of men he had helped to kill.

The field was strewn with equipment of all sorts—muskets, cartridge boxes, fragments of uniforms. Something else was littering the field as well, like an eerie carpet of leaves. These were love letters, and scattered among them were photographs of women. For what is the last thing a dying man wishes to gaze upon if not the image of his wife, his lover, or his mother? Those who still had the strength pulled from their pockets the last letter they had received from home, taking comfort from the pledges of undying love and devotion. When the bodies were collected and tossed into trenches, the letters were left behind to flutter across the field.

Peter made his way to the spot where the Sixth North Carolina had made its charge, and he found the post marking the place where Charles Fisher had fallen, but almost nothing was left of it. The post had been almost completely whittled away by souvenir hunters. He saw a tree close by and cut a piece of it. Back home at Cooleemee, Fanny wrapped the wood in paper and wrote, "Manassas July 21st 1861. A piece of cedar taken from a tree near the spot where my dear brother fell."

The women felt it first—a vague foreboding in the early days of the war, despite the South's success. Signs of it are in the letters from far-flung Hairston sisters and cousins in Mississippi and Virginia. "For me the sky of the Southern Confederacy grows darker, notwithstanding our recent victory," wrote one of the Hairston women, whose brothers were "getting farther off, with a continued prospect of meeting the enemy." Another was unnerved when trophies were brought home from the glorious scene of the South's victory at Manassas and passed around with great hilarity—muskets, grapeshot, and bits of exploded shells. All this passing around of macabre relics troubled her. She retreated to her room and wrote to her sister a letter full of religious sentiments, and full of a sense of doom. "*God is with us.* but oh we must not feel exalted but *humble* or *all will be lost* . . ." How hard it was, she thought, to keep their proud spirit subdued. She urged her sister to fast and pray, to pray even for the enemy, and for the Lord to "revive His work in our hearts and make us humble." The woman who received the letter was Bettie Hairston of Beaver Creek, whose only brother, Jack, had come home after Manassas with some illness.

In 1862, in the second springtime of the war, Jack Hairston left Beaver Creek to rejoin the infantry commanded by his cousin, Colonel Jubal Early. The North had launched another invasion of Virginia, this one by sea. A huge army had landed at Yorktown and was marching west on Richmond, driving the Confederates before them. Jubal Early's Twenty-fourth Virginia took up position outside of Williamsburg in the rear guard of the Confederate army, fighting a desperate delaying action against the invaders. Early thought he had a chance to blunt the federal advance by attacking an artillery battery that was shelling the last fort held by the Confederates on the road to Richmond. Early knew the position of the guns only by their sound—they seemed to be on the other side of a thick woods in front of him. With another officer, he made a quick inspection of the near portion of the woods and found them to be swampy after a full month of rain but free of enemy troops. He ordered his brigade forward at a run and told them to keep running until they hit the enemy.

With Early in the lead, the Twenty-fourth charged into the woods, with other regiments to their right. Despite the boggy ground they kept running—one hundred yards, two hundred yards, three hundred yards, and still they could not see the guns. They emerged from the forest, panting and half-exhausted, and now they could see to their left, across a wheat field and up a slope, the Yankee battery barking shells at the fort. The other regiments were behind them, lost in the thicket. Remembering how his sudden charge had routed the Yankees at Manassas, Early paused only a few moments, then ordered a headlong attack across the field. The Twenty-fourth would go alone.

On they raced into a nightmare. As hard as they ran, they seemed to go slower and slower, as the wet wheat stocks clung to their clothes and seemed to pull them down. What Early did not know was that five regiments of New Yorkers were in the field ahead of him. The Yankees had spotted them now and poured fire into the thin advancing line. Five Northern rifles for every Southern made the odds impossible; but the Yankee commander, General Hancock, was astounded to see that the Southerners would not stop and were actually driving his men back. He ordered his battery officer to stop shelling the fort and lower his guns to fire directly into the attackers. Jubal Early was hit and carried off the field. The other Confederate regiments, at last, came out of the woods and joined the Twenty-fourth, but it was too late; the cannon and the continuous rifle fire of the New Yorkers did their work. The Southerners turned back, their attack a failure. Out of 500 men in the Twenty-fourth Virginia, 180 were killed, wounded, or missing. Jack Hairston, who had just marked his twenty-second birthday, lay dead in the wheat field.

The Confederates managed to halt the invasion that took Jack Hairston's life. With Robert E. Lee newly in command, the Confederate army not only fought the invaders to a standstill outside of Richmond, but launched attacks in northern Virginia that produced stunning victories, including a second victory at Manassas. Peter Hairston had left the army in the fall of 1861, yielding to pressure from his wife and other family members to come home and manage the plantations. The war was going well enough for the South that Peter felt he would be more useful producing food and cash for the cause than serving in uniform.

The continued economic strength of the South in the summer of 1862 greatly concerned President Lincoln. The South's wealth, he knew, derived in large part from slavery, and if he could strike at that foundation, the whole Southern edifice would be weakened. In July he told his advisers that he was considering an executive order freeing the slaves in the rebellious states. Such an order ran against his better judgment—unlike the abolitionists, he wished to end slavery gradually, with compensation for the slaveholders, because he believed that North and South bore responsibility for slavery together; but the exigencies of war forced his hand. When the North won a bloody victory over Lee at Antietam in September 1862, Lincoln published the Emancipation Proclamation, to take effect in January 1863. Confederate slaveholders, naturally, ignored Lincoln's edict; but the Proclamation did have one significant and immediate practical result—it allowed the Union army to recruit escaped slaves.

Two Northern victories in 1863 had a direct effect on the Hairston families. The South lost the battles of Gettysburg and Vicksburg on the same day, July 4, 1863. The Confederate disaster at Gettysburg prompted Peter Hairston to return to active service. Meanwhile, the capture of the strategic port of Vicksburg, Mississippi, made that city a magnet for blacks seeking freedom, one of them being Thomas Harston. As a child, Thomas had been sold to some unknown master when Robert Hairston's estate was divided in 1852. Now a young man, he had escaped from slavery amidst the chaos of the war and would soon have the chance to join in the campaign to smash slavery forever.

To make use of the manpower streaming into Vicksburg, General Ulysses S. Grant had decided to create several all-black units, including the Third United States Colored Cavalry. To lead it, Grant selected Major Embury Osband, who had commanded Grant's personal escort, the Fourth Illinois Cavalry. Osband approached his fellow officers in the Fourth Illinois and asked if any would volunteer to join him in recruiting and leading freed slaves in battle. Forty-four officers stepped forward. "We are getting a very fine class of officers indeed," another commander wrote at the time. "I think they will average better than the officers of white regiments."

From their base in Vicksburg, the officers of the Third Colored (initially designated the First Mississippi Cavalry, African Descent) fanned out into the countryside to find recruits. They didn't have to look hard—the roads teemed with freedpeople making their way to Vicksburg. Many were half-starved and would have died if the army and civilian relief agencies had not fed them. With so many young black men available, the officers had their pick—"none but the finest specimens of physical manhood were accepted," wrote one officer of the Third, Edwin Main, who set down his memoirs after the war. On a recruiting foray in October 1863, a party of officers came upon Thomas Harston and asked him to join.

In his first assignment, not a glorious one, Thomas was detailed to be the servant of Captain Jeremiah Cook. But Thomas was fortunate—Cook was the toughest, hardest-fighting officer in the unit (Cook would soon be promoted to major), and he was quick to recognize fighting qualities when he saw them. He promoted Thomas to company bugler, a post of prestige and high responsibility. Always in the thick of the fighting, the bugler was the backbone of the company's discipline in the field.

The recruitment of freed slaves was an experiment. Officers and civilians alike doubted that it would work. "Will the colored troops fight?" was a universal question. Held in slavery for so long, the freedmen were believed to be too degraded to be useful as anything but labor troops. Despite Grant's commitment to using colored troops, the army bureaucracy remained doubtful, and thus reluctant to "waste" supplies, especially guns and horses, on black recruits. For horses, the Third was pointed to the corrals that held the army's "condemned stock," the tired, lame animals no one else wanted. Not satisfied with these castoffs, the officers led foraging expeditions into the countryside to round up mules and horses.

One item the Third did get was uniforms, which the new recruits proudly wore on the army's regular Sunday-evening parades through Vicksburg. These displays of martial glory by the conquerors irked the townspeople, but nothing bothered them more than to see their former slaves arrayed in Yankee colors. One Vicksburg woman wrote derisively of the black troops on parade—"so grand in their blue uniforms . . . making a fine show." By December the unit's commander, Colonel Osband, decided that they were ready to go along on a short scouting expedition with his former unit, the Fourth Illinois. It would be a good way to test the Third's discipline in the field, with the veterans of the Fourth Illinois at hand to deal with any real trouble that might arise.

The troops hailed a passing steamboat, but the pilot pretended not to notice them. Cook ordered a cannon shot fired across the steamer's bow, which got the pilot's immediate attention and cooperation. The men embarked for their scout on the other side of the Mississippi River. They landed in good order and rode into the countryside, making camp for the night at a plantation. The units made separate camps, with the blacks, oddly enough, getting the finer spot—the yard of the plantation house, with a fence conveniently provided for tethering the horses—while the whites of the Fourth Illinois spread their bedrolls around the cotton gin 150 yards off.

Their sleep was interrupted "by the blinding flash and report of 500 shot-guns followed by the rebel yell." Confederates had crept up on the camp of the Fourth Illinois and taken the veterans by complete surprise. Their horses stampeded into the Third's camp, with the rebels close behind. Never before had the Third come under fire, and the surprise attack in midwinter darkness created an abrupt chaos of shouts, plunging horses, and lethal gunfire. In the eerie light of their campfires, which had seemed so comforting just seconds before, men dropped where they stood, hit by gunfire from the darkness.

The men looked for their officers, who emerged from the plantation house at a run, pistols in hand. Major Cook was shouting, "Kick out the fires! Kick out the fires!" Sergeants screamed for their men as bugles blared the call to "fall in."

With the rebels almost upon them, Cook set up his defensive line along the fence. The tethered horses reared in terror and broke loose. "Shoot the horses!" Cook bellowed. "Use them for cover!" From the darkness the troopers could hear rebel officers call out the order: "Charge the fence!"

In an instant the fighting became hand-to-hand. One trooper at the fence felt his carbine being pulled by unseen hands as he struggled to reload. He slammed a round in the chamber, jerked the trigger, and heard a howl of agony from his invisible enemy, shot through the chest.

Forty men of the Third fell in the first shock of the attack. The wounded, despite orders to get to the rear, refused to leave the fence. They had heard the doubters mutter, "Will the colored troops fight?" They knew full well that if the Third failed this test, they would not get a second chance. But they were barely holding their ground. With the line about to break, one of the lieutenants made a desperate decision. He pulled a company out of the line at the fence and maneuvered them to the rebel flank. With a yell they swept down on the Confederates. Confused by the sudden attack, the Confederates pulled back for a moment, which was all the Third needed. The troopers at the fence line rose up as one and charged. Pressed from two sides, the Confederates broke and ran. The black troopers mounted the surviving horses and raced in pursuit, but held their fire when they saw that the Confederates had positioned prisoners at their rear as a screen.

The Third had proved itself. One of the officers wrote, "Had they suffered defeat on that occasion the morale of the regiment would have been destroyed." Cook was more blunt in his appraisal. Called in to report to the commanding officer, the major declared that the Third would fight "till the last man." A few weeks later, it seemed that his prediction would come quite literally true.

Though the Yankees had captured Vicksburg, beyond its walls lay an unconquered and defiant Mississippi. "Federal authority," wrote one historian, "rarely extended more than a few feet beyond the bayonet-tipped rifle of the Union soldier." The backcountry was the stamping ground of some of the toughest cavalry in the Confederate army—Richardson's Tennessee Brigade, Ross's Texas Brigade, and the cavalry of Nathan Bedford Forrest, the man who would form the first Ku Klux Klan after the war. In an effort to pacify the countryside, the Union command at Vicksburg repeatedly sent expeditionary forces to seek out and engage the enemy. Accordingly, in the winter of 1864, the Third Colored Cavalry boarded steamships for a foray along the Yazoo River. A meandering tributary of the Mississippi, the Yazoo wound beneath tall bluffs through rich cotton country. At some bends of the river the banks closed in so tightly that the transports lost parts of their smokestacks to tree branches hanging over the river. These bends, where the transports were forced almost to a crawl, provided the perfect spots for rebel ambushes; more than once the troopers had to dive for cover as sniper shots whistled down from the bluffs.

Two other units had gone out on this foray—the Eighth Louisiana Infantry, which was another black unit, and the all-white Eleventh Illinois. The white soldiers had initially been skeptical of the fighting qualities of men like Thomas Harston. In letters home they had a great deal of fun lampooning black dialect and describing the greenhorn mistakes of raw recruits fresh from the plantation. But that skepticism turned to respect as the patrol wore on. Together, the black and white troops climbed a hillside thick with brush, braving intense rifle and cannon fire to reach a Confederate breastwork atop a ridge. At the worst moment of that skirmish, the whites saw tired black infantrymen take on fresh rebel reinforcements in a close-range firefight with pistols. Official dispatches mentioned how the blacks "acquitted themselves most handsomely, displaying the courage, coolness, and discipline of the most experienced troops." In a letter home one officer wrote, "The colored soldiers fought with so much bravery and gallantry as to elicit not a few commendations from the officers and men of the Eleventh Illinois." Comradeship with blacks on the battlefield gave at least one white trooper, Henry Uptmor, a remarkable perspective on slavery itself. He saw it as a burden the blacks had borne on behalf of the nation. "We came across some African people," he wrote in his diary, "who have suffered so many hardships for our country." Having forged a bond with the black troops in the brief period of this patrol, the white foot soldiers of the Eleventh Illinois were ready to lay down their lives for them, as events would prove. Veterans of major battles at Fort Donelson, Shiloh, and Vicksburg, the Eleventh would soon "tempt total annihilation," in the words of the historian Jim Huffstodt who studied the regiment, defending a dirt redoubt in an insignificant river town, because they would rather die than live to see their black comrades in the hands of the enemy.

After nearly three weeks of patrolling and raiding the countryside to gather supplies and hunt rebel stragglers, the troops landed near Yazoo City, an isolated river town of several thousand inhabitants. Before marching into the town the federal commander wanted to know that there were no rebel units lurking in the countryside beyond. On February 28 the transports pulled ashore north of Yazoo City and disgorged a forty-man cavalry patrol—Thomas Harston's company, led by Major Cook. They were not magnificently mounted: the Third had been unable to obtain horses for the Yazoo expedition and had to make do with mules they had "requisitioned" from farms upriver.

Thomas's scouting party rounded a turn in the road outside of town and suddenly came upon a few mounted graycoats. Both sides were briefly startled to come upon the enemy at such close range so unexpectedly. When the surprise wore off, Thomas and his comrades exchanged a few shots with the rebels, probably thinking they had bagged the stragglers their commander wanted. Then suddenly more rebel riders appeared, and Thomas heard the unwelcome sound of rebel artillery booming close by. When the shells began dropping, Cook ordered a hasty retreat. More rebels swarmed in. The rapid appearance of the enemy's reinforcements and the presence of artillery meant only one thing—Thomas's patrol had not come upon a gang of stragglers, but a full Confederate brigade. The black troopers bounced awkwardly down the road, getting as much speed as they could out of the reluctant mules. The rebels, mounted on fast ponies, took a short route across a field and cut them off. Thomas watched as the rebels picked off his comrades one at a time, wielding sabers and pistols to knock the troopers from their mules.

When the sound of cannon fire echoed through Yazoo City, the Illinois officers ordered out detachments of skirmishers to cover the retreat of Thomas's patrol. Even so, barely half the forty-man patrol made it into Yazoo City. The skirmishers drove off the rebel cavalry and pursued them down the road until they saw something that made them turn back. They had come upon the bodies of six men from Thomas Harston's unit. They reported that the bodies had been "brutally used," which led their commander to conclude "that they had been murdered after having been taken prisoners."

Thomas's patrol had run into the Texas Brigade, commanded by Lawrence Sullivan "Sul" Ross. The brigade's base had been at Yazoo City, and the Texans intended to get it back. Ross wrote a boasting report of his brigade's encounter with the Third's patrol: "The negroes, after the first fire, broke in wild disorder, each seeming intent upon nothing but his escape. Being mounted on mules, however, but few of them got away. The road all the way to Yazoo City was literally strewed with their bodies. The negro troops after this were timid and never came out to reconnoitre but that they were easily chased back by a few scouts." Ross's wording in this report later became the source of some concern to the Confederate high command. He said that the blacks were intent only on escape and did not try to fight back, which did not account for the fact that no prisoners were taken. His superior, General Stephen D. Lee, offered an amended account of the fight, insisting that the blacks "continued to offer resistance and run."

This was not the first time that Confederate troops had been accused of murdering black prisoners in Mississippi. Not long before, a federal officer reported, "One of the picket stations was suddenly attacked by about eighty rebels. The men were captured and most of them brutally murdered. Fourteen were killed and six wounded. Two white officers were made to strip off their clothing to drawers and stockings and were then shot and left for dead." Ross's policy was plain. One of the brigade later wrote, "As for the negro troops,—well, for some time the fighting was under the black flag—no quarter being asked or given." As one officer of the Third remarked, "It was well known that the Texans took no 'nigger' prisoners."

The federal troops at Yazoo City had taken refuge in a set of earthen redoubts that the Confederates had previously used as their base. The main redoubt stood on a high bluff overlooking Yazoo City. Its earthen walls formed a box about fifty yards square. Outside the walls were rifle pits, where Major Cook distributed eighty men from the Third as "shock troops" to delay any attempt to storm the fort. As a black infantry unit and the white Illinois troops took up their positions inside the walls, a flag of truce was seen on the rebel side. A gray-clad officer rode up to the wall and called out a request for surrender. Major Cook jumped up on the parapet and yelled in reply, "My compliments to General Ross, and say to him that if he wants this fort to come and take it."

Ross's response was not long in coming. As one trooper described in his diary, "In a very few minutes they set up their cannons and began to shell us unmercifully, and we could do nothing in return." A sergeant was dismembered by shrapnel; an officer was thrown in the air by another burst. It quickly became apparent that the smaller redoubts could not be held, and the order was given to abandon them and combine forces in the largest one. Dodging heavy fire, Major George C. McKee of the Eleventh Illinois dashed into the fort and took command, while Cook joined his own men in the rifle pits.

Thomas Harston and the other men of the Third may have had second thoughts about their commander's boastful defiance—another brigade, General Richardson's Tennesseans, arrived to back up the Texans. The Third Colored and Eleventh Illinois, numbering about fifteen hundred men, faced a besieging force of five thousand.

For the next four days the rebels contented themselves with lobbing an occasional shell at the redoubt and testing the Union outposts. The eighty black troopers in the rifle pits were able to prevent the rebels from bringing their artillery close enough to level the fort, but they had to endure nerve-racking fire from rebel sharpshooters. They were the first line of defense, and their comrades inside the fort kept a protective watch over them. When the Confederates tried to storm the pits, a detachment of the Third burst from the redoubt at full gallop and drove the rebels off.

Nighttime must have been hard on the men in that no-man's-land between the lines, exposed and vulnerable. They would have heard the inevitable taunts and threats from the enemy side. But the other sound they would have heard was singing. It was the custom of the colored troops to sing at night around their campfires, so from the walls of the redoubt looming behind them, the men in the rifle pits would have heard the comforting sounds of their comrades' voices raised in song. One of

157

the favorites of the colored troops was a spiritual they had sung as slaves, "My Lord, What a Mornin'." It spoke of a dawn when they would awake to find slavery ended; but it also told of the long night of struggle that would lead up to it, when "the stars begin to fall." The song sprang up among the slaves after a fearsome meteor shower struck the South for three days and three nights in 1833. Each day ten thousand meteors streaked down, some in balls of fire as large and bright as the moon. Whites and blacks alike were amazed and shaken with fear, because it seemed to be the fulfillment of a prediction in the Book of Matthew: "As soon as the distress of those days has passed, the sun will be darkened, the moon will not give her light, the stars will fall from the sky, the celestial powers will be shaken." Accounts of the event appeared in the oral histories of the slaves, who saw it as an unmistakable omen of a war that would free them. A slave from Virginia remembered, "Then the stars commenced a shootin'. A great big star over in the east come right down almost to the earth. . . . It was a sign of war." He said the slaves were glad to see it—"so glad God sendin' war." They made that event into a spiritual, which they sang in the fields and later in the camps, when they were soldiers fighting the war the song had foretold.

Just when it seemed that the Yankees had managed to engineer a stalemate at Yazoo City, the rebel commanders decided to bring matters to a head. At dawn on the fifth day of the siege, the Texas Brigade unleashed a furious artillery barrage against the redoubt, while the Tennesseans stormed into the town. Aided by civilians potshotting at the Yankees from rooftops, Richardson's Tennessee Brigade drove back the federal rear guard, including the Eighth Louisiana Colored Infantry, in vicious street fighting. In short order the rebels gained control of Yazoo City and chased off the federal gunboat guarding the river. The redoubt's defenders were now entirely cut off.

Holding the upper hand, Ross sent a final ultimatum—immediate and unconditional surrender or he would take the fort by storm. In such a situation, he said, "he would be unable to restrain his men." He was presenting McKee with a clear choice—fight for the sake of the black troops, or surrender and save everyone's lives, white and black. In a dispatch to his superiors, Ross made no secret of his intentions: "I would not recognize negroes as soldiers, or guarantee them nor their officers protection as such." It was a shrewd strategy, calculated to make any white commander hesitate to go into the field with black troops, if he faced the constant prospect of having to surrender to prevent their being slaughtered. "You know how it will be," the Confederate emissary said ominously. McKee replied that if the battle resumed under those conditions, his troops too would fight under the black flag—"I would kill every man that fell into my hands." McKee made sure his remarks were heard by his men, and he had the effect he intended. One of the troopers muttered to a friend, "He don't scare a God damn."

After rejecting the rebel ultimatum McKee called out the order: "Fix bayonets!" It was the first time in the siege the defenders had heard that order. It meant that there would be no surrender—the commander expected a fight to the death. In his diary, trooper Henry Uptmor described the moment when the defenders took their positions along the parapets. "Suddenly," he wrote, "there came from Yazoo City a loud alarm of war." The black Louisiana infantry, which Ross had reported as beaten and cowed, along with a company of the Eleventh Illinois, had come back to rescue their comrades in the redoubt. The men launched a systematic attack on Richardson's Tennessee Brigade in the town. Two steamers hove into view, their decks bristling with more black troopers of the Eighth Louisiana. Not waiting for the reinforcements to disembark, the relief force charged into the Tennesseans while a naval gun pounded the town. The Tennesseans turned and ran, which sparked panic in the Texans.

McKee ran from the gate of the fort with a handful of infantrymen and charged the Texans. On his heels came two companies of the Third Colored Cavalry at full gallop. A young lieutenant, racing forward with McKee, called out, "Boys, they are running, they are running!"—then a bullet to the head cut him down. As the colored troops of the Eighth Louisiana swarmed around the fort, the Confederates scattered into the back country.

Both sides admitted that the black soldiers had turned the tide. One Illinois officer wrote with admiration of the black troops, "Scarcely a man of them skulked away, as did several of the white soldiers who made their way as fast as possible." Ross himself was forced to admit in his report, "The negroes who had run down to the river in the commencement of the fight returned and pressed our forces so hard that we were compelled to withdraw." A captured rebel officer was heard to mutter that the black troops "didn't know when they were whipped."

There may have been another element that led to the rebels' defeat. Some of the Southerners had lost their stomach for the kind of war Sul Ross wanted to wage. Ross's Texans were a prickly sort, not afraid to threaten mutiny when their commander displeased them. A historian of the Texas Brigade pointed out that "some of Ross's own men were re-volted by the implications of his grim warning" to McKee about prisoners. A letter from one of the Texans reports that "the news got out that Ross would show no Quarter to prisoners. . . . This caused a great deal of dis-satisfaction among our boys. You would hear it in Every Camp—*Damned if I don't leave if this prisoner Killing is not stopped.*"

But the prisoner killing did not stop. The next month sixteen men of the Third were executed after being captured. In April 1864 the "prisoner killing" culminated in the notorious massacre at Fort Pillow, Tennessee, where Confederate cavalry under General Nathan Bedford Forrest cap-tured about 225 black troops and a roughly equal number of whites. For-rest denied that anyone had been killed after surrendering, but two-thirds of the black troops, and one-third of the white, did not come out alive. The commander of U.S. colored troops in Tennessee scoffed at Forrest's denial and wrote to Washington, "If this is to be the game of the enemy they will soon learn that it is *one at which two can play.*"

The anger and bitterness over Fort Pillow were especially sharp for the officers and men of the Third, who had barely escaped a similar fate at Yazoo City. The whites and blacks of the Third felt extraordinary loyalty to each other; so when one of their number was threatened, they reacted with a harshness that, even in war, was regrettable. One of the army's less pleasant duties in Mississippi was the confiscation of rebel cotton. The officers regarded it as little more than legalized theft and a distinctly unmilitary activity, but the revenue for the government was so great that the army was compelled to do it, willing or not. Like many units, the Third sometimes had to transport and protect civilian cotton traders sent from headquarters in Memphis, including one named Woo-ten, who was a Confederate in everything but uniform. He despised his black protectors. When word reached the unit of the massacre at Fort Pillow, Wooten loudly made known his approval.

One night Wooten came upon a black sentinel chatting with a woman, and he threatened to cut the soldier's throat. The sentinel duly reported the incident to his superior, who brought it to the attention of Major Cook, who was in charge of the regiment in the absence of Colonel Osband. The major did not view the matter lightly—indeed, he took Wooten at his word. He had Wooten arrested and brought on board the unit's steamer, where Cook called together the line officers of the regiment and reported that a death threat had been made against an enlisted man. The officers convened a court-martial, heard testimony, and found Wooten guilty of attempting to impede the war effort. The sentence for this infraction was death. The next morning the steamer put ashore, and with the entire regiment assembled, Wooten was hanged from a telegraph pole.

The master and the former slave, Peter Hairston and Thomas Harston, never faced each other directly in battle, but they were antagonists nonetheless. In the broad tapestry of events, the success of one brought the other low. I found that, late in the Civil War, Thomas's cavalry troop embarked on a campaign to cut off the supplies of a Confederate general who planned to march north and prop up the sagging Confederate defense in Virginia, where Peter Hairston was fighting. In November of 1864, Confederate general John Bell Hood, based in Alabama, assembled an army to strike the federal stronghold at Nashville, Tennessee. His ultimate plan, however, was to make a powerful thrust beyond Tennessee, either to join Lee or to march farther north and compel Grant to give up the siege of Richmond. No federal army could prevent Hood from reaching Tennessee; but the Union forces in Mississippi could do the next best thing—they could destroy the rail lines that provided Hood his reinforcements and supplies.

Thomas Harston's unit, the Third Colored Cavalry, rode out of Vicksburg at daybreak November 23, as part of a 2,200-man strike force. Confederate scouts, watching Vicksburg for just such a move, set fires in the fields to signal their forces in the interior that an attack was under way. The burning grass sent up dense clouds of smoke visible for fifteen miles. The raiders reached the Big Black River and made their way north along its banks until they were close to their goal, the bridge carrying the Mississippi Central Railroad over the river at a place called Way's Bluff. The position was regarded as almost impregnable. It was protected by two wooden stockades, one at each end of the bridge. The bridge was twenty-five feet above the river, which at that point wound through swamps and almost impenetrable canebrakes. Twice before, federal raiders had tried to destroy this bridge and had been driven back. One of the units that had failed was the Third's old comrades-in-arms, the Eleventh Illinois. The officers of the Eleventh thought the job could not be done without artillery, which was impossible to bring up in that terrain. They reckoned that a direct charge against the bridge would cost one hundred men. As one of the officers of the Third later wrote, "It was well known to the

district commander that the bridge could only be taken by the most determined bravery and the sacrifice of many lives." The commander called
for Major Cook and told him that his Third Colored Cavalry had drawn
the task of destroying the bridge. The major regarded the assignment as
a compliment to the Third's reputation. Cook, however, had no interest
in wasting the lives of his men, so he hatched a plan.

Late in the day on November 27, Cook and a few handpicked men
made their way along the tracks until they were in sight of the bridge.
They were reminded again of how difficult their mission was when they
saw the battle scars on the bridge—timbers blackened and bullet-torn
from the previous assaults. With a shout they ran forward, peppering the
near stockade with gunfire. The rebel garrison fired back. Cook's men
withdrew, ran forward again, and then pulled back again under heavy fire.
This time the rebels came out to pursue them. At this point Cook turned
to his bugler—I could only assume that this bugler was Thomas Harston,
who had been with Cook's company since the formation of the Third—
and gave him a signal. The bugler sounded a blast that caused the surrounding swamps and forest to erupt in yells and gunfire. While Cook
and his party had been playing cat and mouse with the garrison, the rest
of the Third had been wading waist-deep through the surrounding swamp
until they had reached the bridge from below. At the sound of the bugle
they opened fire and clambered up the slope to the bridge itself.

"If a thunderbolt had cleft the earth at their feet they could not have
been more dumbfounded," wrote one of the Third's officers, describing
the reaction of the rebels. They ran back toward their stockade, but they
could see chips flying from the walls as the Third laid down a withering
fire to keep the rebels from entering. The rebels ran across the bridge
toward the other stockade, with Cook and his men in pursuit, jumping
from one tie to the next. A relentless covering fire from the Third kept
the defenders' heads down inside the stockade until Cook and his charg-
ing party burst inside. In hand-to-hand fighting they drove out the garrison and took possession of the bridge.

Thomas and the other troopers were all carrying kerosene in their
canteens. Moving as quickly as they could with the rebels potshotting at
them from the woods, the troopers emptied their canteens on the timbers
and piled brush on the bridge. But no sooner had they tossed torches onto
the bridge and seen the flames rise, than bullets came whistling up from
below. A rebel relief force, alerted by the smoke signals outside of Vicks-

burg, had come up and caught the Third in an exposed position. With the job done, Cook ordered everyone off the bridge.

As they made their escape, the troopers had the satisfaction of looking over their shoulders to see smoke rising from the bridge. But in short order the smoke waned, then stopped. The rebels had extinguished the fire and saved the bridge. The mission had not been accomplished. The Third had failed for the first time.

The officers of the regiment took credit for what happened next, but in reading the account it seemed to me that the idea could only have come from the men themselves. As former slaves, they had spent their lives doing hard labor, much of it in gangs. They knew at a glance, looking up and down their ranks and taking the measure of their strength, what they could do all together if they set themselves to it. They laid down their weapons, and as one man, the five hundred troopers of Thomas Harston's unit bent down and ripped the railroad tracks from the earth. They lifted them up and hurled them into the swamp. This part of Hood's lifeline was broken.

More work remained to be done. Hood's army, beaten back from Nashville in mid-December 1864, trudged south to regroup and replenish itself. It was vital to ensure that no supplies of any kind reach them. Accordingly, the federal high command in Washington ordered General Benjamin Grierson, who had won fame for a wide-ranging cavalry raid during the Vicksburg campaign, to assemble another strike force to destroy the remaining lines in Mississippi and Alabama. Grierson dispatched a fast packet boat to summon the Third Colored Cavalry from Vicksburg.

Thomas Harston's unit formed part of Grierson's 3,500-man expeditionary force, which wreaked terrible destruction on Mississippi. On their sixteen-day raid the strike force defeated Nathan Bedford Forrest's cavalry, destroyed 20,000 feet of bridges, 100 miles of track, 95 railcars, 300 wagons, and 32 warehouses. The Third was often in the vanguard of the assault. One after-action report stated that "too much praise cannot be awarded . . . the 3rd United States Colored Cavalry. They alone repulsed several desperate charges."

Hood ordered that attempts be made to repair the damage, but it was too late. His army staggered south, desperately hunting supplies. "We expected to draw clothing at Corinth," wrote one of Hood's soldiers, "but there was none for us." Farther south their rations gave out. Hood released some men temporarily so they could fend for themselves and then come back. But they did not come back. The last hope for a "second front" vanished as Hood's army melted away.

No relief reached the battered Confederates in Virginia, where Peter Hairston was fighting out the last act of the war in the winter of 1865. His kinsman and brother-in-law, General Jeb Stuart, had died a cavalryman's death in battle, shot while commanding his troops outside of Richmond in May 1864. (The epitome of the dashing, fearless cavalier, Stuart had ridden into his last battle singing, "Soon with angels I'll be marching." At word of the beloved Stuart's death, a staff officer wrote, "Brave men bowed their heads and wept like children.") By 1865, Peter Hairston was fighting in the command of another relative, his cousin General Jubal Early, trying to hold the Valley of Virginia for the Confederacy with 1,200 worn-out, ragged men. In March 1865, a month before the South's surrender, they were defending Rockfish Gap in the Blue Ridge Mountains west of Charlottesville. Huddled behind piles of fence rails with a cold drizzle falling on them, they grimly awaited an attack. The federal officers against them, Generals Phil Sheridan and George Armstrong Custer, commanded about ten thousand men "thoroughly equipped in every detail," including the deadly Spencer repeating carbines. From their vantage on a ridge, Jubal Early and Peter watched as three regiments of Custer's men probed their left flank. The federals were heading toward a gap in Early's line. Early sent a messenger with orders to fill the gap immediately, but it was already too late. Custer's men attacked on the left, while a Yankee brigade hit the center. Exhausted, cold, and outnumbered almost ten to one, the Confederates ran. Peter and the rest of the officers made one final attempt to rally the troops at a bridge, but the game was up. The swiftly moving federal cavalry cut off most of Early's command.

The Hairston cousins, Peter and Early, fled the battlefield. They made their way to the mountains of southwestern Virginia, where Early hoped to receive reinforcements and new orders from General Lee. Instead, there came a telegram relieving him of his command. Early left for his home, but along the way he came down with pneumonia. He was jouncing painfully along a country road in an ambulance when a rider stopped him to convey the news that Robert E. Lee had surrendered at Appomattox. To Early, it was news of the end of the world. Groaning with pain and cursing, he yelled out bitterly, "Blow your horn, Gabriel!"

Peter galloped to Oak Hill, just outside of Danville, to be with his family at the end. The landscape he left behind was, he said, "a complete desolation—it has truly been a war of extermination." He had thought that Oak Hill would be a safer place for his wife and his children than Cooleemee, which was isolated. On his last visit to Cooleemee, Peter had hinted to one of his favored slaves, a wagon driver who had been allowed to earn money on his own, that the old order was coming to an end, and that he should be prepared for a catastrophe that would make the most common daily items suddenly precious. Peter asked the slave if he had any money saved up.

"A little," replied the wagon driver.

"Go and buy something with it."

"Buy what?"

"Buy anything you can find—sugar, cloth, no matter what."

Peter was wrong when he thought that the region around Danville would be a safe place to hide. He had no way of knowing that Confederate president Jefferson Davis would flee from Richmond to Danville, with a federal army of twenty-six thousand men in pursuit. At the same time, a separate federal column under General George Stoneman was tearing through central Virginia and making its way toward Martinsville. Jefferson Davis lingered in Danville only a week, staying at the mansion of the banker and slave-trade financier William Sutherlin, before fleeing south and leaving Danville in the hands of Confederate deserters, who systematically looted the place. Eighty of them were in the arsenal, grabbing weapons and filling bags with gunpowder, when some fool struck a match and the building went up in a ball of orange flame. At Oak Hill they would have heard a strange, distant thump, then silence, and from the upper floor they might have been able to see a dense cloud of smoke spreading up from the Last Capital.

The shock of defeat filled some whites with rage, a rage they turned on the blacks. A Hairston woman wrote in a letter that the bodies of seven black men had been found in Danville with their throats cut. Uncounted others, she reported, were being shot and hanged. Supposedly they had been killed for stealing, but there were new categories of crime now, established by embittered Southerners. A letter in the Hairston papers said, "Scales killed a man for impudence last week—shot him down."

The countryside was in upheaval, the roads clogged with freed slaves, some leaving plantations by their own choice, some driven off by former owners who wanted nothing more to do with them. The Union army had orders to force the freedpeople back to the plantations, and to force the planters to feed them. Troops closed the road to Richmond, already engulfed by refugees. Women and children were dragging about in every direction. The Yankee army driving on Danville had its progress slowed by crowds of freed slaves who came out to greet it. In one spot an old man stood by the road with his family, all of them singing and shouting the praises of the vast "Delivering Army"—more numerous, they cried, than "the hosts of David." A Yankee officer on horseback waved at the throngs of people who had not been a hundred hours out of slavery. "You are free now!" he shouted. "You can have anything you want!"

A letter written by a Hairston cousin named Sara Penn contained a vivid account of the abrupt advent of the Delivering Army. In mid-April 1865, Sara happened to be in front of her house at one in the afternoon when a figure came dashing up to the gate. It was the devil she had long feared—a soldier in a U.S. uniform. Until that moment, in the last month of the war, the fighting had not touched Hairston country. This solitary soldier seemed to have dropped from the sky.

The soldier called out to her. Could he get something to eat? She told him to wait by the gate while she went inside and fixed a plate of ham and biscuits. The soldier must have sensed her fear because he stayed patiently outside the gate, not inviting himself to the house or even the porch, and ate his food standing in the road. He struck up a conversation, speaking politely, which put Sara at ease so she was not looking around until some sound or a flicker of a shadow made her glance over his shoulder. "I looked down the road and it was blue with them as far as the eye could search."

A great wave of men rolled down the road, through the gate, into the yard, depositing a group of chattering officers on the front porch. They were Pennsylvanians, they said, as she gave them seats. One was "a nice, clean looking man," about thirty years old. He was General Parsons from Philadelphia; the gentlemen with him were his staff. The Yankees were impressed by the region—"a fine section of the country," they thought. They were pleased to see the heartland of the Virginia aristocrats, and even happier at the abundance of tobacco; all their soldiers, as she could see, were smoking "very fair cigars." Sara Penn offered them some brandy. The general politely refused, but this offer seemed to amuse his staff, who began chuckling among themselves. The general explained that he knew already of a large store of good brandy and had sent some men to get it.

He did not say that the brandy he had in mind was part of the Confederate medical supply, which they were on their way to pillage.

In gratitude for Sara's kindness, Parsons ordered that a guard be posted at her house while the army passed, and then he left and rejoined his column. True to the general's word, guards stood by the fence, preventing any stragglers from touching Sara's house or her livestock, lingering there until the rear of the column passed, vanishing down the road like the Assyrian host. In a twinkling, it seemed, the war was over in a burst of blue-coated courtesy.

But later that night there was a fierce banging on the door. Sara ran to open it and discovered a stout, rough-looking Yankee. He was drunk. He swaggered through the door, followed by a short man, his sidekick in adventure. The large man called for a candle; he was going to search the house. Sara told him she had not two dollars in the house, but with the short man carrying the candle they nosed around and finally marched her into her bedroom and ordered her to open the bureau drawer. The drunk turned to his short companion and told him to search the drawer as he himself would not touch a woman's things. They found nothing among her underwear, so the Yankees went outside to the plantation office, from which Sara could hear the sounds of glass and wood being smashed. A small knot of men appeared in the yard, fellow stragglers, along with a black man who had been dragooned to be their guide. Sara appealed to them for help. A light-haired Yankee took pity on her; he said he would not allow the drunk to disturb her further or to enter the house again. He said he would "spill his blood before they should disturb her any more." The light-haired man led some of his companions into the office and fetched the drunk, whom they led away without further violence, carrying a motley booty of clothes and sheets.

Other cousins did not get off so lightly: "We are now in the Yankee Lines and power," one woman wrote. "The raiders have been at Jeff Penn's—burnt the Gov't meat & all their clothes, everything but what Catherine had on was burnt—their trunks were in the woods where the Bacon was hid & they set fire to it & burnt all . . . they are a terrible foe."

The passage of the Yankees threw the whites into panic. They hastily buried their jewelry, silver, clothing, and food; they drove their horses into the woods; they concealed meat and corn by the wagonload in re- mote barns, wrapping hams in moss so they would look like moss-covered rocks. But the raiders seemed to appear everywhere at once and found willing informers among freed slaves and among whites who wished to ingratiate themselves with the victors or to settle old scores. A friend of the Hairstons' buried his silver, only to have one of his neighbors lead the Yankees to the hiding place. At Martinsville the Yankees destroyed corn and brandy and tore up some documents in the courthouse, but did not burn any buildings. So much bacon was stored at Martinsville that the Yankees couldn't carry it all off. They loaded it onto wagons, which they rolled into the woods and burned—an act of pure vindictiveness against a people already defeated and soon to face starvation.

With the Yankees rampaging through the Hairstons' part of Virginia and North Carolina, one of the Hairston slaves—then actually a free man—carried out a final service to the man who had been his master. John Goolsby, the coachman of Cooleemee Plantation, had accompanied Peter Hairston throughout his combat in the war, acting as Peter's valet and groom. (At one point early in the war, Goolsby actually grabbed a musket to fight off an expected Yankee attack that never materialized.) Sometime in April 1865, Goolsby galloped from Virginia to Cooleemee to save the Hairston family silver from the Yankees—an act that became part of the family lore of the white and black families. Goolsby knew he was risking his life. The federal raiding party under General George Stoneman was pushing rapidly south toward Cooleemee. He had to stay away from them and from any stragglers, who would have no scruples about killing a man hauling a rebel's trunk of silver.

Goolsby made it to Cooleemee ahead of the raiders, loaded the silver into a wagon, and then drove north into the teeth of the Yankee advance to Saura Town Plantation. He buried the silver; but somewhere, someone had observed him and betrayed him to the Yankees. On his way back to Cooleemee a group of mounted Yankees stopped him. They knew what they were looking for—the leader said that they were searching for Major Hairston's coachman. Since the Yankees had not recognized him, Goolsby realized that they did not have a reliable description of him. He kept his wits and said he did not know the man they were looking for. The Yankees resorted to threats. They said that they had heard that the coachman was hiding a load of silver, and that if they found him, they intended to string him up by his thumbs until he revealed the hiding place, and that if the coachman didn't care to give up the silver, they would string him up by his neck.

Goolsby stuck to his story: no, he did not know the man they were looking for. The Yankees rode off. Goolsby turned his wagon around and headed north into Virginia, where he hid in the attic of Chatmoss, the plantation of Peter's sister Alcey.

Goolsby left no clear explanation of what he did; he probably felt that it needed no explanation. He could not refuse his former master in a time of danger. After the war, a Northern woman who came to Virginia to perform charitable work heard stories of slaves risking their lives to protect their master's families and was astonished by them. As someone who hated slavery, she simply could not understand the loyalty of the slaves. So she asked one of them about it, and he replied, "Often we left our own wives and children during the war in order to take care of the wives and children of our absent masters. And why did we do this? Because they were helpless and afraid, while our families were better able to take care of themselves, and had no fear."

It might seem easy now to mock the patience, loyalty, and sense of duty displayed by some of the slaves, except that—in order to survive— African-Americans have always had to be stronger than the system that oppressed them. They learned that lesson in slavery and in what came after.

I wondered why no one in the family had ever mentioned anything about Thomas Harston. It was odd that he had been so thoroughly forgotten. He was, as far as I could determine, the only black Hairston who had served the Union cause in any significant way. Several others had joined up at the very end of the war, but had been detailed to labor units. But Thomas was a hero, and in his old age he must have been a fount of stories about escaping from slavery to fight for freedom and the Union. Where were his grandchildren and great-grandchildren? As I looked into his story, I discovered the kind of reward this country bestowed upon Thomas Harston and the other colored troops for their heroism.

Thomas was mustered out of service at Fort Pickering in Memphis in 1866. That city, like Vicksburg, had been a magnet for freed slaves during the war. The black population had soared from fewer than four thousand in 1860 to more than sixteen thousand in 1865. Blacks formed a solid majority of the citizens after the war, but they were still unable to vote.

The veterans of the colored troops took a leading role in Tennessee after the war. Having served their country and having emerged the victors, they were not inclined to take a backseat and wait patiently for the old power structure to grant them rights they knew were "inalienable."

One former sergeant declared at a political meeting, "We want the rights guaranteed by the Infinite Architect. For these rights we labor. For them we will die. We have gained one; the uniform is its badge. We want two more besides the cartridge box—the ballot and the jury box. We shall gain them."

The blacks had to struggle against two groups, the Southern whites who had difficulty accepting the new status of the former slaves, and a group of newcomers—Irish immigrants. In the first Memphis election after the war, the Irish staged a political coup. With many white males who had served in the Confederate army forbidden to vote, the Irish stepped into the void and elected an Irish mayor, who appointed an Irish police force and fire department. The Irish and the blacks were both on the way up the economic ladder, competing in many spheres of the city's business life. They resented each other. In slavery time plantation owners hired Irish immigrants to perform tasks too dangerous for valuable slaves to do. Some blacks looked on the Irish with contempt: "I think he is very much below me," one former slave said of the Irishman.

Small incidents escalated murderously in 1866. Two black soldiers on a train refused to yield their seats to a white man. The white drew a gun; the blacks drew theirs and shot him. At the next station a gang of whites dragged the blacks off the train and lynched one of them.

Although many blacks owned their own businesses or worked at regular jobs, many could not find work. The black leadership in Memphis endorsed efforts by the city and federal governments to relocate "idle, vagrant, and worthless blacks" to the distant countryside, where they were forcibly hired out on farms. But black leaders drew the line when the authorities announced a large-scale program to round up and relocate up to six thousand black people—almost a quarter of the city's entire population. The federal government stated that Memphis "will not be disgraced by a single black vagrant. Surplus blacks will be relocated to the countryside." A Memphis newspaper stated its wishes more bluntly: "Would to God they were back in Africa."

The police began a strict-enforcement policy of the city's traffic laws and ordinances against cursing, disorderly conduct, fighting, and wife-beating. Nearly all of the defendants were indigent and black. Under the new policy, plantation owners could pay the fines of the convicted and gain their labor for extended periods. One entire family was shipped to Missouri when they could not come up with a $15 fine.

The black troopers—some still in active service and some who had been discharged—decided to put a stop to the relocations. They interfered with arrests. Under military authority they began arresting white vagrants. They beat police officers. They made it known that any black man threatened with arrest could find protection in South Memphis, where many former soldiers had their homes. The police soon hesitated to enter that district.

The commander of the army post at Memphis, General John E. Smith, was one of the chief architects of the relocation program. But after repeated complaints from his black troopers and their white officers, he started an investigation of racial conditions in the city. He concluded that "provocations are frequently given the colored soldiers and resented by them. Their general deportment has been respectful and orderly. The fact cannot be concealed that the negro soldiers . . . and the political freedom of the black are new conditions repugnant to the ancient prejudice of the South." He also said that some groups in the city were determined to provoke "an outbreak among the colored people," and he singled out the mostly Irish police force, "who are animated by a peculiar hatred and jealousy of the colored people."

The black community staged a large celebration on April 30, 1866, when the last colored troop units were discharged from Fort Pickering. Policemen and white idlers watched the event, exchanging insults with the veterans. When the blacks called for three cheers in salute of "Ole Abe Lincoln, the Great Emancipator," the whites shouted back, "Your father Abe Lincoln is dead and damned." What would have been only a war of words became violent when the police decided to go looking for a fugitive in the celebratory crowd. Soldiers punched a policeman and pulled the fugitive away. After a brief brawl the two sides separated and the incident might have ended there, except that as the whites were retreating from the black neighborhood, an Irish fireman fell dead from a gunshot.

As word of the shooting spread, the white community boiled over. Police and firemen joined with thugs and criminals to form a "posse" that poured into South Memphis to "kill the last damn one of the nigger race, and burn up the cradle, God damn them." The posse hit the black community as it slept, breaking into homes and burning them, beating the men and raping the women. Schools and churches went up in flames. In the history of American racial violence, there is little to match the savagery of the Memphis riot. The rioters set fire to one house with the people still in it, then stood outside shooting the occupants as they tried to get out. The mob shot a teenaged girl on the doorstep. She fell across the threshold, wounded but unable to crawl away. With the mob holding back rescuers at gunpoint, they watched as the girl burned to death.

The soldiers of the colored troops had relinquished their arms the day before. Now they rushed to Fort Pickering to demand weapons to protect their families. The officer in charge ordered his troops to fire over the heads of the black veterans to drive them off. Despite the pleas of black leaders, the post's new commanding officer, General George Stoneman, refused to send white troops to quell the riot. The violence continued for a second day and subsided only when Stoneman relented and placed the city under martial law. When military and congressional investigators looked into the causes of the riot, they focused on the shooting of the Irish fireman that had touched off the violence. It turned out that the Irishman had been quite swarthy, and another Irishman had shot him, taking him for a mulatto. The shooter confessed, "I have made a mistake, I thought it was a damned yellow nigger."

Memphis moved forward. In the aftermath of the riot the state government took control of the police department and announced a strict disciplinary code. Among the first people arrested by the reformed department were the mayor and the former chief judge of the police court. Two hundred black carpenters went to work rebuilding South Memphis. To mark the renaissance of their community and to show their determination to join the city's mainstream, the blacks marched en masse in the city's Fourth of July parade, despite the reluctance of the Irish politicians. After the parade the blacks filed off to enjoy their own Independence Day picnic and dance. There was no violence. A few weeks later the community gathered to elect delegates to a statewide convention to press for equal rights immediately. The state assembly passed a civil rights bill recognizing the political equality of blacks, with the exception of voting. That right was recognized for black males the following year.

Despite the easing of tensions in Memphis, friction remained between the white community and the former colored troopers. Having won their freedom on the battlefield, the veterans were quick to assert their rights. To the Irish newcomers and the defeated Confederates, the prickly pride of the black veterans was galling. General Stoneman sized up the situation and offered to pay the transportation costs of any former troopers and their families who wished to leave to make a new life elsewhere. "They have been stationed here a long time," Stoneman said, "and are very much disliked by the lower classes of people whom they have had to control here."

I looked through the masses of postwar records to see what had happened to Thomas, who had been mustered out of the service in Memphis. He was not among the fourteen black soldiers killed in the riot, nor did his name turn up among the hundreds of affidavits filed by survivors. I searched the military records and found nothing—no pension request, no bounty claim, no claim for back pay. I looked in the census records of twenty states and found no trace. I turned to the research of black genealogists for some clue. Their research revealed that many of the soldiers had changed their names after the war, shedding their slave names. The records of their pension requests often state "formerly known as . . ." It became impossible to trace many of these soldiers. Of course, the soldiers did not know that more than a century later others would come looking for them, to resurrect the stories of the heroes who risked their lives during and after the war for the rights "guaranteed by the Infinite Architect." Taking advantage of Stoneman's relocation program, they scattered themselves to the winds. Before Thomas mustered out, he bought a Remington pistol with his soldier's pay. Did he and Annie disappear out West? I found his wife's name, Annie Harston, in Texas, but the rest of the information about her didn't match up with what I knew. He was gone, vanished—leaving, as Faulkner wrote, "no bones nor dust anywhere." He was nowhere and everywhere, one of the thousands of black soldiers who dispersed through the country to become farmers, ranchers, teachers, and builders, carrying with them the memory of victory. Wherever Thomas went, he probably had his old bugle with him, and I wondered if he remembered the spiritual that the troopers used to sing in their camps. It had a verse that spoke to the war they were waging then and the long campaign that unfolded later: "You'll hear the trumpet sound to wake the nation's underground—My Lord, what a mornin'!"

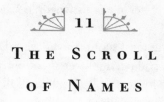

THE SCROLL

OF NAMES

The story of Thomas Harston had come to light because of a chance discovery—I had found his name in a marriage register in Jackson, Mississippi. After finding his name, I went looking for more marriage records to trace the roots of the Hairstons I had met at the reunion in Baltimore. A footnote in *The Black Family in Slavery and Freedom*, a seminal work by Herbert Gutman about African-American families, led me back to Henry County, Virginia, in search of an elusive document from the time of Emancipation.

The clerk at the Henry County courthouse was helpful, but puzzled when I told her I was looking for something called the cohabitation register. She had never heard of such a thing. I told her everything I knew about it. Just after the Civil War, black marriages in Virginia had been recorded in documents called cohabitation registers. Herbert Gutman had found registers from four Virginia counties in the National Archives. The others had been lost or had never been taken in the first place. The records from the counties where the Hairstons lived were among the missing. For black families seeking their origins, the marriage register was often the best hope they had of penetrating what they called "the wall of slavery." The registers listed the names of husbands, wives, and children, giving the ages of all, and the names of their former masters. By studying these records carefully, a researcher could resurrect extended families and find clues for pursuing the search further into slavery time itself. One problem was that the searchers had no idea what the records actually looked like. At another archive I had met an African-American scholar, Professor Barnetta White, who had spent years searching courthouses, libraries, and churches for marriage records. She told me that in some counties the record consisted of a pile of paper strips kept in a folder. In other counties the black marriages had been entered at the back of another ledger. Professor White said that when she went to a courthouse, she took every old ledger she could find, flipped it over, turned it upside down, and opened it. In some places the marriage record had ended up in the care of a local black church many decades ago, perhaps because the county clerk had been about to throw it out.

If the Henry County register had somehow survived but had been mislaid, the most likely place to search for it was the county courthouse. The clerk said she was certain the county archive didn't have the document—everything was catalogued, she said—but she patiently made a thorough search anyway. We looked in every possible nook, including the vault where the most valuable items were kept. Without success, I tried Professor White's technique of reading old ledgers backward. I left the courthouse empty-handed and decided to try my luck a few blocks away at the library.

When I posed my question to a reference librarian, he said that the library had no old documents beyond a few nineteenth-century newspapers. Not wanting my visit to be a total loss, I explained that I was looking for information about black Hairstons and asked if there was an index to the obituaries in the local newspaper. "You won't find any of *those* people in the obituaries," he said dismissively. I found the index and looked anyway. In fact there were several obituaries for black Hairstons in earlier decades, mostly of the "Beloved Old Slave Departs This Life" sort.

Another librarian had overheard my question and the response it got. I was hunched over the microfilm reader when she came over to me and said I should visit a small library out in the country in the town of Bassett, about ten miles west of Martinsville. It had a substantial local-history collection, she said—a collection that many black people from the area had used and contributed to.

The Bassett Public Library was indeed tiny—a brick building by a creek on a narrow road that abruptly swept up into the wild hills of the western part of Henry County. At the back of the library, in a genealogy room crammed with books of family history and cartons of documents, I met an archivist named Pat Ross. She knew the Hairston families quite well and immediately pulled out a box of material about the white Hairstons. As I was examining the papers, Ross began to assemble some material on black genealogy for me. I mentioned idly that it was a shame that the Henry County cohabitation register was lost.

"No, it's not," she said. "I have it right here." She stepped over to a shelf and pulled down a binder. It held a typescript about 150 pages long.

I was dumbfounded. Almost shaking with excitement, I scanned through the pages as Ross narrated the strange tale of this document.

In 1975, a group of volunteers and officials of the Clerk of Court for Henry County had been clearing trash and old boxes from the ancient jail in Martinsville when they found, tossed into a corner, a thick scroll of parchment. The sheets had been carefully lined, and on the sheets of the scroll, in an elegant Victorian script, full of curls and flourishes, were inscribed about three thousand names. Many were names of the leading families of the county—Penn, Gravely, Dillard, Hairston—names that in 1975 still adorned the signs of the county's businesses. But many of the given names were unfamiliar to the modern ear and testified to the exotic antiquity of the document: there was a Shober, a Pelisia, Ithey, Celestia, Askly, and Enidine. There was a Grul, Ras, Aggy, Gency, Viney, Isam, Littelberry, Quince. And Solomon, Sampson, Hezekiah, and Dorcas; Caesar and Pompey; a Columbus and nine Americas. It seemed to be a census of some kind, but it was not something the county had done; and none of the officials who now came to peer at this document had ever seen anything like it, and no one could say how this scroll had come to rest in a corner of the jail, among the old and useless documents called the Dead Papers. When they unfurled the scroll fully, they found a sheet with a title inscribed in large letters: REGISTER OF COLORED PERSONS OF HENRY COUNTY STATE OF VIRGINIA COHABITING TOGETHER AS HUS-BAND AND WIFE 1866. Below the title was the signature of William L. Fernald. Although much about the document was unknown, the discov-erers recognized that it had some importance, so they transcribed it, which was fortunate because when the scroll was handed back to the county government for storage, it vanished.

Over a century before, in August 1866, word spread through the black community in Henry County that the federal government intended to register the marriages that had begun in slavery time. A day had been set when people could come to the courthouse in Martinsville, where Lieu-tenant Fernald, an officer of the Freedmen's Bureau, would take down the names of husbands, wives, and their children. This was momentous news because even after Emancipation, the marriages of slaves had no legal substance. Husbands and wives who might have been together for twenty years were merely "cohabiting" in the eyes of the law, and their children were illegitimate. In the winter of 1866, the Virginia legislature had declared that freedmen and freedwomen who were living together as husband and wife on February 27 would thenceforth be regarded as legally married, and their children would be legitimate. In passing the law, however, the legislature made no provision for registering these old marriages. So the Freedmen's Bureau, charged with monitoring the well-being of the former slaves, took up the task. The commander of the Bureau decreed that his officers make a census of the marriages that had existed among slaves. In keeping with the edict, the great clanking bureaucracy ordered its agents in Virginia to summon the freedpeople and inquire who was married and for how long and who were their offspring.

The officers of the bureau were not enthusiastic about the assignment. Already saddled with writing a host of monthly and semimonthly reports on the state of feelings between blacks and whites, on the amount of rations dispensed to the poor of both races, on the quality of justice meted out to freedpeople, on the condition of the local schools for freedpeople (if there were any), on the condition of the bureau's offices, horses, and anything they had to buy or rent (all leases to be submitted in triplicate), the officers had no interest in more paperwork. Most of the freedpeople could not even write their names, so the officers would have to fill out the registration forms for them, knowing that if they left off any of the required information, they would have to do the whole thing over again. Worse, the planters complained loudly when they heard that their workers might be called away for some trivial business of filling out forms.

Few registrations had been done by August of 1866, and headquarters, growing impatient, dispatched an inspector general to the offices in the isolated parts of central and southern Virginia to get the business done. After a surprise visit to Charlottesville, where at nine in the morning the inspector found the officer in charge too drunk to perform his duties and relieved him on the spot, the inspector made his way 150 miles south to prod the officer in the town of Martinsville, one of the remotest outposts in the empire of the bureaucracy.

At that time Martinsville was an insignificant country village. Mapmakers did not even agree on its name—some called it Martinsville, some called it Henry Court House. Only a couple of hundred people lived in or near it. There were a pair of tiny country stores, twice as many grogshops, two tenpin alleys where gamblers lounged, and a pair of wretched hotels with only a few rooms in each. There were a dozen or so houses and no sidewalks; everywhere there was mud, a foot deep; hogs wallowed in mud holes in every street and slept undisturbed beneath the steps of the Methodist church.

At the center of town, near the courthouse, was the office of Lieutenant William L. Fernald. His presence in Martinsville was the ultimate torment of defeat; he was the very image and sound of the Yankee. This particular affliction had been dropped upon Virginia from the state of Maine; he spoke with the sharpest of New England twangs, in an accent that must have baffled his black clients and grated immeasurably on the ears of the planters. Holding the grand title of Sub Assistant Sub Commissioner of the Bureau of Refugees, Freedmen, and Abandoned Lands for the Seventh District of the State of Virginia, Fernald was responsible for the well-being of the freedpeople of Henry and Patrick Counties. Diligent, energetic, and courageous, he was also a stickler for detail. When the impatient inspector came calling, Fernald explained that he had not conducted the marriage registration because headquarters had not sent him the proper forms. Told now in no uncertain terms to get on with it anyhow, Fernald put his hands on a scroll of heavy paper and proclaimed the day of registration.

He probably didn't expect much response. The Southerners were saying this business of marriage among the blacks was a great joke—"the whites laugh at the very idea of the thing." It would take years of sermonizing, they said, before the freedmen had any notion what a family meant. So one can imagine that Fernald, having lent an ear to this talk, was surprised when he was awakened early in the morning by the rumble and creak of wagons and the expectant murmur of a great and growing throng.

We have the list, so we know who was there at the courthouse when the registration took place. Fernald would have set up a table outside the courthouse, probably in the shade of a tall oak visible in old photographs of the square. Fernald arranged his papers, uncapped his pen, and the long taking of the names commenced. They came forward, each family in turn: Carters, Colemans, Egglestons, Penns, and Redds; the Hollands, Kings, and Martins; but most numerous of all, the Hairstons. Each father stepped up and spoke his name: "I am Shober Hairston, farmer, twenty-five years old, with my wife, Nancy, twenty-three, and daughter Sally Ann, five, and son Mat, four." Now comes Reuben Hairston, twenty-three, with his wife, Fanny, carrying three-month-old Willie. Here is Ras with Charlotte and their Delsy, Sally, and Hardeman. Manuel and Easter Hairston step up, a couple in their fifties. Manuel met Easter over thirty years ago in Mississippi and brought her back to Virginia to be his wife. Together now since 1834, they enter the names of their ten children. This next man and wife have names from the Bible—Hezekiah, the king of Judah whose people were saved when a pestilence struck their enemies, and Dorcas, whom Peter raised from the dead; and Hezekiah and Dorcas have two children.

And now a large family—here are Henry and Barbery Hairston; he is fifty-five and she is forty-nine. Fernald asks what year they "began cohabitation"; they say 1842 and present their children. Rachel was born in 1843, and two years later Anthony, and three years later John, and two years later Joshua, and three years later Gloucester, and two years later Rufus, called Rufe, and four years later Edie, and in the next year Moses, and the next year after that Garms, aged five. Nine children, with the last three in the quickest burst as time was running out for them to put people on this earth—and as it turns out Henry the father would be dead in three years. There is another Henry, aged thirty-one, who comes with his wife. They have been together fourteen years, and there is a twelve-year-old child, but Henry says it is not his—write it down as "wife's child"—but still they are together, so whatever happened he has forgiven. Here is John Goolsby, the man who had buried Cooleemee's silver, with his wife, Athena, known as Theny, and their children—America, Tish, and Nancy. Surry and Esther have come in a cart from Beaver Creek. Among all the farmers and other country people they stand out in their fine clothes, and when Fernald asks Surry his occupation, he responds proudly, "Butler."

Now the old generations approach, the patriarchs, travelers from the distant past. It was said that they were regarded with veneration, "as if they were prophets and seers." Here is Simeon Hairston, born in 1786. He says he was born in Gloucester County, which is not in these parts but in the Tidewater, where they have been planting tobacco 250 years. Simeon can remember the ocean, something these other people of the Piedmont have never seen. In 1840 he married Julia, thirty years younger than he, and Julia bore eight children: Edie, Elick, Simon, Jack, Randolph, Pierson, Saunders, and Gracie. Simeon would live to a great age and suffer one of the sorrows of a long life—he would bury his son Pierson. Grul Hairston, born during the presidency of Washington, has been with Rukey since 1816, and they enter ten children on the scroll.

On and on they come and fill the scroll to bursting with their names:

Samuel and Franky, Garland and Phillis, Pompey and Lucy, Tif and Pelisia—all taking the name Hairston for themselves and their children.
There are marriages of thirty, forty, and fifty years; parents who put thirteen names of children on the roll. They crowd the square to declare
themselves families, to ratify and affirm their connection to each other,
to see it written down and made permanent. The law does not compel
them to come; they are here willingly, to compel the law to recognize
them, to make the law acknowledge and record the families that had long
existed but had until then been outside the concern of the law.

I had read that the days of registration were marked with celebration
and festive music. In the courthouse square there would have been fiddle-
playing to the rhythm of carved bones slapped against the palm, and the
sly and sinuous tones of gourd banjos, homemade with horsehair strings.
As the day slid into darkness, they danced in the square, husbands and
wives bowing and twirling, joining hands and raising up their arms. A
thousand feet tapped the earth in rhythm and made the earth shake to
share the joy.

The strength of family ties in that era was extraordinary. In the years
after the Civil War, thousands of freedpeople went on desperate searches
for lost family members. The Hairstons were among them. In the postwar
letters of Peter Hairston I found an enigmatic account, just a few lines
long, of an epic journey undertaken by a group of black Hairstons from
Virginia. What we know about it comes down to us thirdhand. The black
Hairstons told an overseer about the trek; the overseer described it to
Peter Hairston, and he wrote about it in a letter to his wife. He did not
usually record events in the lives of the black Hairstons, so this journey
must have struck him as astounding.

Some who left and went South have returned. They say they crossed
one big river and got to another they could not see across & they saw
the Sun set in it & people told them if they went across that river
they would be in Cuba & they would sell them. So they concluded
to return. Some of them were drowned in a boat in the Mississippi.

I pulled out a map of the South and tried to get some sense of what
they had done. Since Cuba was on the other side of the "big river" they
could not see across, then the place they had reached, the "big river,"

was the Gulf of Mexico, a direct distance of nearly seven hundred miles from Virginia, and perhaps a few hundred miles more along the meandering route the wanderers presumably took. The letter did not say how many people went on the journey, whether they were all men or if women and children were brought along. They would have set out on foot, perhaps with a wagon to carry supplies they had collected. They probably had little money, if any at all.

The letter says that they had reached the Mississippi River, so from the Gulf they would have headed northwest, walking another five hundred miles, to the Mississippi, which they tried to cross in a boat. Perhaps they lashed together a makeshift raft, just large enough to hold a few people at a time. I could see the first group scrambling aboard, pushing off, and paddling hard against the current. But here, catastrophe struck, and some of them drowned.

We do not know why they attempted such an extraordinary journey. Why would they head directly south if their real intention was to migrate to the West? They must first have gone to the Hairston plantations in Mississippi to find lost relatives—and having gathered their kin, they would have set off in search of western farmlands. No other explanation made sense. But then disaster struck.

In the spring of 1870 they arrived back in Virginia. They had journeyed over two thousand miles and had come home, with their families restored. After a perilous odyssey, they had returned to a homeland equally full of uncertainty and hardship. It is in the American grain to leave behind the old and seek the new, untouched place. But for the people who went to Mississippi and came back, the arc of history was different. Their task was to reclaim an old land—old and burdened with the crimes of previous generations. They had to take possession of a place that had been defiled and purify it. They would renew it by making it their own.

According to accounts in standard history books about Reconstruction, the Hairstons would supposedly have been fortunate. Compared to other parts of the South, the region of Virginia and North Carolina where the Hairstons lived became relatively peaceful; and in the judgment of white historians, race relations were fraught with tension but relatively good. One historian wrote, "The significant fact is not that violence occurred but that there was comparatively little in Virginia. . . . Very few [blacks], if any, were outraged or murdered." He quoted an earlier researcher who asserted, "The great mass of whites felt no bitterness toward the negro for the events of the four preceding years." But in newspaper accounts, government records, the letters of the white Hairstons, the records left by Lieutenant William Fernald, the army officer who had recorded the Hairstons' marriages, and a remarkable set of letters written by a Northern teacher, I began to see a much different history. The Hairstons experienced the birth of America's apartheid. They lived in an atmosphere of extreme hostility and suspicion, with the status of "outlaws," in the oldest meaning of that term—which did not originally mean "criminals," but people outside the protection of the law. They could not get justice; they and their relatives were murdered while the killers went free; their right to marry whom they chose was abrogated; by force and violence they lost the right to vote; and when they sought to improve their lot through education, their teachers were threatened and a school-house was destroyed.

One of the first documents I looked at from the Reconstruction era, a letter in the plantation papers, threatened a group of Hairstons with mass murder. The black people living on the Royal Oak plantation, said the anonymous writer, "shal go to the flames."

> The Negroes at the Royal
> oak plantation must and
> shall leave this country or
> there will not be a house left
> standing upon the place.

The note had been left at Oak Hill plantation in 1868, addressed to the elderly owner, Samuel Hairston, Peter's now senile father, to give him "timely notice" of the planned massacre and an opportunity to prevent it by evicting the black families.

> If you cant move them
> we can and everything else.
> so take warning while you have
> the opportunity.
>
> those vilans that now
> live on the plantation shall
> be burnt to Death if they
> donot move and leave the state.

        we are able to carry out
        our designs we can do so
        and we will do so at an
        unexspected time to you
        remove them and nothing
        will be disturbed   otherwise
        all will be . . . ruin
                        We are many in number

The note characterized the blacks as "a den of thieves" and "villains," without mentioning any specific crime or incident. Since the local court was always ready to impose a harsh sentence on any black for the most trivial of crimes, I could only conclude that no real crime had been committed. The letter also said that the blacks had displayed rascality and meanness, which may have meant that they had been "insolent." The whites probably wanted to get rid of the black Hairstons so they could rent the Royal Oak land themselves. But I found no evidence that any harm befell the Hairstons at Royal Oak in 1868, possibly because the white Hairstons let it be known that they would not tolerate any violence. It would not be surprising if Samuel Hairston or his son Peter had a protective attitude toward the former slaves. One Northern woman who was living in the area at the time said that the blacks were treated most fairly by "the educated gentry," who by tradition looked upon the slaves as "their people," but that the small-scale farmers were for the most part extremely hostile to the freedmen.

Not all the white Hairstons took a kindly view of their former slaves when they abruptly claimed their freedom. Beaver Creek plantation saw a mass exodus at the end of 1865, as all but a handful of black Hairstons left. Ann Hairston recorded the exodus with irritation, and with astonishment that many of the black Hairstons quickly found new employers, while no blacks approached Beaver Creek looking for work. "I have not had a single application," Ann wrote. She began to realize, after a lifetime of paying no attention to what her slaves thought of her, that she had a poor reputation among the blacks. She mentioned that only one man was thinking of staying with her, but she was certain that the other Hairstons "will abuse him out of the notion." One black Hairston irritated the family no end because he refused to address the owner, Marshall Hairston, as "Master" anymore.

In one letter from 1865, I recognized the name of a black woman I had read about in Beaver Creek's slave records. Named Grace, she was the woman who had done much of the spinning and weaving for the mistress, Ann Hairston. The postwar letter referred to her as "Aunt" Grace, which was the title whites usually used to refer to older black women regarded as faithful slaves. But Emancipation had freed Grace from a role she was apparently tired of playing. The letter, written by one of Ann Hairston's daughters, described how "Aunt" Grace came to the big house one day to take her granddaughter away. Before leaving, Grace told Ann Hairston to her face that she "had done a heap" for the white Hairstons "but could never do any more." Ann's daughter watched in shock and remarked grumpily, "I reckon she thinks that she made us rich."

Ann bitterly harangued the departing Hairstons, telling them that "they will never be as free again as they have been here." That declaration summed up the deepest belief of many slaveholders—they had been good masters, and under them, slavery was freedom. The blacks left anyway, in what seemed to Ann to be the ultimate act of disloyalty. She thought that no white person should hire a black who had left a master. The shock of Emancipation rippled through the white family. To see their former servants walk off and start a new life left them stunned. "There has been almost a perfect revolution among the negroes," one Hairston mistress wrote, as if the servants had pillaged the house and set it afire, when in fact all they had done was leave.

The image of blacks as lazy, shiftless people became entrenched in the white mind. In the summer of 1865, just months after the end of the war, a Northern journalist named John Dennett traveled to Virginia to investigate conditions there. He passed through Pittsylvania County, where many of the Hairstons lived. But before reaching that part of Virginia, Dennett had already collected a sampling of impressions about the attitude of whites toward the newly freed slaves. On the canal boat Dennett took from Richmond into the interior, he fell into conversation with a planter who was more than happy to give an outsider the benefit of his experience. "The Negro is doomed to undergo extinction," the planter said with certainty—"less than a hundred years of freedom will see the race practically exterminated. . . . The Negro stands as much in need of a master to guide him as a child does." Without the care of someone superior, the planter continued, "the race will first become pauper and then disappear." Dennett would hear this opinion elsewhere, and it would be repeated in books and magazines for fifty years to come.

Dennett asked another traveling companion how the blacks were behaving. "Sassy and lazy. They go round stealing," was the response. "Don't you believe it," another man interrupted. "They behave well enough. They are pretty much all at work. But some people can't see a nigger go along the street now-a-days that they don't damn him for putting on airs. A good many of the masters forget pretty often that their niggers are free and take a stick to them, or give them a cuff with the fist."

Dennett observed that white Virginians customarily left all manual and menial work to blacks. A railroad contractor told Dennett he simply could not get white laborers. "They're too damned proud to work," he said—"rather loaf around Richmond and Petersburg. But they'll have to come to it. I've had to pull off my coat since peace came." As Dennett was passing through the countryside, he noted, "I have seen at one time and another hundreds of white men, and I doubt if I have seen in all more than ten men engaged in labor of any sort." For the white men, Dennett observed, the main occupations seemed to be drinking apple brandy and keeping a bleary eye on the Yankee troops. In Lynchburg, the number of white idlers grew to such alarming size, with a corresponding rise in petty crime, that the military commander had to modify his order to arrest black vagrants "so as to include all white persons found loafing about the streets."

From Lynchburg, Dennett rode south into Hairston country. On the road to Danville he overtook an old black man driving a cart loaded with peaches, sweet potatoes, and chickens. The cart horse, he noticed, was "very old, very thin, and very galled in many places." The man said he was on his way to sell his produce in Danville and to see the army officer there. He and his family had been thrown off a plantation because they weren't needed for the rest of the year. He had tended the master's vegetable garden; his wife was the cook; two sons were field hands; and the youngest boy was a house servant. The man showed Dennett a contract saying that the total payment for the entire family for the year would be ten barrels of corn. The man hoped that the army officer might be able to persuade, or force, the master to take him back. They had no other place to get work, no winter clothes, and he didn't see how five people could survive through autumn and winter on ten barrels of corn. He said the planters were driving off all the old people and families with too many children and were hiring only the young and strong.

In the days of slavery, no one had actually starved. But under the new system, the ruthlessness of the marketplace prevailed. Those who did find a place to work were not allowed to help the homeless and jobless. The work contracts drawn up by one of the Hairston planters contained a cruel clause—the owner provided food to his workers, but anyone caught feeding someone not working on the plantation would be fired.

Stopping to get a meal at a tavern north of Danville, Dennett found nothing on the dinner table but buttermilk and corn bread. The white proprietor moaned about the troubles of running his farm. He refused to hire blacks and instead relied on the services of his grown sons, a sulky and restless bunch who despised farming. One of them declared that he would rather be in the war ten years than pull fodder two days: "Damn farming—it's just fit for a nigger." The farmers were eloquent on the subject of black laziness, but at the same time they were refusing to give work to blacks so that, in the words of one observer, "they shall be forced to feel what a sore and costly thing it is to be free."

Rumors flew in the months after the war as everyone, white and black, wondered if the government would act on its promise to the freedpeople of "forty acres and a mule," which the government would provide by confiscating the lands of disloyal planters. According to one rumor, the "dividement" would happen at the end of 1865. Indeed a Yankee officer at Martinsville was telling blacks to find themselves homes "until Christmas," lending weight to the rumor. President Andrew Johnson, though he was a North Carolinian himself, took a harsh line against his fellow Southerners when he succeeded Lincoln. Johnson specifically took aim at the backbone of the old slavocracy. Under his Reconstruction policy, owners of property worth $20,000 or more, a range that included nearly all the Hairston planters, would permanently lose their rights as citizens, and their property would be subject to confiscation. In the spring of 1865, the government actually began to list properties in Virginia for confiscation and to schedule auctions—throwing the white Hairstons into a panic and raising the hopes of the freedpeople for their forty acres and a mule. Politics intervened. By midsummer Johnson began to think of his election campaign, which could use the support of wealthy Southerners. He canceled the confiscation of property. New rumors sprouted in response. A federal officer told the blacks in Martinsville that families who had not found places to work by the end of 1865 would be shipped south to the cotton fields. In fact, labor agents hired by Mississippi cotton planters were already prowling the area, asking army officers to turn refugees over to them. The military command issued orders that black men who couldn't find work be arrested and put into chain gangs for roadwork. Some stories had the government itself secretly selling people into slavery in Cuba.

Slavery of children survived in practice. Children who had become separated from their parents for whatever reason were bound over as apprentices to farmers, and even when a child's parents appeared and asked for custody, they could not obtain it. When the black Hairstons left their former plantations to seek better conditions, they ran a terrible risk. If they could not find work fast enough, the county government could legally declare them to be vagrants, which made their children subject to the apprenticeship law—any child who *might* become a burden on the county could be indentured to a planter until the child was eighteen, in the case of girls, and twenty-one in the case of boys. Hundreds of black parents in Henry and Pittsylvania Counties begged the army to rescue their children, but the army did nothing. Some desperate parents kidnapped their children from plantations, only to have the sheriff appear at their door to drag the child back to the planter who held the documents of indenture.

Hundreds of blacks streamed into Danville to get food and jobs in the bleak summer of 1865. Smallpox swept through the town, and then typhoid fever. Homeless men, women, and children were dying in the roads—during the summer word spread through the countryside that "heaps of 'em" were dying in Danville. Still people went there looking for work, and when the tobacco factories reopened, the glut of labor made wages fall and rents double. Leaders of the black community appealed to the federal authorities to persuade the country people to go back to their old homes because the situation had become impossible in town.

Conditions were just as bad in North Carolina in the region around Cooleemee. The army established a camp for white and black refugees about twenty miles from Cooleemee. The displaced and dispossessed crowded into it during the summer and fall of 1865. A Northerner on a tour of inspection passed the ration stand where people were waiting to get their issue of hardtack and found "abject poverty vividly depicted on face, form and clothing." The people lived in tents and log huts, the latter with roofs that could barely keep out the rain. Children and old people huddled around miserable campfires; mothers washed discarded bones and bits of bacon to put into soup.

Most of the blacks, including the Hairstons, became sharecroppers.

After the war the freedpeople embraced sharecropping gladly—indeed, they insisted upon it. If hard work resulted in a good crop, they would share in the profits. They had seen the wealth piled up by the planters before the war, and they felt certain that sharecropping was the path to independence. When the overseer of Beaver Creek was recruiting laborers for 1866, he could find only two men who would work for cash wages—everyone wanted to work for a share of the crop.

As the black people, for the first time, were trying to negotiate the conditions of their labor, they insisted on one point that the planters considered revolutionary—black women and children would no longer labor in the fields. Parents wanted their children to be children, not worm pickers, and there was talk that the government might try to open schools for the black children; they already had them in the eastern part of the state. The married women simply refused to work, and their husbands backed them up, because the planters did not want to pay women equal wages or shares—the working wives of laborers got only their meals in exchange for work. Responding to complaints from planters, a federal officer in Henry County lectured a group of blacks on the subject, telling them that it was "a very mistaken notion of theirs not to make their wives work." An overseer from one of the Hairston plantations listened with approval and reported back to his bosses that the speaker was "the smartest Yankee he had seen." Still the women resisted. They wanted to tend their families and their own patches of land. Some of the black Hairston women became extremely independent-minded after the war—more so than their husbands. One white Hairston planter was driven to distraction by the sassiness and back talk of the freedwomen, and he fired several good workers because he could not endure their wives.

It soon became apparent that the blacks had been wildly optimistic about sharecropping. Women and children were inexorably drawn back into plantation toil, and the profits the blacks expected from working on shares did not materialize. On one hand, the farming economy in the Hairstons' part of Virginia was uncertain, to say the least. Few planters had cash, and those who did have cash did not intend to hand it over to their laborers. On the other hand, the blacks had not counted on the capacity of their former masters for cheating. It became common knowledge among the planters that widespread cheating would occur at the end of the 1865 season, when the time came to "settle" with the freedpeople. Hairston letters of the period are full of dread at a rumored uprising of the blacks that would occur at the end of the year. Even those who

planned to treat the workers honestly were afraid—"the people apprehend rebellion of negroes this winter," as one of the Hairston women
wrote in November. In all the descriptions of former slaves leaving the
plantation, the Hairstons remarked on how they went off "very quietly,"
as if the whites had nervously expected something else.

Lieutenant Fernald, the Freedmen's Bureau officer, tried strenuously
to protect the interests of the black laborers. He called at plantations and
demanded to see the contracts the planters had with their black workers.
He filed suit against two white Hairstons on behalf of freedmen who had
not been paid. Planters routinely ignored court orders to pay their workers, to the extent that Fernald begged his superiors to send troops to impel
them at gunpoint to pay. When the inspector general came to Martinsville to speed up the marriage registration in the summer of 1866, Fernald
took the opportunity to renew his request for troops. The inspector, Colonel Horace Neide, thought that a bit harsh. He went around and talked
with the planters. They were all encumbered with debt, he discovered,
and "cannot dispose of any part of their land except at an almost ruinous
sacrifice." He admitted that the wages paid to the freedmen were extremely low, but he thought the planters were doing the best they could
under the circumstances. "In speaking of this remuneration as fair," he
wrote in his report, "I mean taking into consideration the fact that the
planters . . . are almost totally deprived of the means to pay what would
elsewhere be called remunerative wages." Neide denied Fernald's request
for troops to enforce the labor contracts.

Fernald returned to his task of monitoring the local courts to ensure
that justice was meted out properly to the blacks. In his reports I could
see the creation of the legal double standard that would characterize segregation for the next century. Fernald described one case that helped to
establish the idea that beating a black man was different from beating a
white. Ironically, the man who established this local precedent was a
white Hairston. Fernald wrote a report about a freedman named Caesar
who had received a severe beating at the hands of Colonel P. H. Hairston,
a cousin of the Oak Hill Hairstons. No cause could be found for the
beating except that Colonel Hairston was at that time apparently a very
frustrated man. He had moved his family into a fancy house and couldn't
pay the rent; in fact he could not pay any of his debts and had a pack of
lawyers after him. Possibly Caesar had tried to collect payment for some
work and Hairston had turned on him; perhaps Caesar had been insuffi-
ciently respectful and had gotten his beating for "insolence." In any case,

the beating was bad and Fernald wanted to see what the local court would do about it.

Fernald settled into a bench in the courtroom to watch the trial. Four blacks appeared that day with complaints. A freedman named Garland said that he had been beaten by a white named Shelton. When Garland entered the courtroom to testify before the grand jury, he found that the court had appointed Mr. Shelton himself to be the foreman of the jury! Naturally, the grand jury declined to indict. Next, a black woman said she was beaten by another white man, but "no notice was taken of it by the Grand Jury," according to Fernald. He listened to the circuit court trial of Joel Dillard, a freedman, on the charge of theft. The evidence was of such a trifling nature that the general opinion in the courtroom was that he would be acquitted. The jury, however, convicted Dillard, and he was sentenced to three years in the state penitentiary. The item he had allegedly stolen was a bushel of oats.

When Caesar's complaint against Colonel Hairston was heard by the grand jury, the evidence against Hairston was so overwhelming that nine of the jurors, all white men, were actually inclined to indict the colonel. But then a magistrate rose to make a short speech advancing a new legal doctrine: a white man, he said, ought not to be prosecuted for beating a black "unless in so doing he should disable him." This was food for thought. The jury could see that Caesar had survived the attack. They reconsidered the evidence in light of this extraordinarily flexible new legal standard. Colonel Hairston was not indicted.

Frustrated and angry, Fernald reported to his superior that, for the black people, "it is almost impossible to obtain justice." He said that blacks were beaten if they tried to make a formal complaint to him or to a local magistrate. Even if a magistrate thought that a black man's complaints had merit, the magistrate did not dare to act for fear of incurring the wrath of his white neighbors. Lieutenant Fernald wrote in one of his reports that whenever he confronted a white man with a complaint made by a black, the white would inevitably say that the allegations were fantasies, that blacks simply could not be believed under any circumstance. By repeating this lie often enough, they hoped to plant enough doubt in Fernald's mind about the truthfulness of blacks that he would begin to question anything the blacks told him.

With their own eyes, the black Hairstons learned that whites could murder a black man with complete impunity, because the white community retained total control over the civilian legal system. Whites could manipulate the legal system as they wished, while relying on intimidation to prevent blacks from complaining to the federal authorities. In 1868, a black farmer named Spencer Hairston went into Martinsville to find the justice of the peace, James Barker, and demand an inquiry into the murder of Nelson Wilson, who was at that moment lying dead in front of Spencer's cabin. Barker went out with twelve white men to Spencer Hairston's place and examined the body of Wilson, who was indeed dead, shot through the gut. The wound was a large one, so large that only a shotgun fired at close range could have made it. The men there knew that of all the painful ways to die this was one of the worst. Several black people were waiting. They had witnessed the fatal event and now wanted to see justice done.

The jury held its inquest on the spot, with Wilson's body still lying in the dust in front of Spencer's cabin. They first called Spencer Hairston's wife, Rachael, put her under oath, and asked her what she had seen. She said she had known Nelson. He had come by their house carrying a duck, which he said had been given to his sister, and asked for some water. About an hour later seven mounted white men suddenly converged on the house from different directions. Wilson ran, then turned around and tried to scurry under the corn crib. He was not quick enough. A man whom Rachael Hairston recognized as John Carter saw Wilson and called out, "Here he is!" The others quickly galloped up. Rachael recognized "Mr. Walters and Mr. McGill," whose first names she didn't know. Someone in the group yelled, "Shoot him!" She said John Carter shot Nelson as he was lying on the ground.

Tilda Hairston, another black woman, gave evidence that largely corroborated Rachael's. She did not see who fired the shot, but she heard the victim cry out, "Marse John shot me."

A woman named Phibly Hairston stepped up and took the oath. She saw and heard John Carter say, "Here he is!" and heard Nelson clearly say, "I surrender," just as one of the other white men said, "Shoot him!" Phibly declared to the jury, "The man called John Carter shot him."

The jury heard no further testimony; no one came forward to contradict this account of Wilson's death. Having heard the eyewitnesses to the shooting of Nelson Wilson by John Carter, the jury conferred among themselves and reached a verdict. James Barker recorded their findings, specifically that "the said Nelson Wilson came to his death—upon their oaths do say—that deceased came to his death on the third day of Sept 1868 by means of a wound received in his abdomen from a gun in the hands of some unknown person."

All twelve jurors signed the document, and Barker affixed his signature and seal. Barker filed the transcript with his other papers, confident that no further action would be taken and that he had nothing to fear from filing a demonstrably false document in the public record. Barker did not even bother to note Wilson's death in the county death record, nor did anyone report the incident to Lieutenant Fernald, who was away at the time in the next county, following the events of the September election campaign. Nelson Wilson had become a nonperson. A man had been shot dead, but no one had done it.

Every morning the sound of a bell rolled down from Danville's highest hill, echoing through the town and across the Dan River. A large plantation bell, the kind rung to summon the workers to the field, this bell was rung by a teacher to summon the children to school. The sound rolled into the countryside across the fields, heard there only feebly, but it was heard; because the people far from town were earnestly listening for it. The school was a complex of buildings on the outskirts of the town. The schoolhouse itself, a Confederate hospital during the war, was a tumbledown frame building one hundred feet wide by one hundred and fifty feet long. With its hilltop site the school enjoyed a sweeping view of the river and the landscape beyond it. Just across the Dan River lay the Hairston plantations.

The black people understood very well that they would never be able to improve their conditions if the community remained uneducated. They knew the cost of ignorance—illiteracy made them dependent on whites in every legal and business transaction—and they did not want their children to pay that price forever. The great dream that tantalized them was a schoolhouse. But the Freedmen's Bureau had utterly failed in keeping schools open in Hairston country—in the bureau's education records Henry and Pittsylvania Counties appear in the category of "Destitute Places." Asked to estimate the number of black children who might attend schools if the bureau could open them, Fernald reported that Henry County needed five schools for four hundred children (a low estimate), and the agent for Pittsylvania County put the potential enrollment there at two thousand, a figure that headquarters refused to believe and penciled down to five hundred (perhaps to bring it in line with Fernald's figure). But this exercise with the numbers was futile because the bureau was never able to maintain schools there for any useful stretch of time. A school operated in Martinsville for exactly one month. The country people in Pittsylvania had better luck—a white woman in Chatham ran a school for eighty-four black children in a building she owned herself.

The bureau agents felt that the only way a school could survive in the remote parts of the tobacco country was to have it taught by a local person, who would probably not be attacked. "It would never do in the world to send a teacher from the North," one of them said. If a Northern man came down, no one would give him a place to board; it would be worse if a woman came—"all the young men would take it for granted she was a whore."

The whites also understood the supreme importance of education. If the blacks became educated, they would inevitably challenge and overcome the inequalities that the whites so desperately wanted to preserve. So, among the whites who most hated the blacks, the most hateful thing was a school. From across Virginia reports came in of teachers threatened and beaten, of schoolhouses sacked and burned. Poring over these reports, the bureau's superintendent of education exclaimed that the devil had taken Virginia by the hand "and is making a regular stamping ground of the state." But while the bureau was wringing its hands over the problem of educating the blacks and making no progress in Hairston country, another group came in. This group, most of them women, had an advantage over bureau employees in facing down local bigots because they were utterly fearless. They were Quakers.

The teacher who rang the bell every morning at the Danville school was a Quaker woman from New England named Eunice Congdon. She had been sent by a group of Quakers from Philadelphia, who had formed the Friends Association of Philadelphia and Its Vicinity for the Relief of Colored Freedmen (later shortened to Friends Freedmen's Association of Philadelphia). In 1863, while the war was still going on, they began sending teachers, money, and supplies (blankets, clothes, shoes, seeds, Bibles) to the refugee camps in the coastal areas of Virginia and North Carolina. At the end of the war they sent their emissaries to the places in the interior where the Freedmen's Bureau teachers could not go. Simple in dress, frugal, completely upright in their habits, and blessed with an unshakable faith, they went about their business methodically and effectively. Their activities spawned great interest in the Quaker communities in England, which contributed substantial amounts of support—with the result that bundles of clothes, seeds, and Bibles packed in Manchester or Birmingham, England, were reaching black families as far away as Jackson, Mississippi. They went where the need was greatest, a mission that took them to Hairston country—to Danville and to the region in North Carolina around Cooleemee.

The Quakers opened a school just a few miles from Cooleemee at Mocksville, and another at Salisbury. In the autumn of 1865 the association dispatched two of its members to North Carolina on a tour of inspection. They were overwhelmed by their reception. A huge crowd of children and parents turned out at Salisbury to thank them for opening the school. The crowd closed in, shaking their hands so vigorously that they ached for days—"two or three at a time holding and pulling each hand at once, the crowd literally pressing us down." Later they went to Chapel Hill, where they were met at the train by the black man who ran the town's cab company. Before they could stop him he paid their hotel bill in advance, and then brought the leaders of the black community to see them.

The opening of a school in Lexington, just across the Yadkin River from Cooleemee, was delayed until July 1866 because funds were short and local opposition strong. The blacks built the schoolhouse themselves and paid some of the costs for its two white teachers and eighty-eight students. A local black man named Levi E. Johnson took over as teacher the following year. So many adults wanted to learn to read that the Quakers planned a night school, but feared for Johnson's safety in the night. His was a life they did not care to risk; so they looked for one of their own to run the night school. The building was in a remote place in the country, two miles from town and reachable only over bad roads that were almost impassable in winter. Only one white family was brave enough to board a Northern teacher—a black family who tried such a thing would have been slaughtered—and the Quaker in charge of the district warned, "The teacher sent here ought to be a strong man, otherwise no night school could be kept up." His fears were justified. In March 1868 the local Freedmen's Bureau agent put a brief note in his monthly report that the freedpeople's schoolhouse was "burned by incendiary." It took a year and a half for the community to gather the funds and materials to rebuild it.

The Quakers ran their flagship school at Danville, the very capital of unreconstructed rebel antipathy. They were able to gain a foothold in Danville only because the army still maintained a post there. Indeed, Danville was such a trouble spot that it was one of the last places in Virginia to require a federal garrison. Even so, whenever the troops were called out to quell some problem in the countryside, hell would break loose in town. In a single day when the troops were gone, mobs pillaged six buildings the government was using.

Eunice Congdon, the headmistress of the Danville school, was an intrepid woman who neither shrank from having to live in filthy quarters, which she dubbed "Rat Hall," nor from dealing with "the Rebs," as she jauntily called her Southern tormentors. To her fellow Quakers in Philadelphia she recounted the various threats she received, with a coolness that must have astonished the Northerners: "One [threat] is, 'these Government buildings are not to stand long.' Another is, that we teachers are to be 'rode on a rail for teaching the d_____d niggers.'" A city policeman stopped by, not to offer protection, but to threaten to set fire to the school and sweep the teachers out of town. All this she airily dismissed, saying that if the Rebs had really meant to carry out their threats, they would not talk about it—"so we have settled down in a state of composure," she wrote, "trusting that we shall be taken care of by Him who inclined our hearts to this work." She was also taken care of by the black community. After a nighttime visitation by a gang of whites apparently intent on setting fires and attacking the teachers, black fathers began to patrol the grounds after dark, and no harm came to the school or its teachers.

Every morning, in response to the sound of the school bell, the black children gathered at 9:15. Congdon reported that the children arrived neat and clean, in clothes that were old and scanty but carefully tended. She was well aware of the difficulties faced by these children and their parents. "It is a perfect marvel," she said, "how these people do so much with so little. Their exertions to provide for themselves and families, and pay for their children's schooling, are very great."

The children studied reading, writing, spelling, arithmetic, and geography. With four hundred students and just two teachers and two assistants, individual study was impossible, and the teachers had some trouble with "the thousand pranks that come cropping out of their excessive vitality." In the largest hall of the school building, one teacher would lead as many as one hundred students through exercises in arithmetic. Fifty to one hundred boys and girls would be in a reading class, in which the teacher would write a word on the blackboard, pronounce it aloud, and the students would repeat it in unison. Nevertheless, Congdon said that the children were "on the alert," eager to learn, and displayed "a sense of deep responsibility." The Quakers found that the black children had great natural ability—"the children compare favorably with any white children I ever taught; indeed, I think they excel them in reading and writing."

Although Quakers in the North and in England were paying for the school's books, maps, arithmetic charts, and other supplies, the school was not run as a complete charity—the students themselves were expected to help support the school. Initially there was no tuition, but eventually the Quakers decided to set a fee of five cents a week. This was a great hardship for the families of Danville's factory workers, who were thrown out of their jobs seasonally, sometimes without being paid for work already done. It was even harder on the country families, such as the Hairstons, who had no cash whatever. The solution was simple; if the children could not pay, Eunice said, "we set them to work." The children carried water from the spring, scrubbed floors, and chopped firewood. If a student was absent for several days, an assistant was dispatched to the child's cabin to ascertain the reason; if it was lack of money, then the assistant simply took the child and put him to work at the school.

Eunice had also to contend with the planters for her students. One day a boy appeared at the mission, pouring out a story that he had escaped from a plantation where he was being mistreated. Eunice took him under her wing, only to have a constable turn up in company with the plantation owner. The planter had with him the paper showing that the boy was legally bound to work for him until he was twenty-one. Eunice pleaded and threatened, but to no avail. The planter tied the boy's arms behind his back and led him away. "The Slave Power," one of the Quakers remarked, "is not dead."

Throughout the late 1860s and early 1870s, the Quakers reported that conditions worsened in Hairston country. Their appeals to their sponsors in Philadelphia grew more desperate: "Not one third of our scholars have had a pound of meat in their houses for months. The balance are half-starved. Their tattered rags scarcely hide them now." So dire was the situation that the teachers were cutting up their own clothing to make covers for newborns. The winter of 1867–68 was unusually cold, and the effect was plainly visible in the schoolhouse: "They take the chills at school—three or four lie down by the fire every day—and it rends my heart to think how defenceless they are from disease—no doctor will come to them unpaid. And the shortness of the crops this season will but deepen their miseries. . . . I have seen little children tremble with the cold like a leaf in the wind, without the means to make them comfortable. I saw little children in school stand up and recite, shaking like aspen leaves, with no earthly thing on but short-sleeved cotton dresses." Disease swept the community, and the old people told the teachers that they had not seen anything like it in thirty years. Congdon wrote, "To one of our colored women who had lost a child, I remarked, 'It has been very sickly here.' She replied, 'No, *deathly*, nothing but death.' "

The terrible suffering among the freed slaves during Reconstruction has been overshadowed, in popular literature and film, by the fall of the white planters, exemplified by the figure of Scarlett O'Hara. Her fictional travails, so powerfully rendered in Margaret Mitchell's novel, *Gone With the Wind*, and portrayed by Vivien Leigh in the film version, still appear as the one true story of Reconstruction in the minds of many people. Scarlett's story had a basis in fact, but not all the planters suffered as she did, and Mitchell did not describe the way that bitterness over defeat and economic distress became transformed into racial prejudice.

Peter Hairston, unlike Scarlett O'Hara, did not cling grimly to the land and try to rebuild his old life. He left the South permanently. He believed that the victorious federal government was determined to destroy the South utterly: "The Radicals are not satisfied with [our] humiliation—there is such a thing as driving a people to despair." He thought that a revolution could be at hand, one that would "produce scenes of anarchy and confusion such as we have not as yet witnessed in this country." A visit to the coastal area of North Carolina left him deeply shocked. It had once been a wealthy country, but the freedpeople had departed after the war, and much of the best land lay fallow for lack of laborers. Peter was told that not one out of a hundred of the large planters could pay his debts. "Men who drove their fine carriages now go in carts and wagons," Peter wrote.

The region around Cooleemee was infested with bushwhackers. Cooleemee itself was not touched, but thieves ransacked a house at another smaller plantation Peter owned. The robbers were not identified, and any number of Confederate renegades in the area could have done it, but the Salisbury newspaper did not hesitate to blame it on the freedmen. Whoever the perpetrators were, the incident helped convince Peter that North Carolina was no longer safe. In contrast to almost all of his white Hairston peers, he left his family at his parents' house in Virginia and went to Baltimore, the hometown of two of his wartime friends, a city full of Confederate sympathizers, to look into a new line of work. Feeling far more at home there than in, say, Washington or New York, he was one of many Southerners in the city during the summer and fall of 1865, fleeing the uncertain conditions in plantation country.

In less than ten days he found a business partner and established a commission house, named Herbert & Hairston, which would provide supplies and manufactured goods to plantations and act as broker for tobacco, cotton, and wood products. He estimated that the firm would provide him an income of about $3,000 a year and that his plantation income would be about the same, enough to live quite well in Baltimore. He purchased a house on Charles Street close to the Washington Monument, "the most fashionable and desirable part of the City," as he wrote to Fanny. Clearly excited and eager to fire her enthusiasm, he described the new house glowingly: "It is handsomely furnished and has every convenience of gas, bathroom, hot and cold water, fine dining room with kitchen in the basement." The only drawback he could think of was that it had "but one parlor." There was also the problem of his citizenship. He was still a rebel in the eyes of the law.

President Johnson announced a limited amnesty for former rebels in the summer of 1865, but he would issue pardons only to those who presented their papers to him personally. This announcement led to a deluge of petitioners at the White House, among them Peter Hairston, who had two private interviews with the president. In his first meeting with Johnson, Peter managed to obtain pardons for his father and a few other relatives. Unfortunately, his own papers were not yet ready, and when he returned to the White House nine days later with his application, he found that Johnson had put a hold on issuing the papers. The president was busy and was doing his best to usher his visitor to the door, but Peter was persistent. He recorded his encounter with President Johnson in a letter, now among the Hairston papers in Chapel Hill.

"Sir, I am very much pressed with business," the president said.

"It would be very gratifying to my family if I could carry my pardon home with me."

"There are great many here, sir, just in your situation."

"That is true, sir."

Johnson was a native of North Carolina, and simple courtesy required that he exchange a few pleasantries with his fellow Carolinian before turning him down. Johnson asked where Peter was from.

"Ah!" Johnson exclaimed in nostalgia. "I tramped all through that country once!" He remembered the Hairstons: "Your name was very familiar then, in the days of Jacksonian democracy."

Peter's persistence, and skill at presidential small talk, carried the day. Johnson relented and told Peter he would "do the very best I can for you."

Peter was not alone among many leading Confederates who decided to give up planting after the war and start new careers in law, business, commerce, and railroads. The very men who had led the fight to preserve the plantation system now turned away from it; they peered into the future and saw nothing but futility, recognizing that an era of agrarian dominance had passed with the loss of the war. The plantation days were over, and Peter, for one, felt the loss acutely. "What I dislike more than anything else," he said, "is giving up my horses, but I must cease to be a gentleman now & go to work."

Some of the white Hairstons remained so wealthy that they were barely affected by the fall of the Confederacy. For example, Peter's parents at Oak Hill, Samuel and Agnes Hairston, and Peter's grandmother, Ruth, emerged from the war in good shape. Ann and Marshall Hairston of Beaver Creek had enough cash on hand in 1865 that they were able to give Jubal Early $200 in gold to aid him in his flight from federal pursuers. But not every branch of the family was so fortunate. As the first summer of peace slid into a gray and cheerless autumn, a cousin from Magna Vista plantation in Henry County, Louisa Hairston, noticed that everyone still looked the same but that hearts "had grown old." Nature itself contributed to the gloom, as drought-weakened trees refused to offer much color. Normally it was the time of year to make preparations for the next season, but many of the planters in her part of Henry County had just given up. "Farming is greatly neglected," she wrote to Ruth Hairston at Oak Hill, "very many making no preparation for the coming year." The planters had to endure what she called "insults and injustice" from the Yankee officers, the "vile Provost Guards" who understood nothing of "the

Chivalry of our Land." She asked if Aunt Ruth knew of anyone who needed a governess because she did not want to be a burden on her father any longer. "Some of us," she continued, "are falling neath heavy burdens by the wayside."

When I read this letter, it seemed plain that Louisa was asking for money. She could not actually bring herself to say it, but her pitiable story and the reference to "the Chivalry of our Land" were undoubtedly calculated to prick the conscience of her wealthy aunt. Perhaps she hoped that Aunt Ruth would be moved by the humiliation of having a Hairston go to work in someone else's house as little more than a domestic—managing children was something that blacks had always done at Hairston places. But no help came from Oak Hill.

Six months later Louisa wrote a second time. She had not written in so long, she said, because she had been confined to bed by illness. She hinted that she was starving. She said that nearly everyone in the county was down with disease, "which the Doctor said was owing to their not having any suitable food." A bad wheat crop had created a scarcity of bread. The poor came begging to the big houses for flour, which the wealthy had to buy in Baltimore as there was none to be had in the county. One man had taken his mother's wedding necklace to sell in Baltimore. Later in the spring many large farms would be for sale because no one had cash to pay laborers and buy provisions. Already the next wheat crop looked unpromising, and the doctor predicted an outbreak of cholera when the warm weather came. "Poor suffering Virginians!" Louisa lamented; "who could have predicted such a fate for such a noble race of people?"

One cousin who could not bear his burden during that gray and cheerless autumn was George Pannill, married to a Hairston woman. He had lost all his property in the months after the war. One night near the end of November 1865 he tried to drown himself but was rescued. The next morning he put a pistol in his mouth and pulled the trigger.

Some of the saddest letters were written by Eliza Hairston. She and her husband, Samuel William Hairston, a member of the Hordsville branch of the family outside of Martinsville, had enjoyed an idyllic life until the war. Owner of the Union Furnace ironworks, Samuel lived in a large country house nestled in the mountains and flanked by crystalline streams. The house was commodious, with every convenience of a country home in those days—"beautiful lawn, graveled walks, flower and vegetable gardens, well and spring of purest water, kitchen, laundry, ice, carriage and servants' houses." A daguerreotype of Samuel and his wife, Eliza Penn, taken in 1847, shows a handsome, thoughtful young man with deep-set, inquiring eyes and sensitive features. He dressed for the portrait in a fashionable satin vest, from which dangled a gold watch, while Eliza was more simply dressed, with a demure cameo necklace. She sat stiffly and ill at ease in contrast to her husband, who held himself serenely through the long exposure.

For much of his life he had frail health, but he was an excellent manager who made the forge prosperous. During the war his forge was a major producer of horseshoes and wagon-wheel rims for the Confederate army. After a bout of pneumonia in 1863, Samuel decided that running the forge was too much for him; he sold it for $160,000 in Confederate money—enough to keep him in elegant style for life, had the Confederacy won the war and had he been able to keep it. With the war going badly for the South, Samuel tried to convert all of his cash into tobacco, which he knew would be a negotiable commodity no matter which side won, but he miscalculated in his dealings and lost the money.

Demoralized and ill, Samuel W. Hairston moved his family and their former slaves to southwestern Georgia to recoup by planting tobacco, but he had chosen an area outside the tobacco belt and his first crop came up badly damaged. He quarreled constantly with his field hands and took to drinking. Eliza poured out her fears in a letter to her brother in Virginia. "I cannot express to you," she wrote, "the sad picture that I have to contemplate as the lot of my poor family. I have lived in dread of this. If I had a sober husband I could go with some degree of cheerfulness." Debts pressed heavily upon them. Their teenaged son George went to work as a wagoner for twelve dollars a month, his mother fretting over him as he came down with rheumatism from sleeping outdoors in the rain. "I dread it so much for my poor boy," Eliza wrote. "I feel so discouraged some times that I hardly know whether I would rather live or die. It does seem that our way is completely hedged up."

This family's struggles during Reconstruction made a lasting impression. Eliza and Samuel's daughter Elizabeth grew into adulthood with bitter feelings toward the North and toward the former slaves, whom she regarded simply as unfaithful servants. She contrasted the acts of the freedpeople with her memory of slavery time, when the blacks were faithful to the family unto death. She remembered the night during the Civil

War when her parents were called away because a relative was dying. Her father called four of the servants in and told them that they would have the children in their care. She remembered hearing the servants say that they would protect the family "at the risk of their lives." "They never left the yard, but walked around the house all night, sometimes singing softly so if we awakened, we would not be afraid." Emancipation sundered that relationship, and Elizabeth never forgave the blacks for choosing freedom over fidelity to the old master. In her mind the turmoil of Reconstruction was largely the fault of the freedpeople, and she passed on an oral and written history that contributed to the bitter myth of Reconstruction. In a history of the Hairston and Penn families published in 1940, Elizabeth Seawell Hairston wrote:

> Then followed the awful days of "Reconstruction" when the "Freed-men's Bureau" and Yankee "Carpet Baggers" used every means in their power to over run the South and cause an uprising of the newly freed negroes and cause them to insult men and women and declare themselves equals and to confiscate property. In most cases, it is re-markable how well the negroes behaved, putting to shame the white Yankees; however many negroes who were enticed away by their false promises, etc., became roving beggars, ignorant of any knowledge of self support. To meet these conditions, the Ku Klux Klan was organ-ized and it was a Godsend to many innocent people suffering at the hands of these demons in men's clothes, (read *The Klansman*, by Tho-mas Dixon to understand all this) although many were subjected to insults and tortures as being suspected as members of the K.K.K.

The Klansman, which Elizabeth Hairston thought contained the truth about Reconstruction, formed the basis for the film *Birth of a Nation*, made by D. W. Griffith in 1915. It glorified the Klan and enshrined the worst myths about blacks—the laziness of the race and the sexual rapacity of the black male. The film had a private showing at the White House, where President Woodrow Wilson, a Virginian, declared that it was "his-tory written with lightning." Indeed it was—many Americans took *Birth of a Nation* as the literal truth about Reconstruction. It entered the na-tional memory and determined the way tens of millions of white people who had never set foot in the South viewed blacks.

Elizabeth Seawell Hairston's memoir, like Dixon's novel and Griffith's film, was an exercise in selective memory. South and east of Danville, just across the North Carolina line from Oak Hill plantation, the counties of Alamance and Caswell were the scenes of bestial violence in the years of Reconstruction. The Ku Klux Klan spread terror through the black communities; murdered blacks and whites who supported the Republican, reconstructionist government; and for good measure tortured young white women who they believed were prostitutes (in this manner the Klan got its reputation as the shield of Southern virtue). Appalled by the violence, Governor Holden declared the two counties to be in insurrection, suspended habeas corpus, and called down Unionist mountain men from the western part of the state to subdue the Klan. In another North Carolina county, the federal government indicted the entire white population for hunting the freedpeople with dogs. The real extent of violence will never be known because blacks were often—though not always—too terrified to report crimes to local authorities; and the federal government had neither the resources nor the desire to monitor the vast conquered territory.

The Ku Klux Klan in the 1860s had three councils active in the vicinity of the Hairston plantations in Stokes County, North Carolina, according to an anonymous report sent to Governor Holden. Most of the Ku Klux there were moonshiners and itinerant tobacco peddlers who learned "the diabolical edicts of this order," as the informer put it, on their travels through South Carolina and Georgia. The informer said that "this infamous order of *Thugs*" was responsible for numerous whippings. Masked men dragged a black man out of his house late at night and whipped him on account of his being a Republican. A gang rode through Germanton and fired into a house where a party was going on, wounding one man. In all these cases the local authorities merely stood by: "Nothing has been done more than to make some little pretense."

I read the court records of North Carolina and Virginia with trepidation, because I feared opening one of these old ledgers and discovering that a Hairston had suffered the atrocity that befell thousands of other blacks— death at the hands of a lynch mob. I came across one case from 1881 in Stokes County, where I knew the Klan had been very active, that presented exactly the conditions that could result in a murder. A white woman made the highly charged accusation of rape against a black man in his late twenties, Estes Hairston. The accuser did not resort to the Klan but to the county court. Charges had been brought; Estes Hairston had the aid of a lawyer; and the judge seemed determined to regard Estes as innocent until proven guilty. As I read the transcript of the first hearing, the court seemed to be doing everything in its power to protect his rights, and his life.

According to the testimony, Estes Hairston was walking from Winston to Walnut Cove—then and now a center of the black Hairston family—when he encountered a young white woman named Martha Jenkins, whom Estes already knew. She was going the same way, so they walked together to Walnut Cove. Four days later, Martha's father went to the sheriff and charged that Estes had gotten his daughter drunk on the road and raped her.

Estes was arrested and brought before the circuit court judge in the county seat of Danbury. He pleaded not guilty to the charge of rape and contradicted many of the details of Jenkins's charges. Martha herself did not appear. Her father testified that Estes and his daughter had stopped at a store run by a man named Hall, where Estes bought liquor. Jenkins said Estes gave his daughter two glasses of whiskey at the store, and that Hall had seen her take the drinks at Hairston's urging. Estes denied it before the judge and said that Hall would come and testify that Estes had certainly not bought any liquor from him and that Martha had had nothing to drink in his store. Furthermore, Estes said that numerous people had seen them at various points on the road, and that these people would testify that Martha was entirely sober. Finally, he intended to call a black woman who had evidence that the prosecution was undertaken "for malicious motives."

Estes asked the judge to continue the case to the next session of the court to give him the opportunity to have all his witnesses present. The storekeeper, Hall, was his most important witness and was supposed to have been present that day. However, Estes had received a note that Hall was sick. A lawyer had gone to the sheriff on Estes's behalf to file a subpoena compelling Hall to testify. Estes's strenuous effort to force Hall's testimony suggests that Hall's "sickness" might have been a reluctance to contradict Jenkins.

The judge weighed Estes's statement and what had been said against him. The Hairstons were well-known and the judge was inclined to give Estes the benefit of the doubt, despite the protests of Jenkins. The judge granted the continuance and ordered the sheriff to hold Estes in the county jail until the next term of court.

Another black man, Ed Lindsay, was also before the court that day on a similar charge, and he also wanted additional time to have witnesses brought to court. He said the woman who had accused him was not mentally sound, that he would call two witnesses to testify that the woman "has been in the habit of making charges similar to the one against him, against several other parties, and has done so repeatedly, when she has her spells." He added that his two former employers in Iredell County had written him that they would appear in court and testify to his good character, which he considered essential to his case because no one in Stokes knew him. The judge granted Lindsay's request also. The maximum penalty for rape in North Carolina was death; in cases where a black man had been convicted of raping a white woman, a death sentence was routine. So the county could rest assured that if Hairston and Lindsay were convicted, they would be executed.

Perhaps the most explosive issue at that time was racial "mixing." Although mulattoes already represented a sizable proportion of the black population—the result of centuries of mixing—the white population of Virginia and North Carolina remained scandalized by the possibility of the "mongrelization" of the races. This fear even contributed to the reluctance of whites to allow black men to vote. If the law admitted black men to the polling place, one white remarked, "they'll vote themselves white wives." Some white men were able to get away with having a black wife and children by not insisting that the marriage be legally recognized. But a black man living with a white woman, legally or otherwise, was unthinkable.

In 1868 Wesley Hairston, a black man from one of the Stokes County plantations, and Puss Williams, a white woman, were arrested and hauled into court on the charge that they "did unlawfully and adulterously bed and cohabit together and then and there did unlawfully commit fornication and adultery, in contempt of the rites of matrimony." They were convicted, despite the fact that they were, in fact, married. They had a marriage license issued by a North Carolina county clerk and had been married in a Protestant ceremony performed by a duly empowered minister. But their legal status fell into limbo because the marriage was performed in 1867, when North Carolina was under military government. When the state rejoined the Union, it passed a new constitution, affirming the law against mixed marriages. Mr. and Mrs. Hairston appealed their conviction to the state supreme court, which upheld the law, declared their marriage invalid, and affirmed the conviction for adultery and fornication. In his opinion one justice of the court noted, "It is worthy of remark—and the fact indicates the moral improvement of both races— that since emancipation mulatto births have decreased at least one half." He was not sure of his statistics, so he crossed out that figure and wrote "have almost entirely ceased." Any decrease was good. It was in the interest of the state to keep the white race pure.

Despite the hostility of the white community toward any black man guilty of "mixing" with a white woman, Estes Hairston seemed to have a strong chance of winning his case. If his lawyer could subpoena the white storekeeper and compel him to testify, he might corroborate Estes's claim that Martha Jenkins had not been drinking that day. I could only guess at what had actually happened, but since Estes had not denied having sexual relations with Martha, it occurred to me that they might have had a consensual encounter in what they thought was a secluded spot. They had been observed; the observer gossiped about what he or she had seen; and to rescue what was left of his daughter's honor, Martha's enraged father concocted a story about Estes getting Martha drunk and raping her. Having a rape victim for a daughter was preferable to having one who loved a black man. All of this was speculation, and I was curious to see the outcome of the trial. But when I looked in the record from the following term of court, there was no mention of Estes Hairston; nor was he mentioned in later court records. Ed Lindsay's case—with another potentially strong defense—had also inexplicably dropped from sight. It turned out that the white community did not want these men to come to trial, where they might have won. The final chapter in their cases was written not by a judge, but by the county coroner.

Hairston and Lindsay had been in jail for several weeks awaiting their trials when their jailer was awakened at three in the morning by a knock at the door. Without opening the door, the jailer, John Whitten, told the person to go away, for he was trying to sleep; but the visitor kept knocking. Thinking that the man might be delivering a prisoner, Whitten picked up a pistol and opened the door. In an instant a group of hooded men rushed into the room with their guns pointed at his chest. He laid down his own weapon. One of the hooded men demanded the keys, but Whitten shook his head. If they wanted to break someone out—or kill someone—he wasn't going to help them do it. The intruders ransacked the room and found a ring of keys. They demanded to know which one opened the front door of the jail. The jailer shook his head again. One of the masked men tried different keys on the lock to the passageway and finally got it open. They pushed Whitten into the jail itself.

Now they wanted to know where Hairston and Lindsay were. The jailer said that the cell keys were not kept in the jailhouse at night, which was something the gang had not counted on. At this moment Lindsay and Hairston, held in the same cell, would have heard the commotion and known that something was wrong. The door to their cell was sturdily built of wood. They would have heard the jailer's voice when he told the gang that he didn't have an ax. In just two hours it would be sunrise—the earliest sunrise of the year—and with the light the hooded men would have to scurry away. But then came a scraping sound, and the grunts of men straining with effort. The door shuddered and shook; metal groaned as men worked at the jamb with a crowbar. The door snapped open and the prisoners were taken.

About two miles south of Danbury on the road to Walnut Cove, a black man named Henry Martin was startled from sleep by the sound of a large troop of horsemen passing his house. The moon was just rising. As he stated in his testimony to the coroner, Martin jumped out of bed to have a look. His house was near a stream that powered a gristmill. A small bridge spanned the stream, and the thumping of hooves on this bridge had awakened him. Several hours earlier he had seen a large number of mounted men come up the road from the direction of Walnut Cove. Standing now by his gate, just a few feet from the road, he estimated over a hundred were riding by. From here and there he could hear voices in the darkness.

"Boys, let us get away from this house."

"Close up. Close up."

"Tell that man good-bye."

Martin heard a human sound that came to him not as words. He heard it and remembered it as a noise. "I heard two men," he said later, "making a noise as though they were praying."

Then one of the hooded riders said, "Shoot that Negro if he attempts to follow us." Martin went back into his house.

When the first streaks of light came up, Martin went out onto the road. At that hour the road was quiet. He walked south, in the direction the riders had been heading. About two miles from his house he saw bodies hanging from a pine tree. He went up and looked at their faces to see if he knew these men, but he did not. He left the bodies just as he found them and went into Danbury to find the sheriff.

Estes Hairston and Ed Lindsay hung in the tree through the morning. By midday, a group of officials had made its way down from Danbury—a deputy sheriff, the coroner with a jury of a half dozen men, and the jailer. They stood for a while and looked at the bodies. The deputy sat down in the shade of the pine and spread a small sheet of paper on his thigh and wrote his findings:

"I saw them hanging to a Pine tree about four miles south of Danbury near Mr. Wm Neal's & recognized them as being the prisoners & they were dead."

The coroner called the jurymen forward and they stood by the bodies. They asked the jailer if he knew who had done this, and he said no; and they asked Henry Martin if he had recognized any of the riders, and Martin said no, it was dark. So the coroner sat down and spread a paper to write out the findings of the jury: "We for our verdict do say that Estes Hairston and Ed Lindsay came to their death by violent means to wit hanging by parties to the jurors unknown."

He passed the paper around and all the men signed it, bringing the investigation to a close. But as the jury was signing the document, other men were watching them, black men from Walnut Cove. They had come for the body of their friend Estes Hairston. They stepped forward, took him down from the tree, and carried him to Walnut Cove to lay him away.

More than one hundred men had taken part in the murder; it was not a private act of revenge but a public demonstration of the white community's overweening power. Vigilante murders such as these enforced the unwritten code of racial laws. Estes Hairston had been killed for an alleged rape—the usual provocation for a lynching. But several years earlier, Nelson Wilson had been shot dead merely for the alleged theft of a duck. The Hairstons who witnessed his murder tried courageously and vainly to obtain justice for him, only to see the authorities make some little pretense of an investigation.

Some lynchings were the occasion for celebration, as whites gathered by the hundreds, or thousands, to witness the murder. Photographers snapped pictures to sell as souvenirs. Over time, their meaning has changed—these obscene trophies have become damning historical evidence of heinous racial crimes. When I was researching the story of the Mississippi Hairstons, I met a young white man in Columbus, someone fascinated by his local history, who had acquired a large collection of

Columbus photographs taken by a studio in the 1920s and 1930s. He had not examined all the images before buying the collection; indeed, no one had looked at the pictures in years. As he sorted through the images of weddings, church picnics, and school groups, he found a photograph of a lynching, attended by a crowd of whites. The photographer had recorded that event along with all the other day-to-day activities of Columbus. That discovery led to a question: Which image contained the truth about the people of Columbus—the photo of the public murder, or all the others?

I happened upon another of these photographs at an exhibit in the Atlanta Historical Center. To tell the region's history the curators had chosen a fascinating array of artifacts, paintings, and photographs. They shrank from nothing. As I entered the section of the exhibit concerning the 1930s, I heard the voice of Clark Gable, in his film role as Rhett Butler in *Gone With the Wind*. A tape was playing from a kiosk displaying memorabilia about the film, which had opened in Atlanta. I turned and came face to face with a full-size mannequin in Ku Klux Klan regalia. It stood in a display case filled with signs from the Jim Crow era, such as "Colored Waiting Room" and "Whites Only." Near the case a black veil covered a framed object. A sign said that beneath the veil was an image that might be too strong for some to bear looking at. I lifted the veil and saw a photograph of a lynching victim. A black man had been tied to a tree and tortured to death. His body twisted horribly against the ropes that bound him. Displayed near the segregationist signs and the KKK uniform, the photograph powerfully demonstrated how the threat of murder was an integral part of the Jim Crow culture.

A group of young black girls, about ten to eleven years old, entered the exhibition area with their teacher, an African-American woman in her twenties. She made the girls read aloud the old signs from the Jim Crow era, and explained that their own grandmothers could not use the same washroom as white people and had to sit in a separate train car. I saw that one of the girls was lifting the veil. The others gathered around in silence. The teacher walked over to see what they were looking at. She turned her back, walked away, and burst into tears. The students looked at their distraught teacher and then back at the picture. Spontaneously, not with curiosity but with tenderness, the girls reached up to touch the photograph, as if they could heal the agony they saw.

The teacher composed herself and went back to the picture. She told the girls that the man who had been killed might not have done anything wrong, that he might have been killed just because he was black. The murderers had left her—had left to all of us—the burden of explaining what they had done. In writing about the mass murder of the Jews in this century, the literary critic Alfred Kazin perceived a truth that I thought also applied to that photograph—as well as to the lynching of Estes Hairston and Ed Lindsay, and to the racial murders that continue to befoul the country. "The real despair," Kazin wrote, "arises not out of the burning and the killing and the endless political betrayals but out of . . . so terrible a break in human solidarity." The photograph in the museum was an image of that break, which the children had instinctively recognized and tried, in their innocence, to heal with their touch.

At the turn of the century, the black Hairstons were able to follow the awful course of racial violence in the pages of Virginia's leading African-American newspaper, the *Richmond Planet*. In January 1895 the *Planet* ran a front-page article about the number of lynchings in the preceding year—187 men and 3 women—with a melancholy roster of the previous decade's murders: over 1,700 people had been lynched across the country.

The newspaper sardonically chronicled the double standard of Virginia justice: "Within the confines of humane Danville . . . another white man has murdered a Negro and paid the penalty by spending one week in the city jail." In February 1895 the *Planet* began a series of scathing attacks on the courts for their lenient treatment of a wealthy white tobacco manufacturer who had raped a ten-year-old black girl in Danville. "Thomas J. Penn, the white hyena who raped Lina Hanna, the ten-year-old colored girl, is . . . attending to his tobacco business. No one seems to know where his victim is, and the officers of the law have ceased their efforts to find out. Was it murder, or abduction, or both?" The rape of a black Hairston girl was also ignored by the authorities. Her brother, Samuel H. Hairston of Martinsville, wrote a piteous letter to the *Planet*, revealing the shameful news that his thirteen-year-old sister had been raped by a young white man. The rapist, he wrote, "has gone away to some place and the sheriff does not put himself to any trouble to get him. They have paid my mother fifteen dollars not to say anything, but I can't stand it, for my sister is torn to pieces so bad that she has been in bed ever since. She can't walk at all. Please publish this for me, if you possibly can. My sister is one of the most respected girls in this town."

Samuel Hairston's letter galvanized the black community, as well as some whites, to demand that the authorities investigate, but their demand was spurned. From time to time, the courts did rescue a black man from an egregious injustice, as when the Virginia Supreme Court threw out the conviction and eight-year prison sentence of a black Hairston for making a suggestive comment to a white woman. Nevertheless, the reports in the *Planet*, written with palpable bitterness, record the development of a legal double standard that persisted for decades and perhaps, as some would insist, into our own time.

A half century later, the situation had, remarkably, changed little. Three Hairstons were involved in a landmark case that attracted worldwide attention in 1949 through 1951, when the modern civil rights movement was in its infancy. The case of the Martinsville 7, as the black defendants became known in the press, began in 1949 with the rape of a white woman by young black men—four of them teenagers—in various stages of drunkenness on a Saturday evening. The victim had taken a shortcut along railroad tracks that ran through the black section of Martinsville. Joe Henry Hampton, age nineteen, had been drinking in the woods by the tracks when he spotted the woman, called out to her, and pulled her into the shrubbery. She was raped several times before her attackers released her, dazed, bleeding, and almost naked. She found help at the home of a black family. The police quickly arrested seven men, including Howard Lee Hairston, aged eighteen, James Luther Hairston, twenty, and Frank Hairston, nineteen. All seven admitted to being present at the crime, but three insisted that they had not actually raped the woman. The brutality of the crime, which left the victim with severe internal injuries and psychological trauma, shocked the entire state. The black community of Martinsville shared that indignation.

No one thought that any of the defendants would be acquitted outright, but the general expectation was that several of the men would be convicted of the lesser crime of attempted rape or abetting a rape, either of which called for a prison sentence of three years to life. By and large, the court-appointed attorneys put up strong defenses, challenging the testimony of police and the victim, questioning the validity of confessions, and pointing out mitigating circumstances. The defendants and their families had turned down offers of outside legal help in the belief that local attorneys would have a better chance of gaining fair consideration from local juries than strangers would. The black community as a whole believed that the juries would be able to look beyond race and treat the defendants fairly.

Howard Hairston admitted that he had tried to have intercourse with the victim, but asserted that he had been unable to do so. Frank Hairston, who had not been present when the woman was first dragged into the woods, said that another defendant had told him the woman had been paid for sex and that she did not resist him. Booker Millner testified that he had intended to have intercourse with the woman, but when she begged to be let go, he was stricken with remorse and walked away without touching her. On the witness stand he asked for mercy and attributed his involvement to drunkenness: "I know I did wrong. . . . I should have went and called help. By me drinking though, I don't reckon my mind let me do it so I ask the Court to have mercy on me." Frank Hairston corroborated Millner's statement that he approached the woman but "came straight back." Frank Hairston's attorney challenged his client's confession, which he said contained many errors. Frank Hairston suffered from a speech impediment and maintained that the detective who interrogated him didn't understand what he was saying. He had signed the confession without reading it—indeed, he couldn't read it because he was illiterate.

The men were tried, in six separate proceedings, in only eight days. The trials built their own inexorable momentum, as daily verdicts of "Guilty . . . Guilty . . . Guilty" made it all but impossible for subsequent juries to come to any other conclusion. Six all-white juries convicted all seven defendants of rape and sentenced all seven men to death. The juries' sentences, ratified by the judge, struck the black community as a mass lynching in everything but name. White rapists were never sentenced to death. The judge and jury had not even considered the degrees of the defendants' guilt. All were condemned.

Attorneys from the NAACP joined the case to handle the appeals. In an attempt to save the lives of the Martinsville 7, these lawyers devised a legal strategy that would later become a standard in capital cases involving African-Americans. They advanced arguments, based on statistical evidence, that the state systematically discriminated against blacks in imposing death sentences. Since Virginia had begun keeping records of executions in 1907, forty-five men had been put to death for rape, and another fourteen had been executed for attempted rape. All of them were black. Aided by future Supreme Court justice Thurgood Marshall, the attorneys prepared briefs declaring that Virginia's juries routinely sentenced black men to death for rape, while "white men have always had immunity from such penalty." Such a double standard, they argued, undermined "equal and exact justice to all men of whatever race." The attorneys were able to cite a recent case in which two white men from Richmond—police officers—had raped a black woman and received sentences of seven years. The Virginia courts and the U.S. Supreme Court denied all the Martinsville 7 appeals. The justices refused to believe that there was any systematic discrimination.

The Martinsville 7's supporters launched an international campaign to arouse public opinion in support of clemency, something that could not have been done in 1880 or 1900. The effort was spearheaded by African-American celebrities, including Mahalia Jackson, Ossie Davis, Josephine Baker, and Ruby Dee, and joined by famous writers such as Dashiell Hammett and Howard Fast. The black writer Shirley Graham delivered a petition to the White House pleading with President Harry Truman to intervene. Eleanor Roosevelt urged federal officials to consider stepping into the case. Letters and telegrams of protest arrived at the White House and the Virginia governor's office, signed by more than sixty members of the French Assembly, and by the Russian composers Dmitry Shostakovich and Sergey Prokofiev.

Their protests and pleas for clemency proved fruitless. On February 2, 1951, four of the convicted men—Joe Henry Hampton, Howard Lee Hairston, Booker T. Millner, and Frank Hairston Jr.—were electrocuted at the Virginia State Penitentiary. On February 5, the state executed John Clabon Taylor, James Luther Hairston, and Francis DeSales Grayson. Never before in Virginia had so many people been executed for a single crime.

During the appeals of the Martinsville 7 case, Virginia judges, attorneys, and politicians strenuously denied that race was a factor in the death sentences of the seven men. In one court appearance to argue the state's position, Attorney General Lindsay Almond angrily rebutted the defendants' charge of discrimination. "There's not a word of truth in it and they know it," he thundered. He emphasized the "unspeakable and bestial horror" of a gang rape and defied the Martinsville 7's attorneys to cite any example of seven white men "brutally ravishing a defenseless woman of any color." Almond's challenge went unanswered and helped persuade a judge that the state would never act under a double standard of justice. But some two years after the Martinsville 7 went to their deaths, a case arose that met Almond's criteria. Many of the details of the incident have remained secret, and I only discovered the incident when someone who had inside information about the Martinsville 7 case unexpectedly called me.

In the spring of 1954, twelve young men were involved in the rape of a white woman. Eleven of the perpetrators were students at the University of Virginia; the twelfth was a recent graduate. All were white. Beginning on a Saturday night and continuing into the next day, they confined the young woman to a room at the university and repeatedly raped her. She returned to her parents' home "in a dazed condition, apparently beaten and brutalized, covered with bruises." The woman came from a prominent family; indeed, she was from a family well known to the president of the university, Colgate Darden.

Headed by a Charlottesville judge, a private investigation was launched by President Darden. The rapists were themselves from prominent families. Although crimes had been committed, the university used its influence to ensure that the authorities took no action. The investigation led to suspensions and expulsions for some of the students, who immediately protested their punishments as far too harsh. When it was pointed out that some of the young men might lose their expected postgraduate military appointments, the university modified its penalties to preserve their careers. The similarity to the Martinsville case is obvious, but in a final irony, one of the rapists, whose only penalty was expulsion and who never even saw the inside of a jail, was from the family of a judge who helped send the Martinsville 7 to the electric chair.

The Hairston family has never forgotten the Martinsville 7. One Hairston, an attorney, had followed the case in the newspapers at the time. He compared it to Alabama's famous Scottsboro Boys case in the 1930s, in which eight black teenagers were falsely convicted of rape and sentenced to death. Their sentences were overturned on appeal. He said that the Virginia legal system had been more careful than Alabama's in following correct legal procedure, leaving the defendants no real route for an appeal.

At one of the Hairston family reunions, I was speaking with a group of women from southern Virginia. I wondered if any of them remembered the case, forty years after it happened. At the mention of the words "Martinsville 7," one of the women, a soft-spoken, gray-haired woman in her seventies, flinched as if I had slapped her. The pain of those deaths and her anger at the injustice of it were still fresh. She all but spat out her reply: "It was a *sin* what they did to those boys."

PART III

"OUR BLOOD IS IN THIS SOIL"

Materially, psychologically, and culturally, part of the nation's heritage is Negro American, and whatever it becomes it will be shaped in part by the Negro's presence. Which is fortunate, for today it is the black American who puts pressure upon the nation to live up to its ideals. . . . Without the black American, something irrepressibly hopeful and creative would go out of the American spirit.

—RALPH ELLISON, "What America Would be Without Blacks" (1970)

A Gathering

in Ohio

Once more the Hairstons were gathering for their annual reunion, this time in Columbus, Ohio, at the elegant new convention center on the edge of the revitalized downtown business district. Off the lobby, a huge wall of tinted glass offered a spectacular view of postmodern skyscrapers sharply outlined in morning sun. Two stories below I could see a bus delivering part of the North Carolina contingent, who had driven through the night from the old plantation country. The arrival of Squire Hairston, with the branch of the family from around Cooleemee, meant that the convention could get under way.

A ribbon-cutting ceremony at the entrance to the hotel marked the official start of the convention. A Hairston minister offered prayer, and a representative of the mayor read a proclamation welcoming the family. The adults solemnly conducted this ritual while grandchildren and great-grandchildren romped at the edges of the scene. As the group stood for the opening invocation, I could see in the crowd a score or so people I had already talked to about their families and their history.

I caught a glimpse of Savolia Joyce, who had told me fascinating stories of how her grandparents had migrated on foot from North Carolina to the mountains of West Virginia early in this century. They had gone there to take the toughest, most dangerous jobs in the deepest parts of the mines, "to get the kind of money they had always dreamed of." Seated in a wheelchair was the Reverend Robert F. Hairston Jr., a respected figure in Columbus's African-American community. In the 1920s his father, the descendant of Cooleemee slaves, had migrated here and established a church that remains one of the most important religious institutions in Columbus. During the Depression he had started farms outside the city to raise food for the poor. On the other side of the crowd, I spotted a tall, fit-looking man I recognized as Earnest Hairston. He had talked to me about growing up in rural North Carolina and attending a one-room, segregated schoolhouse. When I asked him what he did for a living, he said he had recently retired from NASA. After peppering him with further questions, I discovered that he had been part of an elite team of computer scientists and mathematicians who had guided the spacecraft that took Neil Armstrong to the moon.

Looking out over the crowd and thinking back on their stories, I was reminded of those patriotic murals that adorn the walls of statehouses, courts, and schools, depicting the onward march of national progress. Typically, at one edge of the scene a column of doughty pioneers makes its way forward. Time passes and the children of the pioneers take their places in an allegory of struggle and progress, mastering the land with physical and mental labor. There is the farmer at his plow, the miner with his pick, the scientist holding up a beaker containing a symbol of nature's power, the soldier with his gun, and the preacher with his book. They represent the core values of the nation, in a scene carefully composed to reveal the interconnections and interdependence of all the figures in the American enterprise.

In many ways, no one symbolized the family's journey more than Jester Hairston, who attended the Columbus reunion despite having to prepare for a concert tour of Spain the following week. Jester had made himself into an international star by his performances of the folk music of the slaves. "I decided that I wanted to make my mark in folk songs," he said, "because my grandparents were all slaves. I wanted to keep that music alive."

Jester had to recapture the spirit of that music when he began singing in Harlem with the Hall Johnson Choir in the 1930s. Johnson nearly fired him because he couldn't manage the slave speech of *dis, dat,* and *dey.* Jester had graduated from Tufts University in Boston in 1929 and was proud to have acquired the polished diction of a college man. He had to relearn the country speech of his parents and grandparents to bring himself back to the spirit and soul of what he had escaped.

Jester Hairston's life had been full of struggle. "I had a hard time all my life," he said, "but people always helped me." It took him nine years to finish college because he never had enough money for tuition. He was accepted first at the University of Massachusetts in 1920, arriving with $50 in his pocket to support himself for nine months. After his freshman year, he withdrew temporarily to earn enough for his tuition. He went to work on the docks in South Boston.

"Tough Irishmen!" he exclaimed. "Nothing but tough Irishmen! Used to fight like dogs. They had a big mill over there. The ships would come in with wheat in boxcars from the West. I got a job shoveling wheat. I'd crawl up in that boxcar and push the wheat into a grate in the middle of the floor. Four boxcars for a day's work. Tough Irishmen! Boy, you talk about fighting! I would teach them songs, barbershop singing. They liked me. They didn't like blacks at all, but they liked me because I could teach them how to sing."

When he returned to the University of Massachusetts, he earned extra money singing at white churches in Amherst, and a white woman who accompanied him on the piano was deeply impressed by his talent. She told him he was at the wrong school, that he should study in one of the schools in Boston that had a good music program. "She started nagging me about going to Boston to study music," he said. "I told her I didn't have the money, and finally she said, 'I have a little saved up, I will lend you money to go to music school.'"

Even with the promised loan, Jester didn't have enough to pay tuition. He left UMass and worked for two years on ships running between Boston and New York, working as a scullery man and cleaning the decks—"worst job you could have," he said. When he had enough money saved, he applied to Tufts and told UMass he was not coming back. He should not have been so quick to announce his decision. "Tufts didn't want any blacks there. They made it sound nice. They wrote me a letter saying, 'The junior class is closed.' I was too embarrassed to go back to UMass."

His plans suddenly dashed, Jester went back to work on the boat. There he encountered a passenger from Tufts, a black man who had been the captain of the football team, basketball team, and track team. "They needed him," Jester said, "that's why he was there. They didn't need me." The man asked Jester when he was going back to college, and Jester reluctantly told him what had happened.

"So, you got the letter," the man said. He had apparently heard the same story from other black applicants. He advised Jester not to quit trying and gave him the name of the head of the music department. "Write him a letter," he told Jester, "and lay it on thick."

More than sixty years later, Jester could still recite that letter from memory. He had indeed laid it on thick: "'Dear Professor Lewis—For years I have been reading every article in the press about the wonderful work you are doing with young people at Tufts College. It would mean a great deal to me if I could meet with you so that I could write to my mother in Pennsylvania and tell her I had at last seen the great Professor Lewis and heard about his wonderful work in person.' Well, that got him!"

Soon Jester received a letter from the same man who had earlier turned him down: "We are honored to announce that your application to the junior class has been accepted."

Jester graduated near the top of his class, with grades he hoped were good enough to get him a Phi Beta Kappa key, but the registrar told him that because he had failed one course, a botany class way back in his freshman year at UMass, he couldn't qualify for the key. Sensing Jester's disappointment, the registrar told him that the college would "keep an eye on" him, and if he distinguished himself in music, they would get him the key.

Jester went to New York during the harshest period of the Depression and found work as a singing coach, which led him to the all-black Hall Johnson Choir of Harlem. They sang in the hit Broadway musical *Green Pastures*, which a Hollywood studio soon acquired to make into a film. The choir, with Jester as its arranger, set off for Hollywood in 1935. The Russian film composer Dimitri Tiomkin heard the choir and invited them to sing his music for the Frank Capra film *Lost Horizon*. But the choir ran into a backstage color bar, for the producers flatly refused to allow the group to perform. Tiomkin told Jester that a studio executive had said, "Who the hell ever heard of niggers singing Russian music?" But Tiomkin remained adamant, refusing to work with anyone else, and he forced the producers to relent. After working on *Lost Horizon*, Jester began a twenty-year collaboration with Tiomkin, arranging the music for such classic films as *Red River* and *Duel in the Sun*. But the work was irregular, and he had to supplement his income with bit parts. He was chosen as an extra for Tarzan movies, a spear-carrying African, because of his coal-black skin. He could not afford to buy a house until 1960, the year John Wayne cast him in *The Alamo* as Jethro, the slave of Colonel Jim Bowie, played by Richard Widmark.

In 1972, Jester was surprised to receive a letter from Tufts. The school had indeed been "keeping an eye on" him. They were not offering a Phi Beta Kappa key, but something greater, an honorary doctorate of music. After receiving the doctorate, Jester regaled the graduation crowd with the story of how he had been gotten into Tufts in the first place. He told the story as a joke, but his point was clear—forty-five years ago I was not good enough for this school, but I am standing here today because I refused to accept that.

The Tufts honorary degree was one of four Jester has received—"all for black spirituals," he said. "That's my field, the music of my ancestors. I've traveled all over the country trying to find songs from the African tradition. I found a song in South Carolina on the Sea Islands outside of Charleston. I had seen it in a book and I went to the islands to see if I could find it. I got to talking with some women who were around my age and a little older. And they sang that song to me, 'Sangaree.' They said they'd been singing the song since they were children, the same way children sing 'Ring Around the Rosy,' but they didn't know what *Sangaree* meant. Generation after generation, the meaning had left." He found the meaning when the State Department sent him to Ghana in the early 1960s.

"I made friends with the head of the music department at the university there. I asked him if he ever heard of a song called 'Sangaree,' and I sang it for him. He said, 'It sounds familiar, Jester.'" The professor listened again as Jester sang, and he recognized it: "You know, that song is in our language. It's Ashanti. It hasn't been sung here in Africa for four or five hundred years. It's archaic."

It was an old parable about an eagle, the Sangaree. In those days the land was a tangle of trees and vines, inhabited by an old, emaciated, and crippled woman. One day an eagle flew down and spoke to the woman: "Old woman, I need to lay my eggs, and I'd like to lay them in your tree. If you will permit me to do that, I can make a nice land for you and let you be the head of a village." The old woman agreed. The eagle flew up and cried "Sangaree!" and the tangle of trees disappeared, replaced by a beautiful garden. The eagle cried "Sangaree!" a second time and a village appeared, and then a third time and people appeared, and the old woman miraculously became young, and she was the head of the village. At the center of the village was the tree where the eagle had made her home, and from it could be heard the sounds of her eaglets. One day a boy came to the woman and said he wanted to cut the tree down so he could eat the birds, and she said no: "I made a promise to the mother that she could raise them in that tree, and don't you touch them." But the boy was angry and started to cry. The woman didn't want him to cry so she said, "You could have one, that's all." The boy went out and chopped at the tree, and the tree began to sway, and one of the eaglets fell out and he ate it. Suddenly the mother eagle flew down and cried out, "Sangaree!" The people disappeared; she cried "Sangaree!" a second time and the houses disappeared, and the land was covered again in impenetrable jungle. She said it a third time, and the woman became as old and crippled as she had been before. The eagle flew down with her babies on her back and said to the woman, "You agreed that you would permit me to raise my family in this tree. If someone does good to you, don't repay them by doing evil." With that, the eagle flew away, leaving devastation behind. "I made an arrangement of that song," Jester said, "and I have sung it all around the country."

Even though the story came from Africa, Jester said, "There's your Bible, right there." It was a parable of good and evil, and a creation myth, with a tree of knowledge and a lost paradise. It also seemed to be a folk tale about some long-ago disaster that had removed all the young people, leaving behind the old ones to wander through an empty land with no one to tend it. It was the lamentation of a people who had endured a catastrophe they could not comprehend.

Later, I heard Jester conduct a choir. The singers had been rehearsing for several weeks, and Jester arrived two days before the concert to put the group through its final paces and put his stamp on them. I was watching one of the rehearsals when Jester suddenly stopped the group and ordered a break. He called aside the young black man who was the soloist. Jester told him he was doing it all wrong. It's not "keep your hand on the plow," it's "keep yo' hand on de plow!" It's not "This old hammer," it's "Dis ol' hammer killed John Henry!" Hall Johnson had given Jester the same lecture sixty years earlier. Now Jester was the one keeping the tradition alive, and he seemed to be saying to the young man, "Don't make it sound pretty; don't make it sound better than it was." To Jester Hairston the spirituals were not just historical artifacts, hateful relics of a hated era. They were hymns of courage, handed down to the generations that needed them next.

Indeed, for years no Hairston reunion had passed without the entire family joining Jester in a rousing version of "Amen," which traditionally served, as it did that weekend in Columbus, as the finale of the reunion's festive Saturday-night banquet. Jester composed the song for the 1963 film *Lilies of the Field*, starring Sidney Poitier. It is a song of redemption, ringing with the hope and sadness of the old spirituals. It is the music of a collective memory—a workman's song, being sung by descendants of field hands. Jester had absorbed this heritage and transformed it into music, sung that night at the Columbus reunion in tones of celebration, strong enough to shake the hall.

The Hairston family's rise from the tobacco field to the banquet hall did not occur by accident. It came about through the effort and sacrifice of community-builders who fought for education, jobs, and basic civil rights. At the reunion, many people suggested that I go to Stokes County, North Carolina, to see John L. Hairston. One of many teachers in the family, he had helped start the county's all-black high school in the early 1950s and had been its principal during the integration crisis of the 1960s. His struggle to bring education to his rural county reflected thousands of similar, unsung campaigns in the small towns of the South. His story portrayed something else as well—the turning point in an African-American community when it resolved to climb out of segregation, what Ralph Ellison called the "hole of darkness." Ellison described the psychological passage of a black man struggling against the identity segregation imposed on him: "Before he could have some voice in his own destiny he had to discard . . . old identities and illusions; his enlightenment couldn't come until then." John L. Hairston was the man who had brought that enlightenment to his community.

THE LIBERATION
OF WALNUT COVE

Walnut Cove lay in the old plantation country, just south of the Virginia border, where one of the founders of the white Hairston empire—the man known in the family as Saura Town Peter—had presided over a twelve-thousand-acre plantation from the end of the Revolutionary War until his death in 1832. He owned a network of smaller plantations here as well, places called Shoe Buckle, Hamburg, Muddy Creek, and Belews Creek, where Jester Hairston was born in 1901. Although I knew him as the man who had purchased the land that would become Cooleemee Plantation, Saura Town Peter remained a shadowy figure in my research.

His lands here in Stokes County came into the possession of the Cooleemee branch of the family in the 1850s. In fact, Judge Peter, one of Saura Town Peter's descendants, was able to pay part of his college tuition during the Depression by the sale of timber from these Stokes County lands.

The county remains one of the most important centers of the black Hairston family. John Goolsby, the former coachman of Cooleemee Plantation, had moved his family here from Virginia and acquired land in the early 1870s. His children married Hairstons and established one of the major lines of the black family. Some of Goolsby's family moved to Cooleemee in the 1880s and later, but many of his descendants remained in Stokes County, in the vicinity of Walnut Cove. By right—since their roots here went back to the era of the Revolution—the black Hairstons and Goolsbys of Stokes should have been esteemed as founding families of this region, but that was not the case in the 1960s.

Although the gritty factories and sleek offices of Winston-Salem were only a thirty-minute drive away, Walnut Cove remained a small town in a rural part of the Piedmont. The town had the largest enclave of blacks in the county, which was overwhelmingly white. The black district, called London, had a Hairston Street, named for the former slaves who had lived there for generations. The commercial district on Main Street consisted of a short stretch of low buildings, constructed mostly of bricks, with not a trace of adornment or decorative flourish. The bricks came from the Hedgecock family's brickyard, just outside of town, which for fifty years had been one of the main employers of the town's blacks, in addition to the pipeyard and sawmill.

Walnut Cove's Main Street was also Route 311, a narrow road that roller-coasted up and down the hills south to Winston-Salem. A road with a long history, Route 311 was part of the Great Wagon Road of colonial times, the road that had brought some of the first settlers to this region from Pennsylvania. In the last days of the Civil War, General George Stoneman's column of federal raiders had used the road as its invasion route into the North Carolina Piedmont. This was the road where John Goolsby had been stopped by some of those raiders and threatened with death if he did not yield his master's silver; it was on this road that Estes Hairston had been lynched in 1881, and it was on this road in 1968 that the black teenagers of Walnut Cove marched in a protest demonstration to save their school and their principal, John L. Hairston. Everyone I talked to, black or white, still remembered that event.

It was around noon that day in March when about sixty students filed silently out of the segregated London School, carrying signs that demanded a fair integration plan for the county. As they walked, they carefully kept to the sidewalk so as not to violate the law by blocking traffic and risk arrest by deputies who shadowed the march in their patrol car. One by one merchants emerged from the stores on Main Street to watch, and to ask the teenagers why they were doing this. "You kids should be in school," one said. "This looks bad for the town," said another, adding, "we don't need this nonsense here." In the previous year, the country had seen 164 race riots, and every protest march summoned images of fire, police clubs, and blood.

People remembered that it was a warm day for that time of year, and one of the marchers at the head of the column, Vincent Withers, announced to his friends that he was thirsty and was going to buy a soda. But there was only one restaurant on Main Street, Vernon's Grill, and by long-established custom, Vernon served blacks only through the back door. It occurred to Vincent Withers, and his friends Mona and Christopher Hairston, that it might be time to walk in the front door, sit at the counter, and buy a Coke. As the students approached Vernon's they could see that the town's two deputies had pulled up at the door, where Willis Vernon was standing with a knot of the lunchtime regulars. Across the street from the grill, the noontime crowd at the pool hall came out, cue sticks in hand, to see what the trouble was. So in the early afternoon of March 18, 1968, the civil rights movement came at last to Walnut Cove.

When I went to see John L. Hairston, I had expected to meet a modern Frederick Douglass, an imposing, stentorian man with a powerful presence. Instead I saw a short, slender, soft-spoken gentleman with the diffident manner of a scholar. It was this man, people said, who had publicly defied the segregationists in 1968 and galvanized the black community to topple the "separate but equal" system that had ruled them for their entire lives. Retired after nearly four decades as a teacher and principal, he lived in a substantial brick house in the hamlet of Pine Hall, just north of Walnut Cove. When he came to the door, I was startled, and certain that I had somehow come to the wrong house: the man greeting me was unquestionably white. It occurred to me that directory assistance had given me the number of the wrong John L. Hairston, a white man. As we settled into chairs in his living room, I looked around for any racial clues, but there were none. Besides, I didn't know what items I could look for to signify blackness. I couldn't spot any family photographs amid the shelves full of books, plaques on the wall, and furniture that anyone of middle-class means might have. I asked about his years as a teacher, but his responses could have come from either a white or black educator. More and more worried that I was interviewing the wrong man, I changed the subject to a topic certain to reveal his race. I asked what his family background was. But he said that both of his parents were Hairstons— an answer either a white or black person in this part of the South could easily have given. I thought I had solved the puzzle when he said his paternal great-grandfather had been a planter in Stokes County before the Civil War—he was white; but then he said another great-grandfather was John Goolsby. "I was born in 1918," he concluded, "in a slave cabin on the old Saura Town Plantation." I had come to talk about segregation with a man as white as the segregationists.

He had learned the bizarre customs of Jim Crow segregation as a small child, when his mother took the family to visit their father, who worked for the Norfolk & Western Railroad in West Virginia. "I can remember riding the train back and forth between here and West Virginia. At Bluefield, on the Virginia–West Virginia border, we were able to get out of the segregated coach, which was the oldest and most dilapidated on the train, and move up to the better cars. On the way back, we would have to change again in Bluefield. Certainly we recognized the fact that we were discriminated against, but it was just a way of life." He had to accept it, just as he had to accept the pitifully limited education available to black children.

Before I arrived at his house, I had stopped to see a relic of the separate-but-equal era—a small, whitewashed frame building just down the road, the Pine Hall Colored School. John L., along with many other Hairstons, had attended it as a boy. Originally built for white students in 1885, the building was moved twice and donated, in dilapidated condition, to the black community in 1905. About 1915 it was moved again to Pine Hall, refurbished by black parents, and enlarged when a black farmer attached a cabin to it. Several of the teachers in the early days were Hairstons, and another was a Goolsby. When John L. was going to school here in the late 1920s and early 1930s, the citizens of Pine Hall built a handsome new brick school, with nine teachers, for the white children.

John L. said that he attended the Pine Hall Colored School for nine years, though it offered only seven grades, explaining that he stayed in the seventh grade three years because he wanted to continue his education but no school was open to him. Finally, in 1933, the adjacent county of Rockingham opened a colored junior high school at Madison that accepted Stokes County students. To get to that school, scores of black children hitched rides on early-morning delivery trucks or rode with workers. John L.'s father paid to have him board with a black family in Madison during the week. But when Fred Hairston became seriously ill and had to quit work, the family could not afford to board him in Madison any longer. At home, in between helping to take care of his father and his younger siblings, he kept up his reading as best he could. He could have continued his schooling if the county had allowed him to attend the new all-white school literally within earshot of his house.

"I could hear the white kids playing at recess," he remembered, "but I couldn't attend—it was just unthinkable." It was 1934, and he would not see the inside of a classroom again until 1946, working in the meantime at a country store and the local brickyard. During World War II he served in the National Guard, doing the unromantic job of guarding bridges and tunnels in New York from saboteurs. On a one-week furlough he raced home to marry Ruth Anderson, who had been his childhood sweetheart in Pine Hall.

His military service in World War II gave John L. a glimpse of life outside the boundaries of segregation, and he was determined to get back to the North. At the age of twenty-eight, he started attending special night classes set up for African-American veterans at the Madison school, while working at the brickyard during the day. Even though Ruth had given birth to two children and the family needed money, she encouraged him to go to college rather than settle into a job. He entered North Carolina Agricultural & Technical State University, an all-black school in Greensboro. "I wanted," he said, "to get away from the brickyard."

With the goal of getting a good job as far away from Stokes County as possible, he enrolled in the school of engineering and majored in electrical engineering, graduating with honors at the top of his class in 1951— one of the first black men from Stokes County to receive a college degree. Getting the highest grades was more than a matter of pride, it was an absolute necessity. The few companies that were hiring black engineers picked only the very best of the crop. John L.'s work paid off when he was informed by letter to report after graduation to the Picatinny Arsenal, a sprawling U.S. Army facility in northern New Jersey that had employed a substantial number of black technicians and scientists to develop weapons systems during World War II. John L. and Ruth packed up and prepared to start a new life.

Just a few days before the scheduled departure, John L.'s grandmother died suddenly and he sent a telegram to his new employers requesting their permission to delay starting the job for several days so that he could attend the funeral. In reply he received a telegram telling him not to bother coming at all. The telegram said that his name was being moved to the bottom of the job roster and that he would be advised when his services were required. There was no question of looking for an engineering job somewhere else—the handful of companies that hired blacks had already filled their small quotas for the year. Stuck in segregated North Carolina, the would-be engineer took a job bagging groceries at an A&P in Greensboro.

As he talked about the subsequent events of his life, I was reminded of *It's a Wonderful Life*, the unabashedly sentimental film by Frank Capra about a man who finds himself stuck in a place he desperately wants to leave. James Stewart, as George Bailey, tries for years to find his way out of the dead-end town of Bedford Falls, only to have one mishap after another keep him there. It seems that fate is punishing him, until it turns out that quiet, unassuming George Bailey is the only man who can save Bedford Falls.

John L. was working at the supermarket one day when a familiar face turned up by chance—his old math teacher from the colored school in Madison County. The teacher had been named principal of a new all-black school under construction in Walnut Cove, London School. He needed a good math teacher and wondered if John L. might be interested in the job. It was certainly better than the supermarket.

Since the end of the war, black parents in Stokes County had been patiently requesting that state school authorities build them a school that went beyond the seventh grade. Delegations of parents made numerous trips to Raleigh to lobby state officials in person. Their efforts bore fruit in 1951, when London School took shape at the edge of a tobacco field. It was a single-story building constructed of cinder blocks, faced on the outside with brick. Its large windows flooded the classrooms with sunlight. To the black community of Stokes County, it was a magnificent sight, literally the answer to thousands of prayers. The faculty, naturally, would be all black, which was not regarded as a limitation but as an opportunity.

As the first months of the school year went by, John L. felt exhilarated to be part of a team that was creating a new institution. So he was taken aback when, just after he had dismissed his students for the long Thanksgiving weekend, a messenger arrived at his classroom with a telegram from the Picatinny Arsenal. The arsenal had an immediate opening for him and he should report for work the following Monday. Fate was presenting him with a second chance. The position at the arsenal offered more than twice the salary he was making as a teacher. This secure job in the field he had trained for was up North, away from the Jim Crow segregation in North Carolina. The job offer, however, came with an instant deadline—report on Monday or not at all.

That evening and all day on Thanksgiving he talked things over with his wife, Ruth. They agreed that this was the chance of a lifetime, the chance to leave behind an impoverished county for almost certain advancement. On the other side of the argument were his students. He liked them, and he had discovered that he enjoyed teaching. But the most important thing was just a feeling, as he recalled it forty years later, that if he stayed behind, he could "make a difference, perhaps a much greater difference teaching black kids in North Carolina than I could do in New Jersey." The day after Thanksgiving he sent a wire to the arsenal turning down the job.

London School, the school where John L. Hairston decided to remain, reflected quite accurately the hypocrisy of the "separate but equal" philosophy that reinforced segregated education at the time. Indeed, London received public funds, but at a rate lower than that of white schools. To alleviate the chronic shortage of funds, teachers were constantly busy with fund-raising. Hardly a weekend went by without a group of teachers running a flea market, car wash, or a barbecue. The students ran their own fund-raising events. Every year the students in each of the high school grades competed to raise money—the class with the highest total won the right to elect the homecoming queen. The white schools, of course, held such fund-raisers, but their proceeds usually went toward sports teams and extracurricular activities; at London the money went into basic equipment and books. Teachers not only gave of their free time, they often reached into their own pockets to buy shoes and clothes for indigent students. With its relatively small enrollment, the high school did not qualify for state grants to fund science labs and programs. John L. made his private library of mathematics and reference books available to all the students at London and tutored students who had trouble with algebra, trigonometry, or geometry. The school instituted a program of home visits by teachers, for discussions with parents whose children were falling behind. Any discipline or academic problem prompted an immediate visit to the student's home—no problem was allowed to languish, and no one was written off as incorrigible or unteachable. The faculty relentlessly preached self-improvement. They urged their students to go on to college or technical school, to find a specialty and advance in it. In 1959, eight years after he became a teacher, John L. was made principal of the school. As the highest-ranking black public official in the county, he was the man the entire black community looked up to and became the unofficial head of the community.

He continued his predecessor's program of assembling a superb faculty—all of them black—by recruiting top students from the state's black colleges, notably A&T and Winston-Salem State Teachers College. At that time London had higher faculty standards than the white schools, where some teachers had not even finished college and received their teaching posts through political connections. Many of London's teachers held master's degrees in education or in their fields of specialty; some were working on doctorates. Attending classes at night and during the summers, John L. received a master's degree in mathematics education and educational administration.

Given the population of the county, it was not surprising that several other Hairstons were on the faculty. John L.'s wife went back to college in the early 1960s for a degree in elementary education and joined the faculty in 1964. John L.'s youngest sister taught at the school along with her husband. A cousin who had been London's valedictorian in 1957 graduated cum laude from A&T with a degree in math, taught for three years in Virginia, and then went to work at his old school.

The black community was more or less left alone to do what it wanted at London, for the white community was not hostile to the idea of blacks getting an education; it was merely indifferent. For the first seven years of his tenure, John L. maintained a tradition begun by his predecessor—a perfect attendance record at the monthly meetings of the county's twelve school principals. His attendance rate was zero. He never attended because the county superintendent, R. M. Green, never sent notifications of the time and place of the meetings. His presence was not desired. Yet Green was not an overt racist in the George Wallace mold, and John L. described him as "a down-to-earth, good person, a very kind person, but he had all these inborn characteristics that were typically Southern—you know your place and just stay in it."

Many of John L.'s former students still live in Walnut Cove. I sought out people who had taken part in the protest march in 1968 to ask what it had been like to attend school in the time of segregation. Born after World War II, they grew up, during the atomic age, under the system of segregation devised in Reconstruction. One man said that the separation of the races was almost total. "You'd walk past each other but you wouldn't speak. You didn't know each other. You didn't interact with each other. Until I went off to college, I had no concept of whites as people. They seemed like—something else. In college it was an insight for me to see that they laughed and cried, that they fell in love and got hurt, that they went through all of the same things that we went through, that some were smart and some were not smart, some were strong and some weren't strong, some were pretty and some weren't."

Another former student recalled that race relations were never discussed in her family when she was growing up. Like many of the black children in the county, she learned about race from experience and learned by example not to question the status quo. Like other children, she was puzzled by the different treatment accorded whites and blacks, but she learned to accept it as a way of life, something one had to adapt to. She found that some shopkeepers in Walnut Cove would be courteous to her when she was the only customer, but they would be rude if other whites were in the store, and she sensed that the whites were trying to prove to one another that they knew how to handle blacks. The lunch counter, the Laundromat, and the movie theater remained segregated in the 1960s. The black Hairstons could go to the movies, but they had to sit in the balcony. Other parts of the county were even more hostile. One man recalled that the town of King, about ten miles west of Walnut Cove, was "as bad as Mississippi or Alabama—you wouldn't want to get caught there after dark." He remembered graffiti scrawled on road signs outside King saying, "Niggers—keep on thru." When he went with some white boys to King for a team physical exam, the doctor refused to touch him.

Inside the walls of their school, however, the students were never allowed to feel that they were second-class citizens. Indeed, the students from that era remembered feeling "special," that they were a "unique group," being groomed by good teachers to "take on the world." Although the rigorous academic program at London imparted a strong sense of self-esteem, their passion and optimism collided with the indifference of the white community to their achievements. No matter what the students accomplished, "we were not supposed to be as good as they were," one of them remembered. "If you were white, it didn't matter what you had or what you did. As long as you were white, you were okay—you would feel a little bit ahead of persons who were not white."

Their second-class status was driven home in the mid-1960s when juniors and seniors at London were assigned, for the first time, to take their standardized tests at the white high school. They were surprised to glimpse a well-equipped science lab and see fresh, up-to-date textbooks— their own books were the obsolete texts discarded by the white school. They were also surprised by the spaciousness of the facility, for London had become severely overcrowded from having to accept black students from the entire county. They knew they were on a par with the white students academically, but they also knew that they were expected to make do with less, and it bothered them.

Segregation in schools had, in fact, been illegal since 1954, when the Supreme Court issued its unanimous landmark decision in the case of

Brown v. Board of Education of Topeka. In 1955, the court decided on the implementation of the decision, declaring that schools must be integrated "with all deliberate speed." The vagueness of that language left the door open to all manner of delaying tactics at the state and local levels. The state of Virginia, for example, launched a program of "massive resistance" to the decision and simply closed schools faced with integration. Some black children were denied education for years while the State of Virginia paid tuition for white students to attend private "academies," which were, of course, segregated. Not as militant as Virginia, North Carolina nevertheless interpreted "deliberate speed" broadly. Stokes County schools operated under a "freedom of choice" policy, which theoretically allowed students of either race to enroll in any school. But the few black students who dared enroll in white schools were harassed by students and teachers alike. It seemed that the unwritten Jim Crow law—"you know your place and just stay in it"—would prevail indefinitely over the written law.

In October 1967, thirteen years after the landmark court decision, three representatives from the Department of Health, Education, and Welfare traveled to Stokes County for a fact-finding tour of the schools. The HEW team consisted of a white man, a black man, and a black woman. The members of the school board could not help but notice that the federal officials who came to check on the status of integration had arrived from the same starting point in two cars—one for the blacks and the other for the white. There might have been an innocent reason for it, but the apparent lack of racial comity on the HEW team brought sour smiles to the Stokes County people.

Leading the federal team into the London School amidst an almost celebratory atmosphere of one-sided banter and backslapping, Superintendent Green trumpeted the achievements of his black principal and staff. "Oh, he bragged and he bragged and he bragged," recalled one person who witnessed the performance, "about what a good principal John L. was and how good the school was." But Green's enthusiasm could not hide the evidence that remained plainly visible and incontrovertible—London School was a sea of black faces while the other county schools were almost entirely white. Not surprisingly, HEW declared that the schools were segregated and ordered the county school board to come up with an integration plan.

The school board consisted of five white men and one white woman, only one of whom was known to be sympathetic to the black community. At the end of February 1968, the chairman, a dentist named Isaac Booe from the town of King, announced the board's decision. The board would disperse London's six hundred students, from grades one through twelve, among schools in Walnut Cove and the tiny settlement of Germanton, five miles away. As for the London School itself, the board was closing it.

By shutting down London School, the white community exacted its revenge for integration. In its seventeen-year life, the school had become the center of black community life and culture. Its faculty, headed by the most respected black man in the county, represented the cream of the county's African-American professionals. By closing the school, the board would eliminate the black community's most notable achievement and contemptuously erase the most potent symbol of black public identity. The loss of the school shocked the blacks; but the stench of Jim Crow supremacy—the whites' routine expectation of complete and humble submission—enraged them. The white people were waiting, as one teacher recalled, "to see if we would do anything about it."

The parents scheduled a public meeting with the board and plunged into the unfamiliar task of rallying protest. PTA members contacted people who had influence in the mountain towns of northern Stokes. Ministers called upon their congregations to attend. Appeals for help went through the all-black Voters League grapevine. Simultaneously, parents circulated a petition throughout the county demanding that the London School be kept open. As it became apparent that a groundswell was building, a few in the white community became nervous. At the sawmill and the veneering plant, black employees were informally advised that "agitators" would lose their jobs.

National events added an atmosphere of urgency, and of fear, to the events in Walnut Cove. The National Commission on Civil Disorders, known as the Kerner Commission, issued a report that President Lyndon Johnson had requested the preceding year. On March 1, 1968, as the black parents frantically organized their protest in Stokes County, the *Winston-Salem Journal* carried the front-page headline: "Racism Splits Nation, Johnson Panel Asserts." The report declared that racism would split the nation into "two societies, one black, one white—separate and unequal," unless action was taken immediately. The commission stated that "discrimination and segregation have long permeated much of American life; they now threaten the future of every American." The country would see "the destruction of basic democratic values," unless it created "common opportunities for all within a single society."

The urgency of the Kerner Commission's message was made evident by another article on the same front page, a report on the anxiety over sending National Guard troops to serve in the Vietnam War—the troops, some governors pleaded, would be needed at home to control racial violence. Already, the nation dreaded the approach of yet another "long, hot summer" of racial protest and rioting on the heels of violent race riots in the three previous years in cities as far-flung as Watts, Newark, and Detroit. Many whites, including President Johnson himself, had become convinced that the unrest in the black communities was being deliberately planned by conspirators with links to American and overseas Communists. Thus, black protest became viewed as un-American and a threat to the republic. Tensions rose so high that spring in North Carolina that when legendary Harlem congressman Adam Clayton Powell spoke in Durham, ten police officers escorted him from the door of his car to the door of the auditorium; more officers surrounded the building; the governor ordered the North Carolina National Guard onto alert; and the U.S. Army dispatched a bomb squad to the scene as a precaution.

As plans for the Walnut Cove protest meeting rapidly went ahead, the force of national events could be felt in the area. Martin Luther King had announced plans for a trip through North Carolina. Simultaneously, white organizers were canvassing Stokes County to drum up support for the presidential campaign of the Alabama arch-segregationist George Wallace. Fearing an outbreak of violence at the London School protest meeting, the county school board considered calling on the state police to patrol the event, but one board member flatly refused to allow it, knowing that blacks in the audience would certainly have taken a heavy police presence as an insult and a provocation. In this atmosphere of rising tension and fear, John L. Hairston prepared a short speech to deliver at the meeting, a speech calling for calm, cooperation, and a spirit of compromise.

At 4:00 P.M. on a Sunday afternoon about six hundred parents and students filled the London School gymnasium. One of the London School seniors, Greg Hairston, remembered that he had never seen so many black people in one place before; he had not even been aware of the size of the black community in Stokes County. Apparently some members of the school board had not been aware of it either. Thirteen-year-old Pamela Hairston, John L.'s niece, saw that the people on the dais looked out upon the crowd nervously: "I could see their faces. They looked like they were scared. They had a gymnasium full of blacks and they had no idea of what reaction they would get from us." Pamela was sitting beside her grandmother Luddie. "She was the type of lady who had a comment about everything," said Pamela; and as the meeting progressed, she did.

The petition demanding that the school be kept open was presented to the board, with 900 signatures attached. Dr. Isaac Booe placed it on the table and stood up to address the crowd. He said that the HEW representatives were "displeased" with the London School because it had no white teachers and no white students. He said that the freedom-of-choice plan had to be abandoned because it had failed to bring an end to the dual system of schools.

George Henry Hairston, the president of the PTA, presented the community's case to the board. He talked about how important the school was to the black community and emphasized the excellent curriculum and physical condition of the school. He expressed the community's puzzlement that such a fine facility was being sacrificed. He then moved on to a more general point—the issue of fairness. The black community, he said, was not being treated fairly and never had been. The planned closure of the school was the culmination of a strategy of neglect. The London School had never been provided the resources that the white schools were given.

"That's not true," Dr. Booe retorted. He said there had never been any discrimination in the county's school system. The facilities were separate but equal. With that, an atmosphere of unreality settled over the debate, and the blacks found themselves fighting a phantom. They had come armed with data showing the quality of the London School's programs and the professionalism of its faculty. They had the names of graduates who held good jobs in Winston-Salem and of those who were attending college. The board merely had to walk through the corridors to see the excellent physical condition of the school—the student artwork and posters on the brightly painted walls, the neat-as-a-pin desks and bookcases, the immaculate cafeteria, and the carefully clipped grounds. Closing such a facility simply didn't make sense.

Pamela Hairston recalled listening with pride as members of the PTA defended the school with forceful and precise arguments. At the time it puzzled her that their crisp logic made no impression on the board. The harder black parents pressed for a logical response to their points, the more illogical the board's responses became—and the more adamant.

"We can close the school and we will close the school," one board member said with finality. "We will not have our people coming to that school. The environment is not appropriate for learning," he said, citing the nearby graveyard, shanties, and cow barns. It occurred to Pamela that these eyesores—properties owned by white people—had not been regarded as a deterrent to education for blacks, but would be harmful if whites attended the school.

Refusing to concede that the board was acting unfairly toward the black community, one member accused the blacks of being ungrateful for being allowed to enroll in the white schools. "We have built these schools for you people," he said with exasperation.

His remark was more than John L.'s mother, Luddie Hairston, could bear. " 'You people!' 'You people!' " she exclaimed. She demanded to know what that meant, what was so different about her.

"Look at our skin. Some of us are as white as you are," she said to the board, whose faces were rapidly turning scarlet. "When we go outside the county, some people don't even know that we're Negroes."

At this point, with the meeting about to deteriorate into a shouting match, John L. Hairston took the microphone and addressed the board in his calm, measured, and conciliatory fashion.

"I've been with this school for seventeen years," he began, "and I'm here today with mixed emotions. I work for you, and I'll support your decisions whether I agree with them or not, but it's becoming more and more difficult to explain your decision to students and friends of the school. I've tried, but I can't convince any Negro your plan will work. Negroes have great confidence in the school board of Stokes County. We can reach an agreement. One measure of greatness in anyone is when he admits his mistake and says, 'Let's talk this over again.' "

He began to summarize all the arguments and to make one final push for a compromise; but after he had been speaking for a few minutes, the students and parents in the audience sensed a change coming over him. One teacher recalled that John L. seemed calm and reasoned at first, "and then he just flipped." Perhaps it was the sight of his mother in the audience, but something brought memories of his childhood flooding back.

He began to talk about having to walk to grammar school while the bus carrying white kids passed by, with boys leaning out the windows of the bus to taunt "the nigger." He reminded the board that the black parents in the audience had not been able to attend high school in their own county because Stokes did not deem it necessary to educate its black children beyond the seventh grade. His voice rose as he confronted the whites of Walnut Cove with their recent history of racism. He declared that the era was over when black people would simply accept whatever decision their government might make for them. His people, he said, would not stand by and let the board close the London School.

Every supporter in the gym recognized the implication of his outburst. They knew that John L. was placing his job in jeopardy. He was one of the few black men in the county who "had it made" with a nice house and a good salary, yet he was willing to lose it all.

The anger that suddenly boiled within him was not just directed at the whites. He was angry at himself and at his own community for having remained passive for so long. Poking the air with his finger for emphasis, he addressed his next remarks to the audience.

"We as a people tend to stand back. We wait until things become critical before we decide to do anything. We stand back, and look, and let life pass us by. We let other people dictate the course of our lives. We move by necessity instead of planning our future. It is time for us to get control of our lives back instead of letting other people make the decisions. We can all work together to be productive citizens. We can have an impact on our society and on America."

The auditorium erupted in applause as John L. took his seat. He had heard Dr. Booe's assertion that there was no discrimination in his school system. At first, John L. had been inclined to let the statement pass, as he had done so many times before, to keep peace. But the boldness of the lie was finally too much for him, and he could see that, if he did not speak out, the lie would be passed on to his own children in the audience and the students he had taught.

The community had been prepared to follow John L.'s lead. If he counseled compromise and delay, then so be it; but he had demanded action. His call had an immediate effect. "That speech just ignited the people," one teacher recalled, "everybody became committed that day." More than the adults, the students in the audience had listened in shock. They had never heard their principal publicly challenge the white community or attack racism so overtly. In school he had urged them to strive for excellence, but he had never alluded to barriers or prejudices that might hold anyone back, or that had impeded his own progress.

John L. had hardly taken his seat when one of the PTA members stood up and faced the board. He put the whole issue into a simple, direct question: "For one hundred years decisions have been made against the Negro. Why not make some now in his favor?"

Dr. Booe shot back that whites everywhere were paying for the sins of their fathers and requested the audience to limit its questions to the educational needs of the county. He said that the board would postpone its final decision until hearing new proposals from the London School PTA, but he cautioned that the board would also have to consider the wishes of committees from other schools. He then adjourned the meeting.

In the aftermath of John L's speech, the core of white resistance to integration hardened. Some whites made certain that their remarks about the London School were overheard by blacks: "It's in a dilapidated neighborhood." "It's right next to the graveyard." "It smells like them." The only hint of a compromise required a concession the black community would never make: some whites began to suggest that London might be smoothly integrated if it did not have a black principal. *The Danbury Reporter* said that "feelings [are] running high and rumors becoming rampant."

John L. discovered just how high feelings were running when he answered the phone at his office and heard a string of curses ending with a warning that there was a bomb in the school. The caller hung up, and John L. stood frozen to the spot. He thought for a minute and decided that the call had to be a hoax. He decided to say nothing to anyone about the call, which would only inflame anger on both sides.

Yet his speech had fallen upon some receptive ears. The students who had been present on Sunday spread the word about what the principal had said. After school on Monday the leaders of the student government, including Greg Hairston (the son of George Henry Hairston of the PTA), Vincent Withers, and John L.'s daughter, Mona, gathered in a classroom to talk over the situation.

Their parents had always been reluctant to talk about the racial atmosphere in the county; but John L.'s impassioned description of his generation's struggle to get an education made the students realize that they had taken their school for granted. "John L.'s speech made us all wake up," recalled Greg Hairston. Their parents had fought to establish it, and they realized that it was up to their generation to fight to save it. To Vincent Withers, the principal's message was, "We have trusted in the past and it has not been to our advantage, and now we have to do something to protect what is ours." Their principal had put his job on the line. "I saw him in a new light," Withers recalled. "We felt we had to do something, to take a stand."

The students talked over various options—calling a mass meeting of the students, sending petitions to the board and to state officials—and concluded that the adults had tried that sort of thing with no results.

Instead of just telling people what they wanted, they agreed that they had to take some dramatic action to prove their determination to save what was rightfully theirs. When someone mentioned that Martin Luther King was scheduled to visit several cities in North Carolina in a few weeks, they decided that only one thing was left to try—a demonstration.

The next day the student leaders broached the idea of a march to their classmates and found unanimous support. Then they approached their senior-class adviser, Edward Hairston, and told him of their plans. They said they were not coming to him for permission—their minds were already made up—but they did want his advice. They said they did not want the faculty to be involved openly because it would cost the teachers their jobs. This protest was something they had to do themselves.

Edward Hairston fully sympathized with these feelings. He had been a student at A&T in Greensboro when the famous sit-in at the Woolworth lunch counter had occurred in 1960, and he had taken part in the demonstrations that supported the sit-in. The A&T administration had come under intense pressure from the state government to stop the protests, but the school's officials were able to claim, accurately, that the demonstrators were acting not as students but as citizens, that they were within their rights to demonstrate, and that the school had no authority to stop them. John L. could expect to come under the same kind of pressure, so he would have to be careful to distance himself from the march. When Edward Hairston informed John L. of the students' idea, the principal readily consented to it. Both men were aware of the risk involved, but they also appreciated that the cause was critical to the new generation of students. "We could not teach them to feel they were worth something and not to stand up for it," Edward recalled.

At John L.'s request, a representative from the Winston-Salem chapter of the NAACP quietly came to Walnut Cove to advise the students. He said they should think of the march in positive rather than negative terms, that they should regard it as a call for increasing their rights rather than as a protest against mistreatment, or as a protest against all whites. If whites viewed the march as a threat, he said, they would only stiffen their resistance. He told the students that they must be respectful if questioned and be prepared to answer questions clearly and politely. If they were heckled, they should ignore it and move on. If there was a threat of violence, they should immediately withdraw. He then coached the students in role-playing techniques. He divided the students into "marchers," "spectators," and "hecklers." With some difficulty he persuaded the hecklers to chant racial slurs as they broke into the line of marchers, pushed a classmate, and pretended to spit on him.

The march was scheduled for lunchtime on the following Monday, two days before the final school board meeting. John L. and the teachers decided that the best place for him to be when the march began was out of town, so that the superintendent could not order him to call the marchers back. John L. thought that he might as well be in the lion's den itself, so he called the superintendent's office and made an appointment with him for a meeting at noon. Although the students had insisted that no teachers take part in the march, John L. told several teachers to keep an eye on the march from a distance and be ready to intervene if trouble did break out.

On Monday morning, students from the high school and the junior high school grades gathered in the gym to finish work on their signs and run through their role-playing exercises one more time. The seniors were in charge. At 11:30, Greg Hairston called for silence and gave the group its final instructions. The emotion of the moment overcame some of the younger students, who began to cry as Greg told the group not to allow anything negative to happen; they should not defeat themselves by resorting to any kind of violence or vandalism. "The only thing we are going to do is march, and the reason we are marching is to express our feeling that the school should not be closed." And then they left.

When John L. arrived at the school board office in Danbury, the acting superintendent of schools, Jack Porter, was waiting for him. Porter had just gotten a phone call from a deputy in Walnut Cove—the students of London School were marching down Main Street. The superintendent curtly asked John L. what was going on. John L. wished that he knew. The thought uppermost in his mind, as he recalled, was that his daughter Mona was walking at the front of the march. He worried for her safety, but he also knew that she and the other students were determined to assert their rights. They had grown up in a world where generations of hard work and achievement counted for almost nothing in the eyes of white people. They came of age in a society that treated them as untouchables—some doctors refused to examine them; white people could not bear to eat a meal in their presence; people said their carefully tended school "smelled like them" and scrawled threatening signs by the road: "Niggers—keep on thru." They saw their elders, people they respected, compelled by custom to address white teenagers as "sir." They intended to change that world with their march. One way or another, by the end of the day Walnut Cove would not be the same town it had been in the morning.

Just as they had planned, the marchers took Walnut Cove by surprise. There were a few Klansmen in town, but they had not had the chance to gather a mob of outsiders. Nonetheless, the students had to contend with a small group of whites who formed up alongside the head of the march and kept pace, not sure of what to do. At first they walked along silently, then the catcalls began.

"That's all that niggers want to do is to start something."

"What are they doing out of school? They need to be in school because none of them know anything."

Pamela Hairston remembered one insult that struck her as especially ridiculous, since the kids in the march had been taught by two men who had master's degrees in mathematics: "I bet you could ask any of them what two plus two is and they can't tell you. Hey! Hey, boy! Come over here and tell me what two plus two is!" The remarks began to irritate Vincent Withers, who said he was going to straighten out those people, but Greg held him back. "No, that's not our purpose," Greg said.

Most of the townspeople just stood silently and watched. Whenever someone asked a question a few seniors detached themselves from the column to explain their reasons for marching.

As the marchers reached the heart of Walnut Cove, Withers said he was thirsty and wanted to get a soda. Mona Hairston told him to wait until they got back to school, but Vincent insisted, "Why can't I buy a Coke in my own town?"

Vernon's Grill was on the next block. It had not been part of their plan to go in there, but they all remembered Edward Hairston's description of the massive Greensboro demonstrations of his student days—demonstrations that had begun when students went into a segregated lunch counter and refused to leave until they were served. Looking at each other, the London School students said, "Why not?"

The town's deputies had pulled up in front of Vernon's, on the block where the most spectators had gathered. The marchers approached Willis Vernon and the crowd of his customers on the sidewalk, and they could see the men from the pool hall, alert for trouble, watching from across the street. Withers went up to Vernon and said he wanted to go inside and get a soda. Vernon looked at the deputies and said, "Put 'em all in jail! That's where they belong!"

The deputies looked out on the line of marchers halted on the sidewalk. They were standing quietly holding their signs. No one had caused any trouble except for the handful of white adults who had insulted the teenagers and spat in their path. Since the day London School had opened, seventeen years earlier, no graduate of the school had ever been in court for anything worse than a traffic ticket. The deputies conferred for a minute and then spoke to Vernon.

"Willis, you have to let them come in your store. They have a right to go in." Ever since Congress had passed the 1964 Civil Rights Act, four years before, segregation in places of public accommodation had been illegal. The deputies knew that; but until that moment no one in Walnut Cove had tested the law.

Vernon stared at the deputies in disbelief. He tried to think of some pretext to keep the marchers out. "The only way you can come in my store is if you leave your signs outside. You can't bring them in my store and you can't leave them on my sidewalk."

Withers wanted to insist on bringing the signs in, but the other leaders knew a victory when they saw one. With Vincent in tow, three of the seniors went around to the alley next to Vernon's, the alley they usually took to get to the back door, and leaned their signs against the wall. Then they went around to the front and walked in. The place was empty except for Mrs. Vernon, who was behind the counter, and the black cook, who was standing at the kitchen door. Through the windows people stared at the scene inside as Vincent Withers put a quarter on the counter and asked for a Coke. He drank his soda, and the four of them walked out into the noontime sun to resume their march.

Superintendent Porter was waiting at the school when the students got back. He met in a classroom with John L. and the leaders of the march. When the students told him that it was not fair to achieve integration by closing a black school, Porter replied that no one had anything against integration, but that some parents were concerned about sending their children to a school in such a run-down neighborhood. He told them that it had been a mistake to leave the building during school hours, and that the march did not present a good image of the Negro people. But the students did not yield, saying that they would march again if necessary.

The final meeting of the school board on the integration issue was supposed to be closed to the public, but sixty members of the London PTA simply showed up, and no one dared tell them that they could not come in. Dr. Booe called the meeting to order and, without making any remarks, asked if the representative of the PTA had any proposals to put before the board. George Henry Hairston stood up and read the text of a plan, which the board had previously rejected, that would keep the London School open as an integrated institution, under the leadership of John L. Hairston. Dr. Booe repeated his opposition to any plan that compelled integration, saying that he still preferred a "freedom-of-choice" system. He then called for a formal vote. One member joined Booe in opposing the plan. The other three members voted to accept integration. There was no applause. The parents savored their victory in silence. Indeed, it was an extremely rare victory, as black principals almost never kept their jobs when Southern schools were integrated.

The students' march had saved their school and their principal. It had also brought segregation to an end in Walnut Cove. As if some signal had gone out over an invisible telegraph, the manager at the movie theater no longer expected blacks to sit only in the balcony; the Laundromat that had recently barred the wife of a soldier home on furlough no longer turned blacks away. On April 4, 1968, the weekly issue of *The Danbury Reporter* published the details of the school integration plan. At the top of the front page of the same issue, the newspaper ran a photograph of John L., with an article saying that he had received a citation from the alumni association of North Carolina Agricultural & Technical State University, praising him for his "high degree of fortitude and outstanding leadership qualities" in the integration campaign.

John L. was at home preparing for a trip to Atlanta to attend a conference on antipoverty programs on the day when the integration plan and his citation were announced in the newspaper. He was at his desk gathering his records from the Yadkin Valley Economic Development District when reports began to come over the radio that Martin Luther King had been shot in Memphis. It occurred to him that King was supposed to be in North Carolina that day and would still be alive if he had not decided to go to Memphis to march with striking sanitation workers. Then John L. felt overwhelmed by an awful sense that the killing had been inevitable.

To John L.'s surprise, the antipoverty conference went ahead as scheduled, so he was in Atlanta when Dr. King's funeral took place. He was sharing a room with a white official from North Carolina, and the two of them were among the thousands of people who filed through Ebenezer Baptist Church to view King's coffin. Back at the hotel, they sat up talking late into the night. John L. remembered saying that the most remarkable thing about King was the great faith that he had. John L. said that "a person with less faith or less strength would have given up along the way—he knew he was a marked man, but he didn't let that stop him." John L.'s friend, groping to find some meaning in the tragedy, hoped that somehow, even in this crime, "the hand of God was working," and for a moment thought of miracles: "You know, I would not be surprised if Martin Luther King could get out of the coffin. God can raise the dead." The next morning they went back to the church and stood outside during the private funeral service. As King's body was brought out of the church and placed on a mule-drawn wagon, the two North Carolina men joined the silent throng following in its path.

Martin Luther King's funeral procession included thousands of men and women like John L. Hairston—people who had sacrificed a great deal for something as simple as a school. Before his death King had spoken of the civil rights demonstrators as conquerors of the Promised Land. The sound of their marching feet, he said, "is the thunder of the marching men of Joshua. And the world rocks beneath their tread." They were ordinary people who, because of their race, had to possess extraordinary courage to achieve seemingly ordinary goals. As a young man, John L. Hairston had held in his hands the ticket to a better life than Stokes County could provide, but he had taken a harder path. He had let his dream go because he thought he could "make a difference" on his home ground—and he did.

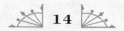

In Search of

the Father

On a warm September afternoon in 1995, when the National Hairston Clan was holding its twenty-second annual reunion in Winston-Salem, North Carolina, about a hundred family members drove south in a caravan of cars and vans to see Cooleemee Plantation. Judge Peter Hairston guided groups of visitors through the house and described the history of the plantation. After everyone had had a chance to walk through the rooms and hear the judge's stories, one of the leaders of the Hairston Clan, Joseph Henry Hairston, gathered as many people as he could fit into the dining room and thanked Judge Peter for taking them around. To an outsider it seemed an awkward moment—a group of African-Americans were standing in a mansion their enslaved forebears had helped build and were hearing the history of the place from the white owner. But after thanking the judge, Joseph went on to explain their presence at the plantation. He declared with firm conviction how important it was, especially for the young people in the group, to visit that place and hear its history, because, he said, *"Our blood is in this soil."* They had, he declared, a bond to their forebears that gave them the privilege, and the obligation, to claim the history of that place.

The history of the black Hairstons had the dimensions of an epic, and not merely in its chronological scope or in the multiplicity of the family's accomplishments and tragedies. An epic is not just a catalog of adventures; it is the story of the foundation of a nation, and an exploration of the character of a nation. The story of the Hairstons reflects the long effort of African-Americans to forge a nation that fully realizes, accepts, and honors the ownership that African-Americans have by right of birth and blood. In the course of that effort, black citizens have been compelled, far more sharply than whites, to ask themselves what it means to be an American. Generation after generation, they have had to grapple with the question, how does one go about repairing a nation that is broken, that was defective from the start?

I thought that the Hairstons had provided a powerful answer: forgiveness. At my first meeting with them in Baltimore, five years before, one of the Hairstons had said, "We are a long-suffering and a forgiving people." But it seemed far too pat an answer, because there was too much to forgive. Ralph Ellison had wrestled with exactly this problem in a speech entitled "Hidden Name and Complex Fate," where he said, "I speak here not of mere forgiveness . . . but of the conscious acceptance of the harsh realities of the human condition, of the ambiguities and hypocrisies of human history as they have played themselves out in the United States." Joseph Henry Hairston, the man who declared at Cooleemee, "Our blood is in this soil," embodied that struggle.

Joseph Hairston was one of the people I had met at the first family reunion I had attended in Baltimore. He had spoken up about the family's mixed origins; later he had given me the genealogy dictated to him by an aged aunt in her cabin in Virginia, and at subsequent reunions I had gotten to know him. He had been particularly gracious and encouraging to me, inviting me to his home for an interview about his family history and bringing me to a reunion of his World War II unit, the all-black Ninety-second Infantry, the "Buffalo Division," which had fought in Italy. After leaving the army in 1960 he had, with difficulty, become a lawyer for the federal government and eventually rose to be one of the highest-ranking black attorneys in the executive branch.

In the extended Hairston family, Joseph Hairston was an esteemed figure, the man to whom the National Hairston Clan looked for advice on legal and business affairs. In his retirement he traveled to Africa and South America on behalf of an African-American legal organization, offering expertise to the governments of developing countries and making business contacts with private industries. He was in many respects the embodiment of the American dream, seemingly the kind of man who had completely transcended his past. But I was only seeing the surface of the man. Joseph had passed through a series of trials that had tested his connection to the past, to his family, and finally, to his country. On a scale large and small, in matters public and private, he had found himself intimately bound to the past and locked in a struggle with it, compelled to grapple with the "ambiguities and hypocrisies" that were part of his inheritance.

Joseph's life was an apparent Horatio Alger story—and that's the way

I thought he wanted me to hear it—the story of a poor boy's rise from poverty to prosperity, lifted on the wings of the American dream. When he was an infant, his family had moved from Virginia to Connellsville, Pennsylvania, a small, working-class town that produced coke for the steel mills in Pittsburgh. His was one of many Hairston families who took the Norfolk & Western rail line up from Virginia through the Shenandoah Valley to Pennsylvania in the 1920s to find work in the steel industry, becoming part of the great migration of African-Americans from the South to the North that began during World War I, an exodus that dwarfed smaller migrations of the late nineteenth century. Yet many of those who made the trek North never intended to remain there permanently, but planned to earn enough money from factory jobs to buy their own farmland back home in the South. Their readiness to leave after they had saved enough for a down payment on a farm sprang from a deep attachment to their Southern homeland and from the dream of owning their own acres, yet many factory bosses attributed such departures to shiftlessness.

In Connellsville, enormous, beehive-shaped ovens provided unskilled men fresh from the South, or others from Italy, Poland, Ireland, or Germany, with jobs "pulling" coke in excruciating heat. The dangers were not restricted to the laborers themselves, for the ovens created a perilous landscape—huge slag heaps that rose up next to the ovens and marred the terrain. Despite warnings from their parents, some children played on the heaps. I found a newspaper account of a small girl who had lost her footing and tumbled down one of these steep, stony hills directly into the mouth of an oven.

Even when Joseph Hairston's father was working, his wages were barely enough to keep the family alive. His father, like millions of other laborers, lost his job during the Depression and went to work at even lower pay for the Works Progress Administration, the federal agency begun by President Roosevelt to provide public works jobs to idle laborers. Joseph remembered his childhood as "poor as hell," but with a stoicism born of the Depression, he made light of the experience: "Everybody was poor, so nobody realized what they didn't have." Only later when I talked to his brother did I realize how poor the family had been—always hungry, sometimes forced to subsist on green apples.

When Joseph was ten in 1932, his mother died, and not long after that his father died on the street of a heart attack. Joseph remembered the day well. "My brother and I were downtown, and we weren't supposed to be there. My father was working for the WPA, and this was during the lunch break. He was standing there on a corner and we saw him. We hotfooted back home. We found out later that he saw us and started to go after us, and that's when he had the heart attack. In fact the ambulance that picked him up passed us on the way to the hospital. He died before he got to the hospital. Now at age twelve I think I'm an orphan."

The orphaned boys were cared for by their father's sister, Dorcas, who by herself supported a household of seven by taking in laundry. Joseph and his brother picked up and delivered the laundry in a little wagon. In a poor town, they were near the bottom of the poor, and they heard quite a few taunts on their rounds from other kids who liked to torment "the wash woman's boys."

Joseph let the humiliation roll off him because, as he recalled it, he had his younger brother to look after. His brother remembered, "Joe was the hustler. He took responsibility for the two of us." Aunt Dorcas made sure that Joseph understood his responsibility. If the young one got in trouble, the old one got the whipping. In fact, Joseph extricated his brother from a gang of shoplifters and put him to work scavenging for any old thing that would bring a few pennies into the house. His brother said, "We picked junk—zinc, jar lids, milk bottles, and soda bottles. We cleaned basements and whitewashed walls, hauled ice in fifteen- to twenty-five-pound blocks, unloaded A&P trucks for twenty-five cents a night." Before school and after school Joseph delivered newspapers; on the weekends he sold them on the streets. "I made three cents the first day. Remember the old movies with the kid yelling, 'Extra! Extra!'? I did that a lot. I'd open the paper and look for something catchy that's easy to quote. 'Extra! Extra! Read all about it!'

"By the time I finished high school, I had corralled most of the business in town because I did something nobody else did. In those days you didn't give credit; you got paid when you delivered the paper. You might take credit for the daily paper but not on Sunday. You handed people the paper Sunday morning and they handed you a dime. That takes a lot of time. I had the idea of leaving the paper and going back for the dime. I'd go out at four A.M. and cover twice or three times the district of anybody else and go back later and collect the dimes. I had a lot of fights about that." With his brother helping him, Joseph built the largest paper route in town and won all sorts of newsboy contests. His brother recalled that they won a trip to Pittsburgh, where they were amazed to see, for the first time, an escalator.

Connellsville was largely white. Joseph remembered it as an ethnic town with little overt racism, though some segregation did exist. There were not enough blacks to fill a separate school system, so Joseph and his brother went to the same schools as white children, although the high school did not guide the blacks toward college. No racism was directed against small children; it started when they got old enough to date. Black teenagers had to stay away from white girls. Joseph's cousin was beaten nearly to death just for walking with a white girl.

Joseph and his brother were denied admittance to a popular diner called the Crawford Tea Room. That it was a forbidden place made it seem all the more exotic to the young boy. The image of it lingered in his memory even when he was grown, and he was determined to go back one day and integrate it. When he finally did sit there and order a cup of tea, he didn't find the deluxe establishment of his imagination: "It was a greasy spoon. It was nothing. I was so disappointed."

When he was about sixteen, Joseph did something—he couldn't recall what it was—that made Aunt Dorcas angry with him, and she blurted out some cryptic remark about his father that he couldn't figure out and can no longer remember. But at the time, Joseph realized that he had stumbled upon something his aunt found deeply embarrassing. There was a secret about his father, which he sensed that his aunt would never talk about. A sudden burst of anger had made her reveal the existence of the secret in the first place, and Joseph didn't want to summon up that anger again. He pondered her remark for a long time, until he finally sent a letter to another family member, part of a branch of the family that had migrated to West Virginia, to gritty towns like Bluefield and Princeton and dead-end valleys like Tams and McComas, which were, in fact, not towns but just names of mines. In reply to his letter Joseph received a note saying, "Your father works in the same mine with me."

The man Joseph had thought was his father, who had died years ear-lier, had not been his father after all, but his stepfather. His real father had abandoned Joseph and his mother when Joseph was an infant. The younger brother he had been diligently watching over and protecting was really his half brother. No one in the family had spoken about it, and only his aunt's chance remark, hurled in anger, had given Joseph the clue that his family was not what it had seemed. His real father was still alive. He was elated. The secret that seemed so shameful to his aunt felt like a rebirth to Joseph. His uncle's letter revealed that his father was married and that Joseph had another half brother and two half sisters in West Virginia.

Too poor to afford train fare to West Virginia, Joseph did not have the chance to meet his father until four years later in 1942, when he was twenty years old. By then World War II had broken out and Joseph was in the army. On leave from his base in Louisiana, he traveled by railroad to the West Virginia mining country. What he experienced then was not a joyous reunion but a bitter disappointment. His father had no interest in him. The only greeting his father could muster was a casual "Hi, Joe."

Only then did the reality finally sink in that for two decades, his father had made not the slightest effort to find him. But for Joseph the connection, once made, was too important to be broken. No matter how much pain that connection brought him, it was better than the pain of blankness, of complete rupture from the past. It was also the first step Joseph would take to come to terms with the truth about his past, for accepting the truth was the key to making himself a man. As Ellison wrote, "The way to create a false identity is to think that you can ignore what went before." Despite his father's indifference, Joseph went to see him on his furloughs from the army. His reconciliation with his father was incomplete and one-sided—his father never really acknowledged him. But his struggle to become reconciled with his father prepared him for something larger—a reconciliation with his country.

Joseph had enlisted in the army in October 1940 when the military was slowly gearing up for war. He didn't wait to be drafted. As he put it, "I'm a flag-waver." After training as a medic he passed the test for Officer Candidate School and graduated with the rank of second lieutenant. On the same day, the army activated the Ninety-second Division, one of two all-black divisions, and Joseph received orders to join the unit at one of its training camps in Louisiana. He had grown up in the North and had thus far received his army training in the North. This trip would bring him his first experience with virulent racism.

Heading south for training in Alexandria, Louisiana, where he met his future wife, Joseph and his fellow soldiers had to change trains in St. Louis. There, they were ordered off the comfortable Pullman cars they had shared with white troops and were herded into segregated coaches. They could no longer eat at restaurants in train stations with the white troops, but had to send out for sandwiches, which they ate in their coaches. When the train arrived at Alexandria, Joseph could hear the whites lounging at the station say, "Look at them Northern niggers; they'll learn how to live in the South."

Examining the official records of the period, I found out that, if anything, Joseph was understating the horrors faced by black Americans in World War II. The attack on Pearl Harbor sparked a patriotic surge of black volunteers, but many were refused induction, in keeping with military policies devised just before the war. When the military draft had begun, before the attack on Pearl Harbor, army headquarters in the supposedly more enlightened New England states sent a classified directive to draft boards ordering them not to accept any blacks. The governor of Connecticut heard of the order, which had been kept secret even from President Roosevelt, and threatened to expose it if the army did not back down. Despite this local setback, the War Department continued to avoid drafting blacks, claiming that it did not have enough segregated facilities.

Following the lead of voter registrars, the military adopted a literacy requirement specifically to exclude blacks, but the program backfired. The secretary of war, Henry Stimson, described the dilemma the military had maneuvered itself into: "The Army had adopted rigid requirements for literacy mainly to keep down the number of colored troops and this is reacting badly in preventing us from getting in some very good but illiterate [white] recruits from the southern mountain states." The poor level of education in the South was a problem for both whites and blacks, although it had a greater impact on blacks because more of them came from the South. Draft boards began quietly accepting illiterate whites, while continuing to exclude blacks who couldn't read.

Training blacks posed problems because the army was using civilian facilities for its programs. A black trainee, sent from New Hampshire to Oklahoma A&M for clerical training, was stopped at the door because the Oklahoma state constitution barred blacks and whites in the same classroom. Training programs for aviation mechanics, engineers, photographers, and bomb disposers all had quotas to limit black enrollment. Many blacks who did manage to receive specialized training never got to use it, with the result that highly trained mechanics, photographers, and medical corpsmen ended up spending the war as common laborers.

The military trumpeted its skill at taking green civilians and, in a short term of concentrated, rigorous training, transforming them into effective fighting machines; but it claimed it could not deal with racial prejudice. For Joseph, who had grown up in a Northern town where prejudice, in his own assessment, had been a minor annoyance, the army came as a terrible shock: "When I got in the army, I had to learn quickly what other blacks had known from birth."

It became official policy to maintain segregation because the War Department felt it could not deal with objections from Southerners. The director of the Selective Service, General Lewis Hershey, stated without apology that "what we are doing, of course, is simply transferring discrimination from everyday life into the army. Men who make up the army staff have the same ideas [about blacks] as they had before they went into the army." The Army General Staff issued a similar statement: "Every effort should be made by the War Department to maintain in the Army the social and racial conditions which exist in Civil life in order that the normal customs of white and colored personnel not in the Army may not be suddenly disrupted." Racial justice would be bad for morale. White officers who took their duty seriously and actually intended to lead the black soldiers under their command were sometimes stymied by their fellow officers. One such officer who spoke of his plans for training a black unit was told, "No need for that. We're just here to baby-sit Eleanor Roosevelt's niggers."

General George Marshall, responding to a suggestion that small units of all-black troops be integrated into larger white units, stated that "the War Department cannot ignore social relationships between negroes and whites that have been established by the American people through custom and habit." Thus, mixing units would be an "experiment . . . fraught with danger to efficiency, discipline, and morale." Marshall believed that the "intelligence and occupational skill of the negro population is considerably below that of the white." While he spoke out against discrimination, the future savior of war-ravaged Europe insisted on separate but equal facilities for the black troops. In fact, when acute manpower shortages after the Battle of the Bulge in the winter of 1944–45 forced the army to attach black platoons as reinforcements to some white units, the result was a great success. The army later polled the white officers who commanded the black troops and found that every one of them praised the fighting ability of the black troops and reported that the experience had been favorable.

Official policy also imposed a strict limit on the number of blacks commissioned as officers and on the manner in which those officers served. This caused great resentment among blacks who had scored high on intelligence and aptitude tests and yet found themselves barred from Officer Candidate School. Though born in New York in 1867, Secretary Stimson expressed a belief widely held in the old-line, Southern-dominated military establishment when he said, "Leadership is not imbedded in the negro race yet."

There was also a more practical consideration to the limit on black officers. As Joseph Hairston put it, when a black man became an officer, "then he would have to command somebody." Inevitably a situation would arise in which a black officer would give an order to a white man, and the white would have to obey. This prospect shook the military culture. The War Department decided that it would allow limited conditions under which a black officer might give orders to white enlisted men, but matters had to be arranged so that a black officer would never command a white officer. One white commander preempted the problem by refusing to promote any black to a rank above the lowest-ranking white. Another commander simply scrapped the officer hierarchy and ordered that in his unit white first lieutenants would be superior to black captains. In other combat units, blacks who achieved the rank of captain were shipped out to all-black labor units. Perhaps more than any other factor, this limit on black officers led to disaster on the battlefield.

The segregation of military facilities infuriated the black troops. As Joseph Hairston discovered, troop trains traveling through the South had to keep blacks out of sight at stops, while white troops were allowed to leave the trains to stretch their legs and take meals sitting down. One group of blacks traveling through Alabama was brought coffee in a large oil can, with oil residue still in it. They took their exercise "penned up between two freight cars so no one could see us, kept us cooped up like animals," as one soldier complained. Camps offered no transportation off-base for blacks; many provided no church for blacks; and commanders sometimes banned black newspapers. "The doctors treat us as if we are dogs," one soldier wrote; "the whites beat and curse the colored soldiers," reported another. "We sleep on sand floors with no boards or anything," complained another soldier at a Southern camp. "We stand up and eat each meal . . . we do not have any running latrines . . . we are nothing but slaves for the people here." One black trooper stationed in Texas near a prison camp for Germans was disgusted to find a "Negroes only" latrine in the prison, the other reserved for white soldiers and Germans: "It made me feel, here, the tyrant is actually placed over the liberator." At one post soldiers were notified that any association with a white woman would be regarded as rape, which was punishable by death. Petty discriminations abounded: white troops in Seattle were issued coal for heating, while the blacks were given wood and told that because of a shortage of coal in the East, no one was getting coal; the black troops knew that was a lie because they had to deliver the coal to the white barracks. Black troops were murdered at Fort Benning, Georgia, and Fort Bragg, North Carolina; shot in their own barracks in Fort Jackson, South Carolina; and attacked by police in Bastrop, Louisiana.

Joseph Hairston's wife, Ann, closely followed military news in African-American newspapers, like the *Chicago Defender* and the *Pittsburgh Courier* during the war. She pasted many articles into a large scrapbook, including a series about the black press's "Double V" campaign to promote a symbol calling for victory in the war and on the home front. Under pressure from black newspapers, politicians, and labor leaders, and with the behind-the-scenes urging of the president's wife, Eleanor Roosevelt, the army reactivated an all-black division, the Ninety-second, known as the Buffalo Division, which had fought in World War I. General Marshall, a Virginian, took a personal interest in the division, though not favorably. To command it he selected a relative and fellow Virginian, General Edward Almond, like Marshall a graduate of the Virginia Military Institute. Though Almond was not a field commander but a staff officer, whose previous combat command experience amounted to exactly one month, his gross inexperience as a leader was not important to Marshall. Almond himself stated Marshall's reasons for choosing him: "I, being from Virginia, had an understanding of Southern customs and Negro capabilities." For the black troops the choice was disastrous. Joseph Hairston, a newly minted second lieutenant, fresh out of Officer Candidate School and eager to fight for his country, was assigned to Almond's unit.

As the Ninety-second entered its training, a series of incidents—some seemingly trivial, some brutal—signaled to the black troops and their black officers that all was not right. The army broke up the Ninety-second Division into four segments for its initial training. As Joseph observed, the military high command did not want to concentrate thousands of black soldiers in one place. Finally the division was brought together in May 1943 at a camp in the Arizona desert called Fort Huachuca, which had been established in the days of the Indian wars. Some white troops from another division were also stationed there. By accident or more likely by design, the white troops lived in whitewashed wooden barracks, while the blacks were assigned to tar-paper shacks. The black quarters were so filthy that the first arrivals had to spend three weeks rebuilding and cleaning them to make them habitable. The army expected that friction between black and white soldiers from the different divisions would result in some clashes. To ensure that any incidents would not get out of hand, the army informally decided to limit access to live ammunition. The white troops always had ammunition in their quarters; the black troops had it only on the firing range.

All officers, in keeping with army custom, were allowed to have their families live on the base. In the evening the officers could have dinner with their wives in the officers' club, until one day a senior white officer called the blacks together and announced a new rule. Joseph remembered the incident because it cost one black officer his career.

"Tell your wives they can't come to the mess hall anymore," the colonel said. Joseph recalled that a young black lieutenant stood up to protest.

"I'll never forget him," Joseph said. "He was what I would consider a born leader. He was about six foot two, two hundred pounds, a very imposing figure, and he was *magic* with the troops.

"He stood up and said, 'Colonel, why can't our wives come into the officers' club?'

"The colonel became beet red. 'Because I said so.'

"The lieutenant said, 'Does that include all the wives or just our wives?'

"The colonel said, 'You heard my order. Don't bring your wives.'

"The lieutenant replied, 'Yes, sir. But if any other officer brings his wife, I'm going to bring mine.'

"From then on, that man was hounded. We found out later that one of the white wives from the South didn't want to eat in the mess hall with black women."

A more serious incident occurred, Joseph recalled, when a black soldier came back from leave so drunk he couldn't stand up. The guards summoned a white captain, who ordered the man to get to his feet. The soldier was simply too drunk to obey the order, whereupon the officer beat him. Word of the beating quickly spread through the post. The black officers met to decide what they should do about the beating, which was a flagrant violation of military law. As Joseph recalled, "We knew the soldier should have been punished for being drunk—drunk in uniform, drunk on the post, all those things—but he should not have been beaten." The officers decided to bring charges against the white officer. "Since I was the battalion adjutant, I wrote up the court-martial papers. Then the army had to deal with the charges. So he was court-martialed. An all-white court-martial found him not guilty."

In three years, Almond conspicuously did not promote a single black officer above the rank of captain, although black officers with college degrees outnumbered white officers with degrees by three to one. The 92nd absorbed the all-black 366th Infantry regiment, which had a black commander, Colonel Queen. Instead of using that regiment intact with Queen in command, Almond broke it up and harassed Queen until he requested a transfer.

Morale sank so low that the army sent its highest-ranking African-American officer, General Benjamin O. Davis, to visit Fort Huachuca and report what he found there. Arriving at a dedication ceremony with General Almond, Davis heard the men boo their commander. He interviewed the men and found serious problems, but he treated Almond delicately in his report, stating that the commander had neglected "the human element" in his dealings with the troops. The report was filed and forgotten.

Almond was, in fact, an unrepentant racist to the end of his days. Almond himself told an army historian in 1972, "I do not agree that integration improves military efficiency; I believe it weakens it. . . . The basic characteristics of Negro and White are fundamentally different. . . . There is no question in my mind of the inherent differences in races. This is not racism—it is common sense and understanding."

Almond's views set the tone for the entire chain of command in his division. In private interviews with officers, a military historian found that the white officers "generally disliked their assignments, had no confidence in their men and believed that the 'experiment' of using Negroes in combat would fail." One staff officer declared, "The Negro could not generally overcome or escape his background of no property ownership, irresponsibility, and subservience. The Negro is panicky and his environment has not conditioned him to accept responsibilities."

The racism of the Ninety-second's officer corps was extreme even for the 1940s. A white officer from the division, who was sympathetic to the black troops, wrote a scathing magazine article denouncing the War Department over the handling of the Ninety-second. Joseph knew the officer who wrote the article and largely agreed with his assessment. The article appeared after the war, when the author was safely beyond the reach of General Almond. The author described officers "often of high rank, with violent and ungovernable prejudices, whose only concern has been to do a poor enough job to get out. In fact, it often seemed in the 92nd that the War Department had chosen exactly the officers who would guarantee the division the least possible chance for success." He described one officer as "irascible and indecisive . . . tactically incompetent." Many of the highest-ranking white officers were Southerners, he wrote, with "conventional Southern attitudes" toward blacks. "They believe and say that colored troops cannot fight; that they are all or almost all cowards, or inept, or both. The white officers . . . endlessly cite alleged examples of cowardice and bungling."

The nation had gone backward. The colored troops of the Civil War had been led by white officers who were proud to volunteer for the assignment. The white officers of the Third United States Colored Cavalry, in which Thomas Harston had served from 1863 to 1866, risked their lives rather than surrender their black troops to an enemy who might summarily put the blacks to death. The black combat troops of the Civil War and World War I had achieved a sterling record of victories and individual heroism. By World War II, the army had erased that history. The African-Americans who wore the U.S. uniform in World War II were not regarded as the heirs of the heroic colored troops. They were, once again, "an experiment," despised as "Eleanor Roosevelt's niggers," token soldiers who were considered an obstacle to the war effort. But they took the abuse and endured the contempt because they wanted the chance to prove themselves on the battlefield.

One Sunday morning Joseph discovered how deep were the "violent and ungovernable prejudices" he and his fellow black officers and soldiers would have to face. Joseph would never forget that moment. A senior commander, Colonel Edward Dill [not his real name] called the black officers together in the camp's chapel. He told them that once the division got into combat, he was going to make certain that they did their duty. His yardstick was going to be a body count—not the enemy's, but theirs. The tradition in the military is to take the objective with the least possible casualties, but Dill declared to the assembled officers, "You people constitute ten percent of the population of this country, and I'm going to see to it that you suffer ten percent of the casualties."

It was an insane vow, absurd; but a senior officer about to lead men into battle does not make idle threats. Having declared his wish that his men fill their quota of graves, he left the chapel. The officers sat stunned.

"I'll never forget the son of a bitch," Joseph said. "I've always been one of these men, when you play the 'Star-Spangled Banner,' I feel good. Wave the flags and pound the drums, I feel good. Now my senior commander is saying that he's going to *see to it* that we pick up our share of the casualties. It devastated me. It ate at me for a long, long time. But right after Dill left, the black chaplain came out. As he walked out, he was reading aloud from the Bible."

The chaplain had heard Dill's remarks and could sense the mood of the men. He had opened his Bible to a passage that summoned the only feeling strong enough to overcome the bitter sense of betrayal in the chapel. It had an immediate effect on Joseph.

"It was First Corinthians thirteen. You need to read that. That's the chapter that says, 'Though I speak in the voice of angels and have not loved,' and then goes on, 'Love is patient . . . it bears all things, believes all things, hopes all things, endures all things.' " In that moment supercharged with bitterness, the chaplain's words pierced directly into the consciousness of the officers. They trusted him, because he had stuck his neck out before to help the men. As the highest-ranking black officer on the post, he had signed the court-martial papers Joseph had drawn up when the drunken soldier was beaten by a white officer. So they listened to his desperate plea to save themselves from falling into the hatred that consumed their commanders. In peacetime his reading would have been just another pious homily—meet hatred with love; do your duty; endure. Words that sounded soft in peacetime carried the hardest meaning in war. As it turned out, these words would later save Joseph's life.

When the Ninety-second arrived in Italy in October 1944, it immediately went up to the front line. The troubles that would dog the division surfaced immediately: Almond's staff sent one of the lead infantry regiments to the front without ammunition. The mix-up arose from Almond's policy of not allowing black troops to have live ammunition unless absolutely necessary—he simply didn't trust them. Even in the combat zone he wanted to withhold issuing ammunition until the last possible moment. The black officers and their men had assumed they would be issued live ammunition on their march, but just moments away from facing the Germans, they had still not been given bullets. They had to halt their deployment until ammunition reached them. Joseph recalled the incident with disgust: "White troops *always* had ammunition. If you don't trust a soldier who is going into combat to have ammunition, what do you expect from him?"

In the weeks before shipping out for Italy, many of the white officers had frantically tried to transfer out of the division, without success. Once the division was at the front, many of the whites fled to the safety of headquarters at the rear, leaving the junior black officers, including Lieutenant Joseph Hairston, in charge.

"My battery commander was afraid of combat," Joseph said as he described what happened when his artillery unit got its first taste of combat. "One of the things you learn in a combat situation is finding some way to live with fear. When you're in an artillery position, you're under artillery or mortar fire periodically, so you have to learn to live with the fact that anytime day or night there's going to be a round coming in. One of the things you learn is how to recognize the sound of the shell. From its pitch you can tell that it's way up or down close. When you hear a boom off in the distance and then you hear the shell coming, you listen for the sound. This captain was so scared he couldn't distinguish. So every time he heard the boom, he's out there screaming, 'Hit the ground!' This is scaring the hell out of the troops, and they're wondering, 'Did I miss something?' He kept them so riled up they couldn't function. He disappeared soon after we got into combat. So I commanded the battery until the war ended.

"I had a group that responded beautifully, without a second thought. Nobody stopped and said, 'I'm tired, we've been shooting too long,' they just did it. I had one person who was beautiful to watch—the loader on one of our guns. He raised morale, but it was dangerous! This guy tossed the shell, just tossed it, and it jumped into the chamber. He was about half again as fast as anybody else, and his crew trusted him implicitly. They were proud that he was their man because it made them the best. My four guns were probably faster than any other guns in the division. I was quite proud of Charley Battery."

Early on, his forward artillery position was hit by a German mortar barrage. Shrapnel tore through the men. "One guy had half his face blown open, and it was just hanging loose. Several of us got him to the aid station. He was smoking a cigarette out of his good side. The aid people moved toward him and he said, 'Take care of my buddy over there, he's worse off than I am.' His face was blown open, just hanging off like a hinge. People talk about courage."

The Army had, as if willfully, deployed the Ninety-second where it could do the least good and at the same time face the greatest danger. The division was spread thinly along a front stretching for more than twenty miles. On the west, the front ended at the Ligurian Sea on Italy's western coast, about ten miles north of Pisa. In this region—the sector where Joseph Hairston's artillery battery took up its station—the coast was a narrow strip of beach overlooked by hills. From the coast, the Ninety-second's front ran inland to the east, into extremely rugged, mountainous territory. In preparation for this assignment, the Ninety-second had been trained in the Arizona desert. The German front line occupied high ground, with approaches made hazardous by rough ridges, deep gorges, and hillsides covered with olive groves. Many of the approaches from the south were steep cliffs. Just beyond all this lay the German army's dreaded Gothic Line—a complex of intricately laid minefields, concrete pillboxes concealing machine guns, artillery emplacements, and trenches. The U.S. Army high command had assessed this sector of the Gothic Line to be impregnable. The U.S. commander in Italy, General Mark Clark, said the Ninety-second was deployed along "the formidable half of the line we had decided not to attack." The Ninety-second's job was to remain in place and hold its position. To keep the Germans occupied, the Ninety-second was expected to throw itself at the Gothic Line from time to time, operations that Joseph described sardonically as "frontal assaults up a hill into German fire." The other, all-white Allied units deployed to the east faced less formidable fortifications, but they too were bogged down in the winter of 1944–45. During that winter, white troops began to desert their units at an alarming rate as morale sank.

The sporadic probing attacks that Almond ordered the Ninety-second to undertake eroded morale as well as men. Some of the best soldiers and officers died in the first months of combat. The army had no system for finding reliable black replacements. When fresh troops were needed in Italy, the army gathered up those who had been left behind in the first place because they were unfit, and the jails were emptied. Some of these men did not know how to fire a rifle, some were cowards, and some were simply demoralized, as Joseph observed: "There were instances when the troops retreated when perhaps they should not have. I believe that if there had been a little less racism and a little better training or cohesiveness that the troops would have performed better." On the eve of an attack, in which Joseph was assigned to be a forward artillery observer, he called for the "meanest, toughest guy in the unit" to be his driver. The soldier came to Joseph sniveling and crying, refusing to go. Joseph unstrapped his sidearm and said he would shoot the man if he disobeyed the order to move out. A few hours later the attack was called off.

The army played up the failures of the Ninety-second, determined to prove that the "experiment" of putting African-Americans in uniform had not worked. A story in the official army publication, *Stars and Stripes*, which was distributed to all soldiers in the army, declared that the men of the Ninety-second "melted away" in combat. The army was perfectly willing to let that phrase set the image of the Ninety-second. On the other hand, the army also hid the unit's successes. Not a single African-American was recommended for the Congressional Medal of Honor in World War II. Of course, the Medal of Honor is not something that should be handed out by a quota. But the African-Americans who fought in the war knew that some of their comrades had displayed extraordinary heroism that had never been recognized. For decades after the war, black veterans' groups lobbied the army and Congress to investigate the stories of the forgotten black heroes. Not until 1992 did the army bow to this pressure and commission an independent study. The panel recommended that ten African-American veterans receive the Medal of Honor. Seven men from this list were ultimately nominated for the award. Two were from Joseph's unit, the Ninety-second Division.

One of the men recommended for the medal, Lieutenant John Fox, was a forward artillery observer when the Germans launched a massive attack across the Ninety-second's front on the day after Christmas, 1944. Fox and his platoon had taken up position on the second floor of a house in the village of Sommocolonia, near Joseph Hairston's sector. Instead of pulling out when he had the chance, Fox held his position to direct artillery strikes on the attackers. He did not have enough men to drive off the Germans, but he knew that he was the eyes of the Ninety-second, and he decided to hold his ground until the end. After several hours of fighting, the Germans were swarming around his position, and he called in his last artillery strike: "Put everything you've got on my post!" The artillery officer on the other end of the radio link was Fox's friend and couldn't believe what he was hearing. He would not give the order. But

Fox was adamant—he requested that smoke shells be fired first to cover the retreat of the men with him, and then a barrage of high explosives. He was determined to stay to make sure that the explosive shells did their work: "Fire it! There's more of them than there is of us!" And so the order was given. The Ninety-second's artillery demolished Fox's position. When a rescue team reached the house, they found Fox's remains, surrounded by the bodies of more than one hundred Germans. Fox's immediate superiors put him in for the Distinguished Service Cross, but Almond's staff managed somehow to "lose" the paperwork. In 1982 one of his comrades from the Ninety-second, Hondon B. Hargrove, wrote up the papers for the DSC, which was bestowed on Fox's widow. It took fourteen more years before Fox was selected for the Medal of Honor.

Joseph Hairston's artillery lent support to another heroic stand by the men of the Ninety-second in February 1945, two months after Fox's death, when Almond ordered a general assault along the Ninety-second's whole twenty-mile front. Some of the white officers would later complain that the plans typified Almond and his staff—they never displayed any imagination nor made a serious attempt to deceive the enemy or even concentrate forces in one place to force a breakthrough. Almond seemed not to really want a victory.

Joseph's artillery battery was at its station near the western end of the Ninety-second's line by the seacoast. His job was to give fire support to an attack by tanks and infantry across the Cinquale Canal, which ran down across the beach and into the Ligurian Sea. On the northern side of the canal lay minefields. Overlooking the canal and the beach was a range of coastal hills, thick with German infantry, machine-gun emplacements, and artillery. Several miles up the beach, hidden in caves, stood immense naval guns designed to defend an Italian base farther north. Like the mythic "guns of Navarone" of Hollywood fame, these weapons could not be bombed and could not be touched by Allied naval fire because, with a range of almost six miles, the guns kept Allied warships far from the beach. The shore was a death trap. Even Almond's own staff thought an attack would be futile. The intelligence report prior to the attack described the Cinquale area as a "heavily mined, fortified and very strong position. . . . [An attack] would not be decisive and would cause only small immediate difficulties to the enemy." Nonetheless, Almond proceeded. One key officer, the white commander in charge of the engineering battalion with the crucial assignment of clearing the minefields around the canal, was so incompetent and so hated by his men that the army had months earlier recommended his dismissal. But Almond had kept him on.

The attack began at night on February 5, 1945, when engineers crept onto the beach and began clearing mines to make a path for the tanks. Under cover of darkness, the work proceeded well, with the engineers able to clear a five-hundred-yard-long lane. The tanks followed slowly behind them. When dawn broke, the German gunners began their work, raining shells down on the engineers and the tanks. Joseph's battery fired back in reply: "I almost burned up a gun in support of that action. The seacoast guns beat the hell out of us. Air Corps couldn't get them. They also had a railroad gun that they'd run into a tunnel. The Germans on the hillsides could see everything down on the coastal plain." Because of heavy cloud cover, the attack had to go on without air support.

Two tanks at the front of the column hit mines, blocking the advance of the column. The tanks and their supporting infantry were sitting ducks. Desperately trying to avoid the high-explosive shells raining down on them, the surviving tanks broke away from the safety zone and tried to get across the minefield. Four of them immediately blew up. Still, the task force pressed ahead. On the second day of the attack the Americans held a zone a thousand yards wide and six hundred yards deep. Twice they drove back German counterattacks. When the Germans attacked a third time, the tanks and foot soldiers fell back to a defensive line. The Americans held the defensive line for three more days, enduring constant machine-gunning and artillery barrages. Joseph Hairston's battery responded with its own relentless barrage, but artillery alone could not dislodge the well-entrenched German defenders. When a salvo from the German seacoast guns made a direct hit on the Americans holding the shore, an officer saw that "the entire mouth of the canal appeared to turn red with blood."

In his wisdom, Almond had not kept any reinforcements in reserve to exploit the foothold the black troops had so courageously gained. After four days watching his men being pounded, Almond ordered a withdrawal. The cost had been heavy. Over two hundred men had been killed or wounded; another forty-eight were missing. Out of the twenty-five tanks that went into the attack, only two came back. Intelligence officers at Fifth Army Headquarters learned that the Germans had unleashed "the greatest single concentration of artillery fire of the entire Italian Campaign" against the Cinquale attackers. One officer noted, "There did not seem to be a single patch of ground anywhere that was not covered with artillery fragments."

Despite the gallantry of the black troops, given an impossible assignment with scant support, the failure of the attack convinced the high command that the Ninety-second was not an effective unit. All blame was fastened on the black troops—no notice was taken of the deficiencies of Almond's planning, nor of the intensity of the artillery assault the men had endured. The army chief of staff, General George Marshall, proposed using the Ninety-second as bait for a trap—as cannon fodder. The man who would later become the architect of the Marshall Plan that saved Europe came up with the idea of placing the black troops in an exposed position that would invite the Germans to attack. He would conceal other units behind them, so when the Ninety-second had been chewed up and forced to retreat, the Germans would pursue them and run headlong into a trap. Marshall's scheme was never carried out, but it reveals the depths of the commander's contempt for his African-American troops.

After the war a black officer of the Ninety-second wrote a private letter to a War Department official, in which he said, "It is my considered opinion that the 92nd was doomed to a mediocre performance of its combat duties from its very inception. The undercurrent of racial antipathies, mistrusts and preconceived prejudices made for an unhealthy beginning." He said that blacks who "fit into the Southern pattern" of automatic deference to whites were promoted regardless of their capability, whereas "those Negroes who exhibit manliness, self-reliance and self-respect . . . are humiliated and discouraged." Prejudice cost the lives of both whites and blacks: "I was astounded by the willingness of the white officers . . . to place their own lives in a hazardous position in order to have tractable Negroes around them." In conclusion, he paid tribute to the patriotism of the men who gave their lives for a country that did not honor them: "They were Americans before all else."

A deep sense of duty had sustained the men of the Ninety-second, trapped in a situation they could only endure and hope to survive. The officers, Joseph among them, carried the special burden of leadership. One black officer who was belatedly awarded the Medal of Honor recalled that he was able to sustain his spirits only through a rigid mental focus. He kept thinking to himself, "Keep going. Keep the men going. Set the example. Complete the mission."

The officers had to keep going with the memory of Colonel Edward

Dill's "10 percent" vow still fresh in their minds. With each snafu—no ammunition for the first troops, no reinforcements, futile assaults up hillsides into German fire—it became easier to think that the real enemy was behind them. Joseph himself, the young flag-waver, came to that bitter conclusion one winter's day, out on a "stupid" patrol along the face of a mountain in full view of the enemy. As he walked along the exposed mountainside, leading a platoon of black men behind him, he remembered Colonel Dill's vow to "see to it" that the blacks picked up their share of the casualties. After the patrol had been out for a while, another officer said it was his turn to take the lead. That officer was Joseph's best friend and did not want Joseph to take more than his share of the risks. They switched places. Only a few feet farther on, a blast knocked the men flat. Joseph looked up to see his friend crumpled and still. He had stepped on a mine and died instantly.

Had it not been for his friend's casual courage and sense of duty in taking his turn, Joseph knew he would have been lying there instead. Joseph did not see this death as an accident of war. Had it not been for Dill, who ordered the patrol, his friend would still be alive. "I blamed Dill for his death," Joseph said, "and I carried that resentment for years."

Joseph stayed in the army after the war, intending to make it his career. The army felt it had too many black officers, so in 1949 Joseph faced a choice: resign as an officer, with an officer's pension, or stay and be broken back through the ranks to sergeant. Despite the humiliation, he chose to stay, in part because he had completed flight school and still harbored hope of advancement. Ambition was not his only driving force: he had a wife and three daughters to support so he was eager to earn flight pay. His pilot's wings, however, were not valid everywhere. When he reported for duty at a base in North Carolina, the adjutant asked him to have a seat while he made a phone call. Joseph could hear the adjutant on the phone to the personnel office in the Pentagon saying, "What do you mean sending me this nigger pilot?" Joseph was transferred that day to California. When the Army Air Corps was detached and made a separate service, the U.S. Air Force, Joseph rushed to apply, only to have the door slammed in his face. "Some racist colonel told me in effect that I was dumb as hell to think that I would get to fly in the air force. What could I do about it? I had to take it."

In 1951, Joseph went to helicopter training school and may have been the army's first black helicopter pilot. During the Korean War Joseph served as a helicopter pilot, assigned to rescue downed pilots from enemy territory. This time, he was decorated for bravery in action. His wife kept a scrapbook with a newspaper photograph from 1952 with the caption, "Capt. Joseph Henry Hairston receives first Oak Leaf Cluster to the Air Medal for services in Korea." Despite the bravery that won him a medal, Joseph was again broken through the ranks to sergeant because the army didn't know what to do with its black officers.

Despite President Harry Truman's 1948 executive order officially forbidding discrimination in the military, the army clung to its culture of segregation. One black officer remembered the day when his commander assembled the black officers, read Truman's order to them, and then said, "Now, gentlemen, as long as I am in command, there will be no changes. There'll be Officers' Club No. 1 and Officers' Club No. 2; NCO Club No. 1 and No. 2; swimming pool No. 1 and No. 2." But the effect of the Army's stubborn refusal to integrate was not just felt in its swimming pools and mess halls. Once again the army's deeply ingrained racism cost lives on the battlefield. While the battlefield was Korea, the architect of the policy was the same man who had commanded Joseph's division in Italy, General Edward Almond. Almond and his cadre of top officers had all been promoted, despite their inadequate performances in World War II. Almond served as chief of staff to General Douglas MacArthur and as the commander of X Corps, one of the largest combat units in Korea and, ironically, a multiracial and multinational unit. The history of the Ninety-second repeated itself in the history of X Corps.

One military historian, Shelby Stanton, looked back on Almond's assignment with amazement. "The Army excused his abysmal record of division command by blaming the quality of his black troops. Despite Almond's pronounced sentiments against racial integration and nonwhite capability, the Army [put him in charge of] the most racially diverse field command in Korea." In the end, Stanton noted, "the Army paid a high price for promoting Almond." His troops once again paid in blood. X Corps suffered repeated defeats, partly due to Almond's refusal to make proper use of his black, Hispanic, and Korean units. As carnage once again engulfed the African-American troops, a twist of fate brought Joseph Hairston face-to-face with his old nemesis.

Joseph had been assigned to a base on Okinawa in 1952. One day the base commander called him and said they had a visiting dignitary who needed an aerial orientation of the island. At the airstrip, Joseph discovered that the dignitary was Edward Dill, the man who had years earlier told the Ninety-second's officers of his intention to "see to it" that the proper percentage of them were killed. Joseph held him personally responsible for the death of his best friend. A high official with the Far East Command, Dill had attained the rank of general. As Joseph saluted, it was evident that the general had no memory of him. Joseph was disgusted that such a man could rise to high rank. "What I saw," Joseph remembered, "was a man who to me was the epitome of evil. Seeing him, the hate just rose up in me. I had carried that resentment for years."

Joseph directed the general toward his plane, a two-seat, tandem aircraft with the pilot in front. Standard procedure required the pilot to buckle a passenger into a parachute, but the general had grown somewhat stout. He glanced at the cramped passenger seat and told Joseph not to bother with a parachute. Joseph hitched up his own parachute, and it suddenly occurred to him, "I've got this son of a bitch under my control.

"Now, I'm very calm. I'm hating this man's guts, but I'm very calm, almost deadly calm as I look at him and put him in the plane. So we go up about five thousand feet and we're over the part of the island which is mountainous and uninhabited. What goes through my mind is, 'I'm going to get this son of a bitch.' And I started through the process.

"I leveled the plane, got it to fly straight, adjusted the throttle, and decided, 'I'm going to bail out of this thing.' I'm going to leave him in here. He doesn't know what's happening. I'm talking to him on the intercom just as calmly as I'm talking to you. And just as I'm about to get out, just as I'm opening the door, the thing that goes through my mind—I hear the chaplain. Now this is crazy, but I hear the chaplain saying the verse from Corinthians: 'Love is patient . . . it bears all things, believes all things, hopes all things, endures all things.' The bottom line of this verse is that love is supreme. I latched the door and went back to flying. He doesn't know how close he came to death that day, but the Scripture is what saved his life. And I got rid of my hate. It was an exorcism of the hate I had carried all those years." Joseph landed the plane, saluted his hateful passenger, and walked away.

Joseph's dream had been to follow in the footsteps of Benjamin O. Davis and become a general. One of his comrades from the Ninety-second did attain that rank eventually. (Another, Edward Brooke, became the first African-American U.S. senator since Reconstruction.) Joseph's army career, however, was stalled by his refusal to accept the slow pace of integration. He kept up a running battle with the military bureaucracy, a battle he knew he was losing, but one he believed he had to fight anyway. "Whenever I saw something that was wrong or unfair, I tried to fix it. I complained, wrote letters. That is not the way to advance in the army. I burned too many bridges." Transferred to Virginia, he obtained permission to attend college at night, and then law school. With two law degrees in hand he reluctantly decided to retire from the army at age thirty-eight. He went to work as a lawyer with the Labor Department and then with the Treasury Department, where he was the first black senior executive in the Office of Chief Counsel for the Internal Revenue Service. Despite the tragic events of World War II and Korea, and the discrimination he fought in peacetime, he never lost his affection for the army. He kept up his military friendships by patronizing a barbershop, also used by many other African-American veterans, at Walter Reed Army Hospital near his home in Washington.

Indirectly, the army had provided Joseph Hairston his first inkling that he was part of a very large extended family. In 1944, a USO touring company passed through his training camp in Arizona. One of the entertainers in the troupe was Jester Hairston. Even then, Jester had the habit of seeking out Hairstons wherever he went, and he unerringly found his way to Lieutenant Joseph Hairston. The two Hairstons spoke only briefly, but Jester made the young lieutenant from a small Pennsylvania town aware for the first time that Hairstons had a long, fascinating history. For a man who had once been haunted by the idea that he was an orphan, with no connection to the past, the notion of a communal heritage waiting to be uncovered was tantalizing.

When he finished his army career and settled in Washington, Joseph finally had the chance to track down his family's history. He began to make periodic visits to the countryside near Martinsville, Virginia, to see his oldest surviving relative, Aunt Mattie Bell, who had generations of history stored up in her memory. Behind her house a family burial ground held the graves of his ancestors, who had been slaves on some of the white Hairston plantations around Martinsville—places such as Camp Branch, a small plantation owned by Peter W. Hairston of Cooleemee, and Chatmoss, a much larger place that had been owned by the cruel master Samuel Harden Hairston. On the wall of Mattie Bell's house hung a large photograph of Joseph's grandmother—a striking woman with long, straight hair and high cheekbones who was clearly part Indian and part black. Her Indian origins remained elusive. Mattie Bell knew her name and birth date, but exactly how Joseph came to be descended from the original proprietors of this land remained a mystery.

Another mystery presented itself to Joseph on one of his visits to the area. "I was at a service station getting a flat tire fixed," Joseph remembered, "and this white man came up and started talking with me. He was there to get something fixed, and we were both sitting there in the waiting room just chatting. I didn't know him from Adam, but I kept saying to myself, 'What is there about this man that seems odd?' As he drove off, I suddenly realized—we looked a lot alike. It was like looking in a mirror." Only later did Joseph discover what kind of ghost he had been seeing.

At first Aunt Mattie Bell had seemed reluctant to tell him very much about his family beyond a certain point. But Joseph persisted. She sensed that he wanted to know the truth about his background—he would rather know the truth than be an orphan—so she told him. One of his great-grandfathers had been a white man.

"Aunt Mattie Bell told me that my great-grandmother had a relationship with the overseer on one of the Hairston plantations. His name was Cheatham. Had the law been different, they would probably have been man and wife, because they stayed together for a lifetime. She had twelve children by this man. They didn't live together because that was against Virginia law. Miscegenation was outlawed in Virginia until 1967. My great-grandfather did the unconscionable thing of recognizing his children. When the boys got to be teenagers, he scandalized the countryside by riding, carousing, and getting drunk with his sons. That wasn't done. It was acceptable for a white person to dabble in the black community for his sexual needs, and everybody knew it was done, but it was not acceptable to recognize a bastard. And by his carousing with his own children, he was breaching a social taboo of that era." The man Joseph had met in the gas station had the name of the overseer. Since then, he said, "I've often wondered if I was seeing something of myself in him."

Pursuing a genealogy can bring anyone face-to-face with uncomfortable truths, but the discovery of a racially mixed relationship in an era when white men enjoyed almost unquestioned supremacy over black women is anguishing. The African-American poet and teacher Carrie Allen McCray described in her memoir, *Freedom's Child*, the anger she felt at her discovery, in the 1960s, that her mother's father had not only been white, but also a Confederate general. She fastened upon her grandfather the rage that welled up in her over the brutal treatment of civil rights demonstrators:

> I tried then to write Mama's story, but finally realized that the Birmingham church bombings, the water hose, the dogs, and the assassination of Martin Luther King had filled me with rage. Debilitated by anger, I could not write an honest story. As I struggled with the narrative, I heaped my rage upon Mama's father. . . . I did not pick the story up again until the late 1980s. And when I did, I decided to go on a search, a search for the father my mother never talked about.

Her search led her, after many years, to a painful acceptance of the ambiguities in her past. Her grandfather had publicly acknowledged her mother as his child—at the cost of his own social ostracism, had paid for her education, and had passed on to her a love of poetry, an artistic heritage that McCray inherited as well. After an internal struggle that lasted decades, McCray was able to reconcile herself to the past. As she wrote in *Freedom's Child*, "We cannot deny our heritage. Then, too, there's the strange reality that hit me in the middle of one night: if it had not been for General Jones, I would not be in this world." The publication of McCray's memoir brought her some unwanted attention. She found herself literally and figuratively embraced by Confederate apologists, who took her story as a sign of a generalized reconciliation of the races. To her dismay, McCray heard herself hailed as a champion of racial healing by people with bumper stickers of the rebel flag—a symbol she loathes. She had become reconciled with the memory of her grandfather, but with this acceptance came a realization that her mother had been one of a lucky few mixed-race children to have a loving father. The general's love did not redeem the evils done by the others all around him. As McCray wrote, "Mama was one of the few fortunate children born of the 'monstrous system.' "

Joseph told a similar story of a private reconciliation in the Hairston family. Mattie Bell had told him of a deceased relative, a black Hairston woman who, many years earlier, had had an affair with a white doctor in Martinsville that resulted in the birth of a daughter. Wishing to keep details of the affair private, Mattie Bell did not mention any names to Joseph. But he repeated the story at a family gathering—with no way of knowing that the daughter of the story was standing next to him at that moment. She listened in silent shock as she recognized the outline of her own life story. Her mother had never admitted who her father was, but because of Joseph's indiscretion she learned the truth and went to meet her father for the first time.

Joseph had no doubt that the black Hairstons of Virginia and North Carolina were related in some way to the white Hairstons, but the link had long been severed. He thought he sensed a tacit acknowledgment of the connection in the closeness of Judge Peter's relationship with the family. "That's the odd thing about Peter," Joseph said. "Peter doesn't come right out and say, 'Yes, it happened,' but he doesn't distance himself." In Joseph's view, there would be no shame in discovering such a connection. "I don't pass judgment, I just accept my kin where they fall." He thought that, if the masters had children by their slave women, it revealed the degradation not of the slave, but of the master. He came to this realization on a trip to Africa. He visited Senegal because he wanted to see the spot where the slaves left Africa. He went to a slave holding house on an island in Dakar harbor where the slaves were brought in, segregated by groups, and chained up "like cordwood." He said the white slave handlers would select the most attractive young women as their servants and mistresses. It fascinated him to hear that if a woman became pregnant, she was freed. The slave traders, he said, "had sufficient respect for themselves that they couldn't sell their own children into slavery."

Joseph had a copy of the book Judge Peter had written about Coolee-mee, with the names of the slaves Peter's grandfather had owned at Coo-leemee and his other plantations in North Carolina and Virginia. Joseph pored over the roster trying to make connections with his own genealogy. The name at the top of Joseph's genealogy, four generations back, was Elias. His name was at the farthest limit of her memory. Elias had been born a slave somewhere in the white Hairston empire, but exactly where, no one knew.

The custom on the Hairston plantations, according to Judge Peter, was for slave parents, not the master, to name their children. Elias was a variation of the name of Elijah, the great prophet, that was used in the old King James Version—the version the enslaved people would have heard from the lips of black and white preachers. A prophet and teacher, Elias had a divine mission to reconcile fathers and sons, mothers and daughters, and thereby save all from destruction. "Lo, I will send you the prophet," says the Book of Malachi. "He will turn the hearts of parents to their children and the hearts of children to their parents, so that I will not come and strike the land with a curse." Joseph Hairston had described that same kind of turning of the heart: "I don't pass judgment," he had said of his ancestors, echoing the message of the Old Testament prophet. I decided that I would try to find Joseph's Elias.

Once more I was drawn back into the chronicle of slavery. I reread and reabsorbed thousands of names—plantation ledgers; death lists; army rosters; census lists; a compilation of all the given names of the slaves of Lowndes County, Mississippi; registers of people who had sent letters to the Freedmen's Bureau; lists of sharecroppers; rosters of slaves who got shoes, who got coats, who gave birth. The name "Elias, Elias" kept me poring over the records in one fruitless search after another. Another thick packet of documents came to me, sent by one of Joseph's cousins. He, too, was descended from Elias, and he had pushed the genealogy back a generation. Through years of tedious research he had found the names and birth dates of Elias's parents, William and Sally. He had also compiled a list of Elias's siblings with their dates of birth:

Julia	1828
Elias	1833
William	1834
Christina	1842
Jerry	1846
Ruth	1850

But even this was a dead end. The names were common ones that turned up numerous times in the plantation books. How could I tell one William from another? I was chasing a phantom through a maze of lists. Genealogy becomes a mania, an obsessive struggle to penetrate the past and snatch meaning from an infinity of names. At some point the search becomes futile—there is nothing left to find, no meaning to be dredged out of old receipts, newspaper articles, letters, accounts of events that seemed so important fifty or seventy years ago. All that remains is the insane urge to keep looking, insane because the searcher has no idea what he seeks. What will it be? A photograph? A will? A fragment of a letter? The only way to find out is to look at everything, because it is often when the searcher has gone far beyond the border of futility that he finds the object he never knew he was looking for. And so it was that a chance remark by Judge Hairston led to the discovery of an extraordinary document.

On a visit to Cooleemee I was having lunch with the judge, reviewing the progress of my research. He asked me if I had had the chance yet to look at the plantation papers Rufus had. I had no idea whom he was talking about. "Rufus Hairston from Oak Hill," he said. One of the judge's cousins, Rufus Hairston had left Oak Hill after World War II and moved to Bristol, Virginia, on the border with Tennessee, taking with him a pile of documents. Rufus had died some years ago, but his widow and son were still living in Bristol. I left the next day.

Rufus's widow, Rosalie, had graciously agreed to see me on short notice. When I entered the colonial-era, brick house, I saw Hairston family portraits from Oak Hill, books from the Oak Hill library, and furniture from the plantation. Rosalie opened a drawer in a sideboard to reveal a cache of old letters and documents. Her son, Thomas, described, with regret, the day over thirty years earlier when he had taken one of the family documents to school for show-and-tell. It was the original royal land grant from the English king to the Hairston family, granting land in Virginia. The document, Thomas recalled, carried a large wax seal with a ribbon. A teacher asked to borrow it, and Thomas never got it back.

Thomas had with him a folder containing a half-inch-high stack of photocopied papers. They had originally belonged to Ruth Hairston, the shrewd, wealthy matriarch of the Hairston family, the wife of Robert Hairston, who had fled Virginia for Europe, and ultimately Mississippi. The papers included legal documents from the court fight over Robert's will, in which he tried to bequeath his estate to his black daughter, Chrillis; a ledger recording births and deaths of slaves; and a two-page slave list from Saura Town Plantation in North Carolina. Ruth had owned that plantation—in 1832 she had inherited it from her father, Saura Town Peter. I quickly glanced through the photocopies, which Thomas said I could keep, and resumed my conversation with my hosts about their family history. Not until I reached home and looked at the papers more carefully did I realize how valuable they were.

The two-page list from Saura Town, which I had taken for a routine tabulation of taxable slaves, was, in fact, a genealogy—a family tree written in slavery time itself. Drawn up by a white Hairston and dated 1854, the genealogy covered at least four and perhaps five generations, giving the names and ages of eighty-eight people, all descended from one person. I had never seen anything like it. A title across the top said, "A List of Sally Blags Decendants at Saura Town N.C. Feb 14, '54." On that day in 1854, the slaveholders had drawn up a roster of all of Sally Blag's living offspring. The copy was faded, and some of the names were difficult to read, but among the eighty-eight names on the list, the word *Elias* leaped out. He was a grandson of Sally Blag.

I had to make certain I had the right Elias. I pulled out the list of Elias's siblings and parents I had received from Joseph Hairston's cousin and laid it next to the Blag list. One by one, the names and the birth dates matched. They were all on the list. Joseph was definitely a descendant of Sally Blag.

But who was she? Why was she so important that the masters would draw up a list of all her descendants, something they never did for any other black woman? Who was this person Joseph was descended from?

I had seen the name Blag before, on another list, on another document. The list of her offspring contained other names I had seen before, the unusual names Gilcrease and Gilblas. Gilcrease seemed especially familiar—and his name finally jogged my memory. Those names were in a book—the book Judge Peter himself had written about Cooleemee. Gilcrease was the slave who had also been known by the nickname Tinker. He and Sally Blag were the slaves of old Saura Town Peter, the judge's great-great-great-grandfather, one of the founders of the Hairston empire. Saura Town was the name of a twelve-thousand-acre plantation in North Carolina.

Saura Town Peter, a whirlwind of energy and enterprise, had prospered in the tumultuous decade after the Revolutionary War and had become a substantial figure in his rough part of the world. He ran an iron forge and a general store and gathered up for sale the commodities of the backwoods—bear skins, ginseng, snakeroot, swine, venison, and hides. He operated a roadhouse, a tobacco inspection station, and a distillery. He was elected four times to the North Carolina state senate, aided by the generous servings of free liquor at the polling place.

Peter became rich enough to commission a portrait, one that shows him as a bulky, bull-necked man with the strong nose and chin characteristics of the Hairston males. He sat for the portrait wearing a fine, dark coat with a high collar, a white shirt, and tie—a man of the frontier, on the edge of gentility. The eyes are large and watchful but not harsh; his lips, oddly feminine, seem to be suppressing a smile. A business acquaintance described him as "a plain man—but very intelligent," but he had a rough temper that made even his own relatives reluctant to cross him. He was a shrewd, tough, and patient bargainer when buying land or slaves. Sometimes he paid cash and sometimes he bartered. Among his papers I found a receipt, dated February 1785, for the purchase of a black girl. Her name was given only as "Sall." Peter bought her for a barrel of tobacco.

In 1815, Peter was considering the purchase of a large plantation on the Yadkin River, about forty miles south of Saura Town. The plantation was Cooleemee. Before making the purchase—a $20,000 investment—Peter had to be certain that the land was suited for growing cotton, so to try out a crop, he sent a group of ten slaves to the Yadkin. He needed the most reliable, skilled, and trustworthy manager he could find, so he placed the task in the hands of Sally Blag's eighteen-year-old son, Gilchrist.

Gilchrist was a remarkable person. He could repair and operate farm machinery; he handled large sums of money; and he traveled on his own across North Carolina and Virginia to conduct Peter's business. Gilchrist married a woman from another plantation and had several children. In 1822, Peter purchased the family for over $1,700 so they could live with Gilchrist. Most remarkable of all, Gilchrist could read and write, and from old documents of Saura Town, there arose that greatest of rarities, the voice of a slave.

Gilchrist wrote to Peter from Cooleemee that he had repaired the ceiling of the mill and was at work on the mill wheel. Many of the Negroes had been sick, he said; a woman named Cintly "lost her child last Sunday." Nevertheless the work was progressing well and Peter didn't have to worry. Gilchrist seemed more concerned about Peter's health—the owner was then sixty-three years old—than with the state of the plantation. "If you cannot come out conveniently," he wrote, "it wont make no difference only we would rather you would be here and see things yourself. . . . If your business is such that you can leave home try to get here next Sunday and by the time you look about a little and get rested I think we shall be ready to go home with you." He wrote in a firm, clean hand, signing his name with a large capital G topped by a neat flourish. He expressed himself more clearly and more fluently than some whites of the time whose letters I had read.

Peter had no white sons to look to for help. He had hopes for a nephew named Woods, but came to rely more and more on Gilchrist. After Peter bought Cooleemee, he put Woods in charge of the place, but he sent Gilchrist down too. Gilchrist wrote to Peter in July 1823 that "everything is well as far as I know and the Plantation is all in very good order—and I dont want you to be in any way uneasy. . . . I am well and hope to find you [well] and all the rest." Indeed, Gilchrist did a better job at Cooleemee than Woods. When Peter wrote the final version of his will, he canceled a bequest that he had earlier made to Woods, "because he has displeased me."

Gilchrist's brother Salem was also highly regarded by Peter and had unusual responsibilities. Another favored slave was Gilblas. He too may have been a son of Sally Blag. His name does not appear on the list of her descendants, but it is likely that he was dead by the time it was drawn up in 1854. Two younger males on the list are also named Gilblas—presumably his son and grandson. In his will Peter gave farms to Gilchrist and Gilblas, "for their use and benefit forever." It was extremely rare for a slaveholder to bequeath land to a slave, and the legality of the bequests under North Carolina law was questionable—but Peter went ahead and did it anyway. He probably thought that it was no one's business but his.

In his will, Peter also commanded his heirs to look after Sally Blag. Peter feared that after his death Sally's children and grandchildren might be sold or moved to other plantations. He did not want that to happen, ever. In the most emphatic language, Peter declared, "It is my positive will and direction that Sally Blag nor none of her children be separated but remain and live with my daughter." When he wrote "separated" he meant "sold." To insure that his heirs carried out his wishes, he bequeathed the *use* of his slaves to his daughter, Ruth Hairston, for her lifetime, but he passed the *ownership* of the slaves to his great-grandchildren, including the judge's grandfather. The youngest heir would not reach legal age until 1850 and so could not give her consent to a sale until then.

Sally's sons were the only slaves to whom Saura Town Peter gave special responsibilities and privileges. It also appears that Gilchrist was the only Hairston slave taught to read and write. Because Sally Blag and her children were named in the master's will and given unique opportunities, it suggested a connection deeper than that of master and slaves. Perhaps Sally's children were Peter's offspring.

After Peter's death in 1832, Gilchrist and Gilblas came into the possession of Robert Hairston, the "lunatic" who later bequeathed his land and slaves to his black daughter in Mississippi. I found a note from a merchant to Robert that referred to Gilblas as "your manager." The note revealed that Gilblas was managing a plantation on his own, and that Robert held him in high regard. In the papers that I had perused, merchants routinely referred to black overseers and drivers as "boy." A merchant would have used the deferential term *manager* only because he knew

Robert Hairston would be furious if he didn't. Robert wanted the white community to treat Gilblas with respect, an unusual level of respect that lent further weight to the possibility that Gilblas was more than Robert's manager, that he was his cousin and the half brother of his wife.

The Hairston males have always had a strong physical resemblance from generation to generation. If Gilblas and Gilchrist were Robert's cousins they might have resembled him; every day might have brought him face-to-face with his own dark-hued image, men just like himself, but slaves. Was it the image of these enslaved cousins that haunted Robert on his deathbed in Mississippi, that compelled him to spare his daughter from their fate? I believed that it was.

From the very first, slaves took an active part in the founding of the great Hairston plantation empire. Gilchrist established the plantation at Cooleemee, planted the first crops, and got the place up and running. Gilchrist and Gilblas were so valuable to Peter that he gave them land. No Hairston ever gave land to a white manager. Because of their race, Gilchrist and Gilblas were unable to claim all that was rightfully theirs—a full share of their likely father's estate, and freedom.

The white Hairstons had drawn up the list of Sally Blag's offspring not from any lingering affection for that black family, but as an inventory. In the aftermath of Robert Hairston's death in 1852, in Mississippi, when the family embroiled itself in bitter feuding over his estate, the Hairstons needed to have an accurate accounting of the slaveholdings in North Carolina. Saura Town Peter had given his daughter Ruth the lifetime use of his slaves in his will of 1832; but Ruth's marriage to Robert complicated the legacy. Lawyers could argue that Ruth actually owned the slaves, that the slaves became Robert's property upon his marriage to her, and that the slaves should be dispersed among Robert's heirs-at-law. As this litigation was under way in 1854, Ruth Hairston ordered that the offspring of her father's slave Sally Blag be called together and counted, their names written down. I could only wonder if Ruth, when the list was handed to her, felt any hint of acknowledgment or shame that these slaves were her half brothers and half sisters, her nieces and nephews, to the fourth generation.

Ironically, just months after Robert Hairston died in 1852 and tried to free his slaves in his will, Harriet Beecher Stowe's *Uncle Tom's Cabin* was published, stirring a hurricane of abolitionist fervor in the North. I wondered what would have happened if Chrillis's plight had become known at exactly that moment. Perhaps the forces of abolition would have dispatched a legal champion to Mississippi to make hers a test case. The people on the list of Sally Blag's offspring might have been freed and sent North. Instead, their names went back into the asset column of the ledgers, and their labor created the wealth that would soon build the mansion at Cooleemee.

The sons of Sally Blag were favored slaves in their father's lifetime and for a while thereafter. But their status was not inheritable. Their bequests of land were not entered into the Stokes County deed books, so their children and grandchildren did not receive the allotment that was rightfully theirs by blood. Eventually the memory of their family's inheritance was lost, and they joined the others in tilling fields they did not own. And so it happened with Joseph Hairston's ancestor Elias.

The records showed that after the Civil War, Elias sharecropped at Camp Branch, near Martinsville, not far from where Joseph's aunt had her cabin, where he was buried. Elias worked alongside his parents, William and Sally, who was the daughter of Sally Blag and Saura Town Peter. According to the Camp Branch ledger, Elias's mother Sally, the daughter of one of the wealthiest men in North Carolina, toiled as a sharecropper when she was in her seventies and ill. The records contained small medical bills for her treatment. Her daughter Julia would die of typhoid fever.

I remembered a remark Judge Peter had made to me years earlier, how landed people have to know where all the third cousins are, because one of those cousins may turn up some day in probate court to challenge a will. The black descendants of old Peter Hairston had no standing in court, but in a deep sense they too were the heirs of Cooleemee. Joseph Hairston, a direct descendant of Sally Blag, was one of them.

Judge Peter had never seen the Sally Blag list. I sent him a copy of it, with my conclusion that, beyond much doubt, the slaves on it were the offspring of his grandfather's great-grandfather. Their descendants were his distant cousins. In his lawyerly fashion Peter said, at first, that the story was doubtful, that there was still no conclusive proof. But Sally Blag, he admitted, had always intrigued him. He had wondered about this woman who had been mentioned so prominently, but mysteriously, in old Peter's will. And then, paradoxically, he pointed me toward a piece of evidence I was unaware of. He suggested that I find an article in an obscure historical journal. It contained, he said, an account of a traveler's visit to Peter's plantation at Saura Town. I looked up the reference. In 1816 the traveler had indeed visited old Peter's place. In his diary the traveler commented on the large number of mixed-race slaves at Saura Town.

The judge wanted all the evidence to be considered, even if he knew he would not like the verdict. His family, it seemed evident, had enslaved their own flesh and blood for generations. It had happened so far back in the past that the whites had apparently been able to forget it, and even among the blacks it was only a dim memory—so dim that it had only the frail substance of a phantom, a voice that whispered only faintly in the roll of begats carried in the memories of the elders.

The judge wished to warn his brother, Nelson, that this "rumor" of Saura Town Peter having children with a slave would soon appear in print. He was shocked to hear his brother say—*it's true*. As a young man Nelson had known an elderly white Hairston who had told him of old Peter's relationship with his slave. Nelson had told no one of it, even his own brother, until that moment.

A Rite of

Reconciliation

A peculiar gravity kept the white and black Hairstons at Coolee-mee. Judge Hairston's grandfather had abandoned the house after the Civil War, but misfortune brought his family back to it. They had no other place to go. When the white Hairstons returned, so did the blacks. Thrown back together by necessity, the Hairstons acted out, in micro-cosm, the long aftermath of slavery. Paradoxically, as the years and gen-erations passed, Hairstons of both families felt the burden of their history grow heavier.

The judge's grandfather had rented Cooleemee to a farmer and moved his family to Baltimore in 1866, seeking a more comfortable life than the ravaged plantation country could offer. From time to time he traveled to Virginia and to Stokes County, North Carolina, to inspect his properties, but it seemed that he never returned to Cooleemee, perhaps because it would stir painful memories.

The future heir of Cooleemee, Judge Peter's father, was born in Bal-timore in 1871. Even as a boy he struck his father as serious and hard-working, prompting the elder Peter to remark, "I feel satisfied he will do something in the world unless he has very bad luck." From his remark about his son's making something of himself "in the world," it seems that the senior Peter did not want his son to return to the plantation. But his other remark about "very bad luck" came true, forcing the family back into the past.

The trading house of Herbert & Hairston, which Peter Hairston had founded in Baltimore after the Civil War, prospered until Peter's partner suddenly died. Peter discovered that Herbert had borrowed $20,000 for his personal use but in the firm's name. Herbert had died broke. Peter could have repudiated the debt since he had never approved it; he could have declared bankruptcy; he could have sued Herbert's widow to take possession of the property he had left. Peter took none of those courses. His unshakable sense of duty required that he honor the debt, even though it was not his. He redoubled his efforts at the firm in a vain struggle to satisfy the creditors. The strain exhausted and finally killed him. He died at his desk of a stroke in 1886 at the age of sixty-seven. His body was returned to the oldest Hairston place in Virginia, Berry Hill plantation, where his first wife, Columbia, and their children were buried. According to a newspaper account of Peter's funeral, a large number of his former slaves attended, "many of whom had walked long distances to see him laid away."

Unable to support the family's fashionable Baltimore town house any longer, Peter's widow, Fanny Hairston, brought her four children back to Cooleemee, which the two youngest children had never seen. The firm's debts trailed them. Fanny would have lost the property immediately except for help from two distant relatives and, indirectly, the Civil War. Peter Hairston had served in the war with Jeb Stuart, whose brother Alexander had prospered from selling salt to the Confederacy. He offered Fanny a loan. Help also came from another relative and wartime comrade, Jubal Early, the old fire-eater, whose Confederate connections had rescued him from poverty. After the war General Pierre Beauregard had been hired to head up a lottery in New Orleans because the organizers needed a distinguished war veteran to lend legitimacy to the operation. Beauregard had never forgotten that Jubal Early's sudden arrival with the Twenty-fourth Virginia had saved the Confederacy at the first Battle of Manassas. He summoned Early to New Orleans to take a position with the lottery. Early amassed a comfortable fortune and gladly advanced Fanny additional funds to satisfy the Baltimore creditors.

The Cooleemee that Fanny returned to had become a wreck. The man who rented the plantation had cheated on the arrangement, cutting large amounts of timber on the property without permission or payment. He had used the house itself to store grain. Fanny won a lawsuit against the tenant but did not recover any money. Fanny took up the task of reviving the plantation. Fanny was fifty-three, while her oldest child was twenty-seven, and Peter was the youngest at seventeen. After his graduation from college at age twenty-one, he returned to Cooleemee and assumed the mantle of "Marse Peter." No one in the family had any experience managing a plantation. For help they called upon the children and grandchildren of John Goolsby, whose family lived on the Saura Town Plantation in Stokes County. Goolsby's son "Harse" took over the day-to-day workings of Cooleemee's farm. One of Goolsby's daughters, Tish, was the cook, and her son, John Winston Hairston, took the position of butler. Cooleemee's former field slaves, and their children and grandchildren, were still living on the plantation, many of them in a tiny hamlet called Petersville, located just across the Yadkin River from the big house. As occurred at many other plantations, the old master-servant relationship was resurrected, almost as if the Civil War had never taken place; but something unusual happened at Cooleemee.

Fanny Hairston recognized that her teenaged butler, John Hairston, was a young man of intelligence and talent. These gifts made him an ideal servant, but Fanny did not want to see him waste his obvious talent by keeping him as one. She paid for him to go to college, sending him to the all-black Livingstone College in Salisbury, North Carolina. In return, she expected nothing. She did not expect him to come back and work for the family, nor did she ask him to repay his tuition. She put him on course to an independent life and wished him well.

John Hairston graduated with a degree in theology, was ordained a Baptist minister, and became pastor of a church in Salisbury. Later he moved to the far western part of North Carolina, taking over a church in Asheville, where he led the largest Baptist congregation, black or white, in the state. He never forgot his former mistress's generosity, nor did the white family forget him. He frequently visited Cooleemee, where he was known to both the black and white Hairstons as "Brer John."

The Reverend John Hairston remained devoted to Fanny. He was at Cooleemee when she died in 1907 and helped carry her coffin from the house. After her funeral he wrote a heartfelt tribute to her and sent it to a North Carolina newspaper for publication. It was customary at the time to publish personal tributes to the dead, and John Hairston wrote, "I should do injustice to my own feelings at this solemn hour were I not to speak." He felt compelled, he said, "to publicly acknowledge her goodness and kindness to me, from my infancy till we looked each other in the face for the last time." He described Fanny as "a tender and faithful mistress to all of her servants . . . beloved and respected by all of them." His tribute contained an indirect, carefully disguised barb, a quiet rebuke to whites who pretended to be a "friend of the Negro," but did nothing to help him.

In her death my race loses a valuable friend. She loved the negro. . . . Those negroes in needy circumstances could be seen at all times coming from far and near making their way to the "white house." They were never sent away empty-handed. She was not the kind that received the negro in a social way and gave him no material aid, but she "fed the hungry and clothed the naked." She did many charitable deeds that even her children knew nothing about. No one knows of the great help she has been to me but myself.

Fanny's generous gesture toward her servant near the close of the nineteenth century came at a time when race relations in North Carolina were making some progress. Many white leaders were doing their best to put a stop to violence against blacks, and white jurors proved themselves willing to convict other whites for vicious crimes against blacks. In 1905 a mob of two thousand whites broke into the jail at Salisbury and lynched three blacks being held for the murder of a white farmer. A prominent local judge and a United States senator tried to stop the mob, literally blocking the jailhouse door until they were shoved aside. The state government tracked down the head of the lynch mob and brought him to trial. Convicted by an all-white jury, he was sentenced to fifteen years in prison. Ten years later the state government took extraordinary measures to prevent another lynching. When word reached Governor Bickett that a mob was threatening a rural jailhouse, he dispatched a machine-gun company of the Durham Home Guard with explicit orders to protect the black prisoners "at all hazards." He directed the Home Guard to "shoot straight" into any mob, which meant no warning shots were to be fired into the air. When the mob attacked the jail, the Home Guard opened up, killing one white rioter on the spot and wounding two more; but the three prisoners were saved. A state court later found the black men innocent of their charges and convicted fifteen of the white rioters. Some rioters received sentences of six years at hard labor on chain gangs. Although the government showed that it would not tolerate mob violence against blacks, it did not attempt to alter the rigid system of social segregation that was deeply ingrained in North Carolinians.

Upper-class Southerners abhorred mob violence against blacks because it subverted the rule of law. But they were not what the Reverend John Hairston would have called "friends of the Negro." Old-line Southerners, including Cooleemee's "Marse Peter," held views that echoed the pronouncement of a Virginia slaveholder and Revolutionary leader: "I am an aristocrat. I love liberty, and hate equality." They upheld segregation as a venerable way of life, handed down from their forefathers.

Such landholding families refused to divorce themselves from the traditions of the past. In 1911, for example, a relative of the Hairstons' from Salisbury, Christian Reid, wrote a novel called *The Wargrave Trust* set at a fictional North Carolina mansion. The novel portrays a profound love of the past that was intimately connected to the house itself: "After the servant had been dismissed, he stood for a moment looking around him, conscious of a thrill of pride, as he realized, more distinctly than ever before, what a fine old house, full of the intangible essence of a wealthy and aristocratic past, this home of his mother's family was." This fictional house was based on Cooleemee. By the time Christian Reid had written those lines, the Southern plantation had become a place of romance in the popular mind. The plantation represented old agrarian values in a country that had rapidly industrialized. The plantation offered memories of the social solidity and safety of antebellum times. Among whites, the cruelties of slavery were forgotten, effectively shrouded in a hazy fog of nostalgia. In this atmosphere of romance and willful forgetting, Judge Peter Hairston was born at Cooleemee in the old master's bed, in 1913.

The countryside Peter Hairston knew as a child had changed little since the Civil War. There were factories twenty miles away in Salisbury, but Cooleemee remained the little capital of a rural province. To cross the Yadkin River, the Hairstons took their small, private ferry, pushed by a former slave using a long pole. As late as World War I, Cooleemee remained so isolated that there were no schools appropriate for the white children of upper-class plantation owners. Peter and his brother were educated at home by their mother and aunt, using the Calvert System, a home-school program devised in Baltimore for the children of Protestant missionaries serving in distant parts of the world. So each month, packets went out from Baltimore to families in China, the Congo, Argentina, and Cooleemee Plantation, North Carolina. When Peter was a child, his playmates were the children of the black servants and sharecroppers. Many older white Southerners speak glowingly of the childhood days they spent playing with black children as equals. But that custom descended directly from slavery time, when the small children of masters and slaves cavorted happily together, until it was time for the black children to take their places in the fields.

Judge Hairston formed friendships with several black Hairstons as a child, but he later came to realize that Cooleemee had not been an oasis of racial tolerance. Looking back as an adult, he realized that he was being groomed to take his place as the master of Cooleemee in a racial hierarchy inherited from slavery, and under a system of rules that never had to be spoken about but were universally recognized and obeyed by both races.

"It was *anything* but integrated," the judge recalled. "Not even *close*. It was perfectly all right for me to play ball with them and go swimming with them in the river. But you could not sit down with them and eat. You did not go in their houses at night. Only one time did I go into a black house at night, and that was when one of Harse's daughters was getting married, and I asked permission." The judge recalled that blacks were not allowed to enter the mansion by the front door under any cir-cumstances—they could not even set foot on the front steps. They were never allowed to sit down, despite age or infirmity, in the presence of a white person. The judge's father, Marse Peter, the son of the slave master, imposed this rigid system.

"He was *very firm*," the judge said. "His prejudice really was deep and broad. It was not a hostility, not the competitive prejudice you see now. It was simply, 'We're better than they are. They're poor, pathetic people, and we have to look after them.' But my father was fair. He treated them all exactly alike, and they respected that. That's one reason why he got along with them. He never said anything that would indicate that he had a very low opinion of most of them, but he did. There were a few he liked, but very few. What did impress him was being absolutely faithful. Be there every morning at seven o'clock to beat the biscuits; be sure you're down there at the riverbank when he wants to cross."

By the 1930s, when Peter was a young man, he began to challenge, slightly, his father's prejudices, with little success. "He had established his views before the First World War. There were so few blacks then with professional standing. When I came along, there were black scientists, doctors, teachers, and lawyers. There was no question but they could do it. Some had considerable ability." When one day Peter played a record-ing by the great black contralto Marian Anderson, his father angrily told him to turn it off. On another occasion, when one of the black Hairstons brought his fiancée, a Northern woman, to meet his family on the plan-tation, the black and white families had to carefully time her visit to the mansion itself, awaiting a moment when Marse Peter was away so the Northerner could walk in the front door unchallenged.

The Depression extended the life of the old system. Southern blacks who had left the farms for work in cities were forced to come back when city jobs disappeared. They were willing to do any kind of work for small wages and tolerate almost any indignity. Prices for farm products dropped sharply, and Cooleemee faced its worst economic crisis since the Civil War. The strain of managing the plantation amidst plummeting prices, a flood, and then drought took a heavy toll on Marse Peter. He suffered a heart attack, recovered somewhat, but remained weak until his death in 1943. His wife, known as Miss Elmer, managed Cooleemee until her own advancing age made it impossible. In 1949, Peter took over Cooleemee, bringing with him his new bride, Lucy, herself the descendant of an old North Carolina family that had fallen on hard times.

When Peter and Lucy took over the plantation, the house was in deplorable condition after many years of neglect. Large chunks of plaster had fallen from the walls of the stair hall and had not been replaced; green mold was growing on the stucco outside; the woodwork on the tower was rotting. Far worse than the physical deterioration was the obsolete economic system by which the plantation was run. Peter realized he had hundreds of tenant farmers, a slight majority of them white, living on the plantation—many of them past the age when they could do useful work. He couldn't, however, just evict them. He was legally able to ask them to leave, but the unspoken pact, left over from slavery time, required the owner to look after servants and tenants for life. Peter shifted from planting cotton to wheat, but profits were not high enough to support what was essentially a small town. Nearly a century had passed since the Civil War, yet this rural economic system, which harkened more to feudal times than the middle of the twentieth century, had hardly changed. Some black Hairstons around Cooleemee owned small patches of land where they raised their own tobacco, but industrious blacks faced a racial barrier to improving their condition. Banks refused to lend them the cash to acquire tractors and other heavy equipment they needed to cultivate large plots.

By the 1960s, the younger black Hairstons were able to get factory jobs in Winston-Salem, or at one of the furniture factories in Lexington or High Point. Eventually only one black family was left at Cooleemee— the butler, William Hairston, his wife, Charming, and their children and grandchildren. The connection between the white and black families ran deep, for Charming was a granddaughter of John Goolsby, the slave who had gone off to the Civil War as body servant to the judge's grandfather.

The judge never alluded to any difficulties in keeping Cooleemee afloat in the 1950s and 1960s. But when I spoke with his son, Pete, who still lives on the plantation and will take it over upon his father's death, I got some sense of the struggle it had been to keep the place alive. "You never hear my dad complain about how poor it was here," Pete said, "but there was no money at all. My parents would drive cars until the wheels were falling off. It was not until the mid-1980s that water worked in this house all winter. I had the lines buried deep enough so they wouldn't freeze or have to be cut off. When I was a kid, if the temperature went to thirty-two degrees, there was no water in the house. You saved it in buckets until the weather warmed up."

Pete explained that his parents had abandoned successful careers to return and save the plantation from ruin. "My mother headed a government office in Washington. Dad was a lawyer for a large insurance company there. They could have easily stayed in Washington and done very well. But it was either he comes back or the plantation is gone. To him there was no choice. Very few people in our day and age would undertake what they did. Very few in *that* day and age would either. The alternatives were much better; but this is just what he felt he should do.

"About 1955, Dad was thrown from a hay wagon and got a concussion. Mom told him it was time to go back to the law. She ran the farm after that. He worked six days a week at his law practice. My father has never been one to hound people for money. I can remember people paying him with guinea fowl, peahens, or quail that still had buckshot in them. We didn't buy *anything*.

"The older generation of black families helped hold the farm together. They did a great deal for it. But it held them together too. My parents were pretty outspoken on the racial issue for this part of the world—to the point where there were threats made against my father. It's hard for people to imagine what the black-white issue was around here as little as thirty years ago. We've come farther in thirty years than we'd come in three hundred years before that. I'm amazed that there's not more backlash than there is. I still find myself shocked when I get invitations to so-and-so's place, 'Confederate States of America.' I was just shown a barn full of Confederate flags, one for every Confederate state."

The judge had described the racial hostility around Cooleemee in the 1950s and 1960s, and his family's role in combating it. "People have gotten used to the fact that blacks vote now. In the 1950s when they went to vote, they would have been turned down cold—there was no question—except Lucy would take them up and walk them in." The judge himself talked the local school board into submitting to integration without a fight in 1964. He knew his community well; he achieved what he wanted not by appealing to their sense of justice, but to their practical side. "I said to them, 'Look, fellas, it's just a question of time. Do you want to catch hell now or do you want to catch it in pieces, down the road? 'Cause you'll catch it every time you make a move, and nobody's going to be satisfied until you just combine the schools.' So we integrated. The only real objection came from the principal of the black high school. He lost his job. He could not conceivably have gone as the principal of the high school here." (The abrupt, automatic dismissal of this black principal showed just how tenacious the Stokes County Hairstons had been in keeping John L. Hairston as their principal.) It was around that time when his son Pete happened to be at the gas station in nearby Mocksville when a white mob was gathering for a raid on the blacks. Pete was just a teenager at the time, but he talked them out of it.

In 1978, amid an atmosphere of racial tension, the black and white Hairstons came together at Cooleemee for a public ceremony. After struggling for thirty years to save the house from ruin, the judge saw the fruits of his effort when the U.S. Department of the Interior declared Cooleemee a National Historic Landmark. The judge planned an elaborate ceremony for the official dedication, sending invitations to hundreds of family members, friends, and state officials, while opening the event to the general public as well. To entertain the throng—about three thousand people attended—and to add historical flavor, Civil War reenactors staged a battle on the grounds of the plantation. Amidst the booming of cannon and the swirling smoke of muskets, rebel troops absorbed a fierce Yankee attack, regrouped, and drove the invaders from the soil of Cooleemee.

But amidst the pomp and Civil War pageantry, a more important event was taking place at the house itself. Peter had invited the National Hairston Clan to be present for the ceremony, not to witness his triumph, but to participate and to claim their rightful share in it. He planned that the keynote speech at the event be delivered not by himself but by Squire Hairston. His invitation to Squire Hairston was an act of courage. He had already received threats when he had helped the blacks vote, and the racial situation in his part of North Carolina had steadily worsened. Cooleemee lay near the strongholds of particularly violent factions of the Ku Klux Klan and neo-Nazi hate groups. Just a year after the dedication of Cooleemee, an appalling massacre took place, in 1979, when a civil rights group staged an anti–Ku Klux Klan march in Greensboro. They had taunted the Klan, defying them to interfere with the march. In the midst of the march a line of cars and trucks pulled alongside. Someone yelled out, "You asked for the Klan and you got 'em." Fourteen demonstrators fell under a hail of gunfire. Five of them died. Captured by police as they sped away, the shooters were acquitted at their trial by an all-white jury.

The dedication of Cooleemee was patrolled not only by police units but by a detachment of the North Carolina National Guard. As far as the public knew, the Guard was present for traffic and crowd control, but Lucy Hairston conferred with the guard's commander about the possibility of violence, and he assured her that nothing would happen with his men patrolling the grounds.

That event was a point of reconciliation between the two families. Peter would never acknowledge it, but for years his actions spoke of a wish for reconciliation and reunion. Peter's legacy had been the myth of the South, born of the Lost Cause. He struggled against the customs imposed by his father to throw off that legacy. When he turned his hand to writing a book about his family's past, he devoted the most effort to recovering the heritage of the slaves, a task he undertook, he wrote, "as a memorial to these people."

I thought that, at last, I fully understood the handshake I had seen between the judge and Squire Hairston at my first meeting with them. I thought that I had indeed witnessed an absolution being uttered over the past. However, some issues had been left unsettled, and one question from the past remained unanswered.

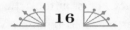

16

A MONUMENT
BY THE RIVER

The Hairstons had filled another large hall for their reunion banquet, this time at a hotel in Greensboro, North Carolina—near the heartland of the family. Both Squire Hairston and Judge Peter had called me weeks before the event to tell me to be sure to attend because the main speaker of the evening would be Ever Lee Hairston, who had grown up at Cooleemee and retained close ties to the white family. She had been born on Cooleemee Plantation in 1944; as a child she had worked there as a sharecropper and a maid. Her grandparents were the house servants William and Charming, Cooleemee's butler and cook, the last survivors of the old order. They had been servants at Cooleemee since the end of the nineteenth century. Their ties to the plantation were venerable: William's grandfather, born a slave in 1828, had been the wagon driver at Cooleemee. Charming's grandfather was John Goolsby. Charming's brother was Brer John, who had been educated by the generosity of Fanny Hairston. William and Charming had served three generations of the white Hairston family until their retirement in the 1960s.

I had seen Ever Lee at the first reunion I attended in Baltimore, but had not been introduced to her. She had sat silently in the room with the rest of the executive board as Squire and Jester talked about the family's history. At that meeting she seemed to be listening intently, but she never said anything, and she never even looked at me. I had interpreted her refusal even to glance at me as a sign of suspicion; but later I discovered a simpler explanation. She was blind. Ever Lee and one of her sisters had lost their sight in adulthood to retinitis pigmentosa, an inherited disease.

In recognition of her connections to Cooleemee and the white Hairston family, Ever Lee had asked the judge's wife, Lucy, to make the introductory remarks before her speech. So, as the reunion guests were finishing their dinner, Lucy Hairston took the podium, tightly clutching a sheet of paper with her prepared remarks. When I had first met her, Lucy was a jaunty, animated woman who took pleasure in lingering at the dining table long after the judge had gone to bed, chain-smoking cigarettes and telling stories, yet this night she appeared frail and tense. Only a few people knew that she was suffering the early stages of Alzheimer's disease. She could have begged off from the invitation, but her affection for Ever Lee was too great. In the days leading up to the reunion she had repeatedly rehearsed her short speech, describing Ever Lee's family background and education:

"After completing high school in the local system, Ever Lee entered North Carolina Central University and took graduate work at Rutgers. Then, because she was losing her sight, she graduated from the Louisiana Center for the Blind. She also changed her job from teaching. She is now a supervisor of counselors for the Camden County Health Department in alcohol and substance abuse. Of the many honors she has received, I shall only mention that she is president of the state chapter of the National Federation of the Blind. She is a national board member of the National Hairston Clan. Please join me in welcoming our own Ever Lee Hairston." With these words, the mistress of Cooleemee yielded the floor to her former servant.

Ever Lee took the podium, and a powerful, ringing voice filled the hall. An experienced speaker, she had delivered talks around the country about the need for educating and employing the blind and the disabled, using her own experiences as an example. She opened by saying the topic of her speech would be "change" and how it comes about, and how her own life had changed. But before she launched into the substance of her talk, she paused to thank Lucy for her introductory remarks. At the time, this seemed a mere formality, but Ever Lee wanted to clearly state her feelings of affection for the white Hairstons before she reached the crux of her speech. She called attention to the old Southern way of addressing an elder with respect:

"This morning I called Miss Lucy. I knew that time has brought about change because she said, 'Just call me Lucy.' Thank you, Miss Lucy. I'm so used to it, I don't mind saying 'Miss Lucy.'" In a different situation, before a different sort of audience, her expression of respect and courtesy would have sounded servile. But everyone in this room knew what she meant.

"The process of life is change," she began. "I received my incentive to change while living at Cooleemee. My two older siblings and I had to stay out of school to pick cotton. I remember very vividly one day when my father dropped us off where the cotton was planted. It was shortly after noon on a fall day. I had gotten about fifty yards down this cotton row, and I leaned forward to pick a ball, when there on the ground was a black snake. I was frightened, but my sister convinced me that we must keep on picking. Farther down the row I leaned over again, and there lay another snake, a brown one. My brother said, 'A copperhead!' I looked around, and there was another, and another. We ran as fast as we could until we reached a trailer packed full of bags of cotton. We climbed up on top and waited until father came for us. While sitting on the bags of cotton, I thought and I thought about my life as a sharecropper. And I thought, 'There must be a better way of life.'"

She paused for just a beat, and then repeated the statement, this time addressing it to a member of the audience sitting right in front of her at the table of honor.

"I thought, 'There must be a better way of life, *Mr. Peter*.'"

There was a murmur, and then applause from the family. With one remark, Ever Lee had cut through decades of encrusted courtesy and decorum to declare in front of the entire family that despite the affection she had for Lucy and Peter, some issues had never been settled.

Peter and Lucy Hairston left the hall immediately after Ever Lee finished, not waiting to hear the long series of award presentations. I heard later that Ever Lee had gone to Cooleemee several weeks after her speech to show some friends the mansion. I found it hard to believe that she would dare approach the house after what she had said about Peter in the presence of the entire family, since no black Hairston had publicly criticized the judge before. But what I still did not comprehend was the depth of the connection between Judge Peter and the black Hairstons. The relationship was not based on mere courtesy. Their links to each other were too close and too deeply rooted to be broken so quickly. In fact, Ever Lee felt no reluctance about calling the judge to ask if she could bring a group of friends to see the mansion. Peter was waiting for her as she made her way up the steps.

"You come on in, young lady," his voice boomed from the doorway, "because I have something to say to you."

Ever Lee did not back away from the confrontation. She reproached him for the lifetime of work he had gotten out of her parents and grand-parents, with scant reward, in her view. Peter replied, "That's all that they could do. They didn't know how to do anything else."

"That may be true, Mr. Peter," Ever Lee responded, "but did anyone encourage them to do anything different?"

Few people, if any, had ever dared speak to Judge Hairston in that fashion, in or out of the courtroom. On another occasion the judge had unceremoniously tossed out a visiting white relative who had committed a minor social offense, but he tolerated Ever Lee's reproach, even in the presence of strangers, with the portrait of his grandfather, the slaveholder, peering down on them from the wall.

Ever Lee's relationship with the judge's family had a great deal more to it than I had suspected. Her blindness was inherited, part of a devas-tating pattern of illness in her family. Not only had a sister gone blind from the same disease, but another had died young from a rare kidney ailment. Rumors in the black family alleged that her blindness resulted from her parents' being close blood relatives, and that their common ancestor was a white Hairston. When her parents had announced their plans to marry, some of the older people tried to talk them out of it. Convoluted and sometimes contradictory—what an old man called "one of the silent things"—the rumors coalesced around the judge's grandfa-ther. No one could offer any proof; there were only whispers repeated over the decades. Ever Lee herself did not know the truth. The burden she carried was the burden of not knowing whether her blindness was a random mishap of nature or one of the last, bitter legacies of slavery.

Ever Lee had thought a great deal about her family's past, about the mentality of slavery and the "slavery-like" time she grew up in. She had also pondered the bond between the white and black Hairstons of Coo-leemee. She spoke of her past in an outpouring of nostalgia and pain, resentment and love—powerful strands of emotion that were contradic-tory but rose up together, so tightly woven that they could not be pulled apart. With her anguish over her history came a determination to em-brace it.

During the 1950s, when Ever Lee was a teenager, Cooleemee had changed little from the nineteenth century. Her parents and grandparents lived in a house without a bathroom. The entire family worked for min-imal wages. The other black families had all left the plantation. But Ever Lee's grandparents were the house servants, still bound by loyalty and custom to serve the white family for life. Her grandparents groomed the children to take their places in a system everyone else knew was dead.

"Everyone had moved away from the plantation except my family. We were the only black family left. My grandparents, William and Charming, were truly dedicated, *but that was the only life they knew.* I saw a way out, despite what my parents and grandparents were saying to me. They had been so brainwashed. It hurts to say it, but it's a fact—they were so brainwashed that they thought, 'If my children go outside of the home and work, Marse Peter is going to get upset.'

"My parents felt stuck. They had seven children, one with a terminal kidney illness. In order to survive, all the children had to work on the plantation. I cleaned the white family's house. But whenever I had a break, I would go into the library and read a book.

"I sat and talked to my grandfather. There was no way that I or anyone else could get him to see how he had sacrificed his entire life to help these people, and how his family may have been neglected. There was no way to get through to him. But after seeing that my grandparents had survived and were happy with the life they'd lived, you let it go. It doesn't mean that I have to be happy with that. But that's how I came to get a grip on all of this. I knew that resenting it would only create hostility, and I didn't want that, because we had built such a bond. And the way we built this bond was that my grandfather never said anything negative about them, ever. He kept harmony and peace in our home, in spite of the hard work that he was doing, and in spite of whatever resentments he may have had. He kept it to himself.

"They believed that they couldn't have made it without someone giving them something, and I understand that. They were grateful because it could have been a lot worse for them. So many other families who didn't have positive images became destroyed. They were churchgoing people. They were positive-thinking people, good role models in the way they spoke and dressed. They believed in maintaining family ties."

Ever Lee spoke of the relationship that had formed between the white and black Hairstons when she was a girl. "At holiday time, especially Christmas, there was such a bonding, because we sang Christmas carols together, we had prayer together, and they gave us gifts. It may not have been very much, but it made us feel special. We were happy to walk over to get those gifts because usually the gifts were very practical. It was Christmas when we got our shoes for the winter. We'd get maybe two outfits that would carry us through the winter, maybe some money to put aside to buy our Easter clothes.

"I knew I had to do something better for myself. I said to myself, 'I am not going to pick cotton for the rest of my life on this plantation.' At age seventeen, when I finished high school, I said, 'I'm leaving the plantation, I'm going to New York, I'm going to work.'

"I had seen an ad in the newspaper: 'Housekeepers. Baby-sitters. Long Island, New York.' And I thought, 'This is my way out.' My grandmother said to me, 'Girl, you go to New York, somebody's going to hit you on your head, and you'll be back here. There ain't no better life than here.' I just kept thinking, 'There *is* a better life.' "

The employment agency sent her a free bus ticket to New York. She didn't know anyone in the city and had no place to stay. She had to get a live-in job immediately or she would have found herself on the streets. As soon as she stepped off the bus in midtown Manhattan, she made her way to the employment agency.

"When I got to the agency, there were all these black girls lined up, and it was another form of slavery. Tears started to roll down my face, but I had to press on. There were all these owners that were looking over the girls and saying, 'I want that one, I want that one.' " (As she told this story, I noticed that she had instinctively thought of these men not as "employers" but as "owners.")

"What I noticed is that they were skipping over the girls who were real dark, and picking the ones who were light, so I had an in. Somebody picked me. He took me to his home to meet his wife and his two kids and told me what my responsibilities would be. What they're supposed to do is take you back to the agency, sign you up, and they take you home with them again.

"On our way back from his home, he's fondling me, putting his hands on my legs and telling me, 'On your days off I can make your stay here worthwhile.' I just sat and I listened, and I was filled up with so much anger and pain, and I thought, 'How can I get out of this?' It was like being back on the plantation in slavery and having to survive that. When we got to the agency, I went to the bathroom and hid from him. I didn't come out until hours later after he had left. I was in there just crying. I heard them announce that all the girls who didn't get jobs today were being taken out to Hempstead, Long Island, to sleep there for the night. I went out with the crowd. They put us in a huge auditorium and threw us some blankets.

"I cried all night. I remembered what my grandmother said: 'You'll be back here. There ain't no better life than here.' But I kept thinking that I will not go back until I've done what I need to do. And I prayed, 'God, please give me a job. I need a job. I want to go to college.' The next morning they gave us a washcloth and took us to an agency in Hempstead. There were maybe one hundred and twenty people, but this guy came and picked me. It was like a miracle. I had a good feeling about him. He had his wife and two children in the car. When we got to their home, they told me they had a daughter who had a terminal illness, and I shared with them that I had sister with a terminal illness, that she had had six operations. And we connected. They were so good to me. And I can see how you get brainwashed—that you feel that somebody has saved your life. Here I went from a plantation to a Jewish home. I think they paid me twenty dollars a week or thirty dollars a week. Which was good money to me! Because I was only making four dollars a week from Mr. Peter and Miss Lucy.

"I stayed there for that summer. Of course they thought they had me for life. I was so depressed at the end of the summer because somehow I had to tell them the truth, that really I wanted to go to college. Finally I broke down and told them, and they said that they would help me to get back to North Carolina. They gave me plane fare.

"I was going to go into nursing. But when I took the eye test, I failed it. My sight was already failing then, but I was in such denial. I was not going to tell anybody; I had so many other things to deal with. My main problem then was night blindness. I could read, but I had a lot of difficulty reading at night. But I was determined. I talked my grandfather into giving me the money to study business education at North Carolina Central College.

"The following summer I went back to New York and worked for the Bronsteins again. That's what helped me see the dedication of my grandfather and my grandmother. I thought about it: How can I resent my grandparents for their dedication and commitment to people who they feel saved their lives? And yet the Hairstons hadn't been as giving as this Jewish family had been to me in such a short period of time. My grandparents had given their entire lives; I had only given a summer, but the Bronsteins were willing to help me. They found people who could give me clothing for college. They told me that I could come back the following summer. At Christmas they sent me one hundred dollars.

"As soon as I graduated from North Carolina Central, I moved to

New Jersey and lived with my older brother. I started teaching business education courses in high school, like typing and shorthand. I taught there for three years, and then I started working with special-education students. My eyesight was failing me more rapidly because of all the reading I had to do. I would have these excruciating pains in both eyes because the cataracts were building and the optic nerve was deadening by the day.

"I remember very vividly the last day that I taught. I was standing in the classroom, writing some shorthand on the board, and all of a sudden, everything just went totally black. I couldn't see. I was so scared. I kept saying to the students, 'Excuse me, I have chalk in my eyes.' Finally, from the fear and the fright, I passed out. They took me to the hospital. The thing that I remember is they kept asking me, 'Are you on drugs?' I had never used drugs. I didn't even drink. I told them I needed to see an eye doctor. I told them that a year before I had been diagnosed as having retinitis pigmentosa, and that I would go blind.

"My sight returned but I had to quit teaching. The doctor said the stress was too much. But I wasn't ready to give up. I was still very good at shorthand, so I got a job in the city courthouse. I worked there for a few years until I just couldn't do it anymore. I was thinking, 'Maybe it will come back.' But it didn't. From there I got a job as an employment counselor for disabled persons. My job was to educate employers that they must hire the disabled. I lost that job when Reagan came in. All those funds were lost.

"In 1983 I had been out of work for a year and a half. I found out about a training position with the county. I got the job, but I was starting at the bottom because people didn't believe in my ability because I was blind. That was the year I went from the sighted world to the unsighted world. That was the turning point for me. I said, 'I'm going to accept this; I'm going to do whatever I can to live a productive life in my unsighted world.' I started using a cane. I took the Civil Service test and just kept moving up, from trainee to counselor, to senior counselor, and now I manage an alcohol and drug rehabilitation program."

Through all the years she had lived in the North, she kept a close connection to relatives in North Carolina and, despite the ambiguities of their relationship, to the white Hairstons as well. On her visits to North Carolina, she often stopped at Cooleemee. "I still want to connect with them," she explained, referring to the white Hairstons. "It's part of your heritage, your growing up, your history. It's what helps to make us who we are today. I truly believe that you don't know where you're going unless you know where you've been. How can you change history? The only thing we can change is what we do about today. So many families have broken up and there's so much hostility and animosity because they're holding on to resentment. It weighs them down. It destroys them. It tears them apart. Although our people were slaves, although they continued to live under the 'slave syndrome' after they were freed, they had a positive attitude about living and making the best of life that they could— in spite of the things that were done to us that were wrong and the abuse that was done to us."

I wondered if the family was holding back from telling me some things because the stories were too painful. I asked Ever Lee, and she said they were not. She said that the leaders of the family had discussed that issue in a meeting, and that they realized that certain things might come out that would be painful or embarrassing.

"Years ago," she said, "the only thing being held back was how the slave owners were using their own blood relatives to work on the plantations. That was the deepest, darkest secret. But it was not being withheld by us, but by the other side."

She brought up the Reverend John Hairston, whom the white family had educated. Brer John was her great-uncle, and she remembered him from his visits to Cooleemee when she was a child. She said her grandmother idolized him, always keeping a photograph of him on her dresser. He had very fair skin.

"As a little girl, I thought he was a white man. We always felt that his father was a white Hairston. I went to talk with Peter himself about it. He said, 'Now, Ever Lee.' " She lowered her voice to mimic the judge's skeptical growl. " 'You mean your family didn't tell you?' I said, 'No, they didn't, so I need to know from you.' But I never got it from him."

I told her how the judge had denied to me that there had been any "mixing" at Cooleemee.

"Maybe it's time to ask him again," she said. "I think he feels he's living his last days. Go and ask him, 'Who was Brer John's father?' Now is the time to set him free."

Her request had a peculiar urgency. Both Squire Hairston and Judge Peter had recently suffered strokes. Squire's was not as severe as the judge's. For weeks Peter had lost his sight and was confined to a nursing home. Although he was recovering, had regained his sight, and was back at Cooleemee, Ever Lee felt anxious about his health. She had called him to make certain that no hard feelings were left between them, and he assured her there were none. These sudden illnesses, so close together, had reminded her that the old generation would soon pass, and that little time remained to recover truths that had carefully been hidden.

Ever Lee's concern increased my own sense of urgency—that in a matter of perhaps months, the secrets possessed by the family's elders would go to the grave. I opened the judge's book about Cooleemee and its people. He had sifted through 150 years of documents to reconstruct the history of his family. He had gone about his investigations without sentiment. He never said, nowhere wrote, and never even hinted that he thought that the masters "loved" their slaves. He had no patience for the sentimental myth of the Old South. Like the dedicated lawyer he was, he had searched the chronicle of slavery for evidence, and as I reread his findings, I was struck by how carefully he qualified his conclusions. When he cited the long-standing tradition, passed down by the oral history of both the blacks and the whites, that the Hairston slaveholders generally treated their slaves well, he was careful to add, "But this tradition was probably started and was kept alive by those former slaves who stayed with the family after freedom."

On his family's plantations "a considerable effort was made to keep families together each in its separate house, not herded into barracks." He evaluated the living conditions of the blacks at Cooleemee and concluded that their physical care was "adequate." To reach that conclusion he went to unusual effort, examining the ledgers, account books, and county records until he could calculate the plantation's death rate for a ten-year span. He found that the mortality among the slaves at Cooleemee was lower than that of the white population throughout the United States.

He found many instances of what he called "true caring" for the slaves, such as medical bills, which showed treatments for both masters and slaves. In all the records he could find only five times, in the ninety years between 1775 and 1865, when slaves had run away. He was careful not to say that slaves were never whipped, only that he could find no record of it. From examining the names black parents chose for their children, he ventured into some speculation about how the slaves might have felt toward his family. "Naming of children was, as always, a matter of some importance. There were Columbias, Ruths, Agneses and Sams as well as

Peters. These names may have been given in an effort to curry favor, but even this indicates an attitude not entirely one of resentment at the condition of slavery."

The judge had left one item of evidence out of his book, and I could not figure out why he had omitted it because it reflected favorably on his family. The blacks had told Peter many years earlier that the old people remembered bodies floating in the Yadkin River. Unlike Peter Hairston, Sheriff March, the master upriver, was unspeakably cruel. His punishments sometimes resulted in death, and he flung the bodies into the river with contempt.

The judge was not, however, aware of everything. For example, I found a letter, written by an anonymous slave, in the official records of the county where Cooleemee is located. Dated October 6, 1845, the letter revealed that the tranquil calm of the plantation country was false. It contained detailed plans for an uprising, what the slave called "the trial to get our freedom" by the blacks on the Yadkin River.

The plans were elaborate. The first part of the plan involved breaking open the jail in a nearby town to release the black prisoners and obtain guns and powder. The rebels would then seize control of the bridge across the Yadkin River, all the ferryboats, and the road to Lexington. They planned to stop stagecoaches and take travelers hostage. The leader insisted in the letter that they should not kill anyone if they could help it. He said many runaway slaves were prepared to come out of hiding to join the uprising. All together, they could count on three hundred men. Their ultimate plan is unclear, but that they did not want to indiscriminately kill whites suggests that they intended to take the whites only as hostages to use as bargaining chips to exchange for their freedom.

The letter writer was well aware that the penalty for conspiring to rebel was death. He said in the letter, "Dont let a single whit person see this or we will all get killed." That may have been what happened. The letter rested in the county records, so somehow it had fallen into official hands. The archives held no record of any arrests for conspiracy; and the Salisbury newspaper of the time made no mention of any trouble. But the authorities knew of the conspiracy, so they must have moved against the rebels in secret.

In his book, Judge Hairston did not attempt, as many descendants of masters had done, to put a kindly face on slavery. He declared it outright to be "a curse." He stated that there was no way "for a slave to improve his lot within the condition of slavery. There was no freedom, no choice of assignment, and the ever-present requirement . . . that the servant must be completely subject to the master's will." What he had written was a lawyer's brief—scholarly, thorough, and dispassionate. He stopped short of pleading anyone's case. He laid out the evidence and invited history to judge.

It seemed that the white Hairston family had indeed been judged, by precisely the jury Peter had wanted. I had seen the handshake between Squire Hairston and Peter, the handshake that seemed to seal a pact of reconciliation between the two families of this plantation. The slaves had passed down an image of benign masters that had made that reconciliation possible.

Brer John was the emblem of the bond between the two families. The white Hairstons had indeed loved their servant, and he had loved them in return. Brer John had led the way toward the reconciliation of the families. In the judge's book about Cooleemee he had written, "The Rev. John W. Hairston was a remarkable man indeed. His affection and example may have much to do with the unusual developments which have taken place between the descendants of the . . . owners and the slaves."

Brer John was born in 1878. At that time the judge's grandfather was living in Baltimore, but he visited North Carolina occasionally to check his properties. Brer John was born on the old Saura Town Plantation. I knew from family letters that the judge's grandfather had visited that plantation, sometimes staying for days at a time. Would he, then a fifty-nine-year-old man, have forced himself on one of the young black women who worked on the place? Brer John's mother was Tish Hairston, who was married to a man named Winston. She was the daughter of Peter's former slave and comrade-in-arms, John Goolsby. I wondered whether Peter would have repaid Goolsby's loyalty by raping his daughter.

If Brer John had really been the son of the master, then the white family's benevolence toward him was not the selfless generosity of the master's widow toward a young black man she loved, but blood money, paid to ease the guilt of discarding a colored son. If Brer John was the master's son, and Peter could deny the truth to Ever Lee, then the reconciliation was false. Before going to Cooleemee I searched archives and libraries to find information about the Reverend John Winston Hairston. In an old book about prominent ministers of North Carolina, I found a photograph of him. To my eye, an outsider's, he looked like the judge.

The judge, having suffered his stroke, warned me that he would come to the door in a wheelchair, but he told me not to worry, that he was fine. His greatest difficulty now was that it was almost impossible for him to read. He spent his days listening to books on tape and to music.

He wheeled himself into the library, passing underneath the portrait of his grandfather. As soon as I settled into a chair, I asked him the question I had come with: "Was your grandfather the father of Brer John?"

He answered directly, "I don't believe Grandfather had anything to do with it. I'm not putting it above Grandfather. I just don't think so. His father was Winston Hairston. My grandmother educated him."

"Why did she pick him?"

"Because he was bright. He was the son of her cook. I've never heard anything in this family, any suggestion of that sort of connection, a physical connection with any of the blacks. There is the suggestion in the Sally Blag papers, which you found, that Old Peter, grandfather's great-grandfather, may have engaged in these practices. But I do not think Grandfather did. I have too many day-by-day accounts of him. I can't help but believe that there would have been something, somewhere slipped. I don't find it. Maybe so. I don't know. I'm not defensive about it, but I doubt it very much."

"I have a picture of Brer John. And I think he looks like your family. You knew him."

"I never saw any resemblance at all. However, I wouldn't have looked for one."

He looked at the photograph.

"I would be very much surprised. I can't say it's not, because there's no way of proving a negative. But I don't think Grandmother would have educated a black who was any kin at all. No, I don't think she would. She was a very straitlaced lady. That would have ended him."

I was not sure whether I could believe him. I had hoped to break through his pride and coax from him an admission of guilt for what his forebears had done, and an admission that he had acted as he did toward the black Hairstons out of a sense of responsibility. But my fixation on this quest of mine blinded me to the truth. I only had to take him at his word: he had no feelings of guilt about the past. He acted as he did out of his sense of honor and justice, and from the affinity he felt for people who shared the history of this place along with him. He believed that black people should be treated as he would treat anyone: honorably and justly.

He denied that his grandfather had black children because he didn't see any evidence for it. But he didn't need to have a lightning-bolt revelation of a blood tie to the black Hairstons to invite them into his home, to serve them meals, to invite Jester to sleep in his bed. He endured Ever Lee's outburst because he loved her. Even after she had delivered her public rebuke, Peter welcomed her into his house as a friend. He shook hands with Squire Hairston because he respected him. His friendship with the blacks was not staged for newspaper writers or television cameras; it was private. But when the writers and cameras were present, he did not hide that friendship. There was nothing deeper to it than simple humanity. The extraordinary thing was that his history had prepared him to cling to custom and the shreds of his family's old status as lords of this part of the world.

I thought that he would never accept evidence of his family's blood tie to the black Hairstons. He had always insisted that the events in Mississippi—Robert's deathbed emancipation of Chrillis and his gift to her of all his land and slaves—were proof not of love but of lunacy. But as Peter wheeled himself out of the master's library at the end of our talk, he stopped and asked, "Did you ever find out what happened to old Robert's child?"

I crossed the Yadkin River to see Squire Hairston. He lived in the hamlet of Petersville, founded by former Cooleemee slaves. It is so small it appears on no maps. In its entirety the community consists of about a dozen brick houses, centered on a Baptist church and its graveyard, where many of the old slaves had been buried. Some of these people had lived to a great age. When Squire and some of the other leaders of the Hairston family were children, the former slaves were still alive. Squire had talked with them. I thought perhaps something the former slaves had told him and the other children had led to the reconciliation of the black and white families in our own time.

Squire was waiting for me with another leader of the Clan, Verdeen Hairston, whom I had met years earlier at the Baltimore reunion. When I asked them about their relationship with the judge, Verdeen answered, "We think a lot of Peter. We have no grudge against him for what happened. It wouldn't be right for me to hold a grudge against him for what his granddaddy did. That's one spirit that the Lord gave us—not to hold a grudge."

Squire stood up and said there was something we should go and see. He wanted to look at the graves. I thought we were going to walk over to the church's graveyard, but instead he got into my car. We drove only a short distance along a quiet country road until Squire directed me to pull over in a grassy spot at the edge of a forest. This was the site of the first church the Cooleemee slaves had built after Emancipation. The church was gone, but what remained were the graves of the people who had built it. Someone was still tending these graves—fresh flowers had been placed on several of the graves, making bright clusters of color in the shadows cast by the trees.

This was where the Hairston Clan had started. As early as the 1920s, a group of Hairstons began holding a memorial service every Easter at this cemetery. They would gather in the forest before dawn and wait for the sunrise that heralded the day that celebrates resurrection. After sunrise they would start a bonfire to keep them warm through hours of preaching and hymn singing.

When we had been at the cemetery for a while, Squire told me what he had learned from the slaves. One day when he was a child, an old woman named Annette called him and some of the other children together. She lifted the side of her dress to show them places where the flesh was knotted and scarred. This was where she had been whipped, she said—whipped with chains. Another former slave, Victoria, told them that the master watched the people from his tower atop Cooleemee, and if a slave was not working hard enough, he would give the order for the slave to be whipped. Squire Hairston had seen the marks. He knew the truth of slavery by the marks the chains and whips had left.

"We understand these things," Squire said. "I don't think that Peter really knows."

I asked Squire about Brer John. I told him I had heard that he might have been the son of the judge's grandfather, and I asked if he had seen a resemblance between Brer John and the judge's family. Like the judge, he said there was none—no resemblance at all.

The question that troubled Ever Lee Hairston had no definitive answer. Like the origins of her blindness, Brer John's paternity remained uncertain, one of "the silent things," obscured in a tangle of memory and rumor several generations old. He might have been the slaveholder's unacknowledged son, or he might not. The white family's generosity to him might have been simple kindheartedness; and Brer John's affection for the white family might have been exactly what it seemed—warmhearted gratitude. And yet, any such gesture between whites and blacks seemed suspect. That was the burdensome legacy of Cooleemee—that the simplest human gestures seemed fraudulent and corrupt. What is known is that Brer John laid the foundation for a reconciliation, a foundation that Squire Hairston built upon.

I left Petersville and drove down to the Yadkin River. There was a narrow dirt road that led from the highway down to the rich bottomland. Broad and sluggish, the Yadkin twists through this section of North Carolina, becomes narrow and rocky for a short distance, and eventually joins the Pee Dee River and empties into the Atlantic. At one time the white Hairstons had dreamed of establishing a town of their own on the Yadkin. They drew up the plans for Hairstonburg, parceled out lots, and sought other investors. Their scheme envisioned a prosperous river port that would send their tobacco and cotton directly to markets in the East and Europe. But no one could come up with a way to bypass or clear the shoals farther down the river. The plans for Hairstonburg were rolled up and put away. Cooleemee Plantation and its people would remain isolated, an island of the past left alone to ponder its history. The descendants of slaves and slaveholders remained rooted here until a generation arose that could try to throw off the burden of slavery. Such a task—to create something new for the future—required a man of courage, someone with full knowledge of all the evils of the past.

As a child Squire Hairston had worked in the fields with his father, who owned thirty-five acres and rented additional land from the judge's father. Squire remembered his father's encounters with the judge's father, when his father would say, with rigid respect, "Yes, sir, Marse Peter. . . . No sir, Marse Peter." Squire remembered the times he had accompanied his father to the back door of the mansion to pay the rent. Sometimes Marse Peter was slow in coming. Squire's father had a hernia and was unable to stand for long periods. He could not leave or stroll around the grounds, and it was unthinkable for him to sit; so he would get down on his knees to wait. Squire never forgot the image of his father on his knees at the doorway of the mansion. When Squire reached manhood, he was determined to force a change in this part of the world.

When he turned twenty-one, he was legally allowed to vote, but in Davidson County, in 1941, blacks did not vote. One night, when he had just turned twenty-one, Squire put his father and five other people in his father's Model A Ford and drove to the house of the voting registrar. He said they were there to put their names in the voting book. The registrar was prepared for this. He said the literacy regulation required that Squire be able to read the Constitution of the United States. He placed a copy on the table. Squire picked it up and read it. The registrar looked at Squire and realized he had no choice. He entered Squire's name in the book. He was the first black to register in the county. The second was his father, because Squire would not leave until his father's name, and the names of the five others, were put in the book. That was not enough. The next day Squire brought more people to the courthouse, where he faced a different clerk, who refused to register the people. Squire told him, "I believe you ought to register these folks. They're able to read. Not all of your folks coming in here can read."

The clerk looked at Squire and said, "Why do you want to get in trouble?" The meaning of this threat was plain, but Squire was determined to go ahead despite the cost.

"We want to see it done," Squire replied. "We don't want any trouble, but we want the people to be registered. If you don't register these folks today, I'm going to see why. I have a group of people who will go to work on it." For the first time the county government encountered a man who would not budge from his belief in his rights. Squire got the people registered.

At his house Squire had given me a copy of the speech he had delivered at the dedication of Cooleemee as a National Historic Landmark in 1978. He paid tribute to Judge Peter for his leadership, and he quoted the turn-of-the-century leader Booker T. Washington on the necessity of reaching out "in every manly way" to people of all races. He alluded to "our grievances" and to "problems and misfortune." But he said that "if they are dealt with rightly, they will turn out to be a blessing." Finally he declared Cooleemee to be a sacred place. He called it an altar—"the altar that represents the result of the struggle of your race and mine."

At the Hairston family reunion I attended in White Plains in 1997, the organizers in New York had invited the noted preacher and activist, the Reverend Al Sharpton, to speak at the awards banquet. I had expected that he would deliver a fiery speech on race relations, but instead he talked about the importance of family gatherings, because families, he said, were the repositories of so much history that would be lost if families didn't pass it down. "It is a blessing for families to be able to pause and exchange memories, and stories—to understand where you come from. It gives you a firmer base for where you are going. People who don't know where they are coming from don't know where they are going. In order to go forward you've got to understand what brought you this far. Many of us in this era become lost because we forget what brought us this far. . . . That's why families need to convene and draw the continuity from one generation to the next."

Then Reverend Sharpton took up his main theme—the story of Joshua's conquest of the Promised Land, and more important, the theme of remembering that conquest. In telling these stories he evoked the old connection African-Americans felt in slavery time to the story of the Children of Israel.

"The Children of Israel were slaves for three hundred years. They prayed, they fasted, they asked God to hear their cry and deliver them from Egyptian bondage. In the wilderness, after the miracle of the Red Sea, after plagues had been put on Egypt to loosen Pharaoh's grip, you would have thought that they would never, ever have forgotten how they got free. But as soon as they got in the Wilderness, they started worshiping false gods, and they got lost in the Wilderness. And the same has happened to us. We were slaves and we marched and fasted and prayed and went to jail. God brought us across the Red Sea. Those values, those principles, and that spiritual power are what you need to pass down from one generation to the next.

"When Joshua finally led the Children of Israel out of the Wilderness, over the Jordan River, God made the same miracle he made at the Red Sea. God made dry land in the Jordan. Then God said, 'Wait a minute, Joshua, we're doing something different this time. Tell them to gather stones from the river and build a monument on the bank.' Somebody said, 'Why should we do this? We know that God brought us across.' And God said, 'I'm not doing this for you. I want a monument so your children will know how you got over the Jordan, so that they will always know that God opened the waters and made a way for them.'

"So that's why it's important for the Hairston Clan to meet. You need to collect the stones and build a monument, so your children will know the story, and know the struggle, and know what price was paid for this.

They will know they come from a clan that expects them to do great things, because they come from great things. If you don't teach them, how will they know?"

A price was paid at the Yadkin River, and it was remembered. On its bottomlands the slaves had worked. Here a group of them had planned "the trial for our freedom," which they never attained. Here the slaves of Cooleemee could see the bodies of their murdered brothers floating past. In the old days, when infants were baptized at the Petersville church, the deacons went down to a branch of this river to draw the water.

In January 1998, three months after my visit to Squire Hairston, I received a call with the news that he had died. On the day of the funeral, a snowstorm threatened Virginia and North Carolina, but it dissolved into a heavy rain that was not enough to deter the mourners. When I reached the outskirts of Petersville in the early afternoon, the road into the hamlet was already clogged with parked cars, and Buncombe Baptist Church was jammed with some three hundred people. I saw that the family had placed Judge Hairston, in his wheelchair, at the front of the church. As rain pounded the church, the congregation prayed and sang for three hours. Four ministers declaimed four impassioned eulogies. Friends, both white and black, rose to pay tribute. Judge Hairston staggered to his feet from his wheelchair to speak of his love for Squire and broke into uncontrollable tears. At the end, Masons in their regalia stepped forward to perform the rites of the order, as a sixteen-voice choir, sounding in the packed country church like sixteen hundred, sang a final hymn, more joyous than somber, for the departed patriarch.

I sent the list of Sally Blag's offspring to several people whose ancestors were on it. They were experienced genealogists who had shared their findings with me when I was just beginning my research. They pounced on this document, which brought back the names of their foreparents from the far corners of the past. In the hands of its rightful heirs, a hateful artifact of slavery was transformed from a roster of property into a gathering of families. The enslaved revealed themselves as the mothers, fathers, and children who had paid a terrible price for posterity. With the list in hand, the descendants of Sally Blag embarked on further searches to find more names and to honor more of the people who had given them life, and whom they would one day join.

Several years ago a small group of Hairstons had held a private service at Cooleemee. A line of cars wound to the bank of the Yadkin, and a family stepped to the edge to release the ashes of their father into the water, because he had asked that his ashes be scattered into the river from the shore of the plantation where his foreparents had been slaves.

NOTES

HAIRSTON FAMILY PAPERS

Nearly all the Hairston family papers are held at the Southern Historical Collection (SHC), Manuscripts Department, Wilson Library, University of North Carolina at Chapel Hill. A few Hairston items reside in the collections of the Virginia Historical Society, Richmond, and the Alderman Library Special Collections, University of Virginia, Charlottesville.

The Hairston papers at UNC are divided into two large collections: Wilson and Hairston Papers, collection #4134, and Hairston and Wilson Family Papers, collection #3149. The latter includes numerous subcollections, such as Peter Wilson Hairston Papers (#299); Elizabeth Seawell Hairston Papers (#1518); and George Hairston Papers (#4477). Subcollections are identified in the notes when necessary.

Notes to the Wilson and Hairston Papers refer mainly to the SHC microfilm copy (71 reels), which is unpaginated but arranged chronologically. The Hairston and Wilson Family Papers have been microfilmed only in part. Thus, some notes refer to the documents at SHC, while others (designated "Stampp, ed., Hairston and Wilson Papers") refer to the microfilm edition (22 reels): *Records of Ante-bellum Southern Plantations from the Revolution through the Civil War* (microfilm), general editor, Kenneth M. Stampp; associate editor, Randolph Boehm. Frederick, Md.: University Publications of America, 1985– Series J. Selections from the Southern Historical Collection, Manuscripts Department, Library of the University of North Carolina at Chapel Hill. Part 11. Hairston and Wilson families.

Abbreviations used:

RH—Robert Hairston (1783–1852)
RSH—Ruth Stovall Hairston Wilson Hairston (1784–1869)
SH—Samuel Hairston (1788–1875)
PWH—Peter Wilson Hairston (1819–86)

CHAPTER 1: COOLEEMEE PLANTATION

3ff: Interview with Judge Peter W. Hairston.

3: "Harston": Nineteenth-century records indicate the blacks also said "Harston" or "Hosston." In Mississippi today the name is often pronounced "Hosston"; in Georgia, "Hurston" (the writer Zora Neale Hurston may have descended from black Hairstons). Some blacks stress every consonant and say something close to "Harriston." Many whites have yielded to the spelling and say "Hairston."

5: Traveling through the South: Henry Wiencek, with photographs by Steve Gross and Susan Daley, *Old Houses* (New York: Stewart, Tabori & Chang, 1991).

5: "the deep South dead since 1865": William Faulkner, *Absalom, Absalom!* (New York: Vintage International, 1990), 4.

6ff: Hairston family history: Peter W. Hairston, *The Cooleemee Plantation and Its People* (Lexington, N.C.: Davidson County Community College, 1986); "largest slaveholder": Frederick F. Siegel, *The Roots of Southern Distinctiveness* (Chapel Hill: University of North Carolina Press, 1987), 117. Siegel writes "Samuel Hairston was often described as the largest slaveholder and wealthiest planter in the South." Ervin L. Jordan Jr., *Black Confederates and Afro-Yankees* (Charlottesville and London: University Press of Virginia, 1995), 11, 330 n. 24. Jordan examined the 1860 federal census and found that the largest slaveholding enumerated in Virginia was eight hundred slaves, owned by a Mr. Morson of Goochland County. Jordan continued, "But apparently this same census missed Samuel Hairston of Henry County who in 1860 owned 1,600 slaves." Sixteen hundred slaves would have been worth about $1.4 million in 1860, extrapolating from figures used by Jordan. Clement Eaton, *The Freedom of Thought Struggle in the Old South* (New York: Harper & Row, 1964), 35.

11ff: Interview with Squire Hairston.

13ff: Interview with the Executive Board of the National Hairston Clan.

CHAPTER 2: "DAMN YOUR SOULS, MAKE TOBACCO"

22: "Damn Your Souls, Make Tobacco": Workers of the Writers' Project of the Work Projects Administration in the State of Virginia, *The Negro in Virginia* (Winston-Salem, N.C.: J. F. Blair, 1994), 64–5.

22: Land of Eden: William Byrd, *A journey to the land of Eden, and other papers* (New York: Macy-Masius, 1928).

22: Saura Indians: Stokes County Historical Society, *The Heritage of Stokes County, North Carolina, 1981*, vol. 1 (Germanton, N.C.: Stokes County Historical Society), 3–4. "Sorrow Town": Stampp, ed., Hairston and Wilson Papers, Peter Perkins to Peter Hairston, 1792, reel 5, p. 845.

23: "No crop is so well adapted": Ora Langhorne, *Southern Sketches from Virginia* (Charlottesville, University Press of Virginia, 1964), 83.

23–24: curing barns and colors of tobacco: Siegel, *Roots of Southern Distinctiveness*, 97; tinderboxes: Philip A. Bruce, "A Tobacco-Plantation," *Lippincott's Magazine*, December 1885, 539.

25: courtship of Jeb Stuart and Bettie Hairston: Hairston and Wilson Papers, subseries 1.2, folder 4, September 23, 1852.

25: ex-slave interviews: George P. Rawick, ed., *The American Slave: A Composite Autobiography*, Contributions in Afro-American and African Studies no. 11, 19 vols. (Westport, Conn.: Greenwood Publishing Company, 1972); George P. Rawick, ed., *The American Slave: A Composite Autobiography*, Contributions in Afro-American and African Studies, no. 35, 12 vols. (Westport, Conn.: Greenwood Publishing Company, 1977); Ira Berlin, Marc Favreau, and Steven F. Miller, eds., *Remembering Slavery* (New York: Free Press, 1998).

25: "Lots of old slaves": Paul D. Escott, *Slavery Remembered* (Chapel Hill: University of North Carolina Press, 1979), 8.

25–26: Virginia interviews: Charles L. Perdue Jr., Thomas E. Barden, and Robert K. Phillips, eds, *Weevils in the Wheat: Interviews with Virginia Ex-slaves* (Charlottesville: University Press of Virginia, 1992), xix–xxxvi; Roscoe Lewis and questionnaire, 367–76.

26 Danville woman (Henrietta Perry): Ibid., 223.

26: runaways in the woods, "like a dog": Ibid., 153; dances: Ibid., 224–25.

26: spies and "bugs in the wheat": Ibid., 297.

27: patrollers whipping at will: Stokes County Patrollers Records, North Carolina State Archives; ambush for the patrol: Perdue, Barden, and Phillips, *Weevils in the Wheat*, 290; cutting horses' throats: Ibid., 241.

27: "we bought you to serve us": Ibid., 290.

28: Gilblas and "Tinker" Gilchrist: Hairston, *Cooleemee Plantation*, ix, 11–13, 17.

28ff: Interview with Daniel, Betty, and Arthur Hairston.

30: burning fence rails: Hairston and Wilson Papers, PWH Papers, subseries 4.1, folder 79, vol. 12, PWH Diary Nov.–Dec. 1845, December 31, 1845, pp. 142–43.

34–35: use of pots: Perdue, Barden, and Phillips, *Weevils in the Wheat*, 93, 119, 141, 161, 196, 198, 203, 214, 217, 230, 242; African origin: Rawick, *The American Slave*, vol. 1, *From Sundown to Sunup: The Making of the Black Community*, 40–45.

35ff.: Interview with Ronald Dean Hairston.

39: taking of names: Eugene D. Genovese, *Roll, Jordan, Roll: The World the Slaves Made* (New York: Pantheon Books, 1974), 446.

39–40: Memoir of Rachel Hairston, August 20, 1952, courtesy of Jerome Hairston and Ronald Dean Hairston.

41: A clipping in the Hairston papers from an 1859 *Richmond Dispatch* describes Samuel Hairston's Oak Hill estate: "His residence . . . overlooks one of the finest river views of its kind imaginable. The broad low grounds of the Dan there appear magnificently. . . . What a blessing to be the Robinson Crusoe of such gloriously wide alluvial dominions! and yet the calm and quiet, yet strong-minded and wise owner takes all this and an immense deal besides, in the quietest style imaginable."

CHAPTER 3: BEAVER CREEK

44: Martinsville: Martinsville–Henry County Woman's Club, *Martinsville & Henry County Historic Views* (Winston-Salem: Hunter Publishing Co., 1976).

45: Marrowbone: Interview with O. E. Pilson.

45: "All are gone": Elizabeth Seawell Hairston, *The Hairstons and the Penns and Their Relations* (Roanoke: 1940), 11–12.

45: Hordsville: Interview with O. E. Pilson, *Martinsville Bulletin*, July 4, 1976.

45: Texas relative: Interview with Joe B. Hairston.

45–46: Chatmoss: Interview with O. E. Pilson, *About Chatmoss, 1992* (pamphlet) (Chatmoss Country Club); slave struck by Samuel Harden Hairston: *Commonwealth* v. *Miles*, Auditor of Public Accounts, Condemned Blacks Executed and Transported, 1781, 1783–1865, November 1859, Library of Virginia; cruelty of S. H. Hairston: Memoir of Rachel Hairston.

46: capitol collapse: George L. Christian, *The Capitol Disaster. A Chapter of Reconstruction History in Virginia* (Richmond: Richmond Press, Inc., 1915), 38.

46: Ann Hairston's house: Woman's Club, *Martinsville & Henry County Historic Views*, 140.

47: George Hairston: Ibid., 14, 89.

47: "File, hell!": Hairston, *Cooleemee Plantation*, 2; George Hairston rescues the widow of Letcher: Letter written by John Letcher, August 2, 1856, courtesy O. E. Pilson.

48: "Tower of Duty": Hairston, *Cooleemee Plantation*, 20.

48: slave rebellion: Virginia, *Calendar of Virginia State Papers*, vol. 10, pp. 120–21; "Inquisition taken on the body of John Smith"; Henry County Court Records, Loose Papers, Inquests, folder 3, Library of Virginia.

49: Two of Ann Hairston's sons died in infancy: Beaver Creek tombstones and Hairston family genealogy, courtesy Robert E. Hairston Jr.; Bettie Hairston married James Thomas Watt Hairston (known as J.T.W.): Hairston family genealogy; Watt killed in a wreck: Interview with O. E. Pilson.

49ff: Interview with Floretta Cahill.

51: Interview with Gloria Hairston.

53ff: Interview with Dr. J. Michael Bestler. Interview with Clara Hairston Dodson.

CHAPTER 4: THE LIVES OF THE HAIRSTON SLAVES

57: slaves aged twelve to fifty were taxable: Hairston, *Cooleemee Plantation*, 18.

57: Beaver Creek records: Hairston and Wilson Family Papers, subseries 2.2, folder 38, volume S-6, 1831–69, household accounts for Beaver Creek and other plantations, hereafter referred to as "Ledger."

57: slaves clothed twice a year: Ledger, pp. 18, 20, 28, 29, 35; Elizabeth Fox-Genovese, *Within the Plantation Household* (Chapel Hill: University of North Carolina Press, 1988), 128.

57: profit per slave: PWH to SH, December 15, 1848, Wilson and Hairston Papers, reel 26.

57: slave lists: the antebellum Hairston family papers contain hundreds of pages listing slaves, e.g., Stampp, ed., Hairston and Wilson Papers, reel 7, p. 783; Hairston, *Cooleemee Plantation*, 93–138; Ledger, pp. 14–17, 75–78.

57–58: absent family: Genovese, *Roll, Jordan*, 450ff.; Herbert Gutman, *The Black Family in Slavery and Freedom, 1750–1925* (New York: Pantheon Books, 1976); Nicholas Lemann, *Promised Land* (New York: Alfred A. Knopf, 1991), 172–77; Brenda Stevenson, *Life in Black and White: Family and Community in the Slave South* (New York: Oxford University Press, 1996), 206–58.

58: tax lists: Ledger, p. 122–29.

58: blankets: Ibid., 6–12.

58: "Jinny's blanket": Ibid., 69.

58: Mat and Kit: Ibid., 71

58: Patrick and Grace: Ibid., 6, 72.

58–59: Sam and Kate Lion's ten children: Ibid., 7, 69.

59: Sam Lion's relationship with overseer: Testimony of Craven Wyatt, *Commonwealth* v. *Sam Lyon* [sic], 1843, Auditor of Public Accounts, Condemned Blacks Executed or Transported, 1783–1865, Library of Virginia.

59: Ned the wagon master: Ledger, pp. 3, 5.

59: fifty horses: Ibid., 54.

59: carrying mail: Wilson and Hairston Papers, reel 26, August 22, 1849, letter to RSH "By Clem"; $500 in cash carried by Booker: September 2, 1840, letter to RH from Nowlin, Wilson and Hairston Papers, reel 23.

59: payments to wagon drivers: Hairston, *Cooleemee Plantation*, 68.

59–60: Clem haggling: Wilson and Hairston Papers, reel 21, October 1833; Clem's beekeeping: Ibid., reel 23, August 1839.

60: Slaves buying goods at Christmas: Stampp, ed., Hairston and Wilson Papers, reel 4, p. 679.

60: livestock and crops at Beaver Creek: Ledger, p. 19, 36, 42, 62.

60: a thousand yam plants: Ibid., 35, 42.

60: tallow: Ibid., 32.

60: weighing and measuring: Ibid., 18–20, 27–30, 60, 65–67.

60: mistress and slaves barter: Ibid., 33, 62.

60: cotton, flax, sheep: Ibid., 35, 59.

61: stuffing shoes with cotton: Perdue, Barden, and Phillips, *Weevils in the Wheat*, 288.

61: 3,700 pounds of cotton: Ledger, p. 25.

61: Grace and Julia: Ibid., 6, 18, 20, 25, 31, 35.

61: lumber house and attic: Ibid., 19–20.

61: sizes: Ibid., 105.

61: shoes: Wilson and Hairston Papers, reel 21, October 1833; Perdue, Barden, and Phillips, *Weevils in the Wheat*, 82.

61: cow's hair: Ledger, p. 25.

61: linens: Ibid., 23, 28.

61: summer and winter clothes: Ibid., 18, 20, 28, 29, 35.

62: children plowing: Perdue, Barden, and Phillips, *Weevils in the Wheat*, 288; worms in the mouth: Ibid., 322; Stampp, ed., Hairston and Wilson Papers, reel 7, p. 789, contains a short, puzzling list of children "that dont work."

62ff.: Bruce, "A Tobacco-Plantation," 537–41; tyrant crop: William Cabell Bruce, *Below the James* (Boston and New York: Houghton Mifflin Company, 1927), 125.

64: songs set the pace: Genovese, *Roll, Jordan*, 324.

64: importance of families: Ibid., 450ff.; Fox-Genovese, *Within the Plantation Household*, 296–99.

65: Sam Lion in jail: Ledger, p. 69; Craven Wyatt: Testimony of Craven Wyatt.

65: clearing new land: Bruce, "A Tobacco-Plantation," 538; while men felled trees, women and children did the less strenuous but still arduous tasks of clearing brush and burning debris: Ira Berlin and Philip D. Morgan, eds., *Cultivation and Culture* (Charlottesville: University Press of Virginia, 1993), 162.

66: killing of Brown: Testimony of Craven Wyatt; Henry County Court Records, Loose Papers, Inquests, December 22, 1842, Library of Virginia.

66: hid in a cave: Woman's Club, *Martinsville & Henry County Historic Views*, 23 caption. Caption states Lion was hanged, which is incorrect, and that he had been captured; it is likely he gave himself up.

66: Underground Railroad: August 1832 letter from [illegible] to SH, Wilson and Hairston Papers, reel 20; 1840 letter about the slave "Jack" arrested in women's clothes in the company of a white woman who was dressed in men's clothes and had her two daughters with her, Box 5, "Papers on Slavery," Richard J. Reid Collection, Special Collections, Alderman Library, University of Virginia; the route north: the slave "Tom" who killed John Smith was traveling this route when he was captured in Montgomery County, *Calendar of Virginia State Papers*, vol. 10, pp. 120–21.

67: trial: Henry County Minute Book 3, p. 159.

67: attempted escape: "Inquest on the body of Sam Lyon [*sic*] a slave under sentence of death," Henry County Court Records, Loose Papers, Inquests, March 7, 1843, Library of Virginia.

67: "Condemned to hang" and Kate Lion's death: Ledger, p. 69.

68: "Sold": Ibid., 75, 102, 105. Because Ann's records of spouses are erratic and obscure, it is difficult to tell conclusively if the people sold—Polly, Jim, Molly, Joe, Claibourne, and Ruth—were married or not.

68: Marshall intends selling slaves: PWH Diary Nov.–Dec. 1845, December 24, 1845, p. 144.

68: slave traders: Philip Thomas letters, William A. J. Finney Papers, Special Collections, Perkins Library, Duke University.

68: auction: Philip Thomas, February 1 and January 20, 1859, Finney Papers.

68: Danville Bank: Philip Thomas, October 6, 1859, Finney Papers; 1999 equivalents: "Inflation Calculator" (www.westegg.com/inflation).

69: slaves heading south: Perdue, Barden, and Phillips, *Weevils in the Wheat*, 153.

69: Sale of Jim Hairston by M. Hairston, 1833: recorded in two places—Jarratt-Puryear Family Papers, Isaac Jarratt, Account Book, Stampp, ed., Series F, Part 3, reel 15, p. 348; and Tyre Glen Papers, Stampp, ed., reel 15, p. 742.

69: Slave sale 1834: James A. Mitchell Account Book (Slave Coffle), 1834–35, Mitchell Papers, Special Collections Library, Duke University.

69: Description of conditions on journey and need for cash: James A. Mitchell to Sarah Mitchell, December 10, 1834, Box 3, Richard J. Reid Collection, Special Collections, Alderman Library, University of Virginia. Mitchell's concern for his family: Callie V. Mitchell to "My Precious Brother," April 30, 1854, Mitchell Papers, Special Collections Library, Duke University; refund for Henry Lang: Mitchell Papers, January 9, 1836.

70: "Remember thy *Creator*": Hairston and Wilson Family Papers, subseries 1.2, folder 2, December 31, 1847.

71: "fatal to the master": Alexis de Tocqueville, *Democracy in America* (New York: Harper & Row, 1966), 317.

CHAPTER 6: THE EDUCATION OF A SLAVE MASTER

75: PWH's black playmates: This was customary in planter families. PWH's daughter played with slave children and taught them to read, and I assume she was continuing a practice her father was familiar and comfortable with: Hairston, *Cooleemee Plantation*, 51.

75: Politics at school: February 1, 1833, PWH to Agnes Hairston, Wilson and Hairston Papers, reel 20.

75: PWH inspects plantation and buys shoes: Interview, Peter W. Hairston.

75: some murmured: Robert H. Thompson to SH, May 20, 1853, Wilson and Hairston Papers, reel 27.

76: Peter Wilson: Siegel, *Roots of Southern Distinctiveness*, 27, 180 n. 25 (much of the Hairston genealogical information in the footnote is incorrect).

76: Saura Town Peter arranges marriage: Hairston, *Cooleemee Plantation*, 3.

77: ownership muddled: Attorney James M. Whittle to PWH, April 15, 1852, Cooleemee Papers, which states there was scant legal precedent for untangling the Hairston legacies and that "the law of nations" might provide guidance; Attorney John A. Gilmer to RSH, May 27, 1853, Cooleemee Papers, which states that the Hairstons' legal muddle "ascends to the metaphysical."

77: marriage veto: Hairston, *Cooleemee Plantation*, 25.

77–78: UNC and UVA: Ibid., 22–23.

78: dower: PWH 1837 lecture notes from law school, Wilson and Hairston Papers, reel 22.

78: PWH's inheritance: Gilmer to RSH, May 27, 1853, Cooleemee Papers.

78: PWH at UVA: PWH to RSH, November 6, 1837, Wilson and Hairston Papers, reel 22; SH to PWH, December 21, 1837, Wilson and Hairston Papers, reel 22.

78: Agnes's isolation: Agnes Hairston to PWH, September 27, 1838, January 24, 1838, Wilson and Hairston Papers, reel 22.

78: Ruth complaining: Agnes Hairston to PWH, May 2, 1839, Wilson and Hairston Papers, reel 23.

79: shopping trip: August 21, 1848, Agnes Hairston to RSH, Wilson and Hairston Papers, reel 26.

79: "please your Papa": December 12, 1838, Wilson and Hairston Papers, reel 22; spending habits: SH to PWH, May 1838, Wilson and Hairston Papers, reel 22; Byron: Stampp, ed., Hairston and Wilson Papers, PWH to George Hairston, reel 4, p. 66.

79: betrayal of Christ: PWH to RSH, January 20, 1849, Wilson and Hairston Papers, reel 26; PWH assumes business responsibilities: Hairston, *Cooleemee Plantation*, 29; land purchase: June 4, 1847, Wilson and Hairston Papers, reel 26; Tennessee lawsuit: Wilson and Hairston Papers, reel 23.

80–81: $12,000 balance: February 22, 1840, Wilson and Hairston Papers, reel 23; Danville bank: Stampp, ed., Hairston and Wilson Papers, reel 4, p. 241; "deranged state of the currency": October 23, 1847, Wilson and Hairston Papers, reel 26; "advices via steamer": April 10, 1849, Wilson and Hairston Papers, reel 26.

81: tended sick: September 21, 1837, Wilson and Hairston Papers, reel 22; approving slave marriages: September 27, 1838, Agnes Hairston to PWH ("Your father has bought Green, America's husband"), Wilson and Hairston Papers, reel 22; also, Greenberg Thornton to SH ("Dear Sir, My Boy Henry wishes to take one of your servants for a wife. I have no objections he is a Boy of good caracter & obedient"), May 15, 1859, Wilson and Hairston Papers, reel 29; "I feel their situation": Hairston, *Cooleemee Plantation*, 27.

81: Grief Mason: Hairston, *Cooleemee Plantation*, 23–25.

82: grand tour: Ibid., 25–27.

82–83: Roosevelt: PWH Papers, subseries 4.1, folder 72, vol. 7, travel diary, October 1843–February 1844, hereafter "Travel Diary," p. 11, 13, 18; hitch slaves to the plow: Ibid., 9; "fanatic bigot": Ibid., 7–8; Manchester: Ibid., 29; Liverpool, "Palaces and poverty": Ibid., 23.

83: factory: Ibid., 36; "White Slaves": Ibid., 33–35; countryside, farmers: Ibid., 29.

83–84: Glover, Napoleon's veterans, Raphael, queen dowager, Naples: Hairston, *Cooleemee Plantation*, 25–27.

84: "God has marked [him]": Travel Diary, 25.

85: Christmas 1845: PWH Diary, November–December 1845.

85: Powhatan Hunter: Ibid.

85: "path of duty": Ibid.

85: PWH visit to RH: Ibid.

86: "do rite and justice": Hairston, *Cooleemee Plantation*, 2. (In his will, Peter Perkins set four slaves free and bequeathed property to them: January 1813, Wilson and Hairston Papers, reel 12.)

87: not a hog was moved: December 16, 1853, Wilson and Hairston Papers, reel 27.

87: "You and I know not": July 17, 1851, Wilson and Hairston Papers, reel 27.

88: Rives: September 30, 1832, Wilson and Hairston Papers, reel 20.

88: "They have all been raised": RH to R. R. Gurley, Records of the American Colonization Society (ACS), Manuscript Division, Library of Congress (LOC).

89: "This day your six": October 16, 1832, Jonathan McPhail to RH, Wilson and Hairston Papers, reel 20.

89: dower and RSH's plan: Hairston, *Cooleemee Plantation*, 21.

89: RH trains a slave: RH to RSH, February 14, 1837, Wilson and Hairston Papers, reel 22.

89–90: McKenney speech: W. McKenney to J. Wilkeson, November 6, 1840, ACS, LOC.

90: RH and RSH argue: Probate Book K, Lowndes County Court, 647, 649.

90: "I am not satisfied"; instructions; "I am on the decline": PWH to SH, May 3, 1852, Wilson and Hairston Papers, reel 27.

90: daguerreotype: Hairston, *Cooleemee Plantation*, 21.

CHAPTER 7: THE LOST CHILD

91: Jackson and the Choctaw: John Ray Skates, *Mississippi: A History* (New York: W. W. Norton, 1979), 80–83.

91: first view of Mississippi, like an ocean: Stampp, ed., Brownrigg Family Papers, Series J, Part 12, reel 17, p. 903; thirty miles of prairie: "Memoranda of My Trip to Mississippi," 1835, Richard Thomas Brownrigg, reel 18, journal, p. 24; E. H. Rowland to RSH, January 14, 1840, Wilson and Hairston Papers, reel 23.

92: RH in Mississippi: Lowndes County Probate Book K, pp. 650, 653–54; E. H. Rowland to RSH, January 14, 1840.

93: cruel overseers and runaways: Nelson Goolsby (white overseer) to RH, May 21, 1836, July 25, 1836, Wilson and Hairston Papers, reel 21; "1 negro whip": RH's account, June 1839, reel 23; "taken up": Wade to RH, June 4, 1840, reel 23.

93: "slaves virtually free": John Hope Franklin, "Slaves Virtually Free in Antebellum North Carolina," *Race and History: Selected Essays 1938–1988* (Baton Rouge and London: Louisiana State University Press, 1989), 73–91.

93–94: RH's men whipped: Robert H. Thompson to SH, May 20, 1853, Wilson and Hairston Papers, reel 27; "composed entirely of servants": Lowndes County Probate Book K, p. 654; RH's black wife: Robert A. Hairston (Harden's son) to George Hairston (PWH's brother), April 13, 1852, Cooleemee Papers; Bluff was a death sentence: Robert H. Thompson to SH, May 20, 1853.

94–95: Account of RH's death: Robert A. Hairston to George Hairston, April 13, 1852, Cooleemee Papers; PWH June 8, 1852, to George Hairston, Cooleemee Papers; transcript of wills, April 7, 1852, Wilson and Hairston Papers, reel 27; Lowndes County Probate Book K, pp. 693–94, 698, 710–11, 720. The suggestion to send Chrillis to a free state was not as outlandish or impractical as it may sound. The *Greensboro* (N.C.) *Patriot* of October 18, 1845, reported that the executor of the estate of John Randolph of Virginia was "seeking a place in a free state" to send slaves who had been freed in Randolph's will and given a bequest of $25,000. The freed slaves could not legally stay in Virginia.

95: one of the richest women: Indeed, Chrillis would have been a millionaire. PWH estimated RH's Mississippi estate to be worth $166,000: PWH to RSH, June 8, 1852, Wilson and Hairston Papers, reel 27. Major George later estimated, under oath, that RH's slaveholdings in Virginia and North Carolina were "upwards of 1000" (worth perhaps $875,000) and that his land in Henry County, Virginia, alone was worth $80,000: Lowndes County Probate Book K, p. 657. RH's Virginia bank deposits, bank stock, and receivables were about $33,000 in the fall of 1851: Probate Book K, p. 674. In addition, he had other bonds, receivables, and land.

96: PWH learns of RH's death: undated fragment (signature page) of letter from PWH to unknown person, Cooleemee Papers.

96: Dispute over RH's estate: The legal wrangling went on for years, generating hundreds of pages of documents, including Stampp, ed., Hairston and Wilson Papers, reel 4, pp. 125–227, reel 8, pp. 322–98. The following illuminate the outbreak of the dispute: Attorney James M. Whittle to PWH, April 15, 1852, Cooleemee Papers; fragment of letter, PWH to James Harrison, attorney in Mississippi, Cooleemee Papers; James Harrison to PWH, May 13 and 27, 1852, Cooleemee Papers; PWH to his brother George, June 8, 1852, Cooleemee Papers.

96: Saura Town Peter's will reopened: John A. Gilmer, Greensboro attorney, to RSH, May 27, 1853, Cooleemee Papers; RSH becomes executrix: county court documents naming RSH executrix of estates of her father and husband, September 1852 (she posted bonds totaling $700,000), Cooleemee Papers.

97: PWH sells Elizabeth to Major George: PWH to RSH, January 26, 1853, Wilson and Hairston Papers, reel 27; PWH sells the slaves: Stampp, ed., Hairston and Wilson Papers, reel 4, p. 203. At the division of RH's property in Virginia, RSH took in all the old and valueless slaves belonging to RH in Virginia, with the obvious intention of maintaining them at her expense for the rest of their lives, as was customary in the Hairston family.

CHAPTER 8: A MINGLING OF ROOTS

106ff: Interviews with Carolyn Henderson, Nicholas Hairston, Eleanor Swoope Hairston, Mary Alice Gibson, Lamar Hairston, Frances Hairston, Joy Hairston, Robert Ervin Hairston Jr., Alice Edwards, William B. Hairston Jr., Sarah Cox Husband, Reuben Triplett, Dr. John T. Frazier, Rosie Stevenson, T. P. Harkins, Rev. B. McCarter, Dan Spann, Daryl Glenn, Catherine Jones, Jubal Hairston, Birney Imes, Blewett Thomas.

108–109: Laura May's memoir: In "Mississippi Memories," compiled by Carolyn Henderson.

112: "maintained": Will Card #2, abstract of will of Robert Hairston, March 6, 1852, Lowndes County Archive.

113: Chrillis had died: Lowndes County Probate Book K, p. 691.

117: minds enslaved: Papers of the NAACP, supplement to part 1, 1951–55, reel 2, p. 421.

118: Ellison: "Homage to William L. Dawson," *The Collected Essays of Ralph Ellison* (New York: Modern Library, 1995), 435.

119ff: Interviews with Thattis Hairston and Helen Hudson; diary of Elizabeth Hairston Bridgeforth, courtesy William B. Hairston Jr.

121ff: Interviews with Aldia Hairston Adams, Jean Neal. Chancery Court Papers, Lowndes County Archive: documents filed under "Elizabeth Anthony," which is the full name Elizabeth/Chrillis went by: Bill of complaint, *Elizabeth Anthony vs. P. C. Hairston et al.*, August 10, 1888; Decree sustaining demurrer, *Elizabeth Anthony v. P. C. Hairston et al.*, October 16, 1888; Deposition of Elizabeth Anthony, February 20, 1889; Summons for George W. Hairston et al., February 23, 1889, *George Calloway v. George W. Hairston*; Deposition of Dr. A. H. Barkley, August 29, 1889; Deposition of Constant Hairston, September 19, 1889.

124ff: Lowndes County violence: 42nd Congress, 2d Session, House Report 22: ("The Ku-Klux Conspiracy") "Testimony Taken by the Joint Committee to Enquire into the Condition of Affairs in the Late Insurrectionary States, Mississippi," pp. 224–27, 232–33, 276–81, 285, 416–19, 423–28, 442, 461, 470–72, 483, 719–22, 799; "Annual Report of the Superintendent of Public Education," *Mississippi Senate Journal*, 1872, pp. 182–83; James Wilford Garner, *Reconstruction in Mississippi* (Baton Rouge: Louisiana State University Press,

1968), 346–47, 360–61; Vernon Lane Wharton, *The Negro in Mississippi 1865–1890* (Chapel Hill: University of North Carolina Press, 1947), 95, 192–97, 217, 245.

125: stealing election: 44th Congress, 1st Session, Senate Report 527, "Mississippi in 1875," pp. 790–831, Documentary Evidence, pp. 56–57, 66–67, 73, 98–99; *Reconstruction in West Alabama: The Memoirs of John L. Hunnicutt*, Confederate Centennial Studies, no. 11 (Tuscaloosa: Confederate Publishing Company, 1959), pp. 72–77. (Racial violence did not subside in the Hairstons' area after the 1875 election. There were seven lynchings in the eight-year period between 1885 and 1893 just in Lowndes County, including a triple murder on May 11, 1891. NAACP Lynching Files, #1568, Part 7, Series A, reel 19, p. 1143.)

126: "We want peace": William C. Harris, *Day of the Carpetbagger* (Baton Rouge: Louisiana State University Press, 1979), 30 n. 80; "exterminate the Negro": J. T. W. Hairston to Bettie Hairston, Hairston and Wilson Family Papers, SHC, subseries 2.1, folder 32.

126: Elizabeth prospered: Chancery Court Papers, Lowndes County Archive: Deposition of A. F. Vaught, *Elizabeth Anthony vs. P. C. Hairston et al.*, September 23, 1889; Depositions of Pleasant Hairston, George Hairston, J. T. W. Hairston, *Elizabeth Anthony v. George W. Hairston et al.*, October 16, 1889; Decree, *Elizabeth Anthony v. P. C. Hairston et al.*, October 23, 1889.

131: feet froze: John Westerfield to RH, December 6, 1839, January 26, 1840, Wilson and Hairston Papers, reel 23.

132: one of the children: Appraisal of the estate of RH, Lowndes County Probate Book K, p. 537.

CHAPTER 9: "NO MAN CAN HINDER ME"

135: Faulkner: *Newsweek*, February 21, 1977, p. 87

135: "presence of the past": Cleanth Brooks, *William Faulkner: The Yoknapatawpha Country* (New Haven and London: Yale University Press, 1963), 314.

137: slavery strengthening and little evidence of moral qualms: Professor Edward L. Ayers of the University of Virginia has remarked upon this in lectures. Tony Horwitz, *Confederates in the Attic: Dispatches from the Unfinished Civil War* (New York: Pantheon, 1998), 135–37.

138: "spirit of the master": Thomas Jefferson, *Notes on the State of Virginia* (Chapel Hill: University of North Carolina Press, 1955), 163.

139: mystical turn: Professor Harold S. Forsythe, Fairfield University, drew my attention to this observation made by Professor Robert Dawidoff, Claremont Graduate School.

140: "knew but still did not believe": *Absalom, Absalom!* 267–68.

141: "does not hate": Brooks, *William Faulkner*, 299.

141: "the holiest cause": Robert J. Trout, *With Pen and Saber: The Letters and*

Diaries of J. E. B. Stuart's Staff Officers (Mechanicsburg, Pa.: Stackpole Books, 1995), 7; *"guaranteeing us our slaves"*: Hairston, *Cooleemee Plantation*, 51; "bloody battleground": Ibid., 23.

142: Vicksburg marriage register: Bureau of Refugees, Freedmen, and Abandoned Lands (hereafter "BRFAL"), Records of the Assistant Commissioner for the State of Mississippi, Registers of Marriages of Freedmen, vol. 1, July 19, 1864.

142: Cooleemee construction: Hairston, *Cooleemee Plantation*, 41–42.

143: Columbia's death: Ibid., 44; Sammy was already a master: Ibid., 49, 54; "Went to war": Ibid., 56; "should we never return": Trout, *With Pen and Saber*, 6.

144: Eighty-three Hairston Confederates: Index to Confederate Service Records, National Archives; Prairie Guard: David Chelsea Love, "The Prairie Guard: A History of Their Heroism, Their Battles and Their *Triumphs*" (pamphlet), courtesy Sarah Cox Husband; fell at Shiloh: George Stovall Hairston; Jack Hairston drummed out: VMI Archives, Outgoing Correspondence of the Superintendent, Letters Sent January 1860–June 1860, 60A30 VMI-2, January 9, 1860, to Marshall Hairston.

144: "I can see": Hairston, *The Hairstons and the Penns*, 169.

CHAPTER 10: "TILL THE LAST MAN"

146: John Brown's knife: Hairston, *Cooleemee Plantation*, 57.

146–147: Manassas: Shelby Foote, *The Civil War*, vol. 1 (New York: Random House, 1958), 73–82; M. Emory Thomas, *Bold Dragoon: The Life of J. E. B. Stuart* (New York: Harper & Row, 1986), 77–81; W. W. Blackford, *War Years with Jeb Stuart* (New York: Scribner's, 1946), 26–39; Burke Davis, *Jeb Stuart* (New York: Rinehart, 1957), 61–65.

147: Hairston doctor: Elizabeth Seawell Hairston Papers, box 2, folder 15, UDC nomination form.

148: Early's approach: Charles C. Osborne, *Jubal* (Chapel Hill: Algonquin Books, 1992), 67–71.

148–49: "a horrid spectacle": Trout, *With Pen and Saber*, 44; battlefield: George Hairston to Bettie Hairston, July 30, 1861, Hairston and Wilson Family Papers, subseries 1.2, folder 9; G. W. Penn to "Dear Jo," August 3, 1861, Stampp, ed., Hairston and Wilson Family Papers, reel 1, p. 318; post cut away: Trout, *With Pen and Saber*, 44; "piece of cedar": Stampp, ed., Hairston and Wilson Papers, reel 5, p. 603.

149: Manassas trophies and "sky of the Southern Confederacy.": "R. A. H." to Bettie Hairston, October 6, 1861, Hairston and Wilson Family Papers, subseries 1.2, folder 9; *"God is with us"*: unknown to "My Dear Sister," August 9, 1861, Elizabeth Seawell Hairston Papers, subseries 1.2, folder 5; Jack Hairston: Charles D. Walker, *Biographical Sketches of the Graduates and Élèves of the Virginia Military Institute Who Fell During the War Between the States* (Philadelphia: J. B. Lippincott, 1875), 259–61; Tom McMahon directed my attention to an anonymous tribute to Jack Hairston in the *Richmond Daily Dispatch*, May 13, 1862.

149–150: Williamsburg: sketch of the battlefield, Finney Papers, Duke; Osborne, *Jubal*, 75–83; Richard L. Maury, *The Battle of Williamsburg and the Charge of the 24th Virginia, of Early's Brigade* (Richmond: Johns & Goolsby, 1880); Ralph White Gunn, *24th Virginia Infantry* (Lynchburg: H. E. Howard, Inc., 1987), 14–21.

151–52: Third USCC formed: Edwin M. Main, *The Story of the Marches, Battles and Incidents of the Third United States Colored Cavalry* (New York: Negro Universities Press, 1970), 58; officers: Joseph T. Glatthaar, *Forged in Battle* (New York: Free Press, 1990), 58–59; "finest specimens": Main, *Story of the Third*, 12; Harston recruited, his assignments: Unbound Regimental Records, 3rd U.S. Col'd Cavalry, box 9, and Compiled Service Record, Thomas Harston, National Archives.

152: Vicksburg parades: James T. Currie, *Enclave: Vicksburg and Her Plantations, 1863–1870* (Jackson: University Press of Mississippi, 1980), 43.

153: first battle: Main, *Story of the Third*, 81–91.

154: "till the last man": Ibid., 91; "Federal authority": Jim Huffstodt, *Hard Dying Men: The Story of General W. H. L. Wallace, General T. E. G. Ransom, and Their "Old Eleventh" Illinois Infantry in the American Civil War* (Bowie, Md.: Heritage Books, 1991), 193; Yazoo expedition: Main, *Story of the Third*, 92ff, and *The War of the Rebellion: A Compilation of the Official Records of the Union and Confederate Armies* (hereafter *OR*), vol. 32, pt. 1 (Washington, D.C.: Government Printing Office, 1902), 320–26; Huffstodt, *Hard Dying Men*, 201.

154–55: white skeptics and black heroics: Huffstodt, *Hard Dying Men*, 194–95, 198–200; "We came across": Henry Uptmor, "Diary of Henry Uptmor," unpublished MS, Chicago Historical Society, p. 12.

155: "tempt total annihilation": Huffstodt, *Hard Dying Men*, 213; scout: Ibid., 205–6; Douglas Hale, *The Third Texas Cavalry in the Civil War* (Norman and London: University of Oklahoma Press, 1993), 106; *The Negro in the Military Service of the United States 1639–1886* (hereafter *Military Service*) microfilm publication, National Archives, p. 3031; Main, *Story of the Third*, 112ff.

156: "brutally used": *OR*, vol. 32, pt. 1, p. 327; Ross's report: *Military Service*, 3032–33; murdering blacks: *Military Service*, 3018; Hale, *Third Texas Cavalry*, 204; S. B. Barron, *The Lone Star Defenders* (New York: Neale Publishing Co., 1908), 183; Main, *Story of the Third*, 120. Some sources say the Texans were in a murderous mood because they had heard some of their men had been taken prisoner and killed by black troops.

157: fort and rifle pits: Huffstodt, *Hard Dying Men*, 203; Main, *Story of the Third*, 119, 144; "My compliments": Main, *Story of the Third*, 120; shelling: Uptmor, "Diary," 21; Main, *Story of the Third*, 121; forces present: Main, *Story of the Third*, 118; Huffstodt, *Hard Dying Men*, 206.

157: sharpshooters: *OR*, vol. 32, pt. 1, p. 331 (map); black troops singing: Main, *Story of the Third*, 156; stars falling: I am indebted to several people, including Robert Kaylor, associate pastor, Allison United Methodist Church, Carlisle, Pennsylvania, Professor John Michael Vlach, George Washington University, and Professor David L. Carleton, Vanderbilt University; slave accounts: Perdue, Barden, and Phillips, *Weevils in the Wheat*, 82, 118.

158–60: final assault: Main, *Story of the Third*, 118, Huffstodt, *Hard Dying Men*, 212–14, OR, vol. 32, pt. 1, pp. 327–28; Uptmor, "Diary," 22, *Military Service*, 3042; "no Quarter": Hale, *Third Texas Cavalry*, 208; "prisoner killing": *Military Service*, 3067, 3072.

160–61: Wooten incident: Glatthaar, *Forged in Battle*, 200; *Military Service*, 2674–75.

161: Big Black River bridge: Glatthaar, *Forged in Battle*, 151–52; Edwin C. Bearss, *Decision in Mississippi* (Jackson: Mississippi Commission on the War Between the States, 1962), 504.

161–62: impossible without artillery: Huffstodt, *Hard Dying Men*, 218; "most determined bravery": Main, *Story of the Third*, 201.

161–63: fight at the bridge: Main, *Story of the Third*, 199–217; Hood's lifeline broken: Ibid., 63; Ronald A. Mosocco, *Chronological Tracking of the American Civil War per the Official Records* (Williamsburg: James River, 1994), 282.

163–64: Grierson raid: Edwin C. Bearss, "Grierson's Winter Raid on the Mobile and Ohio Railroad," *Military Affairs*, spring 1960; Main, *Story of the Third*, 233; Wiley Sword, *Embrace an Angry Wind* (New York: Harper Collins, 1992), 425; William H. Leckie and Shirley A. Leckie, *Unlikely Warriors* (Norman: University of Oklahoma Press), 125; Richard M. McMurry, *John Bell Hood and the War for Southern Independence* (Lexington: University Press of Kentucky, 1982), 353; OR, vol. 45, pt. 1, p. 1000; pt. 2, pp. 552, 741–42.

164: Stuart's death: Trout, *With Pen and Saber*, 253–54.

164: Rockfish Gap: Osborne, *Jubal*, 386–91.

165: "a complete desolation": PWH to SH, October 17, 1863, Wilson and Hairston Papers, reel 29; "Buy anything": Hairston, *Cooleemee Plantation*, 68.

165: "killed a man for impudence": Elizabeth Seawell Hairston Papers, box 1, folder 7.

166: Sara Penn: Stampp, ed., Hairston and Wilson Papers, reel 1, pp. 395ff.

167: "We are now in the Yankee Lines": unknown to Eliza Hairston, April 16, 1865, Elizabeth Seawell Hairston Papers, box 1, folder 7; panic: "L" to "My Dear Ma," April 6, 1865, Green W. Penn Papers, folder 4, Duke University Library.

168: Goolsby grabs musket: Trout, *With Pen and Saber*, 12; hides silver: Hairston, *Cooleemee Plantation*, 68–69.

169: "we left our own wives": *Freedman's Friend*, December 1868.

169–172: Memphis riot: 39th Congress, 1st Session, House Report 101, 1865–66, "Report of the Select Committee on the Memphis Riots and Massacres," Bobby L. Lovett, "Memphis Riots," *Tennessee Historical Quarterly*, spring 1979, 9–33; Gutman, *Black Family*, 24–28; BRFAL, Records of the Assistant Commissioner for the State of Tennessee, Memphis Office, Reports and Affidavits Relating to the Memphis Riots; Reports of Outrages, Riots, and Murders, April 1865–December 1868; Reports of Transportation; Reports Relating to Bounty Claims and Disbursements, National Archives.

CHAPTER 11: THE SCROLL OF NAMES

176: marriage registration: Elaine C. Everly, "Marriage Registers of Freedmen," *Prologue*, fall 1973, 150–54; Gutman, *Black Families*, 11–24 and passim; Gutman located the registers for Rockbridge, Nelson, Goochland, and Louisa Counties in the National Archives. Since then the registers of Henry, Rappahannock, and Hanover Counties have been discovered.

177: inspector: United States, BRFAL, Records of the Assistant Commissioner for the State of Virginia, BRFAL, 1865–1869 (Washington, D.C.: National Archives and Records Service, General Services Administration, 1977), microfilm publication M1048 (67 reels) (hereafter "BRFAL-VA, M1048"), reports of Colonel Horace Neidy, reel 18, items N35, N43, pp. 89, 106ff.

178: Fernald's office, paperwork: BRFAL-VA, M1048, reel 8, vol. 6, items L317, L347, L373.

178: method of registration: Ibid., reel 18, N43.

180: great trek south: PWH papers, box 1, folder 14, PWH to Fanny, April 11, 1870.

181–182: conditions: James D. Smith, "Virginia During Reconstruction" (Ph.D. thesis, University of Virginia, 1960), 410.

183: "We are many in number": Wilson and Hairston Papers, SHC, box 22, folder 202.

183: "educated gentry": *Freedman's Friend*, November 1865; BRFAL-VA, M1048, Records Relating to Murders and Outrages in Virginia, reel 59, p. 157.

183–84: Beaver Creek: Ann Hairston to Marshall Hairston, December 14, 1865, Hairston and Wilson Family Papers, SHC, subseries 1.2, folder 10; Aunt Grace: "Yr. Afft. Sister" to "My Dear Sis Bet," Christmas 1865, Hairston and Wilson Family Papers, SHC, subseries 1.2, folder 10.

184: "perfect revolution": Louisa H. Hairston to SH, April 1866, Elizabeth Seawell Hairston Papers, SHC, subseries 1.3, folder 7.

184: "doomed to undergo extinction": John Richard Dennett, *The South As It Is: 1865–1866*, ed. Henry M. Christman (New York: Viking, 1965), 15.

185: old black man: Ibid., 96–98; BRFAL-VA, paper records at National Archives, Entry 3947, January 1866, has an account of elderly man turned out by former owner after losing both hands and one eye in a fire.

186: tavern: Dennett, *South As It Is*, 94–95.

186: "sore and costly": *Freedman's Friend*, November 1865; "dividement": "Yr. Afft. Sister" to "My Dear Sis Bet," Christmas 1865, Hairston and Wilson Family Papers, SHC, subseries 1.2, folder 10.

187: labor conditions: Lynda J. Morgan, *Emancipation in Virginia's Tobacco Belt, 1850–1870* (Athens: University of Georgia Press, 1992).

187: slavery of children: Rebecca Scott, "The Battle over the Child: Child Apprenticeship and the Freedmen's Bureau in North Carolina," *Prologue*, summer 1978, 100–113.

187: smallpox and labor in Danville: BRFAL-VA, paper records at National Archives, Entry 3947, January 20, 1866, January 1867; conditions near Cooleemee: BRFAL, Records of the Assistant Commissioner for the State of North Carolina, microfilm publication M843, reel 5, Register 2 of letters received, items H3, H16; refugee camp: *Freedman's Friend*, December 1865.

188: sharecropping: Thavolia Glymph, "Freedpeople and Ex-Masters," *Essays on the Postbellum Southern Economy*, eds. Thavolia Glymph and John J. Kushma (College Station: Texas A & M University Press, 1985), 48–72; cash wages: Ann Hairston to Marshall Hairston, n.d. (probably December 1865), Hairston and Wilson Family Papers, SHC, subseries 1.2, folder 10; "mistaken notion": "Yr. Afft. Sister" to "My Dear Sis Bet," Christmas 1865, Hairston and Wilson Family Papers, SHC, subseries 1.2, folder 10.

189: "people apprehend rebellion": Louisa H. Hairston to RSH, November 24, 1865, Elizabeth Seawell Hairston Papers, SHC, subseries 1.3, folder 7.

189: Neide: BRFAL-VA, M1048, reel 18, item N43.

189: court report: Ibid., letters and telegrams received, reel 16, item L244.

189–191: justice system: Ibid., reel 45, pp. 131, 267–68; conditions in Hairston country: Ibid., letters and telegrams received, reel 16: vast poverty in region: p. 92; blacks sent South lest they become wards of the BRFAL: p. 96; white Hairstons sued for nonpayment of workers: pp. 151–52; beating and murder: pp. 153, 156–57; blacks finding work: p. 293; beating a black "merely to make a display of hatred": p. 297; fight at Baptist picnic: p. 355; Fernald requests troops: p. 542. BRFAL-VA, M1048, Register of Outrages Committed on Freedmen, reel 59, p. 38 (rape in Pittsylvania), p. 50 (whipping in Pittsylvania), pp. 55–56 (shooting in Pittsylvania); BRFAL-VA, paper records at National Archives: black Hairstons not paid: Entry 2706; "universal antipathy of white people," planters will drive off any black who votes: Entry 4101, March 31, 1868.

191–92: murder of Nelson Wilson: "Commonwealth Inquisition upon the dead body of Nelson Wilson," September 4, 1868, Henry County Coroner's Records, Library of Virginia. bell: *Freedman's Friend*, February 1866; school: *Freedman's Friend*, December 1868.

192: "Destitute Places": BRFAL, Records of the Education Division, microfilm publication M803, "Virginia: Monthly Miscellaneous Buildings and Teachers," reel 32, pp. 117, 130; Danville school supported by Philadelphia group: BRFAL-VA, M1048, reel 16, p. 500; schools in Hairston region: BRFAL, M803, reel 32, pp. 16, 108, 111, 113, 117, 130, 159, 184, 186, 200, 218, 244, 277, 303–5, 397, 418, 434, 439, 488 (lists Danville teachers). BRFAL-VA, M1048, "Monthly Narrative Reports of Operations and Conditions," reel 47, p. 193: blacks in Danville raised $600 to buy land for a school.

194: tour of inspection: *Freedman's Friend*, December 1865; N.C. schools: BRFAL, M803, "North Carolina: Monthly and Other School Reports," reel

28, pp. 10, 12, 19, 25, 98; BRFAL, Records of the Superintendent of Education for the State of North Carolina, microfilm publication M844, "State Superintendent's Monthly Reports," reel 13, pp. 4, 32, 84–88; *Freedman's Friend*, December 1867.

195: Danville garrison: Smith, "Virginia During Reconstruction," 439–40; buildings pillaged: BRFAL, Registers and letters received by the Commissioner of the Bureau, microfilm publication M752, reel 25, p. 139.

195: "Rat Hall": *Freedman's Friend*, February 1866, July 1866.

195–96: school conditions: Ibid., March, December 1868.

196: "we set them to work": Ibid., March 1868; bound boy: Ibid., April 1866.

196–197: conditions: Ibid., November 1865, February 1866, December 1867, February 1869; *"deathly"*: Ibid., December 1872.

197: "[our] humiliation": PWH to Fanny, September 18, 1866, PWH Papers, SHC, box 1.

198: bushwhackers: Hairston, *Cooleemee Plantation*, 71; Herbert & Hairston: Ibid., 72–73.

198–99: PWH at the White House: Ibid., 72.

199: $200 in gold: Jubal Early Diary, Jubal Early Papers, Library of Congress; hearts "had grown old": Louisa H. Hairston to RSH, November 24, 1865, Elizabeth Seawell Hairston Papers, SHC, subseries 1.3, folder 7.

200: "Poor suffering Virginians!": Louisa H. Hairston to SH, April 1866, Elizabeth Seawell Hairston Papers, SHC, subseries 1.3, folder 7; suicide: Ann Hairston to Marshall Hairston, December 4, 1865, Hairston and Wilson Family Papers, SHC, subseries 1.2, folder 10.

201: "sad picture": "E. A. H. [Eliza Hairston]" to unknown, December 9, 1867, Green W. Penn Papers, folder 4, Duke University Library; George working as wagon driver: "E. A. H. [Eliza Hairston]" to "My Dear Ma," September 20, 1870, Elizabeth Seawell Hairston Papers, box 1, folder 9.

202: "at the risk of their lives": Elizabeth Seawell Hairston, *Hairstons and the Penns*, 170; "awful days": Ibid., 172.

203–204: Estes Hairston: Stokes County, Minute Docket, Superior Court, pp. 162–66; Stokes County Miscellaneous files, Coroner's Reports, North Carolina State Archives.

205: "white wives": Dennett, *South As It Is*, 31; Wesley and Puss Hairston: *State v. Wesley Hairston, Puss Williams*, Bill of Indictment, 1868; Appeal, June 1869, North Carolina State Archives.

208–210: lynchings: Edward L. Ayers, *The Promise of the New South* (New York, Oxford: Oxford University Press, 1992), 155–59; Columbus photographs: Interview with Birney Imes.

210: lynchings: *Richmond Planet*, January 19, 1895.

210: "humane Danville": *Richmond Planet*, July 23, 1898; Thomas J. Penn: *Richmond Planet*, February 23, March 9, 16, 23, April 20, 27, May 11, June 1, 1895.

210: Samuel Hairston's sister raped: *Richmond Planet*, September 20, October 18, 1902.

211–14: Martinsville 7 case: Eric W. Rise, *The Martinsville Seven: Race, Rape and Capital Punishment* (Charlottesville: University Press of Virginia, 1995); interview with Oliver Hill; "Martinsville 7 Pain Remains," *Richmond Times-Dispatch*, June 20, 1993; Charles W. Simmons III, "Virginia Justice and the Martinsville Seven" (master's thesis, Virginia State University, 1985); Press Releases Concerning the Martinsville 7, Special Collections, Alderman Library, University of Virginia.

214: UVA case: *Cavalier Daily* (UVA), May 21, 25, 1954; *Charlottesville Daily Progress*, May 28, 1954; Minutes of the Board of Visitors, April-May 1954, Special Collections, Alderman Library, University of Virginia; confidential interviews.

Chapter 12: A Gathering in Ohio

Interviews with Jester Hairston, Squire Hairston, Collie Hairston, James Hairston, Rhenetta Hairston Davis, Janet White, Jerome Hairston, Savolia Joyce, Alonzo Hairston, Dorothy Hairston Crockett, Marvin Hairston, Deborah Hairston Taylor, Frances Hairston, Adam Hairston, Thurman Hairston, Palvonia Borders, Bernard J. Hairston, Charles Hairston, Nelson Hairston.

Chapter 13: The Liberation of Walnut Cove

Interviews with John L. Hairston, Ruth Anderson Hairston, Edward Hairston, Mabel Johnson, Frank Dalton, Ralph Mitchell, Mary Catherine Foy, George Henry Hairston, Pamela Hairston Matthews, Mona Hairston Willis, Vincent Withers, Christopher Hairston, Rev. J. T. MacMillan, Judge Leonard Van Noppen, Jack Gentry, Gregory Hairston, Barbara Tuttle, Leroy Smith.

236: "Racism Splits Nation": *Winston-Salem Journal*, March 1, 1968; also "Planned School Closing Is Protested in Stokes," *Winston-Salem Journal*, March 4, 1968; "London School Backers Give Plan to Save It," *Winston-Salem Journal*, March 11, 1968; *Danbury Reporter*, March 7, 21, April 4, 11, June 13, 1968.

Chapter 14: In Search of the Father

251: Interview with Charles, Nona, and Elena Hairston.
254: blacks refused induction: Phillip McGuire, *Taps for a Jim Crow Army* (Santa Barbara, Calif.: ABC-Clio, 1983), xvii, xxix.
254–55: literacy: Ibid., xxx; trainees barred: Ibid., 2–3, 59–60, 66; official policy: Ibid., xliii, 5.
255: Marshall: Bernard C. Nalty, *Strength for the Fight* (New York: Free Press, 1986), 146–47.
256: limit on black officers: McGuire, *Taps*, 32–33; Hondon B. Hargrove, *Buffalo Soldiers in Italy: Black Americans in World War II* (Jefferson, N.C.: McFarland & Company, 1985), 8–9.

256: training incidents: McGuire, *Taps*, 5, 11, 18, 19, 20, 27, 51, 145, 167, 186.

257: Almond: Shelby L. Stanton, *America's Tenth Legion: X Corps in Korea, 1950* (Novato, Calif.: Presidio, 1989), 8–9, 14–15, 170–71, 318–19; Ninety-second's training: Dale E. Wilson, "Recipe for Failure: Major General Edward M. Almond and Preparation of the U.S. 92nd Infantry for Combat in World War II," *The Journal of Military History*, July 1992, 476.

258: officers' wives and promotions: Interview with Joseph Henry Hairston.

259: low morale: Wilson, "Recipe for Failure," 483–84; McGuire, *Taps*, 45; Hargrove, *Buffalo Soldiers*, 9; "human element": Nalty, *Strength for the Fight*, 173; unrepentant racist: Wilson, "Recipe for Failure," 488; officers disliked assignment: Ulysses Lee, *The Employment of Negro Troops* (Washington, D.C.: Office of the Chief of Military History, United States Army, 1966), 561–62, 588–89.

259–60: extreme racism: Warman Welliver, "Report on the Negro Soldier," *Harper's Magazine*, April 1946.

260–61: colonel's remarks: Interview with Joseph Henry Hairston (Almond himself made similar remarks on another occasion: Hargrove, *Buffalo Soldiers*, 47).

261: no ammunition: Interview with Joseph Henry Hairston.

263: terrain: Lee, *Employment of Negro Troops*, 544–45.

263–64: sporadic attacks: Ibid., 549–51; replacements: Ibid., 552–53; Jehu C. Hunter and Major Clark, "The Buffalo Division in World War II," unpublished memoir, p. 39; "experiment": *Time*, September 20, 1943.

264: "melted away": Lee, *Employment of Negro Troops*, 556, 560–61, 576–79; Hargrove, *Buffalo Soldiers*, 140; Fox and other medal winners: *New York Times*, January 14, 19, 1997; *Washington Post*, April 28, 1996, January 12, 14, 1997; Lee, *Employment of Negro Troops*, 564–65; Stanton, *America's Tenth Legion*, 13; Hargrove, *Buffalo Soldiers*, 64–65.

265: Cinquale attack: Lee, *Employment of Negro Troops*, 568–72.

265: coastal guns: Hargrove, *Buffalo Soldiers*, 98–99; Paul Goodman, *A Fragment of Victory in Italy* (Nashville, Tenn.: Battery Press, 1993), 99; incompetent officer: Lee, *Employment of Negro Troops*, 554.

266: no reinforcements: Ibid., 571.

267: 92nd as bait: Ibid., 573; "92nd was doomed": Ibid., 588–89.

269: Almond's abysmal record: Stanton, *America's Tenth Legion*, 320.

272–73: Carrie Allen McCray, *Freedom's Child* (Chapel Hill: Algonquin Books, 1998), 16.

275: Elias list: Courtesy Beverly R. Millner.

277: Saura Town Peter: Hairston, *Cooleemee Plantation*, 1.

277–78: purchase of "Sall": Wilson and Hairston Papers, reel 1, February 1785; Gilchrist at Cooleemee, Peter buys his family: Hairston, *Cooleemee Plantation*, 11–13.

278–79: Peter's will: Hairston, *Cooleemee Plantation*, 17.

279: "your manager": Wm Barnett [?] to RH, February 19, 1835, Wilson and Hairston Papers, reel 21.

281: Camp Branch: PWH Papers, SHC, subseries 4.3, box 6, ledgers, vols. 19–23, 26.

281: Saura Town: "Diary of a Journey by George Izard, 1815–1816," *South Carolina Historical Magazine* 53 (1952): 74.

CHAPTER 15: A RITE OF RECONCILIATION

283: "I feel satisfied": PWH to Agnes Hairston, April 25, 1882, PWH Papers, SHC, subseries 1.5, folder 15.

284: death of PWH: Hairston, *Cooleemee Plantation*, 74.

284: Fanny returns: Ibid., 75–81.

285: John Hairston: Ibid., 81–83.

286: Rev. Hairston's tribute: PWH Papers, SHC, series 3, folder 60.

286: lynch mobs: Papers of the NAACP, Lynching files, part 7, series A, reel 5, p. 832ff.

287: Christian Reid, *The Wargrave Trust* (New York: Benziger Brothers, 1911), 32.

CHAPTER 16: A MONUMENT BY THE RIVER

302: treatment of slaves: Hairston, *Cooleemee Plantation*, 13–18.

303: plans for revolt: Davidson County, Miscellaneous Records, Records of Slaves and Free Persons of Color, folder 032.928.9, North Carolina State Archives.

303: "a curse": Hairston, *Cooleemee Plantation*, 18.

305: photo of Rev. J. W. Hairston: M. W. Williams and George Watkins, *Who's Who Among North Carolina Negro Baptists*, 1940, p. 191.

308: plans for Hairstonburg: PWH Papers, SHC, subseries 2.4, folder 53.

BIBLIOGRAPHY

BOOKS

Ayers, Edward L. *The Promise of the New South*. New York, Oxford: Oxford University Press, 1992.

Barron, S. B. *The Lone Star Defenders*. New York: Neale Publishing Co., 1908.

Bearrs, Edwin C. *Decision in Mississippi*. Jackson: Mississippi Commission on the War Between the States, 1962.

Bearrs, Edwin C. "Grierson's Winter Raid on the Mobile and Ohio Railroad." *Military Affairs*, spring 1960.

Berlin, Ira, Marc Favreau, and Steven F. Miller, eds. *Remembering Slavery*. New York: Free Press, 1998.

Berlin, Ira, and Philip D. Morgan, eds. *Cultivation and Culture*. Charlottesville: University Press of Virginia, 1993.

Blackford, W. W. *War Years with Jeb Stuart*. New York: Scribner's, 1946.

Brooks, Cleanth. *William Faulkner: The Yoknapatawpha Country*. New Haven and London: Yale University Press, 1963.

Brownrigg Family Papers, in Stampp, ed., Series J, pt. 12.

Bruce, Philip A. "A Tobacco-Plantation." *Lippincott's Magazine*, December 1885.

Bruce, William Cabell. *Below the James*. Boston and New York: Houghton Mifflin Company, 1927.

Byrd, William. *A journey to the land of Eden, and other papers*. New York: Macy-Masius, 1928.

Christian, George L. *The Capitol Disaster. A Chapter of Reconstruction History in Virginia*. Richmond: Richmond Press, Inc., 1915.

Currie, James T. *Enclave: Vicksburg and Her Plantations, 1863–1870*. Jackson: University Press of Mississippi, 1980.

Davis, Burke. *Jeb Stuart*. New York: Rinehart, 1957.

Dennett, John Richard. *The South As It Is: 1865–1866*. Edited by Henry M. Christman. New York: Viking, 1965.

Eaton, Clement. *The Freedom of Thought Struggle in the Old South*. New York: Harper & Row, 1964.

Ellison, Ralph. *The Collected Essays of Ralph Ellison*. New York: Modern Library, 1995.

Escott, Paul D. *Slavery Remembered*. Chapel Hill: University of North Carolina Press, 1979.

Everly, Elaine C. "Marriage Registers of Freedmen." *Prologue*, fall 1973.

Faulkner, William. *Absalom, Absalom!* New York: Vintage International, 1990.

Foote, Shelby. *The Civil War*. New York: Random House, 1958–74.

Fox-Genovese, Elizabeth. *Within the Plantation Household*. Chapel Hill: University of North Carolina Press, 1988.

Franklin, John Hope. *Race and History: Selected Essays 1938–1988*. Baton Rouge and London: Louisiana State University Press, 1989.

Garner, James Wilford. *Reconstruction in Mississippi*. Baton Rouge: Louisiana State University Press, 1968.

Genovese, Eugene D. *Roll, Jordan, Roll: The World the Slaves Made*. New York: Pantheon Books, 1974.

Glatthaar, Joseph T. *Forged in Battle—The Civil War Alliance of Black Soldiers and White Officers*. New York: Free Press, 1990.

Glymph, Thavolia, and John J. Kushma, eds. *Essays on the Postbellum Southern Economy*. College Station: Texas A & M University Press, 1985.

Goodman, Paul. *A Fragment of Victory in Italy*. Nashville: Battery Press, 1993.

Gunn, Ralph White. *24th Virginia Infantry*. Lynchburg: H. E. Howard, Inc., 1987.

Gutman, Herbert. *The Black Family in Slavery and Freedom, 1750–1925*. New York: Pantheon Books, 1976.

Hairston, Elizabeth Seawell. *The Hairstons and the Penns and Their Relations*. Roanoke: 1940.

Hairston, Peter W. *The Cooleemee Plantation and Its People*. Lexington, N.C.: Davidson County Community College, 1986.

Hale, Douglas. *The Third Texas Cavalry in the Civil War*. Norman and London: University of Oklahoma Press, 1993.

Hargrove, Hondon B. *Buffalo Soldiers in Italy: Black Americans in World War II*. Jefferson, N. C.: McFarland & Company, 1985.

Harris, William C. *Day of the Carpetbagger*. Baton Rouge: Louisiana State University Press, 1979.

Horwitz, Tony. *Confederates in the Attic: Dispatches from the Unfinished Civil War*. New York: Pantheon, 1998.

Huffstodt, Jim. *Hard Dying Men: The Story of General W. H. L. Wallace, General T. E. G. Ransom, and Their "Old Eleventh" Illinois Infantry in the American Civil War*. Bowie, Md.: Heritage Books, 1991.

Hunnicutt, John L. *Reconstruction in West Alabama: The Memoirs of John L. Hunnicutt*. Confederate Centennial Studies no. 11. Tuscaloosa: Confederate Publishing Company, 1959.

Hunter, Jehu C., and Major Clark. "The Buffalo Division in World War II." Unpublished memoir.

Izard, George. "Diary of a Journey by George Izard, 1815–1816." *South Carolina Historical Magazine* 53 (1952).

Jarratt-Puryear Family Papers. In Stampp, ed., Series F, pt. 3.

Jefferson, Thomas. *Notes on the State of Virginia*. Chapel Hill: University of North Carolina Press, 1955.

Jordan, Ervin L., Jr. *Black Confederates and Afro-Yankees*. Charlottesville and London: University Press of Virginia, 1995.

Langhorne, Ora. *Southern Sketches from Virginia*. Charlottesville: University Press of Virginia, 1964.

Leckie, William H., and Shirley A. Leckie. *Unlikely Warriors*. Norman: University of Oklahoma Press, 1984.

Lee, Ulysses. *The Employment of Negro Troops*. Washington, D.C.: Office of the Chief of Military History, United States Army, 1966.

Lemann, Nicholas. *Promised Land*. New York: Alfred A. Knopf, 1991.

Love, David Chelsea. "The Prairie Guard: A History of Their Heroism, Their Battles and Their *Triumphs*." Pamphlet.

Lovett, Bobby L. "Memphis Riots." *Tennessee Historical Quarterly*, spring 1979.

Main, Edwin M. *The Story of the Marches, Battles and Incidents of the Third United States Colored Cavalry*. New York: Negro Universities Press, 1970.

Martinsville–Henry County Woman's Club, *Martinsville & Henry County Historic Views*. Winston-Salem: Hunter Publishing Co., 1976.

Maury, Richard L. *The Battle of Williamsburg and the Charge of the 24th Virginia, of Early's Brigade*. Richmond: Johns & Goolsby, 1880.

McCray, Carrie Allen. *Freedom's Child*. Chapel Hill: Algonquin Books, 1998.

McGuire, Phillip. *Taps for a Jim Crow Army*. Santa Barbara, Calif.: ABC-Clio, 1983.

McMillen, Neil R. *Dark Journey—Black Mississippians in the Age of Jim Crow*. University of Illinois Press, 1990.

McMurry, Richard M. *John Bell Hood and the War for Southern Independence*. Lexington: University Press of Kentucky: 1982.

Millner, Beverly R. *History of the Lampkin-Millner and Related Families*. Privately printed.

Mississippi Senate Journal, 1872.

Morgan, Lynda J. *Emancipation in Virginia's Tobacco Belt, 1850–1870.* Athens: University of Georgia Press, 1992.

Morgan, Philip. *"Don't Grieve After Me": The Black Experience in Virginia 1619–1986.* Hampton, Virginia: Hampton University, 1986.

Mosocco, Ronald A. *Chronological Tracking of the American Civil War per the Official Records.* Williamsburg: James River, 1994.

NAACP Lynching files, #1568, Part 7, Series A.

Nalty, Bernard C. *Strength for the Fight.* New York: Free Press, 1986.

The Negro in the Military Service of the United States 1639–1886. Microfilm publication, National Archives.

The Negro in Virginia. Compiled by workers of the Writers' Program of the Work Projects Administration in the State of Virginia. Winston-Salem, N.C.: J. F. Blair, 1994.

Osborne, Charles C. *Jubal.* Chapel Hill: Algonquin Books, 1992.

Perdue, Charles L., Jr., Thomas E. Barden, and Robert K. Phillips, eds. *Weevils in the Wheat: Interviews with Virginia Ex-slaves.* Charlottesville: University Press of Virginia, 1992.

Phillip, A. Bruce. "A Tobacco-Plantation." *Lippincott's Magazine.* December 1885.

Rawick, George P., ed. *The American Slave: A Composite Autobiography.* Contributions in Afro-American and African Studies no. 11. 19 vols. Westport, Conn.: Greenwood Publishing Company, 1972.

Rawick, George P., ed. *The American Slave: A Composite Autobiography.* Contributions in Afro-American and African Studies no. 35. 12 vols. Westport, Conn.: Greenwood Publishing Company, 1977.

Reid, Christian. *The Wargrave Trust.* New York: Benziger Brothers, 1911.

Rise, Eric W. *The Martinsville Seven: Race, Rape and Capital Punishment.* Charlottesville: University Press of Virginia, 1995.

Scott, Rebecca. "The Battle over the Child: Child Apprenticeship and the Freedmen's Bureau in North Carolina." *Prologue,* summer 1978.

Siegel, Frederick F. *The Roots of Southern Distinctiveness*. Chapel Hill: University of North Carolina Press, 1987.

Simmons, Charles W., III. "Virginia Justice and the Martinsville Seven." Master's thesis, Virginia State University, 1985.

Skates, John Ray. *Mississippi: A History*. New York: W. W. Norton, 1979.

Smith, James D. "Virginia During Reconstruction." Ph.D. thesis, University of Virginia, 1960.

Stampp, Kenneth M., ed., and Randolph Boehm, assoc. ed. *Records of Ante-bellum Southern Plantations from the Revolution through the Civil War* [microfilm]. Frederick, Md.: University Publications of America, 1985.

Stanton, Shelby L. *America's Tenth Legion: X Corps in Korea, 1950*. Novato, Calif.: Presidio, 1989.

Stevenson, Brenda. *Life in Black and White: Family and Community in the Slave South*. New York: Oxford University Press, 1996.

Stokes County Historical Society. *The Heritage of Stokes County, North Carolina, 1981*. Germanton, N.C.: The Stokes County Historical Society, 1981.

Sword, Wiley. *Embrace an Angry Wind*. New York: Harper Collins, 1992.

Thomas, Emory M. *Bold Dragoon: The Life of J. E. B. Stuart*. New York: Harper & Row, 1986.

Tocquevillle, Alexis de. *Democracy in America*. J. P. Mayer and Max Lerner, eds., translation by George Lawrence. New York: Harper & Row, 1966.

Trout, Robert J. *With Pen and Saber: The Letters and Diaries of J. E. B. Stuart's Staff Officers*. Mechanicsburg, Pa.: Stackpole Books, 1995.

Tyre Glen Papers. In Stampp, ed., Series F, pt. 3.

United States Bureau of Refugees, Freedmen, and Abandoned Lands. Records of the Assistant Commissioner for the State of Virginia, Bureau of Refugees, Freedmen, and Abandoned Lands, 1865–1869. Washington, D.C.: National Archives and Records Service, General Services Administration, 1977. Microfilm publication M1048;

Records of the Assistant Commissioner for the State of North Carolina. Microfilm publication M843;

Records of the Superintendent of Education for the State of North Carolina. Microfilm publication M844;

Records of the Education Division. Microfilm publication M803;

Registers and letters received by the Commissioner of the Bureau. Microfilm publication M752.

United States congressional reports:

39th Cong., 1st sess., House Report 101, 1865–66: "Report of the Select Committee on the Memphis Riots and Massacres."

42nd Cong., 2d sess., House Report 22: ("The Ku-Klux Conspiracy") Testimony Taken by the Joint Committee to Enquire into the Condition of Affairs in the Late Insurrectionary States, Mississippi.

44th Cong., 1st sess., Senate Report 527: Mississippi in 1875.

Virginia. *Calendar of Virginia state papers and other manuscripts preserved in the Capitol at Richmond.* New York: Kraus Reprint Corp., 1968.

Walker, Charles D. *Biographical Sketches of the Graduates and Élèves of the Virginia Military Institute Who Fell During the War Between the States.* Philadelphia: J. B. Lippincott, 1875.

The War of the Rebellion: A Compilation of the Official Records of the Union and Confederate Armies. Washington, D.C.: Government Printing Office, 1902.

Welliver, Warman. "Report on the Negro Soldier." *Harper's Magazine*, April 1946.

Wharton, Vernon Lane. *The Negro in Mississippi 1865–1890.* Chapel Hill: University of North Carolina Press, 1947.

Wiencek, Henry, with photographs by Steve Gross and Susan Daley. *Old Houses.* New York: Stewart, Tabori & Chang, 1991.

Williams, M. W., and George Watkins. *Who's Who Among North Carolina Negro Baptists.* 1940.

Wilson, Dale E., "Recipe for Failure: Major General Edward M. Almond and Preparation of the U.S. 92nd Infantry for Combat in World War II," *Journal of Military History*, July, 1992.

NEWSPAPERS

Cavalier Daily (UVA)
Charlottesville Daily Progress
Danbury Reporter
Freedman's Friend
The New York Times
Richmond Daily Dispatch
Richmond Times-Dispatch
Richmond Planet
Washington Post
Winston-Salem Journal

OTHER

Lowndes County Courthouse, Columbus, Miss.: Probate Book K.

Lowndes County Archive, Columbus, Miss.: Chancery Court Papers.

Library of Virginia, Richmond: Auditor of Public Accounts, Condemned Blacks Executed or Transported, 1783–1865; Henry County Court Records, Loose Papers, Inquests; Henry County Minute Book 3.

North Carolina State Archives: Stokes County, Minute Docket, Superior Court; Stokes County Miscellaneous files, Coroner's Reports; Davidson County, Miscellaneous Records, Records of Slaves and Free Persons of Color; Stokes County Patrollers Records, Cohabitation Certification Certificates, Criminal Action Papers, Grand Jury Records and Presentments.

University of Virginia, Special Collections, Alderman Library: Press Releases Concerning the Martinsville 7; Minutes of the Board of Visitors; Richard J. Reid Collection.

Duke University Library: Green W. Penn Papers; Mitchell Papers; William A. J. Finney Papers.

Library of Congress: Jubal Early Papers; Records of the American Colonization Society.

National Archives: Index to Confederate Service Records; Records of the Assistant Commissioner for the State of Mississippi, Registers of Marriages of

Freedmen; Records of the Assistant Commissioner for the State of Tennessee, Memphis Office, Reports and Affidavits Relating to the Memphis Riots; Reports of Outrages, Riots, and Murders, April 1865– December 1868; Reports of Transportation; Reports Relating to Bounty Claims and Disbursements; Letters Sent by the Dept. of Justice: Instructions to U.S. Attorneys and Marshals 1867–1904; Unbound Regimental Records, 3rd U.S. Col'd Cavalry; Compiled Service Record, Thomas Harston.

Chicago Historical Society: "Diary of Henry Uptmor," unpublished MS.

Virginia Military Institute Archives: Outgoing Correspondence of the Superintendent.

PRIVATE COLLECTIONS:

Cooleemee Papers, courtesy Judge Peter W. Hairston.

Rufus Hairston Papers, courtesy Rosalie Hairston.

John W. Hairston Papers, courtesy Marvin S. Hairston.

Rachel Hairston Memoir, courtesy Jerome Hairston and Ronald Dean Hairston.

Elizabeth Hairston Bridgeforth diary, courtesy William B. Hairston Jr.
Family records courtesy Carolyn Henderson. Joseph Henry Hairston Papers.

"Descendants of Peter Hairston," compiled by Robert Ervin Hairston Jr.

Hairston family tree, compiled by Frances Hairston.

ACKNOWLEDGMENTS

This book would not have been possible without Peter W. Hairston and the late Squire Hairston, who courageously opened the doors to their family histories, not knowing what would be found. Both men continued to lend support even after it became apparent that my research was heading into painful territory and that they might not agree with my interpretations. I am grateful also to members of their immediate families: the late Lucy Dortch Hairston, a brilliant and gracious woman who embodied the best of the Old South; Elnora Hairston, whose many years of community service won recognition from the North Carolina governor; Robert Hairston, who took up the torch passed from his father's hands; and Pete Hairston, whose stewardship will take Cooleemee into the next millennium. Thanks to his involvement with the Land Trust of Central North Carolina (P.O. Box 4284, Salisbury, North Carolina 28145), Cooleemee's scenic beauty, wildlife, and historic features will be preserved for future generations.

In the notes I have acknowledged the many people who granted me interviews and information. I am deeply grateful to Eleanor and Nick Hairston, Frances and Lamar Hairston, Mary Alice and Leonard Gibson, Louisa and Bill Hairston, and Pat and Marvin S. Hairston, who took me into their homes and shared family stories. Joseph Henry Hairston and Ever Lee Hairston both offered encouragement when others wondered what was taking so long. Carolyn Henderson, Alice Edwards, Reuben Triplett, the late Dan Spann, and the Reverend Bobby McCarter provided vital leads to sources in Lowndes County. Many family members offered important support and insights, including the late, greatly missed Collie L. Hairston Sr., Verdeen Hairston, Clarence Hairston Sr., Rev. Clarence Hairston Jr., Beverly R. Millner, Thelma Pearson, Mildred Jamison, Will Hairston, Waller Staples Hairston, Robert Sims, Louisa

Hairston Breeden, Ruth A. Hairston, Dorothy Crockett, Dr. Charletta
A. Ayers, Carol Latham, Warren G. Hairston, Helen Hairston Enoch,
Cecile B. Hairston, Alonzo P. Hairston, Esq., Annie Goolsby Burke, John
Will Hairston, Bernard Hairston, James H. Hairston, Rev. Otis L. Hair-
ston, Joe I. Hairston, Nelson G. Hairston, Frank Hairston, Phyllis Buie,
Marie Carter, Betty H. Scales, Rev. Robert A. Hairston, Harold Gorrell,
Alma R. Hamilton, Roger Edmunds, Dr. Raleigh Hairston, Christine
Foreman, the late Bertha Hodge, Mattie Bell Hairston, the late Adam T.
Hairston, and Ann Hairston, who displayed many kindnesses over the
years and whose own fascinating stories must someday be told.

One of the major breakthroughs of my research came about through
Pat Ross, Supervisor at Bassett Historical Center, who is deeply committed to preserving the history of her region. She also led me to Douglas
Belcher and Desmond Kendrick, two other important sources. Mary Bess
Paluzzi guided me through the intricacies of the Lowndes County Archive. The research staff at Jefferson-Madison Regional Library in Charlottesville provided all manner of help for several years. I thank Jim Barns
and Marsha Frick for their forbearing attention to my increasingly frantic
interlibrary-loan requests. I made frequent use of the magnificent re-
sources at the University of Virginia's Alderman Library (notably the
Special Collections room, directed by Michael Plunkett), the Library of
Virginia in Richmond, and the National Archives. At the Southern
Historical Collection, University of North Carolina, Chapel Hill, John
White provided valuable assistance and many courtesies.

I owe a great debt to Robert Weil, my editor, for his scrupulous and
indefatigable work on the manuscript, and to Andrew Miller for his
equally indefatigable work. Jennifer and Karl Ackerman, Jane Colihan,
Ellen and Paul Wagner, Mariflo Stephens, Fred Heblich, and Beth Neville
Evans all read portions of the manuscript and offered their help. I am
grateful to Lucia C. Stanton, Senior Research Historian at Monticello,
Phyllis K. Leffler, Director, Institute for Public History, UVA, Prof. Edward L. Ayers, Prof. Peter Onuf, and the other participants in the Central
Virginia Social History Project for the many spirited discussions on issues
of race and slavery. Prof. William Elwood shared his insights into the
hidden byways of Virginia politics and law. Prof. John Unsworth provided
important information about the music of the Colored Troops. Mary Cas-
sell and Scott Jones offered much assistance, editorial and personal. Rand-
all Boehm went far beyond duty to send materials from the NAACP

Papers. Richard Hatch sent photographs and encouragement. Douglas Winter saved the entire project in ways known only to him. Stow Lovejoy was another savior—blessings upon him.

Howard Morhaim, my friend and literary agent, supported this project through many dark days, providing encouragement, crucial insight, and direction for years. I am grateful beyond words to my parents, Helen and Henry Wiencek, without whose support I would have fallen by the wayside long ago. But my greatest debt is to my wife, Donna, and my son, Henry, my companions in the wilderness, who endured each fresh agony with patience. Donna read every word a dozen times, wrote drafts of critical sections, and edited the manuscript before anyone else saw it, remaining steadfast despite wolves howling at the door. I love you and owe all to you.

INDEX

ABOUT THE AUTHOR

Henry Wiencek was series editor of the *Smithsonian Guide to Historic America*, a twelve-volume descriptive guide to the country's historic sites. He is the author of *Old Houses*, with essays on the histories of eighteen American houses and the families who built them, published in association with the National Trust for Historic Preservation; two books on Southern architecture—*Mansions of the Virginia Gentry* and *Plantations of the Old South*; and several books for Time-Life. He has contributed articles to *American Heritage*, *American Legacy*, *Smithsonian Magazine*, and *Connoisseur*. Born in Boston and educated at Yale, he lives in Virginia with his wife, the writer Donna Lucey, and their son, Henry.